Apocalyptic Crimes

Critical Issues in Crime and Society

RAYMOND J. MICHALOWSKI AND LUIS A. FERNANDEZ, SERIES EDITORS

Critical Issues in Crime and Society is oriented toward critical analysis of contemporary problems in crime and justice. The series is open to a broad range of topics including specific types of crime, wrongful behavior by economically or politically powerful actors, controversies over justice system practices, and issues related to the intersection of identity, crime, and justice. It is committed to offering thoughtful works that will be accessible to scholars and professional criminologists, general readers, and students.

For a complete list of titles in the series, please see the last two pages of the book.

Apocalyptic Crimes

WHY NUCLEAR WEAPONS ARE ILLEGAL AND MUST BE ABOLISHED

RONALD C. KRAMER

RUTGERS UNIVERSITY PRESS
New Brunswick, Camden, and Newark, New Jersey
London and Oxford

Rutgers University Press is a department of Rutgers, The State University of New Jersey, one of the leading public research universities in the nation. By publishing worldwide, it furthers the University's mission of dedication to excellence in teaching, scholarship, research, and clinical care.

ISBN 978-1-9788-3934-2 (cloth)
ISBN 978-1-9788-3933-5 (paperback)
ISBN 978-1-9788-3935-9 (ebook)

Library of Congress Cataloging-in-Publication Data is available
for this book.

A British Cataloging-in-Publication record for this book is available
from the British Library.

References to internet websites (URLs) were accurate at the time of writing. Neither the author nor Rutgers University Press is responsible for URLs that may have expired or changed since the manuscript was prepared.

♾ The paper used in this publication meets the requirements of the American National Standard for Information Sciences—Permanence of Paper for Printed Library Materials, ANSI Z39.48-1992.

rutgersuniversitypress.org

For Jane

Contents

FOREWORD

ALL HUMANS AND nonhuman animals within six miles of a one-megaton bomb killed instantly by blast, firestorm, and intense radiation. Third-degree burns, most of them fatal, for those remaining alive up to fifteen miles from the initial explosion. Near total destruction of the infrastructure for food, water, and shelter in the immediate area. Slow, excruciating death from radiation sickness for many far from the bomb site. Later-life cancers caused by radioactive fallout for still others, including people more than half a world away.[1]

This level of horror was beyond imagination. Until, that is, the United States exploded atomic bombs over the populations of Hiroshima and Nagasaki in order to demonstrate to Japan *and other nations* the presumed irresistible power of the United States.[2]

The debate over whether mass slaughter of civilians in Japan was a justifiable act of war will be never resolved, just as those surrounding mass killings of Palestinians in the 2023–2024 Gaza war will remain an open moral wound as long as there are people to remember that war. What is indisputable, however, is that the use of atomic weapons against Japan, and the subsequent nuclear arms race between the United States and the Soviet Union, placed all life on earth under a nuclear "Sword of Damocles."[3] As Margaret Mead presciently observed, "The atomic bomb exploded over Hiroshima in the summer of 1945. At that point I tore up every page of a book I had nearly finished. Every sentence was out-of-date. We had entered a new age."[4] Indeed. For nearly four decades after those explosions, American and global consciousness was haunted by a profound fear of nuclear war and its aftermath.[5]

For many Americans over fifty, air raid sirens and "duck and cover" drills, erroneously presented as ways of protecting our young bodies from nuclear blasts, remain vivid images from childhood. I, for one, can easily summon the memory of hiding under my desk in a Catholic school, praying it was only a drill, and promising that I would never disobey my parents again if I could live to make it home.

Beginning in the 1980s, fear of nuclear annihilation was gradually replaced in public consciousness by other worries, including economic instability and global climate change.[6] The degree to which this change is an expression of "worry burnout," high hopes for arms control treaties that seemed to signal a retreat from the nuclear precipice, or shifts in mass media focus is unclear.[7] Whatever the reason, the desire to resist "full comprehension" of the massive death and annihilation from nuclear conflict is now commonplace.[8] This remains true even though we have "entered a new age where the risk of nuclear use—deliberately or by accident or miscalculation—is growing."[9]

With nine nations possessing a total of thirteen thousand nuclear weapons, with twenty-two countries having weapons-grade nuclear fuel, with (at this writing) an ongoing war between Russia and a Western-backed Ukraine, with a China-backed North Korea flexing its nuclear muscles, with the collapse of the Iran nuclear arms control agreement, with an increasingly threatened, nuclear-armed Israel, with rising tensions between the nuclear powers of India and Pakistan, and with the rise of authoritarian leaders worldwide, including the threat of a shift toward totalitarian government in the United States, the odds that nothing will go wrong in the nuclear arena are vanishingly small.

The level of risk was made clear by Russian president Vladimir Putin on February 28, 2024, when he threatened that Russia might be compelled to use nuclear weapons against Western nations if they continued to support Ukraine's resistance to Russia's invasion of its territory, bringing about, in his words, "the end of civilization."[10] Despite this growing threat of nuclear conflict, "There is no mass international anti-nuclear movement of the kind that existed 30 years ago. We hear nothing about scientists calling on their governments to stop nuclear escalation. In the euphoria that greeted the end of the Cold War, it seems, the world has lost its awareness and understanding of the possible consequences of a global conflict."[11]

What are we to make of the contradiction between a growing nuclear risk and declining concern among populations and their leaders about the possibility of destruction and death that would make the bombings of Hiroshima and Nagasaki look like a border skirmish? More directly related to this book, what are we to make of criminology's relative inattention to the profound threat nuclear-armed states pose to life on planet earth, given that it is presumptively concerned with the causes and control of harm?

The question of why criminologists study lesser harms rather than greater ones is not new. Since its beginnings, criminology has largely focused on interpersonal crimes that harm one or a few individuals at a time, while giving far less attention to sweeping wrongdoing by corporations or political states that, with a single decision or stroke of a pen, set in motion processes that result in death, injury, illness, and financial loss for hundreds, thousands, and even millions.[12] The result, as noted by David Friedrichs, has been an "inverse relationship" between levels of harm and levels of criminological attention.[13]

The intellectual limitations of focusing criminological inquiry only on acts designated as crimes by law, however, has not gone entirely unnoticed. Since the beginning of modern criminology in the late nineteenth century, there have always been a few criminologists who have recognized the conceptual limits imposed by letting the law determine their subject matter. In 1885, eminent Italian criminologist Raffaele Garofalo noted, "The attempt to show us what the law views as crime ends in our being told that crime, in the eyes of the law, is doing that which the law itself forbade" (in other words, the law is a hermetically sealed theoretical framework that can see only what lawmakers have chosen to criminalize).[14] Maurice Parmelee, the author of what is arguably the first American criminology textbook, proposed that because law varies widely according to place and time, it is a weak foundation on which to base criminological inquiry.[15] Edwin Sutherland and Thorsten Sellin, influential early twentieth-century criminologists, similarly recognized that law imposes blinders that limit criminological vision.[16] Despite these dissident views, criminology was, and remains, largely corralled within whatever boundaries lawmakers chose to set.

In 1939, Edwin Sutherland, then president of the American Sociological Society (now the American Sociological Association), pushed at what were, at the time, the accepted boundaries of criminological inquiry. In his presidential address to the society (later published in the *American Sociological Review*), he argued that violations of law by white-collar workers of high status were no less crimes than the kinds of interpersonal theft and violence that were the routine concern of both the criminal justice system and criminology.[17] Sutherland thus instigated two debates in criminology.

A full-throated challenge to Sutherland's expanded view of crime came in 1947, when another eminent criminologist, Paul Tappan, countered with the argument that only behaviors prohibited by *criminal* law and subject to *criminal* sanctions could analytically be considered crimes, and therefore as appropriate topics for criminological inquiry.[18] Violations of fair trade and other regulatory laws were, in Tappan's view, not objectively criminal because they had not been designated as such by criminal law. Tappan's riposte to Sutherland was also published in the *American Sociological Review*, the official journal of the American Sociological Society, indicating that this debate was no sideshow but rather signaled a significant controversy in the field.

This debate was still alive in the 1970s when Ron Kramer and I were graduate students. By that time, however, many criminologists agreed with Sutherland that violations of law governing the behavior of businesses *is* white-collar crime, even though the acts in question most often violated regulatory, civil, or administrative rather than criminal law. Still, because criminology was and largely remains a discipline focused more on unraveling the social psychology of criminals than understanding the societal causes of crime, Sutherland's own work, and many early studies influenced by his approach, tended to focus on the individual motivations and interpersonal dynamics that led people to violate the laws governing businesses and corporate activities, often for personal gain.[19] It also worth noting that few early studies of white-collar crime focused on violations by people working for institutions of the political state.

The second and more enduring debate about what constituted crimes by "people of high status" arose from a contradiction within Sutherland's work. Sutherland was primarily concerned with understanding white-collar *persons* who broke the law in the course of their occupation, as a way of demonstrating the general applicability of his theory of differential association.[20] However, the data on which he based his groundbreaking book, *White Collar Crime*, consisted primarily of *businesses* that were alleged to have violated regulatory law.[21] While this could have led to greater attention by criminologists to the ways *corporations* themselves could be criminal, initially it did not. Instead, as Ron Kramer noted, the idea of corporations as criminals received "little theoretical or empirical" attention for the four decades following Sutherland's introduction of the concept of white-collar crime.[22]

By the 1980s, however, organizational studies had clearly established that formal organizations used routinized procedures to channel individual behavior in ways favorable to the organizational goals.[23] Following this theoretical lead, some criminologists began to consider how corporate practices, policies, and standard operating procedures could motivate employees to engage in unlawful or wrongful behavior in pursuit of corporate goals.

The idea that institutions, rather than individuals, can be the source of wrongdoing challenges a fundamental "imaginary" of modern capitalist society.[24] All cultures and subcultures within them rely on stories to tell themselves who they are.[25] These stories are not mere ephemera. They are ideological explanations of the practical conditions of life. In class-divided societies, the dominant stories reflect how dominant classes understand the practical conditions of life and explain why those conditions, as harmful and hurtful to some as they may be, are natural and right.[26] In doing so, these dominant narratives work to ensure the most advantaged continue to enjoy their advantages.[27]

Social imaginaries, however, are not immutable. Changes in actual conditions, changes in the understanding of them, and the dynamic interplay between these two processes can sometimes result in new explanations, what historian of science Thomas Kuhn termed "paradigm shifts."[28] The emergent debate around whether corporations could be considered criminogenic entities shaping actions of their employees was a paradigm shift within criminology because it required that scholars ask a new set of questions. It was also an expression of a much larger paradigm shift underway in Western societies.

As the nineteenth century was ending, French sociologist Émile Durkheim formalized the proposition that human behavior was shaped by what he termed "social facts" that preexisted actual persons and that collectively constituted the social structures and cultures within which and according to which people acted.[29] Twenty-five years later, German political economist Max Weber theorized that emergent industrial societies were constellations of bureaucracies that had become dominant structural realities capable of shaping individual will and action.[30]

While these ideas were established in the social sciences prior to World War II, they found increasingly receptive audiences within wider society as the 1950s shaded into the 1960s. The reasons are complex and multifocal, but one question that deserves consideration here is whether the fear of nuclear war planted the idea in the minds of more than a few members of the duck-and-cover generation that forces shaping our lives, indeed that shaped whether or not we would live to adulthood, were far larger than the volition of good or bad people.

The idea that structural arrangements were central to understanding social life became more commonplace as a new wave of mid-twentieth-century public intellectuals questioned post–World War II triumphalism, the capitalist narrative of the self-made person, and the beliefs that the poor caused their poverty, the behavior of Black and Brown people caused racism, and the physical, emotional, and intellectual incapacities of women led to their subordinate status. Key public voices challenging dominant ideologies about class, race, and gender included writers such as Simone de Beauvoir (*The Second Sex*), Kenneth Clark (*The Dark Ghetto*), Michael Harrington (*The Other America*), C. Wright Mills (*The Power Elite, The Sociological Imagination*), and William H. White (*The Organization Man*). These interpretations intersected with an expanding civil rights movement that challenged the long-unquestioned ideology of white supremacy,[31] while a reinvigorated feminist movement sought to rewrite the imaginary of male superiority.[32] Together these forces coalesced into the "long sixties," a period that ushered in society-changing cultural and political paradigm shifts.[33]

This cauldron of social forces led to the increasing popularity of sociology as a field of study. Although structural analyses of social systems by Marx and by Marx and Engels predated Durkheim and Weber, their theories played a relatively small role in the intellectual development of American sociology. The reasons were political, not academic. During the Red Scare of the 1920s and the McCarthy period (Second Red Scare) of the 1950s and early 1960s, left-leaning scholars were purged from universities, otherwise silenced, or self-censored to avoid condemnation as communists or anarchists.[34] This pattern is now being repeated in what I suggest is a Third Purge of leftist thinkers, this time portrayed as a battle against "woke" thinking rather than communism per se.

The heyday of sociology's public popularity lasted from the 1950s to the mid-1980s, when the neoliberal ideology of humans as individualized, competitive actors and capitalist markets as the only path to human well-being began to displace a more sociological/anthropological view of human societies as collective creators of multiple social realities.[35] However, the "sociological imagination" remained alive and well within sociology, laying the theoretical foundations for the study of corporations as criminal actors. By the 1980s criminology included a small but emergent subset of criminologists who saw corporate crime, state crime, and state-corporate crime as part of their portfolio.

Ron Kramer was among the earliest contributors to the emergence of corporate crime studies within criminology. In the early 1980s he articulated a foundational framework for the study of corporate crime that offered an affirmative answer to the question of whether corporations could be considered criminals in themselves, apart from the intentions of specific people working on their behalf.[36] He was also among the first group of criminologists to make the important step of extending the accumulating knowledge about corporate crimes to the realm of state crime and the study of state crimes to the question of possessing, using, or threatening to use nuclear weapons.[37]

In this volume, Kramer focuses his analytic gaze specifically on actions by political states to develop, stockpile, use, or threaten to use nuclear weapons, actions that he argues are unequivocally not only state crimes but perhaps the most threatening to life of all state crimes. In doing so, this work addresses two key theoretical challenges posed by state crime studies: What acts can legitimately be considered state crimes? Who are the state criminals?

In his 1988 presidential address to the American Society of Criminology, William (Bill) Chambliss answered the question of "what constitutes state crime" by describing it as "acts defined by law as criminal and committed by state officials in the pursuit of their job as representatives of the state."[38] Chambliss's initial approach focused primarily on acts by governmental officials that violated the laws of their own countries, such as the CIA's involvement in drug trafficking, which would have been clearly illegal if committed by anyone else. The limitation of this definition, however, was that many of the most harmful actions undertaken by political states are *not* defined as criminal by the laws of those states. Stark examples are domestic political and economic repression of the kind that was legalized in the United States by Jim Crow legislation in the South for nearly a century, racist housing policies in the North, and international wrongs such as initiating wars of aggression.

A legalistic approach to relying on state law to determine if any given act was a state crime also raised the questions of whether states are guilty of crimes if they facilitate actions in other countries that would be illegal under their own laws but are legal in countries where they are being committed. Ron Kramer and I argued that the "space between laws" that enables one country, such as the United States, to engage in acts that would be domestic crimes but that are not prohibited under the laws of the "victim" country cannot adequately be encompassed within a purely legalistic frame of reference. Examples of such state "crimes" include creating trade laws that facilitate the sale of products outlawed in the United States in countries where they are still permitted or that incentivize U.S. companies to pursue exploitative labor practices in other countries, even though these same practices are outlawed at home.[39]

Many criminologists of state crime found the solution to the question of "what law" in the realm of international law, particularly the legal ideals embodied in the United Nations Universal Declaration of Human Rights, the conventions that flowed from it, and international humanitarian law.[40] The idea that human rights, not state law, should serve as the basis for determining what constitutes crime was not new. In an influential article that helped galvanize the intellectual movement first known as "radical criminology" in the 1970s and 1980s, and later rebranded as "critical criminology" in the 1990s, Herman and Julia Schwendinger proposed, "All persons must be guaranteed the fundamental prerequisites for well-being, including food, clothing, medical services, challenging work and recreational experiences, as well as security from predatory individuals and repressive or imperialistic social elites. These material requirements, basic services and enjoyable relationships are not to be regarded as rewards or privileges. They are rights!"[41] In their view, any violation or denial of these rights was both a crime and a legitimate subject of criminological inquiry. The list of rights posed by Schwendinger and Schwendinger can be found explicitly in or derived from international human rights laws as well as other multilateral agreements such as the European Charter of Human Rights.

A *half century* has passed since the Schwendingers argued that criminology should devote itself to the protection and promotion of human rights. While their once radical claim no longer raises bitter objections among criminologists as it once did, the sad reality is that the bulk of criminology and the vast majority of criminologists remain focused on the narrow-reach offenses that are available to individuals acting alone or with a few others. The sweeping harms wrought by corporations and states, up to and including widespread destruction of life due to climate change or nuclear conflict, remain a sideshow in the criminological literature and at criminology meetings. This is not the result of intellectual or moral failings on the part of orthodox criminologists. Rather, it is an example of what organizational theorists of corporate and state crime understood. Institutions, including ones like academic criminology, universities, justice system agencies that hire criminologists, and governments that fund criminological research, create channels of action that appear natural and normal and that only those willing to pay the price would seek to escape.

This brings us to the second question regarding state crime: Who are the state criminals? The study of organizational forms of harm has long suffered from what I term a *mens rea* problem. The blame for most corporate and state crimes is not easily attributed to just one or a few people as it often is in cases of street crimes. This is true even when a specific state harm is caused by a specific state actor. Few, for instance, would place the ultimate blame for the bombing of Hiroshima on Thomas Ferebee, the bombardier of the *Enola Gay* who guided the plane to its fateful rendezvous with horror. One might be tempted to say the real blame rests with President Truman, who authorized the bombing. This, however, overlooks the organizational reality of a complex bureaucracy of military, science, and policy institutions that made it unlikely that a president, who learned of the existence of the bomb only after taking office, would veto the use of a weapon backed by the work and rationale of so many organizations focused on winning the war. In reality, most cases of state and corporate crime lack clear, ultimate decision makers. From the standpoint of how organizations actually work, the search for individual corporate or state criminals who fit the guilt model of street criminals is a fool's errand.

A fundamental principle of Anglo-American jurisprudence, from its beginning in English common law to the present, has been the concept of mens rea—the guilty intention of the wrongdoer. Foundational English legal thinker William Blackstone concretized the principle of mens rea, claiming that "an unwarrantable act *without a vicious* will is no crime at all."[42] In a nod to Blackstone, U.S. Supreme Court justice Oliver Wendell Holmes offered the folksy observation that "even a dog distinguishes between being stumbled over and being kicked."[43]

The proposition that a guilty mind is the sine qua non of crime is a good example of H. L. Mencken's adage that "every complex problem has a solution which is simple, direct, plausible—and wrong."[44] More people around the world are gravely harmed by actions rooted in organizational and systemic arrangements than by those committed by evil minds. The jurisprudential homage paid to mens rea, however, has long been a barrier to condemnation and legal control of these actions. Mens rea has long been a legal and conceptual firewall protecting criminogenic organizations and social systems from state sanction and, I might add, criminological scrutiny.

One might be tempted to assume that Anglo-American jurisprudence was ill-suited to address the emergence of acts that, while harmful and wrongful, were not committed by identifiable actors motivated by "vicious will" because English common law developed at a time when most human wrongdoing occurred as face-to-face conflicts. However, by the time Blackstone penned his foundational statement about mens rea, wealthy merchants and traders had already learned how to combine their wealth into collective trading enterprises that would multiply their power and divide their losses, often to the everlasting harm of many others.[45] The English trade in Africans stolen from their homes and sold into slavery began 250 years before Blackstone mused about mens rea and crime.[46] The enclosure movement that deprived serfs of land from which to extract their livelihood began before Blackstone's era.[47] Yet these stages in what folk singer John Prine sardonically termed "the progress of man" held no place within the concept of crime—regardless of their human toll. Or at least it was not in the minds of the powerful who benefited from these harmful practices and who philosophized about law.

It was quite otherwise, however, for those who were the victims. A seventeenth-century English folk poem captured this distinction between the harms of the powerful and the harms of the powerless under the English law of enclosure:

> They hang the man, and flog the woman
> That steals the goose from off the common;
> But let the greater villain loose
> That steals the common from the goose.
> The law demands that we atone
> When we take thing we do not own,
> But leaves the lords and ladies fine
> Who take things that are yours and mine.[48]

Nor was there any shortage of white people who criticized the emergent institutional practice of enslaving Black Africans.[49] And although no one asked their opinion, we can be fairly certain that those who were enslaved would have found the laws that ripped them from their homelands, stole their labor, and sought to strip them of their humanity to be fundamentally criminal.

What does this distant history have to do with contemporary problems of state crime and nuclear weapons? Just this: In the same way that the legal frameworks of early mercantile and later machine capitalism sanctified social structures that benefitted a few at the expense of many, contemporary social structures and the ideologies they advance ensure and protect malign distributions of the power that ensure only some will fully enjoy the human rights that national, multinational, and international laws hold as our common human patrimony. Others must make do with less or with no rights at all.

As Kramer argues here in *Apocalyptic Crimes*, we cannot claim to support human rights while supporting, promoting, or tolerating nuclear weapons that threaten to destroy access to the "fundamental prerequisites for well being" for hundreds of thousands, perhaps millions of people. In addition, developing, keeping, and threatening to use them are, as Kramer makes clear, also juridical violations of a panoply of existing international laws and treaties. These laws serve as the Archimedean point for this volume, the place where the author has chosen to stand as he applies his analytic lever in an attempt to move the weighty sphere of a nuclear-armed world in a safer direction. While operating primarily from a legalist framework rather than a more sweeping "social harms" or zemiological model proposed by some, Kramer's approach is far removed from the orthodox criminological view of what constitutes crime. Rather, he blends a prophetic voice calling for the absolute abolition of nuclear weapons with a firm grounding in existing law, the law of nations. While these laws often lack the enforcement capability of the laws of individual states, they represent, by far, the better angels of human nature. This book is a clarion call to criminologists and other concerned citizens to recognize that the current state of nuclear armament not only violates international laws but threatens to destroy any chance that as one people living in one world, we can achieve the aspirational, moral goals so clearly set forth in the Universal Declaration of Human Rights.

Raymond J. Michalowski
Regents Professor Emeritus
Northern Arizona University

PREFACE AND ACKNOWLEDGMENTS

THIS BOOK STARTED out as a COVID-19 project in March 2020 as my wife and I hunkered down in our home to ride out the global pandemic. It was not the first time I had focused on the topic of nuclear weapons. As I explain in these pages, I started to explore the nuclear threat in the early 1980s, when the bellicosity and nuclear saber-rattling of the Reagan administration brought this critical issue back to public attention. I was galvanized by the Nuclear Weapons Freeze Campaign and my attendance at the June 12, 1982, march and rally in New York City against the arms race to both join the disarmament movement and start to analyze nuclear weapons from a sociological perspective. Later I began to write about the crimes of the American nuclear state and examine the issues related to these deadly weapons through the lens of the concept of state-corporate crime. With this book I wanted to bring together my scattered observations about nuclear weapons and bring the analysis up to date. I initially planned a much smaller book, but the project seemed to take on a life of its own and grew into the present volume.

Despite the isolation imposed by COVID-19 early on, this book was still a collective endeavor, and I have many people to thank. The last four chapters were written while I was on sabbatical leave from Western Michigan University, and I want to thank WMU for the opportunity to take that sabbatical and finish the project. I want to express my appreciation to the chair of the Department of Sociology, David Hartmann, and my colleagues in the department, for their support. I also want to express my gratitude to the members of the WMU Climate Change Working Group for their support and the opportunity to present my ideas about the nexus between nuclear weapons and climate change during the 2023 Climate Crisis Month series the Working Group organized.

Much of the early research I performed on the nuclear weapons issue was in collaboration with several of my graduate students at the time (all of whom have gone on to influential academic careers). I want to thank Dave Kauzlarich (University of North Carolina at Greensboro), Brian Smith (Henry Ford Community College), Dawn Rothe (Florida Atlantic University), and Elizabeth Bradshaw (Central Michigan University) for their contributions to my thinking about these critical issues.

Good friends and great scholars Paul Clements, Ray Michalowski, and Brian Smith read the entire manuscript and provided excellent feedback. Special mention must be made of my wonderful friend David Friedrichs, a great white-collar crime scholar, who was one of the first to encourage me to study the important topic of nuclear weapons from a criminological perspective back in the 1980s. Shortly before his death in 2022, David read several of the early chapters of this book and gave me the kind of critique that only he could provide. I wish he were still here to read the final version.

Although it has become somewhat of a cliché, Isaac Newton's observation that those who do intellectual work can often see farther ahead because they "stand on the shoulders of giants" is still apt. In analyzing the nuclear danger, I have stood on the shoulders of giants such as Jonathan Schell, Daniel Ellsberg, Robert Jay Lifton, and Richard Falk. My intellectual debt to these great scholars and anti–nuclear weapons activists is great.

My early interest in issues of war and protest was sparked by one of my high school teachers, Jane Charette, who while still a young nun introduced me to the Catholic peace movement. Within that movement, Catholic priests Dan and Phil Berrigan and their colleagues inspired me with their courageous Plowshares Actions against nuclear weapons. Later, others connected to that powerful peace movement in Kalamazoo, such as Father John Grathwohl, Don Cooney, Jean Gump, and Joe Gump, would continue to influence my thinking about nuclear weapons and disarmament.

Additional inspiration to work on abolishing nuclear weapons comes from my children and grandchildren. My son Andrew Kramer, his wife Dr. Sarah Endrizzi, and their children Truman, Malcolm, Calvin, and Clementine provide love and support and always remind me why working on this issue is so important.

My daughter Sarah Kramer was, once again, indispensable to one of my writing projects. She was a skillful editor, assisted me in locating and securing permissions for the images and photos in the book, suggested cover designs, and then prepared the index. She made this a better book. Sarah and her husband Chris Cowgill also provided love, support, and encouragement along the way.

My great friend Ray Michalowski also shaped my thinking and influenced this project. He read every chapter and, as usual, gave me excellent substantive and editorial feedback. I thank him for writing the foreword to the book and always serving as my major sounding board. What a pleasure it was in the summer of 2023 to have Ray for an extended visit in Kalamazoo where we could talk about the book (and many other things) on my backyard patio and over pancake breakfasts.

This book is dedicated to my wonderful wife Jane. More than anyone she influenced the writing of this book in a hundred different ways. I cannot thank her enough. For over fifty years now, she has been the love and light of my life.

Abbreviations

ABM	anti–ballistic missile
AEC	Atomic Energy Commission
ASC	American Society of Criminology
CIA	Central Intelligence Agency
CND	Campaign for Nuclear Disarmament
CTBT	Comprehensive Test Ban Treaty
CTR	Cooperative Threat Reduction
DLC	Democratic Leadership Council
DOD	Department of Defense
DPG	"Defense Planning Guidance"
DPRK	Democratic People's Republic of Korea
EU	European Union
FAS	Federation of American Scientists
FDR	Franklin Delano Roosevelt
GAC	General Advisory Committee
GATT	General Agreement on Tariffs and Trade
HRC	Human Rights Committee
IAEA	International Atomic Energy Agency
IALANA	International Association of Lawyers Against Nuclear Arms
ICAN	International Campaign to Abolish Nuclear Weapons
ICBM	intercontinental ballistic missiles
ICCPR	International Covenant on Civil and Political Rights
ICJ	International Court of Justice
ICL	international criminal law
ICRC	International Committee of the Red Cross
IHL	international humanitarian law
IHR	international human rights
IMF	International Monetary Fund
INF	Intermediate Nuclear Forces

IPB	International Peace Bureau
IPPNW	International Physicians for the Prevention of Nuclear War
JCPOA	Joint Comprehensive Plan of Action
JFK	John Fitzgerald Kennedy
LBJ	Lyndon Baines Johnson
LCNP	Lawyers Committee on Nuclear Policy
LTBT	Limited Test Ban Treaty
MAD	mutually assured destruction
MET	Chicago Metallurgical Laboratory
MIRV	multiple independently targetable reentry vehicle
NATO	North Atlantic Treaty Organization
NDRC	National Defense Research Committee
NGO	nongovernmental organizations
NNWS	non–nuclear weapons states
NPR	Nuclear Posture Review
NPT	Nuclear Non-Proliferation Treaty
NSA	National Security Agency
NSC 68	National Security Council #68
NSDD	National Security Decision Directive
NSPD	National Security Presidential Directive
NSS	National Security Strategy
NWS	nuclear weapons states
OPLAN	U.S. Military Operations/Operational Plan
OSRD	Office of Scientific Research and Development
PDD	Presidential Decision Directive
PLA	People's Liberation Army
PNAC	Project for a New American Century
PRC	People's Republic of China
PSR	Physicians for Social Responsibility
PTBT	Partial Test Ban Treaty
RAF	Royal Air Force
RDJTF	Rapid Deployment Joint Task Force
ROK	Republic of Korea
SAC	Strategic Air Command
SALT	Strategic Arms Limitation Treaties
SANE	National Committee for a Sane Nuclear Policy
SDI	Strategic Defense Initiative
SIOP	Single Integrated Operational Plan
SLBM	submarine-launched ballistic missiles

SORT	Strategic Offensive Reductions Treaty
START	Strategic Arms Reduction Treaty
ToD	treadmill of destruction
ToP	treadmill of production
TPNW	Treaty on the Prohibition of Nuclear Weapons
UCAM	United Campuses to Prevent Nuclear War
UDHR	Universal Declaration of Human Rights
UN	United Nations
UNAEC	United Nations Atomic Energy Commission
UNGA	United Nations General Assembly
UNSC	United Nations Security Council
UNSCOM	United Nations Special Commission
USAAF	U.S. Army Air Force
USSR	Union of Soviet Socialist Republics
WHO	World Health Organization
WMD	weapons of mass destruction
WMU	Western Michigan University

Apocalyptic Crimes

CHAPTER 1

"It Is 90 Seconds to Midnight"

NUCLEAR WEAPONS, APOCALYPTIC HARMS, AND STATE CRIME

> What I am arguing is that we need to recognize the *intrinsic* criminality of any threat or use of nuclear weapons . . . whether we look backward in time to World War II or forward to possible situations where it serves political or military goals to threaten or actually use such weaponry.
>
> —Richard Falk, *At the Nuclear Precipice: Catastrophe or Transformation?*

> Abolishing nuclear weapons, absolutely as soon as possible, is probably the single most important task the human race can pursue right now to ensure our long-range survival.
>
> —Tad Daley, *Apocalypse Never: Forging the Path to a Nuclear Weapon-Free World*

ON JANUARY 23, 2020, the *Bulletin of the Atomic Scientists* dramatically moved the hands of its metaphorical Doomsday Clock ahead a full twenty seconds to one hundred seconds before midnight (nuclear apocalypse), which at that time was the closest the clock had ever been to "doomsday." The organization, which publishes the journal of the same name, was created in the momentous year of 1945 by Albert Einstein, J. Robert Oppenheimer, and University of Chicago scientists who had just helped develop the first atomic weapons as part of the famed Manhattan Project. These atomic scientists, many of whom worked in the project's Chicago Metallurgical Laboratory (Met Lab), had not only developed the atomic bomb but also then protested the use of that bomb against Japan after the war in Europe had ended and the threat of Hitler and Nazi Germany obtaining and using such a weapon was over. Now, seventy-five years after these catastrophically destructive bombs were dropped on the

Japanese cities of Hiroshima and Nagasaki, atomic scientists were warning the world of nuclear danger and the need for political action to avoid the annihilation of human civilization—reminding us once again that "human possession of nuclear weaponry is beyond reckless."[1] In fact, many of these scientists concurred with international law scholars like American political scientist Richard Falk that the use or threat to use these weapons is "criminal" in the most fundamental sense of the word.

The *Bulletin of the Atomic Scientists* started as a newsletter in 1945 and was first published as a journal in 1947. According to its founding editor, Russian-born American biophysicist Eugene Rabinowitch, the *Bulletin* was "a creation of conscience" and one of its aims was "to preserve our civilization by scaring men into rationality."[2] As American historian Lawrence S. Wittner observes, "Even at the start of the Manhattan Project, there was a built-in conflict between the approach of the scientists and that of top government officials."[3] By late 1945, many of the atomic scientists "shared an intense fear of what lay ahead" now that these terrible weapons had been used in wartime by political leaders.[4] American psychiatrist and public intellectual Robert Jay Lifton has referred to these concerned scientists as "prophetic survivors of the catastrophic destructiveness of their own creation."[5] After the war, they set out to engage in a political struggle to control the apocalyptic monster they had brought to life.

The now iconic image of the Doomsday Clock was created in 1947 for the first cover of the *Bulletin* by Chicago landscape painter Martyl Suzanne Schweig Langsdorf, whose husband, Alexander Langsdorf Jr., was a physicist who had worked on the Manhattan Project. He was one of the many scientists who signed a petition to President Harry S. Truman pleading with him not to use the new atomic bomb against the Japanese people. After the war, Alexander Langsdorf became an early founder of the *Bulletin of the Atomic Scientists*, and the organization commissioned his talented wife to design the cover for its new journal.[6] The artist, who went by the single name Martyl professionally, said she designed the dramatic clockface image to convey a sense of "urgency and the time of essence."[7] Martyl sought to symbolically communicate the seriousness of threats to humanity and the planet posed by atomic weapons—and she was successful! Since its debut on the June 1947 cover of the *Bulletin of the Atomic Scientists*—set at seven minutes to midnight—the Doomsday Clock "has become a universally recognized indicator of the world's vulnerability to catastrophe from nuclear weapons."[8] It is a symbolic countdown to the apocalypse.

In its 2020 "Doomsday Clock Statement," addressed to "leaders and citizens of the world," the *Bulletin*'s Science and Security Board (which determines the setting of the clock in consultation with its Board of Supervisors) asserted that "humanity continues to face two simultaneous existential dangers—nuclear war and climate change."[9] These twin dangers, which both pose "the threat of destruction of organized human life in any recognizable or tolerable form,"[10] are phenomena new in history. So, in addition to its original focus on the nuclear danger, the *Bulletin of the Atomic Scientists* has also attempted to promote an increased awareness of the threat of global warming since 2007, when it moved the Doomsday Clock from seven to five minutes to midnight. With this "clarion call for greater attention to the growing climate crisis," the scientists "made clear that the Clock was not about nuclear weapons alone. It was fundamentally about existential risk."[11]

In that 2020 statement, the atomic scientists contended that the current international security situation is dire, not only due to these two apocalyptic threats but also because of a third danger—the undermining of democracy. They argued that "the means by which political leaders had previously managed these potentially civilization-ending dangers are themselves being dismantled or undermined, without a realistic effort to replace them with new or better management regimes."[12] The world's chance to turn back the clock has been severely diminished by the failure of state officials to take necessary actions to address these dangers.

In January 2021, in the midst of what the *Bulletin* termed the "COVID-19 wake-up call," the Doomsday Clock remained at one hundred seconds to midnight, although the scientists added "more virulent pandemics and next-generation warfare" as other dangers "that could threaten civilization in the near future."[13] In its 2021 statement, the *Bulletin* emphasized that "the existential threats of nuclear weapons and climate change have intensified in recent years because of a threat multiplier: the continuing corruption of the information ecosphere on which democracy and public decision-making depend."[14] In January 2022, the famous clock again remained at one hundred seconds to midnight, although the scientists emphatically stated, "This decision does not, by any means, suggest that the international situation has stabilized. On the contrary, the Clock remains the closest it has ever been to civilization-ending apocalypse because the world remains stuck in an extremely dangerous moment."[15]

One month later, the existential danger escalated even more. On February 24, 2022, after weeks of a threatening military buildup, Russian president

Vladimir Putin ordered his military forces to invade the sovereign nation of Ukraine. The invasion itself was a flagrant violation of international law, a crime of aggression, what the Nuremberg judges in 1945 called the "universal crime."[16] Even critical American analysts, like peace activist Medea Benjamin (cofounder of CODEPINK) and independent journalist Nicolas J. S. Davies, who attempt to provide the broader historical context for the development of the conflict and analyze the irresponsible role that the United States and the North Atlantic Treaty Organization (NATO) also played in facilitating the war, charge that "the Russian invasion of Ukraine was not only criminal, but also a catastrophic move and a terrible miscalculation."[17] Putin then compounded this crime on February 27 by placing Russia's nuclear weapons on a higher state of alert ("a special regime of combat duty") and making multiple thinly veiled threats to use these weapons against Ukraine or any other state that interfered with his attempt to overrun the country.[18] As the Russian war effort faltered in the fall of 2022 and throughout the next two years, Putin made additional threatening statements concerning the possible use of nuclear weapons and even reached an agreement with Belarus to station tactical (so-called battlefield) nuclear weapons on its territory.[19]

With these nuclear threats, also illegal under international law, the world has entered what American security expert Michael Klare calls "a New Nuclear Era, in which the risk of nuclear weapons use by the major powers has reemerged as a daily fact of life."[20] He goes on to note, "Whatever the outcome of the conflict in Ukraine, this new or repurposed use of nuclear weapons will remain an inescapable feature of any major-power crisis. And, once the threat of nuclear weapons use has been normalized in this way, it is hard to believe they will not be used, sooner or later, to demonstrate the credibility of threats like those issued by Putin."[21] With the war in Ukraine in mind at the opening of a key Nuclear Non-Proliferation Treaty (NPT) review conference in August 2022, United Nations secretary-general António Guterres warned, "Today, humanity is just one misunderstanding, one miscalculation away from nuclear annihilation. We have been extraordinarily lucky so far. But luck is not a strategy. Nor is it a shield from geopolitical tensions boiling over into nuclear conflict."[22] The international community has come to realize, once again, that given the continued existence of nuclear weapons—estimated at 12,500 warheads by the Federation of American Scientists (FAS) in 2023—we live life on the brink of destruction. And the best way to move back from the brink is to abolish these "indefensible weapons."[23]

Then, on January 24, 2023, the Doomsday Clock was moved again. This time, the *Bulletin* warned, "It is 90 seconds to midnight"—a new record for the closest the clock has ever been to "global catastrophe." The *Bulletin*'s Science and Security Board moved the hands forward ten more seconds "largely (though not exclusively) because of the mounting dangers of the war in Ukraine."[24] Describing Russia's threats to use nuclear weapons in the war against Ukraine as "a terrible risk," the *Bulletin* warned, "The possibility that the conflict could spin out of anyone's control remains high."[25] The scientists also contended that the war in Ukraine threatens the New START (Strategic Arms Reduction Treaty) accord, the last remaining nuclear weapons agreement between Russia and the United States (suspended by Russia in 2023 and set to expire in 2026). The conflict also undermines the world's response to climate change and hampers international efforts to deal with other global problems. But despite the heightened concerns of the scientists and security experts over the war in Ukraine, the threat of nuclear war (like the climate crisis) still lurks below the level of public consciousness, not even making a recent list of the top ten biggest fears of Americans.[26] In January 2024, the Doomsday Clock remained set at ninety seconds to midnight, although the scientists warned that "ominous trends continue to point the world toward global catastrophe."[27]

The Doomsday Clock set at "90 seconds to midnight" in 2023. Courtesy Jamie Christiani / *Bulletin of the Atomic Scientists.*

Even before the Russian invasion of Ukraine and the rise of this new nuclear reality, the editors of the *Bulletin* made the claim in recent "Dooms-day Clock Statements" that global leaders have repeatedly failed to respond appropriately to both nuclear and climate threats, and "the result is a height-ened and growing risk of disaster."[28] The scientists have asserted that "lead-ers around the world must immediately commit themselves to renewed cooperation in the many ways and venues available for reducing existential risk."[29] After the clock was reset to ninety seconds to midnight in 2023, American writer Jon Kelvey observed, "If you're going to pay attention to the Doomsday Clock, one way to think of it is as a measure of how the world's leaders are responding to global risks in a given moment, rather than a measure of when catastrophe might strike."[30] This book argues that the failure of world leaders (state officials) to cooperate and respond to these interrelated "apocalyptic twins"[31] by abolishing the thousands of nuclear weapons that still exist and drastically mitigating carbon emissions can be described and analyzed as forms of *state crime*—what I call the crime of "political omission."[32]

TOWARD A CRIMINOLOGY OF NUCLEAR WEAPONS

In his 1988 Presidential Address to the American Society of Criminol-ogy (ASC), William J. Chambliss defined "state-organized crimes" as illegal acts "committed by state officials in the pursuit of their job as representatives of the state."[33] As one form of state crime, political omission or criminal negligence is the failure of government officials to act when they are legally or morally required to do so to prevent harm (here, to achieve nuclear disar-mament and reduce global warming). States can also engage in the "com-mission" of specific harmful actions (illegal wars of aggression, the actual use or threat to use nuclear weapons, or the promotion of an energy system that is creating a climate crisis). These extremely harmful political omissions and intentional state actions can and should be examined from a criminological perspective.

This book outlines such a criminology of nuclear weapons. I argue that there are four sets of political actions and/or omissions that can be labeled and analyzed as *apocalyptic nuclear state crimes*: (1) the actual use of atomic bombs in 1945 by the United States against Japan; (2) the threat to use these destructive weapons implied in the doctrine of nuclear deterrence; (3) spe-cific state threats to use nuclear weapons in various conflict situations throughout the post–World War II era (including U.S. threats during the wars in Korea and Vietnam and the most recent threats by Vladimir Putin during the war in Ukraine); and (4) the continued possession of these dangerous devices (the failure to disarm when obligated by law to do so) by the United States, Russia, and the other nuclear-armed countries.

Regarding the fourth category—the state crime of continuing to possess nuclear weapons—it is important to note that many criminologists have previously conceptualized the failure of states to prevent or control blameworthy harms they have a moral and legal responsibility to address as a form of state crime. American white-collar and state crime specialist David O. Friedrichs used the term *negligent state criminality* and argued that "the most serious form of negligent state criminality involves the unnecessary and premature loss of life that occurs when the government and its agents fail to act affirmatively in certain situations."[34] The failure to disarm could potentially lead to nuclear warfare, which would obviously cause enormous destruction and catastrophic loss of life.

Other criminologists prefer the concept *state crimes of omission*.[35] According to Australian criminologist Rob Watts, "State crimes of omission occur when states and their officials fail to act, or neglect to notice bad things happening, or even enter into a state of denial. This leads to significant, even life-threatening occasions for harm to particular groups of people simply because state officials have not acted."[36] State crimes of omission concerning nuclear weapons could also clearly result in apocalyptic harms.

This book uses the term *state crimes of political omission* to emphasize the fact that state decisions not to disarm are part of what American sociologist C. Wright Mills called the "basic problem of power."[37] In *The Power Elite*, Mills argued that the failure to make decisions is also an exercise of political power by elites: "Their failure to act, their failure to make decisions, is itself an act that is often of greater consequence than the decisions they do make."[38] Other scholars have also focused attention on "non-decision making" and the setting of public agendas that exclude critical issues, what British social theorist Steven Lukes calls the "second dimension of power."[39] While state officials do make explicit and consequential decisions—that is, they choose to take actions that protect their material and ideological interests in direct conflict situations (the first dimension of power)—it is important to recognize other situations where a "mobilization of bias" operates to limit or exclude issues from public consideration and action in a way that benefits certain groups at the expense of others.[40] The political failure of the U.S. government to fulfill its legal obligation to disarm (under the NPT) often involves this second dimension of power—non-decision making. Various demands for the reduction of nuclear arms have been suppressed before they gained access to the policy arena. These nondecisions constitute a significant portion of the state crimes of political omission related to nuclear weapons and climate disruptions.

In the epigraph opening this chapter, international law scholar Richard Falk declares that "we need to recognize the *intrinsic* criminality of any threat or use of nuclear weapon."[41] Following Falk, I argue that the use, threats to use, and continued possession of nuclear weapons by any government can be defined as state crimes because they involve decisions, actions, or omissions by government officials, acting as representatives of the state, that violate specific public international laws such as international humanitarian law (IHL), the NPT of 1968, human rights laws such as the 1966 International Covenant on Civil and Political Rights (ICCPR), and the 2017 Treaty on the Prohibition of Nuclear Weapons (TPNW). According to the Nuremberg (London) Charter of 1945, many of these illegal state actions (violations of international law) can be designated as "war crimes" and/or "crimes against humanity." The crimes of the nuclear state also increasingly intersect with and amplify the climate crisis in specific ways, intensifying the overall threat of apocalyptic harms.

Although the field of criminology has generally ignored these state-produced harms, a few criminologists have argued that state criminality related to nuclear weapons can and should be brought within the purview of the discipline.[42] As Friedrichs observed, "It is quite remarkable that the vast criminal potential in the use of nuclear weapons has been neglected by criminologists."[43] He also notes that "the nuclear threat going forward in the twenty-first century is quite certain to be a monumentally important issue" that should be part of what he envisions as a "prospective criminology" of state crime.[44] According to Friedrichs, within such a forward-looking criminology, a basic question is, "Can criminological students of state crime identify the most constructive approaches to minimizing the chances of an apocalyptic future?"[45] Yet despite the existential threat and calls for scholarship on the topic, the number of criminologists who have engaged in criminological inquiry concerning nuclear weapons issues, retrospectively or prospectively, remains quite small.[46]

What would a criminology of nuclear weapons look like? What would it focus on? Edwin H. Sutherland, the father of American criminology, asserted in his famous introductory textbook that "criminology is the body of knowledge regarding crime as a social phenomenon. It includes within its scope the processes of making laws, of breaking laws, and of reacting toward the breaking of laws."[47] Sutherland's prescription provides the framework for this book. The analysis that follows first examines the making (creation and application) of laws that are relevant to nuclear weapons, such as those international laws previously mentioned (IHL, NPT, ICCPR, and TPNW) as well as important legal decisions, general comments, and advisory opinions concerning these laws. This examination will establish that nuclear weapons are indeed illegal under international law and that the breaking of these laws can be considered crimes just the same as violations of domestic criminal law.

Evidence will then be presented that these public international laws have been repeatedly violated by the United States and other nuclear states by both intentional state actions (the use of atomic bombs against Japan in 1945 and the repeated threats to use nuclear weapons in a variety of situations in the post–World War II era) and crimes of political omission (the continued possession of these weapons despite a legal obligation to disarm). This process of breaking laws concerning nuclear weapons (by intentional acts or political omission) will be described and analyzed from a sociological perspective.

These significant state violations of international laws related to nuclear weapons have generated a variety of societal reactions (social control efforts to reduce or prevent illegal acts). Those reactions toward the breaking of laws include (1) political attempts to establish international controls over atomic energy and the "ban the bomb" movement in the early post–World War II years; (2) the campaign to stop atmospheric testing of nuclear weapons in the 1950s and 1960s; (3) the nonproliferation and "arms control" treaties negotiated in the 1960s, 1970s, and later decades; (4) the "nuclear freeze" movement of the 1980s; (5) requests in the 1990s for an advisory opinion concerning the legality of nuclear weapons from the International Court of Justice (ICJ); and (6) the recent effort by the United Nations General Assembly (UNGA) to explicitly prohibit these apocalyptic weapons by formal treaty. These past and current international efforts to confront, control, and ban the bomb will be examined and their relevance for future actions to prevent crimes by nuclear states and abolish nuclear weapons will be assessed.

The Apocalyptic Harms of Nuclear State Crimes

While Sutherland provides the intellectual scaffolding for developing a criminology of nuclear weapons, his outline of disciplinary tasks related to the study of crime does not provide the proper human and moral framing for such a critical project. His prescription does not allow us to fully appreciate and address the enormity of the actual physical and social harms that are generated by states "breaking laws" related to these weapons. In the early days of the atomic age, it was award-winning American writer John Hersey's book *Hiroshima* that first revealed the "horrific human cost" exacted by the bomb.[48] But over the years, due to the acceptance and "normalization" of the bomb in U.S. political culture, Americans have been prone to succumb to the process of "psychic numbing,"[49] closing themselves off from thoughts and feelings concerning the terrifying consequences of the use of nuclear weapons.

Analyzing what they call "human nuclear annihilation" and the "lived consequences" suffered by so many from the use and possible use of these bombs, British criminologists Ross McGarry and Sandra Walklate argue for the use of the stronger term *degenerate war* to more fully capture the disproportionate targeting of civilians involved in nuclear warfare.[50] Nuclear weapons are inherently criminal because their purpose is to kill masses of innocent civilians and induce terror among the enemy population (both prohibited by international law). The use in any form of these catastrophically destructive weapons constitutes, in the words of American writer Tad Daley, "a crime of infinite magnitude."[51] Writer and peace activist Jonathan Schell once noted, "The birth of nuclear weapons in 1945 opened a wide, unobstructed pathway to the end of the world."[52] Nuclear warfare as well as climate disruptions are referred to as *existential* threats because they do indeed threaten human existence itself. These twin threats confront us with what Lifton calls the "imagery of extinction,"[53] the extinction of what elegant American scholar Robert Heilbroner called "the human prospect."[54]

Many who write about the nuclear threat use the term *apocalyptic* to refer to these crimes in an allusion to the biblical apocalypse—the complete final destruction of the world, which is forecast in the book of Revelation. As American writer Robert Jensen observes, while the term *apocalypse* has become associated in the minds of some with a reactionary form of theology espoused by conservative and evangelical movements, in a more secular context, "responsible apocalyptic thinking . . . reminds us of the importance of dealing honestly with reality even when it's frightening."[55] Those writers dealing honestly with the reality of nuclear danger search for a concept or word that can denote the unique destructiveness, the world-ending consequences, and the existential nature of the crime of using nuclear weapons.[56] Would it be a crime against humanity, a war crime, genocide, or ecocide? American philosopher John Somerville proposed the term *omnicide* (the killing of all life, destruction of all things), noting that "the supremely ironical fact is that today we live in fear and in possible sight of the human committing of this crime so unspeakable that it does not have a name, this crime so enormous it can be committed only once."[57] Even if a nuclear war or the resulting climatic effects called "nuclear winter"[58] did not entirely kill off all life on the planet, it would destroy human civilization and leave behind, in the words of Schell, only "a republic of insects and grass."[59] It is also important to recognize that nuclear weapons are *uniquely* apocalyptic. As science writer Mark Wolverton concludes, "Because the destruction they can wreak is so much more than any other weapon, because they can, at a single blow, kill more people than anything else humans have devised or built, they simply have to be considered on their own terms."[60] The use of nuclear weapons would indeed be a world-ending apocalyptic crime.

Most conventional criminologists shy away from analyzing social actions that produce, or threaten to produce, such large-scale and notably horrific harms, especially if these destructive acts are committed by powerful states or corporations. Friedrichs proposed an "inverse hypothesis" for criminology, which states that "the level of criminological attention to crime varies inversely with the level of harm (i.e., the larger the scope of harm, as in the case of genocide, the less criminological attention)."[61] Given this pronounced and regrettable tendency within the discipline, it is important to incorporate the element of "morally blameworthy harm" into the definition of the concept of crime more generally, as American criminologist Robert Agnew has suggested, and into any prospective criminology of nuclear weapons.[62]

According to Agnew (a past president of the ASC), a morally blameworthy harm is an act that threatens physical security, or a failure to prevent physical harm when one has a legal or moral duty to do so; is voluntary and intentional; and is unjustifiable and inexcusable. He notes that some blameworthy harms (but not all) are condemned by the public (generate a societal reaction) and are legally defined and sanctioned by the state or international bodies (subjected to lawmaking efforts). Agnew argues that "any behavior classified as a blameworthy harm, subject to at least modest condemnation by a significant portion of the public, or classified as a crime or 'crime-like' civil violation by the state should be viewed as a proper part of the subject matter of criminology."[63] But akin to Friedrichs's notion of a "prospective criminology,"[64] he goes further and boldly asserts that it is part of the "major mission" of criminology as a discipline to bring "unrecognized" blameworthy harms to the attention of the public and legal authorities, thus expanding the core of the field.[65] Following Agnew, I use this "integrated" definition of crime to supplement Sutherland's conception of the tasks of criminology, allowing us to assess (1) the critical nature of the morally blameworthy harms (retrospectively or prospectively) involved in state violations of the laws that have been created to address the threat of nuclear weapons; (2) large-scale societal reactions to the nuclear threat (public condemnations), such as the long struggle against these weapons engaged in by the world nuclear disarmament movement; and (3) the origins and development of the public international laws and legal sanctions intended to limit or ban the bomb and prevent apocalyptic harms. Such an analysis may contribute to the expansion of the core of criminology hoped for by Agnew and to Friedrichs's call for a prospective criminology of state crime.

In addition to the concept of state crime as developed by Chambliss and others,[66] I also draw on the important and overlapping conceptualization of *geopolitical crimes* as outlined by Falk.[67] He contends that it is misleading to think about international relations as a state-centric world order. Instead, Falk argues that there are "two intersecting and overlapping systems of rules and diplomatic protocols that are operative in international relations: a *juridical* system linking sovereign states on the basis of equality before the law; and a *geopolitical* system linking dominant states regionally and globally with other states on the basis of inequalities in power, scale, wealth and status."[68] Within this "structural dualism," it is the horizontal and nonhierarchical juridical system (best exemplified by the UNGA and the ICJ) that "make laws," and the vertical and hierarchical geopolitical system (composed of powerful nations like the United States and Russia) that are most likely to act in ways that "break laws" and produce serious harms (what Falk calls geopolitical crime). Not only do the dominant states in the geopolitical system tend to commit the most serious crimes, they also generally have the political power to successfully block most forms of accountability or social control under international law (the juridical system) for their geopolitical crimes.

According to Falk, geopolitical crimes involve "patterns of deliberative behavior by leading governments . . . that inflict severe harm on the individual and collective well being of people, and do so knowingly and or negligently."[69] He adds that these government actions "violate core norms of international law, diplomatic norms or the protocols of international relations, and fundamental principles of international ethics."[70] Falk's conceptualization of the structural dualism that pervades world order, as well as his concept of geopolitical crimes, is central to the analysis of the criminality of nuclear weapons. As Falk grimly asserts, "Nuclear weapons are geopolitically legal, while being considered juridically unlawful."[71] The juridical system makes laws related to nuclear weapons; powerful states in the geopolitical system break these laws; and to the consternation of much of the international political community, the juridical system is often powerless to enforce its rules and hold the nuclear weapons states accountable for their apocalyptic geopolitical crimes.

To conclude this brief discussion of the concepts of state and geopolitical crime, several additional points need to be made. First, the concept of "crime" is often used by members of the general public as a symbolic device or expressive term to convey a deep concern over actions regarded as moral transgressions or blameworthy harms (acts that are evil, shameful, or wrong). In the opinion of the public, those harms should be condemned and perhaps legally sanctioned. Many participants in the disarmament movement over the years have used the concept of "nuclear crimes" in just this way—as a rhetorical move within the larger social and political effort to control or abolish nuclear weapons. My hope is that the criminological analysis presented in this book, in addition to advancing scholarship in the field of state crime, can also meaningfully contribute to the social movement to abolish nuclear weapons by showing how state policies concerning these weapons are illegal under international law and that these blameworthy harms (crimes) can be understood from a sociological perspective and prevented by organized political action.

British criminologist Robert Reiner has observed, "To call something a crime is to register disapproval, fear, disgust or condemnation in the strongest possible terms and to demand urgent remedies—but not necessarily the pain of criminal penalties."[72] This raises a second point about popular conceptions of crime and social control. The public often expects that someone who is guilty of a crime should experience legal punishment within the traditional criminal justice system. This does not often happen with state or geopolitical crimes, despite some efforts in this direction within the nascent field of international criminal law (ICL). But even if specific state officials are prosecuted, convicted, and punished for international crimes, it may not be the most effective way to reduce or prevent this form of criminal behavior. Such crimes are organizational crimes (acts engaged in by complex, formal organizations) rooted in larger historical social structures such as the capitalist political economy or the geopolitical state system.

A sociological explanation of crimes of the nuclear state must identify the specific organizational actors involved, such as presidential administrations or other government agencies like the U.S. Department of Defense (DOD), as well as the individual officials who occupy key decision-making positions within these organizations. Such an analysis must also examine the specific political and economic structures or institutional environments that these organizations are located within (such as the political economy of global capitalism, Falk's hierarchical geopolitical system, or the American Empire and its national security apparatus). By focusing on military organizations (such as the Pentagon), their relationships with capitalist corporations in the defense industry, and connections to other state agencies, we can identify a military-industrial complex or "nuclear-industrial complex" as still another historical social structure that often drives decision making within the "warfare state."[73] Given the decisive impact of these larger social and organizational structures, a concern with individual criminal punishment may be misplaced. As American criminologist Donald Taft argued in the immediate aftermath of World War II, punishing war criminals (as individuals), however gratifying, would be ineffective. What needed to be done instead, he argued, was "to understand and attack the war system—the social process by which aggressive war is produced."[74] As Taft further observed, there are larger historical social structures that produce apocalyptic crimes, and unless those larger systems are understood and changed, aggressive war and nuclear weapons will not be abolished. This book contributes to that larger sociological understanding and advances public policies to prevent and control nuclear state-corporate crimes and foster nuclear disarmament.

OVERVIEW OF THE BOOK

This book addresses the three criminological tasks outlined by Sutherland as they relate to the nuclear threat. Chapter 2 explains why nuclear weapons are illegal by focusing on the making of international laws related to these weapons. The chapter defines public international law (Falk's juridical system) and surveys the treaties, legal decisions, general comments, and advisory opinions that are relevant to the use, threat to use, and continued possession of nuclear weapons. While the discipline of criminology does not normally draw on this body of law to designate behavior as criminal for study, many criminologists have argued that the general principles and substantive content of various forms of international law do constitute critical standards that can be used to classify the socially injurious actions (blameworthy harms) of states as crime for the purpose of criminological analysis.[75] As Chambliss argued, "Criminologists must develop a disciplinary vision which defines crime sociologically as behavior that violates international agreements and principles established in the courts and treaties of international bodies."[76] Such a vision is indeed critical to any attempt to develop a criminology of nuclear weapons.

Using this expanded legal definition of state crime, I contend that the 1963 *Shimoda* decision by a Japanese court and the 1996 advisory opinion of the ICJ are key to the application of IHL (also known as the laws of war) to the question of the legality of nuclear warfare. The NPT of 1968, as reaffirmed by the ICJ opinion, imposes a legal duty of disarmament on the world's nuclear weapons states, a solemn responsibility they refuse to fulfill in direct violation of the pact. International human rights (IHR) law such as the ICCPR is an underused branch of international law. However, the concept of "the right to life" contained in Article 6 of the ICCPR has also been applied to the use, threat to use, or continued possession of nuclear weapons by the UN Human Rights Committee (HRC). Finally, the TPNW, negotiated and adopted by 122 countries at the United Nations in 2017, is also key to the analysis presented here. This accord entered into force on October 24, 2020, when Honduras became the fiftieth country to ratify the treaty, and then became binding law for participating states on January 22, 2021. The TPNW is the first explicit international law to completely prohibit nuclear weapons, although the nine states that possess these weapons refused to participate in the negotiating process or acknowledge its outcome. Chapter 2 concludes with a brief consideration of the "paradox" of international law—the fact that these laws allow us to conceptualize the use, threat to use, and continued possession of nuclear weapons as crimes (to explain why they are illegal), while the historical record shows that this juridical system has failed to prevent these geopolitical crimes from occurring or to hold the guilty parties accountable.

Chapter 3 describes the consequential and controversial use of atomic bombs against Japan by the United States during World War II and offers a sociological explanation for why these geopolitical crimes (the breaking of IHL by a powerful state actor) took place in 1945 and then became normalized within U.S. political culture shortly thereafter. It is important to first place the atomic attacks against Hiroshima and Nagasaki in the broader historical context of the widespread and illegal conventional bombing of cities and civilian populations that took place both in Europe and in Asia earlier in the war. This chapter examines the social processes of "interpretive denial"[77] and the "normalization of deviance"[78] as they relate to the practice of "area," "morale," or "terror" bombing during World War II.

This analysis shows how both American and international outrage over the terror bombing of civilians at Guernica and other places prior to World War II was morally transformed in a very short time into a general acceptance of and normative support for such deadly state practices as terror bombing, the use of atomic bombs against Japan, the threats to use nuclear weapons during the wars in Korea and Vietnam (and elsewhere), and the stockpiling of thousands and thousands of thermonuclear devices.[79]

In addition to the social processes that led to the normalization of terror bombing during World War II and the interpretive denial concerning the decision to drop atomic bombs on Japan in 1945, the broader structural forces that drove these geopolitical crimes must also be examined. I argue that the imperial goals of an emerging American Empire—or "World Order,"[80] to use American historian Alfred McCoy's more expansive concept—led the United States to engage in an intense form of "power politics"[81] during World War II and to practice "atomic diplomacy"[82] concerning the Soviet Union at the end of the conflict. The structural forces driving the nuclear policies of the U.S. Empire would come to be cloaked in the comforting myth of American Exceptionalism and shielded from criticism by the normalization of the bomb that resulted from the outcome of the so-called "Good War"[83] and the interpretive efforts of U.S. political leaders after the war.

The following three chapters (4, 5, and 6) describe and analyze the other major categories of nuclear crimes: the continued possession of weapons that cannot be legally used and a variety of "threats" to use nuclear weapons either for general deterrence or in specific conflict situations. Societal reactions to and public condemnations of these forms of state criminality are also explored. Chapter 4 covers the immediate post–World War II period through the end of the Truman administration in 1953. Political events related to nuclear weapons from the Eisenhower administration (1953–1961) to the end of the Cold War in 1991 are examined in chapter 5. Throughout the entire Cold War era, American and Soviet leaders were, in the words of American historian Martin Sherwin, "gambling with Armageddon."[84] Chapter 6 then explores the lost opportunities for disarmament at the end of the Cold War, the rise of a policy of nonproliferation by military force, and the paradox of Barack Obama's Prague Promise.

As chapter 4 describes, following the bombings of Hiroshima and Nagasaki, a campaign emerged to establish international controls over the atomic bomb to avoid an arms race and prevent any future use of such destructive weapons (considered by many already at that time to be "criminal"). Despite the best efforts of the nascent world nuclear disarmament movement, organized and led initially by the atomic scientists who created the bomb, this campaign would fail due to the imperial "quest for American atomic supremacy"[85] and the emergence of a set of "attitudes, institutions, and dangers" that Lifton and Falk identified as "nuclearism."[86] As Lifton later explained, "By nuclearism I meant an exaggerated dependency on the weapons to keep the peace or even the world going, to the point of near worship of their godlike world-destroying power."[87]

As for the atomic scientists, after their internal attempt to prevent atomic weapons from being used against the Japanese people did not succeed, they organized committees, wrote reports, lobbied government officials, developed the FAS, launched the *Bulletin of the Atomic Scientists*, and, as previously noted, created the iconic Doomsday Clock in a heroic effort to convince governments to establish international controls over atomic weapons and avoid a costly nuclear arms race. Despite being aided by pacifists, World Federalists, prominent public figures such as British philosopher Bertrand Russell and American journalist Norman Cousins, and a variety of national peace organizations, the movement failed to "ban the bomb"—a slogan of the British Campaign for Nuclear Disarmament (CND).

The onset of the Cold War, the repressive political paranoia of McCarthyism, the impact of the Korean War, the rise of the national security state, the full emergence of the American Empire, and the testing of the hydrogen superbomb all operated to undermine and thwart the goals of the atomic scientists and the world nuclear disarmament movement. These historical developments also reflected larger structural and cultural forces— the U.S. decision to pursue global military supremacy within the world geopolitical system in 1940, the quest for American atomic supremacy during the Cold War, the rising power of a military-industrial nuclear complex (driven by the organizational interests of the Pentagon and corporate military firms), the continued normalization of the bomb (as a lifesaving, war-winning, freedom-defending peacekeeper), and the powerful influence of the cultural narratives of nuclearism and American Exceptionalism. These historical factors constituted what British sociologist Mike Savage calls the "weight of the past,"[88] and they would repeatedly derail the disarmament movement and decisively shape the Cold War world and the arms race. The United States (and eventually other countries) would continue to possess more and more powerful nuclear weapons (more than 65,000 at one point), block any political and legal moves toward disarmament, and threaten to use these weapons to achieve nuclear deterrence and in a variety of conflict situations in violation of international law.

Chapter 5 details some of those specific concerns, starting with President Eisenhower's threat to use nuclear weapons to end the Korean War. As American author and activist Joseph Gerson has documented, "On at least 30 occasions since the atomic bombings of Hiroshima and Nagasaki, every U.S. president has prepared and/or threatened to initiate nuclear war during international crises, confrontations, and war—primarily in the Third World."[89] These threats, he argues, have been used to illegally "expand, consolidate, and maintain" the American Empire.[90] The former American "nuclear war planner" turned peace activist Daniel Ellsberg produced an even more comprehensive list of the times that the United States has considered or threatened to use nuclear weapons in conflict situations since 1945.[91]

As chapter 5 argues, the state crime of threatening to use nuclear weapons also includes widespread organizational planning by the American military during the Cold War for a preemptive "first strike" against the Soviet Union, or the "first use" of nuclear weapons in response to a conventional Soviet military attack against NATO in Western Europe. The development of the fusion hydrogen (super) bomb and the production of new weapons delivery systems—such as intercontinental ballistic missiles (ICBMs) and multiple independently targetable reentry vehicles (MIRVs)—are also considered within this category of criminality.

After the Soviets developed their own atomic weapons and then the hydrogen bomb, a fearsome nuclear arms race ensued. In pursuit of American atomic supremacy, President Eisenhower oversaw a vast buildup of the nuclear arsenal in the 1950s and threatened the Soviet Union with "massive retaliation" in any military confrontation. It was during the Eisenhower administration that nuclearism—"psychological, political, and military dependence on nuclear weapons, the embrace of the weapons as a solution to a wide variety of human dilemmas, most ironically that of security"[92]—fully emerged.

During the John F. Kennedy administration, the two superpowers came to the brink of thermonuclear war during the Cuban Missile Crisis in 1962, and by the late 1960s (during the Lyndon B. Johnson administration) the Soviet Union had achieved nuclear parity with the United States. Thereafter, the two superpowers attempted to deter or check each other with "mutually assured destruction" (MAD). Commentating on this policy, Jonathan Schell notes that "moralists pondered the virtue of threatening a crime in order not to commit it; strategists wondered how a threat of 'suicide' (McNamara) could be 'credible' to the one so threatened."[93] Recognizing the "madness" of teetering on the nuclear abyss in this way, the Cold War protagonists began to take some steps away from the edge of extinction after the Cuban Missile Crisis (installing a "hotline" between Washington and Moscow, agreeing to a ban on atmospheric testing, and signing the NPT of 1968).

Under President Richard M. Nixon (who threatened to use nuclear weapons in Vietnam in 1969), a surprising period of "détente" then took place, and arms control agreements like the Strategic Arms Limitation Treaties (SALT I and II) would be negotiated with the Soviet Union in the 1970s. Despite these welcome but limited developments, both countries would still be "guilty" of the state crime of continuing to possess thousands of nuclear weapons and threatening to use them for the sake of deterrence or in imperial geopolitical conflicts throughout the period of the Cold War. After 1968, the state crime of continued possession of nuclear weapons was a violation of the legal obligation to negotiate in good faith a complete nuclear disarmament imposed by Article VI of the NPT.

Chapter 5 also analyzes the crimes of the American nuclear state in the late 1970s under President Jimmy Carter and in the 1980s during President Ronald Reagan's two terms in office. During these years, détente ended, the Cold War heated up, the "Carter Doctrine" concerning the Middle East was announced, and the threat of nuclear war loomed large in public consciousness once again. The Reagan administration confronted the Soviet Union on many geopolitical fronts, engaged in nuclear saber-rattling with an arms buildup and the threat to deploy a "Star Wars" defensive shield (the Strategic Defense Initiative or SDI), and talked about building "peace through strength." In response, the world disarmament movement was revived and attempted to impose a "nuclear weapons freeze" on the geopolitical system. The pressure of the global peace movement and anti–Cold War cultural activism, as well as the personal and political persuasion of the new Soviet leader, Mikhail Gorbachev, forced President Reagan to the bargaining table, where, to the astonishment of many, he and Gorbachev came close to abolishing all nuclear weapons in 1986. Although that did not happen (due to the political obstacle of the SDI program and the opposition of the imperial system within both countries), the two leaders did sign an important arms control agreement—the Intermediate Nuclear Forces (INF) Treaty in 1987. Shortly thereafter (during the presidency of George H. W. Bush), dramatic events unfolded—the Berlin Wall came down, the Soviet Union collapsed, and the Cold War ended.

Chapter 6 analyzes the lost opportunities for disarmament following the end of the Cold War, when the Doomsday Clock was set back all the way to seventeen minutes to midnight. After the Cold War ended, diminishing the immediate threat and the necessity for nuclear deterrence, the United States and the other nuclear powers squandered what Schell called the "Gift of Time"—the opportunity to change their nuclear policies and move toward disarmament and the complete abolition of nuclear weapons.[94] The nuclear peril receded from public concern as the Cold War vanished and stockpiles were reduced. But thousands of the weapons would be retained, and the potential existential danger they posed remained with them. Despite the removal of the Soviet threat, American political, military, and corporate leaders (the military-industrial nuclear complex) sought to fill what was at that time called the "threat blank" and sustain the nuclear arsenal by focusing on "rogue states and nuclear outlaws."[95] During the George H. W. Bush and Bill Clinton administrations, the Rogue Doctrine would be developed and then confirmed by the 1991 Persian Gulf War (Operation Desert Storm), leading eventually to the use of preemptive military threats against rogue states.

President Clinton would also promote the capitalist penetration of Russia and Eastern Europe and encourage the enlargement of NATO eastward toward the borders of Russia. These policies, along with a continuing obsession with the issue of missile defense, would undermine the process of arms control negotiations between the two major nuclear powers. The George W. Bush administration, aggressively in pursuit of imperial designs in a now "unipolar" world, would craft a policy of "preemptive counterproliferation" by military means and develop new strategic policies that would sweep away most arms control agreements between the United States and Russia.[96] And while President Barack Obama would promise a world free of nuclear weapons at a speech in Prague and sign a New START agreement with Russia, paradoxically he would also end up authorizing the modernization and expansion of the U.S. nuclear arsenal. I argue that, despite his good intentions, Obama remained trapped in a national security state that still pursued global imperial domination, a culture of nuclearism that still clung to the bomb for security, and an ideology of American Exceptionalism that blocked him from achieving his grand promise of abolishing nuclear weapons.

The final chapter describes the current apocalyptic threats the world faces and charts a pathway toward the reduction of the nuclear threat and the eventual abolition of nuclear weapons. The disintegration of the Cold War rationale for the possession of nuclear arms did not result in the embrace of abolition. Instead, imperialism and other structural and cultural factors have led the United States to continue to illegally possess more than five thousand warheads and threaten to use these deadly weapons still today. The existential risk that these weapons pose is heightened by a variety of current apocalyptic threats including recent efforts to expand and modernize the existing nuclear arsenal and withdraw from previous arms control treaties negotiated between Russia and the United States. With the Russian invasion of Ukraine and Putin's repeated threats to use nuclear weapons, the world is now facing a "new nuclear reality,"[97] and tensions between the United States and Russia have escalated. Chapter 7 also discusses other factors that heighten the current nuclear danger, including the antagonistic relationship between the United States and China; an authoritarian chain of command concerning the decision to launch the weapons; the possibility of the use of nuclear weapons by either rogue states or nonstate terrorists; the chance of nuclear warfare by accident, miscalculation, or mistake; and, finally, the intersection of the "apocalyptic twins"—nuclear weapons and climate disruptions. I argue that we must be concerned with both of these apocalyptic crimes, not only because each is a blameworthy harm that poses an existential threat to the survival of humanity in its own right, but also because they intersect with and intensify the risks of each other.

Finally, chapter 7 assesses the prospects for nuclear abolition and outlines intermediate steps the international political community could take toward turning back the hands of the Doomsday Clock and ultimately ridding the world of the scourge of nuclear weapons. Following Schell, I argue that we must turn abolition from a far-off goal into "an active organizing principle that gives direction to everything that is done in the nuclear arena."[98] While abolishing nuclear weapons may seem like a pipe dream to many, I argue that it can be achieved if the major powers in the geopolitical system are forced by intense political pressure from the disarmament movement—and Falk's juridical system—to take very difficult but necessary and achievable intermediate steps. These steps include reducing tensions between the United States and Russia and restoring some form of international dialogue and cooperation between the two. That dialogue and cooperation could then be used to restart and extend the arms control regime to reduce the number of existing weapons through negotiated agreements. As part of this process, a ban on the modernization and expansion of current nuclear arsenals must be enacted. Reforming the United Nations to make it a more democratic and effective body is also necessary, and it will likewise be crucial to revive a pathway toward the implementation of Article VI of the NPT, which requires disarmament. Finally, the most important step is to convince the nuclear states to join the TPNW to rid the world of existing weapons and create safeguards against rebuilding them.

All these intermediate steps toward the eventual abolition of nuclear weapons would require the United States to take a strong leadership role. Only the United States has the power and position in the current geopolitical system to achieve these steps toward disarmament. Despite a recent decline in American power, the United States remains the pivotal nation and the central nuclear power. While Russia, China, and the other nuclear powers have an enormous responsibility to act as well, American leadership is primary and indispensable in moving the world toward nuclear abolition.

Yet I argue that U.S. political leaders have repeatedly shirked their moral and legal responsibility to bring about a world without nuclear weapons. The United States has refused to take the necessary steps toward disarmament because of the pursuit of global economic and political domination. The American state functions to serve capitalist interests and secure the political hegemony of the United States in the world system. Operating within the confines of the historical social structure of the American Empire, U.S. political leaders are unable to take the steps necessary to reduce the nuclear danger and move toward the ultimate goal of abolition. Unless the American Empire is challenged by a strong domestic social movement and powerful pressure from the international political community, nuclear weapons will not be abolished, and the apocalyptic threat will remain.

CHAPTER 2

Nuclear Warfare Is Illegal

The Lawyers Committee on Nuclear Policy believes that
nuclear weapons must be abolished. We believe the use or
threat of use of nuclear weapons is a grave violation of
many provisions of legally binding international law.
—Lawyers Committee on Nuclear Policy, *Statement
on the Illegality of Nuclear Warfare*

The reality of the situation is this. International law is
clear that there exist strong rules prohibiting threat or use
of nuclear weapons and an even clearer obligation to negotiate a treaty obligating their elimination.
—Richard Falk, *At the Nuclear Precipice*

This October 24th [2020] will go down in history as the
day nuclear weapons were declared illegal with the ratifi-
cation of the U.N. Treaty on the Prohibition of Nuclear
Weapons.
—Robert Dodge, "Nuclear Weapons
Banned—Illegal at Last"

IN 1862, AS President Abraham Lincoln deliberated over
his forthcoming Emancipation Proclamation and wrestled with the question of how to develop a more aggressive strategy to conduct military operations during the Civil War, his administration launched an ambitious and
far-reaching project. At this "low moment of the Union's fortunes,"[1] Secretary of War Edwin Stanton and his general-in-chief, Henry Halleck, asked
Francis Lieber, a German-born Columbia College (now Columbia University) professor of history and political science, to draw up a set of rules to
govern the conduct of the Union Army in fighting the war. The professor
agreed and worked furiously at the task. The resulting Lieber Code

23

Professor Francis Lieber, author of the Lieber (Lincoln) Code, ca. 1855–1865. Brady-Handy photograph collection, Library of Congress, Prints and Photographs Division.

(sometimes referred to as Lincoln's Code)—consisting of 157 articles and issued as General Orders Number 100 in 1863 by President Lincoln—would, according to American historian John Fabian Witt, "lay the foundations for the modern laws of war."[2]

While American historian Samuel Moyn has critiqued Lieber's work and argued that he "was not really part of the tradition of making war more humane,"[3] the rules and prohibitions concerning warfare laid out in the Lieber Code soon reached Europe, where they would prove to have a huge influence on diplomats and international lawyers. Building on the Lieber Code, conventions at Geneva, Saint Petersburg, and The Hague would flesh out laws applicable to war and armed conflict, creating the rules that would eventually become known as international humanitarian law (IHL). Many years later, it would be this body of public international law that was first applied to the use of and threat to use nuclear weapons, although other international legal bans on the possession and proliferation of and threat to use these deadly weapons would follow. While Lincoln and Lieber were not the first to grapple with the complex issues that arise from the idea that the conduct of war can be regulated by law, the seminal code they brought to life would come to have an important impact on questions concerning the illegality of nuclear warfare.

PUBLIC INTERNATIONAL LAW

Public international law governs interactions between nation-states. It is defined as "the body of rules binding on States in their relations with one another, and determining their mutual rights and obligations."[4] This form of law consists of both customary state practices and specific treaties negotiated by two or more states. International law is a vast, fragmented, and decentralized system that contains multiple subdisciplines, many of which took their contemporary form following the creation of the United Nations in 1945. These subdisciplines, such as the laws of armed conflict, international criminal law (ICL), international environmental law, the international law of the sea, and international human rights law, among others, "often have their own distinct institutions and occasionally also adjudicatory bodies."[5] This book argues that decisions by government officials (acting as representatives of the state) that violate public international law can be classified as state crimes and subjected to criminological inquiry. More specifically, the book contends that governmental decisions to use, threaten to use, or continue to possess nuclear weapons can be classified as state crimes (morally blameworthy harms committed on behalf of the state) and brought within

the boundaries of the discipline of criminology because they are illegal—
that is, they violate one or more of these various forms of public international law. As Agnew notes, "The international law is especially useful for
identifying harms committed by states," in this case state harms related to
the use, threat, and possession of nuclear weapons.[6]

The term *international law* was first used in 1780 by British philosopher
Jeremy Bentham, a name familiar to criminologists who study what is
known as the classical school of criminology.[7] Yet the history of "the creation of more or less formal practices and mutual expectations that may be
considered the early traces of what we today call international law" can
be tracked to Europe in the late Middle Ages.[8] Dutch jurist Hugo Grotius
(1583–1645) is considered to be the founder of the modern doctrine of
international law. He argued that international rules governing states could
be derived from the concept of natural law, "principles of justice which had
a universal and eternal validity and which could be discovered by pure reason, not made through human choice."[9] The international state system that
emerged from the 1648 Peace of Westphalia—which ended the Thirty
Years' War in Europe and brought peace to the Holy Roman Empire—
advanced the idea that a body of international rules was necessary to govern
relations between sovereign nation-states (an emerging modern conception). In the nineteenth century, the concept of natural law was challenged
by a form of legal positivism, which argued that law was man-made or
state-created, not of divine or natural origin. As Danish legal scholar Anders
Henriksen points out, "Positivism attached primary importance to state
consent, whether expressed explicitly in the form of a treaty or implicitly by
customary state practices adhered to by states due to a belief that the practice was legally binding."[10]

Following the foundational development of the Lieber Code in 1863, it
was the formation of the International Committee of the Red Cross (ICRC)
and the resulting Geneva Convention for the Amelioration of the Condition
of the Wounded in Armies in the Field in 1864 that would be decisive in the
formation of the laws of war. Working through the ICRC, Swiss notables
Henry Dunant and Gustave Moynier played important roles in the establishment of the "first set of treaty rules for war."[11] The Saint Petersburg Declaration of 1868 (renouncing the use, in time of war, of explosive projectiles)
and the two important peace conferences held at The Hague in 1899 and
1907 would push the international community further down the path
toward the development of IHL. The original objective of the two Hague
Conventions was to create rules to limit the use of force in international

affairs (jus ad bellum), but as American legal scholar William Slomanson states, "Once the conference participants realized that there would be no international agreement to eliminate war, the central theme became how to conduct it."[12] The Hague Conventions then produced the first multilateral treaties that addressed the conduct of warfare (jus in bello), built on the rules first set down by Lieber, Dunant, and Moynier.

The catastrophic Great War of 1914 to 1918 (World War I) shattered Europe and the Middle East and brought renewed efforts to outlaw war itself. The most significant result of the 1919 Paris Peace Conference following the "war to end all wars" was a new organization of states called the League of Nations. The United States—despite its new centrality and global power and the strenuous efforts of President Woodrow Wilson—did not join the League of Nations due to the rejection of the required treaty by the U.S. Senate.[13] The covenant of the newly created international league did not prohibit war or the use of military force, but it did attempt to reduce their likelihood through a process of consultation and arbitration. The novel experience of aerial bombing during the First World War also led to the creation of a commission of jurists that met in 1923 at The Hague to draft the Rules of Aerial Warfare.[14] These rules were never formally adopted, however, and future efforts to constrain the bombing of civilians from the air (eventually including the use of nuclear weapons) would attempt to use the more general concepts in IHL concerning noncombatant immunity.

The horrific experience of the Great War also led to a "War Outlawry" movement in the 1920s that was both popular and powerful enough to produce an international accord renouncing war. The Kellogg-Briand Pact outlawed war as "an instrument of national policy" and, despite various criticisms and misgivings, was ratified by the U.S. Senate and signed into law by President Calvin Coolidge in January 1929.[15] But neither the structures of the League of Nations nor the Kellogg-Briand renunciation of war was a strong enough legal instrument to prevent the start of a second world war in 1939. This global conflict, even more catastrophic than the first, likewise produced strong international efforts to create new institutions and laws to prevent war or at least limit its destructiveness. In 1941, President Franklin Delano Roosevelt (FDR) and British prime minister Winston Churchill developed the Atlantic Charter, which was intended to serve as a blueprint for a new "rules-based approach to the international order."[16] Following World War II, the major principles contained in the Anglo-American Atlantic Charter would be enshrined in the charter of a new world organization, the United Nations (UN). As British international lawyer Philippe Sands notes, the creation of the UN in July 1945 "was the starting point for the system of modern global rules."[17]

The creation of the International Military Tribunals at Nuremberg and Tokyo to hold personally liable senior German and Japanese officials accused of crimes against peace, crimes against humanity, and war crimes during World War II was also a transformative moment for human rights and humanitarian law. The constituting treaty for the Nuremberg trials of Nazi officials, the London Charter (Charter of the Nuremberg Tribunal), was agreed to on August 8, 1945, by the victorious Allied powers. The principles contained in this charter were later approved by the UNGA (Resolution 95-1), which explicitly incorporated them into international law. While the UN and Nuremberg Charters generally outlawed the recourse to war (with a few limited exceptions), the four Geneva Conventions of 1949 advanced international law concerning how "legal" wars are to be fought, providing protections for "those persons who are *hors de combat*, that is, those who are not, or are no longer taking an active part in the hostilities, in particular the wounded and sick members of the armed forces, prisoners of war, and the civilian population."[18] The Geneva Laws, and the additional protocols of 1977, are an important part of IHL. It is this general body of international law, which dates back to the Lieber Code and the work of the International Red Cross in the nineteenth century and the Hague Conventions at the start of the twentieth, that requires parties to an armed conflict to protect civilians and noncombatants, limits the means or methods that are permissible during warfare, and sets out the rules that govern the behavior of occupying forces.

Although both courts argued that they were "not making new international law but merely upholding the law as it was,"[19] the International Military Tribunals at Nuremberg and Tokyo, by focusing on the personal accountability of German and Japanese government and military officials, also helped give rise to a new rudimentary body of international law— international criminal law (ICL). ICL is "the body of law that assigns individual criminal responsibility for breaches of public international law."[20] Historically, public international law regulated the behavior of states at the international level, while domestic criminal law held individuals accountable for their illegal actions by meting out criminal penalties. ICL proposes using criminal sanctions against individual state officials for violations of international law. As Canadian international law scholar Bruce Broomhall observes, "Another use of the phrase 'international criminal law'—not adopted here—would encompass the responsibility of States, characterized as *criminal* responsibility, arising from certain exceptionally serious violations of international law."[21] Like Broomhall, most legal scholars view ICL as an emerging body of law that assigns *individual criminal responsibility*, not state responsibility, for serious violations of international law.[22] Others, however, such as the renowned Belarus-born Columbia Law School professor Louis Henkin, have concluded that "at Nuremberg, sitting in judgment on the recent past, the Allied victors declared waging aggressive war to be a state crime (under both treaty and customary law) as well as an individual crime by those represented and acted for the aggressor state."[23]

ICL frequently overlaps with another emerging body of international law known as international human rights law, as well as with the older humanitarian law (the laws of war).[24] In recent years, the development of ICL has been a catalyst for the creation of the International Criminal Court.[25] Since this book focuses primarily on legal norms formulated as obligations upon nation-states, I do not discuss the implications of ICL concerning individual criminal responsibility related to nuclear weapons.

But are any of these forms of international law really *law* properly called? There is a long-standing controversy over this question. As British senior law lecturer Alexander Orakhelashvili points out, "This controversy has focused on the relevance of the lack of *sanctions* in cases of violation of international norms as compared to municipal law."[26] He goes on to argue, however, that the question of whether sanctions are applied or not confuses the issue of whether international law is law (it is) with the very different issue of the effectiveness and enforcement of these rules. Violations of international law are indeed rarely sanctioned, but this does not negate the existence of these laws as law, properly called, or the real power and moral influence that these legal instruments can exert. I return to this problem later with a discussion of what I call the paradox of international law.

The Application of IHL to Atomic Weapons: The *Shimoda* Case

After the atomic bombings of Japan at the end of World War II, the question arose, does public international law, specifically IHL (the law of armed conflict or the law of the Hague) apply to the use of or threat to use atomic weapons? Stated differently, is nuclear warfare or the use of nuclear weapons illegal? The first court case to address the issue was the *Shimoda* decision, handed down by the District Court of Tokyo on December 7, 1963. This important case came about due to the efforts of Japanese lawyer Okamoto Shoichi, who had been a member of the defense counsel during the Tokyo War Crimes Tribunal. Okamoto had hoped to file a legal action against the U.S. government over the atomic bombings of Hiroshima and Nagasaki in an American court. Confronted with significant political and legal obstacles, he abandoned that plan of action and turned instead to the Japanese courts to try to obtain relief for the victims of the atomic attacks.[27]

In May 1955, five Japanese nationals, represented by Okamoto and his team, instituted a legal action against their government to recover damages for the injuries they had suffered because of the atomic bombings of Hiroshima and Nagasaki. The lead plaintiff was Shimoda Ryuichi, a fifty-seven-year-old man from Hiroshima who lost five children and suffered serious health problems from the bombing. Part of the claim of the plaintiffs for compensation was based on the assertion that the dropping of the atomic bombs as an act of hostilities was illegal under the rules of positive international law. The case dragged on for eight years, but in its important ruling the Japanese court held that the atomic bomb attacks on Hiroshima and Nagasaki were clear violations of international law (although it rejected the plaintiffs' claims for compensation). In his classic appraisal of the *Shimoda* case, Richard Falk clearly summarizes the principal reasons the court gave for its decision that the attacks were illegal:

(1) International law forbids an indiscriminate or blind attack upon an undefended city; Hiroshima and Nagasaki were undefended;

(2) International law only permits, if at all, indiscriminate bombing of a defended city if it is justified by military necessity; no military necessity of sufficient magnitude could be demonstrated here;

(3) International law as it has specifically developed to govern aerial bombardment might be stretched to permit zone or area bombing of an enemy city in which military objectives were concentrated; there was no concentration of military objectives in either Hiroshima or Nagasaki;

(4) International law prohibits the use of weapons and belligerent means that produce unnecessary and cruel forms of suffering as illustrated by the prohibition of lethal poisons and bacteria; the atomic bomb causes suffering far more severe and extensive than the prohibited weapons.[28]

According to Falk, the Japanese court based its ruling of the illegality of the atomic attacks on the following legal documents: the Saint Petersburg Declaration (1868); the Hague Conventions on the Law and Customs of Land

Warfare (1899 and 1907); the Declaration Prohibiting Aerial Bombardment (1907); the Treaty of Five Countries Concerning Submarines and Poisonous Gases (1922); the Draft Rules of Air Warfare (1923); and the Protocol Prohibiting the Use of Asphyxiating, Poisonous or Other Gases (1925).[29] These declarations, rules, and protocols are parts of the larger body of IHL. As the Lawyers Committee on Nuclear Policy (LCNP) later concluded, "The *Shimoda* court ruled the bombings illegal. Among other reasons, the court held that the atomic weapons produced **unnecessary and cruel forms of suffering**, in violation of the laws of war."[30] Revisiting the issue years later, Falk asserted that "the use of atomic bombs in World War II was not merely a violation of the laws of war, a conclusion confirmed in a historic and persuasive judicial decision in the *Shimoda* case in 1963, but was also *a criminal act of the greatest severity* for which the perpetrators were given impunity."[31] Yet most Americans have never heard of the *Shimoda* litigation and remain resistant to the idea that the use of atomic weapons against Japan constituted a criminal act by the U.S. government.

American legal scholar Francis Boyle has argued an additional point of law concerning the bombings of Hiroshima and Nagasaki, which also touches on the issue of ICL. He posits that the various international legal rules for the conduct of warfare that the Japanese court relied on had also been accepted (codified and promulgated) by the U.S. government itself in the War Department's Field Manual 27-10. Titled *Rules of Land Warfare*, the document was issued on October 4, 1940 (and amended on November 15, 1944). As Boyle notes, the principles of international law spelled out in detail in Field Manual 27-10 were binding on U.S. officials throughout World War II and thus prohibited the use of atomic weapons against Japan.[32] All American military personnel did know, or should have known, the laws of war. Therefore, he concludes, "all U.S. civilian government officials and military officers who ordered or knowingly participated in the atomic bombings of Hiroshima and Nagasaki could have been (and still can be) lawfully punished as war criminals."[33] But as the following chapter argues, the critical legal observations of scholars like Boyle and Falk (whether asserting individual or state criminal responsibility) have been undercut and all but blocked from public view due to the denial and normalization of the use of atomic bombs within American political culture.

Since the *Shimoda* ruling, a significant number of international law scholars have concurred with its analysis of the illegality of nuclear warfare.[34] These legal analysts all agree that the modern law of armed conflict did apply to the atomic bombings of Japan in 1945 and continues to apply today. The LCNP summarized this law in the following six rules, which they argue "are generally accepted and considered binding by the vast majority of countries."[35] According to the LCNP, under the rules of the just conduct of war (jus in bello), it is prohibited for states to

1. Use weapons or tactics that cause indiscriminate harm as between combatants and noncombatants, and military and civilian personnel;
2. Use weapons or tactics that cause unnecessary or aggravated devastation and suffering;
3. Use weapons or tactics that violate the neutral jurisdiction of non-participating countries;
4. Use asphyxiating, poisonous or other gases, and all analogous liquids, materials or devices;
5. Use weapons or tactics that cause widespread, long-term and severe damage to the environment; and
6. Effect reprisals that are disproportionate to their provocation.

Within the United States, these legal claims are generally ignored, met with a silence that attempts to delegitimize them and render them invisible to the public. Yet soon after the Lawyers Committee published this summary, a major international court ruling would bolster its conclusions and concur that nuclear weapons are illegal.

The Advisory Opinion of the International Court of Justice

The legal analysts who argue for the applicability of IHL (the law of armed conflict) to the use of and threat to use nuclear weapons received a tremendous boost on July 8, 1996, with the delivery of an important decision by the International Court of Justice (ICJ). The ICJ (also known as the World Court) is the judicial organ of the United Nations and has the power to decide "contentious" cases, which are usually disputes between two different member states, and to provide advisory opinions on important legal matters. The ICJ gives these advisory opinions when it is asked a "legal question" by the General Assembly or one of the specialized agencies affiliated with the United Nations. An advisory opinion is intended to clarify some aspect of international law related to the work of the agency requesting the opinion. Fifteen judges usually sit on the ICJ, but only fourteen participated in the nuclear weapons case due to a recent vacancy.

In the advisory opinion *The Legality of the Threat or Use of Nuclear Weapons*, the ICJ ruled that the threat or use of nuclear weapons by states would generally be "illegal" under international law. As international legal scholars Laurence Boisson de Chazournes and Philippe Sands note, "In addressing the issues the Court made its most direct foray into peace and security issues, touching upon some of the most contentious questions of international law."[36] The ICJ decision, which has been called "the most important opinion by a court in the history of the world,"[37] came in response to requests from the World Health Organization (WHO) and the UNGA for advisory opinions on the legality of nuclear weapons. In a complicated and controversial ruling, the ICJ stated that "the threat or use of nuclear weapons would generally be contrary to the rules of international law applicable in armed conflict, and in particular, the principles and rules of humanitarian law."[38]

The two requests for advisory opinions on the legality of the threat or use of nuclear weapons were stimulated by the efforts of various nongovernmental organizations (NGOs) dedicated to the goals of peace and nuclear disarmament. The World Court Project, as it was called, was the result of the work of the International Physicians for the Prevention of Nuclear War (IPPNW), the International Peace Bureau (IPB), and the International Association of Lawyers Against Nuclear Arms (IALANA).[39] Three small Pacific states (the Marshall Islands, Samoa, and the Solomon Islands), along with a worldwide network of private citizens, were also influential in bringing this important question to the ICJ.[40]

The first international agency to request an advisory opinion on the legality of nuclear weapons was WHO. On May 14, 1993, WHO adopted a resolution that asked, "In view of the health and environmental effects, would the use of nuclear weapons by a State in war or other armed conflict be a breach of its obligations under international law including the WHO constitution?"[41] Later that year, the UNGA commenced a debate on the issue that culminated in the passage, on December 15, 1994, of Resolution 49/75K, which asked the ICJ to provide an advisory opinion on the question, "Is the threat or use of nuclear weapons in any circumstances permitted under international law?"[42] Despite fierce opposition from nuclear powers like the United States, the United Kingdom, and France—who argued that the request was "vague and abstract" and might "adversely affect disarmament negotiations"— the measure passed (seventy-eight in favor, forty-three opposed, and thirty-four abstaining) and was sent on to the ICJ.[43]

The Court dealt with the two requests together. In such advisory matters, the ICJ first asks for written submissions and then later holds hearings for those states that wish to make oral arguments. More than forty countries submitted written briefs concerning one or both of the requests, and then between October 30 and November 15, 1995, twenty-two states participated in the oral proceedings (the largest number in the ICJ's history). As Boisson de Chazournes and Sands point out, "Haunting the proceedings, but rarely articulated, [was] a key question: What are the limits of international law when faced with a subject that goes to the core of the exercise of state power?"[44] Despite the momentous significance of the issue and the case, or as one commentator observed, "perhaps because of it," the hearings were almost completely ignored by the world's mainstream media.[45]

On July 8, 1996, the ICJ delivered two opinions. In the first, the Court concluded that WHO lacked competence to request an advisory opinion on the legality of nuclear weapons and thus it would not rule on the substance of the WHO request. In the other opinion, however, the ICJ did rule on the request it had received from the UNGA and declared that, broadly, the threat or use of nuclear weapons was illegal. It was a complex ruling.

In the first part of the opinion the ICJ took up a series of preliminary issues. First, the Court determined that it does have the jurisdiction to respond to the UNGA request, that the UNGA has the competence to ask such a question, and that the request itself was indeed a "legal question." The ICJ thus found no compelling reasons to exercise its discretion not to respond to the request. After a brief discussion of the meaning of the UNGA request, the ICJ then addressed the question of the burden of proof: "The nuclear weapon States appearing before it either accepted, or did not dispute, that their independence to act was indeed restricted by the principles and rules of international law, more particularly humanitarian law, as did the other states which took part in the proceedings. Hence, the argument concerning the legal conclusions to be drawn from the use of the word "permitted," and the question of the burden of proof to which it was said to give rise, are without particular significance for the disposition of the issues before the Court."[46] In its substantive analysis of the UNGA question, the ICJ began by addressing a series of human rights, health, and environmental arguments that had been advanced by several states. First, it was argued that the use of nuclear weapons would violate the "right to life" guaranteed by Article 6 of the International Covenant on Civil and Political Rights (an issue I will return to later). Some states also contended that the prohibition against genocide contained in the Convention on the Prevention and Punishment of the Crime of Genocide (1948) was a relevant rule that the Court could apply. Other states argued that the use of nuclear weapons violated various principles of international environmental law.

The ICJ rejected the arguments based on specific human rights and limited environmental laws and instead turned to the more general law relating to the use of armed force as the basis on which the legality of the threat or use of nuclear weapons should be judged. The ICJ concluded, "The most directly relevant applicable law governing the question of which it was seized, is that relating to the use of force enshrined the United Nations Charter and the law applicable in armed conflict which regulates the conduct of hostilities, together with any specific treaties on nuclear weapons that the Court might determine to be relevant."[47] The Court then added, "In consequence, in order correctly to apply to the present case the Charter law on the use of force and the law applicable in armed conflict, in particular humanitarian law, it is imperative for the Court to take account of the unique characteristics of nuclear weapons, and in particular their destructive capacity, their capacity to cause untold human suffering, and their ability to cause damage to generations to come."[48]

The ICJ then considered the provisions of the UN Charter relating to the threat or use of force. The judges came to a unanimous conclusion that any use of nuclear weapons contrary to Article 2(4) of the UN Charter (generally prohibiting the threat or use of force in international relations) and not vindicated by Article 51 (recognizing every state's inherent right of self-defense if an armed attack occurs) is unlawful. Turning to the law applicable in situations of armed conflict, the Court faced two questions:

1. Are there specific rules in international law regulating the legality or illegality of recourse to nuclear weapons per se?
2. What are the implications of the principles and rules of humanitarian law applicable in armed conflict and the law of neutrality?

The ICJ began by noting that international law (customary or treaty based) does not contain any specific prescription authorizing the threat or use of nuclear weapons. Likewise, the Court also concluded (by a vote of eleven to three) that "there is in neither customary nor conventional international law any comprehensive and universal prohibition of the threat or use of nuclear weapons."[49] It is important to emphasize that this conclusion was true at the time, but the approval of the Draft Treaty on the Prohibition of Nuclear Weapons at the UN in 2017 and its ratification in 2020 (discussed later in this chapter) would most likely change that judgment today. At the time, however, to reach the conclusion that no comprehensive or universal prohibition of the threat or use of nuclear weapons existed, the ICJ took up a series of arguments that the use of nuclear weapons is specifically prohibited by various legal instruments such as the limits on the right of self-defense, the ban on the use of poisoned weapons, specific arms control agreements, customary law since 1945, and UNGA resolutions.[50] The Court rejected these arguments as too limited and specific to deal with the larger issue of the legality of nuclear weapons.

Not having found any specific rules in international law prohibiting nuclear weapons per se at that time, the ICJ then turned to the issue of whether recourse to nuclear weapons could be declared illegal considering the general principles and rules of IHL applicable in armed conflict and of the law of neutrality. The cardinal principles of humanitarian law according to the Court are the protection of the civilian population and civilian objects, the prohibition of weapons incapable of distinguishing between combatants and noncombatants, and the prohibition of causing unnecessary suffering to combatants. The judges all agreed that there could be no doubt as to the applicability of these general principles to a possible threat or use of nuclear weapons, even though these principles and rules had evolved prior to the invention of nuclear weapons. This is a key point that I will also return to later in this chapter.

While all fourteen judges agreed that these principles apply to nuclear weapons in general, there was a sharp divergence of opinion concerning their specific application. There were two points of view.[51] According to one view, the fact that recourse to nuclear weapons is subject to and regulated by the law of armed conflict does not necessarily mean that such recourse is as such prohibited. The other view holds that recourse to nuclear weapons could never be compatible with the principles and rules of humanitarian law and is therefore always prohibited. Although, the Court admitted, "In view of the unique characteristics of nuclear weapons . . . the use of such weapons in fact seems scarcely reconcilable with respect for such requirements. Nevertheless, the Court considers that it does not have sufficient elements to enable it to conclude with certainty that the use of nuclear weapons would necessarily be at variance with the principles and rules of law applicable in armed conflict in any circumstance."[52]

Given the dispute, the ICJ's overall finding on this point (by a vote of eight to seven, decided by the second vote of President Mohammed Bedjaoui) was a qualified one: "It follows from the above-mentioned requirements that the threat or use of nuclear weapons would generally be contrary to the rules of international law applicable in armed conflict, and in particular the principles and rules of humanitarian law."[53] The Court went on to say, "However, in view of the current state of international law, and of the elements of fact at its disposal, the court cannot conclude definitely whether the threat or use of nuclear weapons would be lawful or unlawful in an *extreme circumstance of self-defense*, in which the very survival of a State would be at stake."[54]

Several points need to be made about this qualified finding. First, of the seven dissenting judges, three voted against the finding because it does not go far enough to prohibit the threat or use of nuclear weapons in all circumstances. Second, the qualification in the finding applies only to the most extreme cases where the survival of a state is at stake. Finally, as Falk points out, "The court is clearly not validating a threat or use of nuclear weapons in an extreme circumstance of self-defense but asserting that it cannot conclude definitely one way or the other with respect to the legality of such a claim even in that situation."[55] The conclusion that follows from Falk's point, then, is that all past state actions threatening or using nuclear weapons, and the vast majority of all such potential state actions in the future, would clearly be illegal under international law according to the ICJ ruling.

As previously noted, it is important to stress that the World Court's advisory opinion in this case did not create *new* law. Rather, the decision clarified that *existing* public international law, particularly the general principles and rules of IHL applicable in armed conflict (the laws of war), did apply to the use of or threat to use nuclear weapons. The Court's ruling could be characterized as, in the words of Justice Robert H. Jackson, U.S. chief of counsel at the Nuremberg Tribunal, "declaratory of existent law."[56] This legal position also supports the ruling of the Japanese court in the *Shimoda* case that the United States did violate international law by dropping atomic bombs on Japan.

As the Nuremberg Tribunal itself made clear, the violation of the laws or customs of war are *war crimes*, and inhumane acts committed against civilian populations are *crimes against humanity*. Thus, I argue that the use of and threat to use nuclear weapons are not only illegal but also *criminal*. As Boyle reflects on the ICJ ruling,

> Whenever the court discusses violations of the laws and customs of war; or violations of the Hague Conventions and Protocols; or violations of international humanitarian law, etc. with respect to the threat

and use of nuclear weapons, the reader must understand that such violations are not just "illegal" and "unlawful" but are also "war crimes"
and thus "criminal" under basic principles of international law that
have been fully subscribed to by the United States government itself.
Hence my basic conclusions (1) that both the threat and use of nuclear
weapons are criminal; and (2) that nuclear deterrence itself is
criminal.[57]

Following Boyle, we can confirm that nuclear weapons are both illegal and
criminal.

Concerning Boyle's first conclusion, the idea that the "threat" to use
nuclear weapons is also criminal needs further explication, and chapters 4
to 6 describe numerous occasions in which the United States has threatened
to use nuclear weapons for the sake of deterrence or in various conflict situations. All these threats by the American nuclear state, regardless of the circumstances, are unlawful. First, as previously noted, the ICJ explicitly ruled
that in all but the most extreme circumstances, the threat to use nuclear
weapons would be illegal under international law. The legal logic here, as
the LCNP has argued, is that "if a given use of nuclear weapons is judged to
be contrary to the humanitarian rules of armed conflict, then logically any
threat of such use should be considered contrary to the humanitarian rules
of armed conflict as well."[58] In the view of several legal scholars, these
threats, as violations of international law, constitute state crimes. Boyle concludes that "the threat to use nuclear weapons (i.e., nuclear deterrence/
terrorism) constitutes ongoing international criminal activity: Namely,
planning, preparation, conspiracy and solicitation to commit crimes against
peace, crimes against humanity, war crimes, as well as grave breaches of the
Four Geneva Conventions of 1949, their Additional Protocol One of 1977,
the Hague Regulations of 1907, the Geneva Gas Protocol of 1925, and the
International Convention on the Prevention and Punishment of the Crime
of Genocide of 1948, inter alia."[59]

Boyle's conclusion about the criminality of nuclear deterrence itself also
raises the question of the legal status of the continued *possession* of nuclear
weapons. The following chapters describe and analyze the political struggles over the question of the international control of atomic weapons in the
post–World War II era and the resolution of that question in favor of the
continuing possession of nuclear weapons by the major geopolitical powers,
even after the end of the Cold War. International law and the 1996 advisory
opinion of the ICJ can inform us on that critical issue as well.

THE NUCLEAR NON-PROLIFERATION TREATY

Given that both the use of and the threat to use nuclear weapons are illegal under IHL and "criminal" according to Falk and Boyle, would not the mere possession of weapons that cannot be legally used in any practical way also be illegal and criminal? An international law scholar could certainly attempt to make that argument. However, there is another legal agreement that can be used to evaluate the lawfulness of the continued possession of nuclear weapons under international law: the Nuclear Non-Proliferation Treaty (NPT), which was concluded in 1968 and entered into force as international law in 1970. The former UN chief weapons inspector, Swede Hans Blix, has observed that the NPT was a "double bargain."[60] The non–nuclear weapons states agreed not to develop the weapons and accepted international inspection. On the other side, the five nuclear weapons states at the time committed themselves to negotiations that would lead to general and complete nuclear disarmament. Or, as Jonathan R. Hunt, assistant professor of strategy at the United States Air War College, observes, "In exchange for legitimation under international law, the five legacy members, now authorized as nuclear-weapons states, would make concerted efforts to reduce and ultimately eliminate the world-threatening arsenals that distinguished them from the atomic unarmed."[61] But those efforts were never made. The nuclear arsenals were not eliminated. Instead, Hunt argues, the NPT became a "warrant" for the "nuclear club" to defy the UN Charter's prohibition on the use of military force in international relations and intervene militarily to prevent others from joining "the world's most exclusive club."[62] Despite the solemn legal obligation imposed by the NPT to disarm, Falk finds that the United States and the other nuclear weapons powers have, to this day, "materially and flagrantly breached" the treaty.[63]

After the United States dropped atomic weapons on Japan in 1945, and the existence of the bomb was revealed to the world, the American government and the international political community were faced with what Schell called "the nuclear predicament."[64] This apocalyptic weapon existed; it had been used and was available to be used again; the scientific findings that led to the development of the bomb could never be repealed (the genie could not be put back in the bottle); and thus "no one could ever abolish the bomb in the mind."[65] Having created this deadly weapon, the United States now had to make a fateful choice. According to Schell, given the bomb's "long-term universal availability," the central choice was whether to "address the bomb as a common danger afflicting all nations or whether, denying the fact of that availability (at least for a while), to try to assert national ownership of the bomb and seek military advantage from it."[66] Prominent scientific advisors to Roosevelt and Truman, particularly Vannevar Bush (director of the Office of Scientific Research and Development) and James B. Conant (head of the National Defense Research Committee), argued for some form of international control of atomic energy.[67] But in 1945, U.S. political leaders instead sought to maintain their monopoly. For geopolitical and economic purposes that I analyze more fully in chapters 4 and 5, the United States decided to cling to the bomb.

Despite the buildup of nuclear weapons and the extensive military planning for the use of these weapons against the Soviet Union that took place in the early years of the Cold War during the Truman and Eisenhower administrations, John F. Kennedy (JFK) campaigned for the presidency in the fall of 1960, warning of an ominous "missile gap" that did not exist.[68] JFK was a committed Cold War warrior who was determined to continue the arms race against the Soviet Union. As Kennedy took office, Ireland was endeavoring at the United Nations "to establish an international instrument to prevent the proliferation of nuclear weapons,"[69] although this seemed unlikely at the time given the Cold War international climate. But a dramatic and frightening nuclear confrontation inadvertently created a new opportunity for a nonproliferation accord.

In October 1962, President Kennedy and his government teetered on the brink of nuclear war with the Soviet Union during the Cuban Missile Crisis.[70] But JFK's successful resolution of that crisis (analyzed in chapter 5) and its frightful prospect of a nuclear holocaust—coupled with a worldwide movement to ban atmospheric testing of nuclear weapons, which led to the Limited Test Ban Treaty (LTBT) in 1963—created the political space for him to finally consider Irish foreign minister Frank Aiken's 1958 proposal for "nuclear restriction," a global treaty to stop the proliferation of nuclear weapons. After Kennedy's assassination, President Lyndon B. Johnson (LBJ) continued to participate in the international quest to limit the spread of nuclear arms at the UN and on July 1, 1968, signed "the diplomatic crown jewel of his presidency,"[71] the Treaty on the Non-Proliferation of Nuclear Weapons. While incoming president Richard Nixon had some criticisms of the treaty (related to the provision for disarmament negotiations), he still secured its ratification in the Senate and then formally signed the NPT in a Rose Garden ceremony in March 1970.

Blix argues that the NPT is "a contract in which all parties commit themselves to the goal of a nuclear-weapon-free world."[72] The non–nuclear weapons states agreed to forgo the pursuit of these weapons, while the five nuclear powers pledged to reduce their arsenals and pursue complete disarmament. Some have criticized the treaty for setting up a "social nuclear hierarchy" and reifying nuclear weapons as "a currency of power for a privileged few."[73] In his critical study of the "nuclear club," Jonathan Hunt argues that "the NPT's founding purpose was not peace but rather to nip the revolutionary potential of atomic physics in the bud. The global nuclear nonproliferation regime established more than a set of laws, rules, and norms to regulate atomic power worldwide—it sanctified UNSC [UN Security Council] permanent members' nuclear arsenals and also their right to intervene to save humanity from the Promethean handiwork they themselves had wrought."[74] The historical evidence supports this critique.

At the time, however, most legal analysts saw the NPT as a "grand bargain," an important advance in international law.[75] According to national security analyst Joseph Cirincione, "The critical importance of the NPT is that it provided the international legal mechanism and established the global diplomatic norm that gave nations a clear path to a non-nuclear future."[76] Yet that hard-won legal norm would be violated and that promising path blocked by the United States and the other nuclear weapons states in the years to come. More than fifty years later, the nuclear club has still not disarmed and has instead expanded. Although the terms of the NPT have not been fully implemented, it remains important for the scholarly effort to create a criminology of nuclear weapons and the political objective of abolishing nuclear weapons.

To more fully appreciate the significance of the NPT to the criminological and political question of the legality of the possession of nuclear weapons, I return to the 1996 ICJ advisory opinion. One of the most important aspects of the Court's ruling on the illegality of nuclear weapons is the call, by all fourteen judges, for the complete abolition of these weapons. The ICJ concluded its opinion with an examination of the duty of states to negotiate in good faith a complete nuclear disarmament. The relevant treaty obligation the Court relied on is found in Article VI of the NPT, which states, "Each of the Parties to the Treaty undertakes to pursue negotiations in good faith on effective measures relating to cessation of the nuclear arms race at an early date and to nuclear disarmament, and on a treaty on general and complete disarmament under strict and effective international control."[77] On the basis of this provision, a unanimous Court found that "there exists an obligation to pursue in good faith and bring to a conclusion negotiations leading to nuclear disarmament in all its aspects under strict and effective international control."[78] The ICJ interpreted the NPT provision as imposing a legal obligation to achieve a precise result—nuclear disarmament in all its aspects. This part of the opinion can be interpreted as a strong rebuke of the nuclear weapons states. As Falk observed at the time,

> The unanimity of the Court as to the disarmament obligation thus goes against the prevailing outlook of the declared nuclear weapons states, especially that of the United States and the United Kingdom, and could become substantively important at some subsequent time. Indeed, it gives indirect encouragement to peace groups around the world that have been calling for nuclear disarmament ever since the first atomic explosions in 1945. This legal endorsement of disarmament also amounts, even if unwittingly, to a sharp criticism of the nuclear weapons states of their abandonment of any serious pursuit of disarmament goals in recent decades.[79]

And as Boyle also notes, "Since 1968 it cannot be said that the world's nuclear weapons states have ever pursued negotiations on nuclear disarmament in good faith. . . . Hence, all of the nuclear weapons states currently stand in material breach of these twin obligations under NPT Article VI and/or customary international law as authoritatively determined by the world court itself."[80] In other words, the United States and the other nuclear powers are breaking the law. By refusing to pursue disarmament, they are engaged in an international crime.

In 1995, the NPT was extended indefinitely and the nuclear states that were signatories reaffirmed their legal obligation to pursue negotiations leading to disarmament. According to a strict interpretation of the NPT, the continued possession of nuclear weapons, more than fifty years after the treaty went into effect, is illegal under international law. The very existence of today's nuclear arsenals, their costly "modernization" and upgrading, and the abrogation of arms control agreements that mandate limitations of the growth of these arsenals are all geopolitical nuclear state crimes. The NPT remains in existence today, and despite the continued legal violations of Article VI by the nuclear powers, I argue that it could still become important to a future political effort to abolish nuclear weapons.

INTERNATIONAL HUMAN RIGHTS LAW

In addition to IHL and the NPT, some legal analysts have argued for the application of international human rights law to the question of the legality of nuclear weapons. Human rights are those political, legal, economic, and social rights that individuals possess simply by virtue of being human, and the long history of the concept of human rights stretches from ancient times to the globalization era.[81] As Micheline Ishay, the distinguished professor of human rights and international studies at the University of Denver, points out, "They are rights shared equally by everyone regardless of sex, race, nationality, and economic background. They are universal in content."[82] While there is a massive literature on the general concept of human rights and the specific "human rights revolution" that took place after World War II,[83] I examine only a small part of that literature as it bears on the question of the relationship between human rights law and nuclear weapons. According to South African legal scholar Stuart Casey-Maslen, "International human rights law is an as-yet underused branch of international law when assessing the legality of nuclear weapons and advocating for their elimination."[84] Of relevance to the discussion of this issue is the legal concept of the "right to life."

The concept of human rights "stayed on the margins of high-level international politics throughout World War II," but then was "enshrined" in the preamble to the UN Charter in 1945.[85] A great leap forward occurred on December 10, 1948, when the UNGA ratified the Universal Declaration of Human Rights (UDHR). Since then, individuals and organizations concerned with advancing human rights around the world have regarded the UDHR as "the moral anchor" for these efforts, a "secular bible."[86] Following the ratification of the declaration, seven international human rights instruments have attempted to translate its general principles into specific treaties and international rules.[87] Concerning nuclear weapons, the most important of these instruments is the 1966 International Covenant on Civil and Political Rights. The ICCPR "is one of the most widely signed treaties in the UN system,"[88] and Article 6 of the treaty states, "Every human being has the inherent right to life. This right shall be protected by law. No one shall be arbitrarily deprived of his life." This article's declaration of a fundamental right to life has been interpreted as a legal ban on the use of nuclear weapons, although as previously noted the ICJ declined to use this specific legal principle in its advisory opinion, sticking strictly to general humanitarian law issues.

However, the UN Human Rights Committee (HRC), a group of independent experts in charge of the implementation of the ICCPR, decided to consider whether the principle applied to nuclear weapons. The HRC issues occasional general comments representing the experts' interpretation of the legal meaning of the treaty. In the 1980s, the committee issued two general comments on the Article 6 "right to life" and the possession and use of nuclear weapons, but these comments were criticized as "incomplete and unsatisfactory" by antinuclear activists who wanted a more forceful statement about the relationship between the right to life and the threat posed to that right by nuclear weapons.[89] In 2016, on behalf of Swiss Lawyers for Nuclear Disarmament, international lawyers Daniel Rietiker and John Burroughs submitted a set of "observations" to the HRC on the "incompatibility of WMDs with the right to life (Article 6 ICCPR), proposing 'a concrete new wording of the paragraph' relating to nuclear weapons."[90] In October 2018, the HRC adopted General Comment 36 related to Article 6. Paragraph 66 of General Comment 36 states, "The threat or use of weapons of mass destruction, in particular nuclear weapons, which are indiscriminate in effect and are of a nature to cause destruction of human life on a catastrophic scale, is incompatible with respect for the right to life and may amount to a *crime* under international law." The HRC continues, "States parties must take all necessary measures to stop the proliferation of weapons of mass destruction, including measures to prevent their acquisition by non-state actors, to refrain from developing, producing, testing, acquiring, stockpiling, selling, transferring and using them, to destroy existing stockpiles, and to take adequate measures of protection against accidental use, all in accordance with their international obligations. They must also respect their international obligations to pursue in good faith negotiations in order *to achieve the aim of nuclear disarmament* under strict and effective international control."[91]

Paragraph 66 not only declares that the threat or use of nuclear weapons would violate the right to life enshrined in the ICCPR (and would generally be an international crime) but also buttresses both the ICJ advisory opinion and the NPT concerning the legal obligation of nuclear weapons states to achieve disarmament. And while human rights law in general and this Comment 36 paragraph do not outlaw the use of nuclear weapons altogether, they do advance the principles of civilian protection from harm and state legal accountability for international crimes. In doing so, the paragraph may represent a dynamic advance over humanitarian law (the laws of war). As Casey-Maslen observes, "Human rights law acts to ensure that humanitarian protection increases, not recedes, over time. Thus, it may be said that the static nature of IHL stands in stark contrast to the progressive dynamism of human rights."[92] Paragraph 66 also reinforced the 2017 TPNW (discussed later), demonstrating the "interconnection" between different fields of international law and confirming the growing "humanization of arms control."[93]

From a criminological perspective, it is important to note that there have been increasing calls by sociologists and criminologists to use the specific standards found in human rights law to classify behavior as criminal for the purpose of study. For example, American sociologists Judith Blau and Alberto Moncada argue that "the violation of human rights of any kind is a criminal act or practice."[94] And American criminologist Joachim Savelsberg has observed that "the emergence of HR law and the criminalization of atrocities is one of the most important developments in recent criminology and penal law."[95] American critical criminologist Gregg Barak has also recently outlined an integrative approach to the study of international crimes and state-corporate criminality as "gross human rights violations."[96]

Insofar as international law in general, and IHR law specifically, evolves through a process of multilateral reasoning, debate, and treaty formation, it has been argued that it constitutes the best available standards for determining when states behave criminally. There is disagreement, however, over whether the international legal framework created in the post–World War II era reflects genuine "universal" standards. In particular, postcolonial and feminist theorists have argued that the understanding of human rights that grounds the contemporary system of public international law is little more than a Trojan horse for essentialist doctrines of white, Western liberalism.[97] Some have gone so far as to challenge the current international order as human rights imperialism.[98] Supporters of the human rights model of international law counter that foundational documents such as the UN Charter and the UDHR, as well as the many accords subsequently derived from them (such as the ICCPR), were forged through genuine international debate and, despite uneven implementation, remain the best available global standard for distinguishing legal and illegal state actions.[99] As Agnew notes, "The international law represents the closest thing we have to a universal consensus regarding rights and rights violations. This provides compelling justification for its use and gives some moral force to the work of criminologists who draw on it."[100] And in 2017 criminologists concerned with analyzing the crimes of the nuclear state had a new international treaty to utilize in doing this work.

The Treaty on the Prohibition of Nuclear Weapons

Shortly after World War II, the UNGA was determined to eliminate the production and possession of atomic weapons through the promotion of international agreements. In 1946, in its very first resolution, the UNGA proposed that atomic weapons should be eliminated. In 1961, the group went further and passed a resolution declaring that the use of nuclear weapons was illegal. Given the Cold War and the technical problems of monitoring, inspection, and enforcement, it proved impossible for the UN to accomplish the goal of banning the bomb by international law (through the juridical system) at that time. Recall that the ICJ concluded in 1996 that "there is in neither customary nor conventional international law any comprehensive and universal prohibition of the threat or use of nuclear weapons."[101] And as Blix once admitted, "We have not been able to achieve rules specifically banning the production, stockpiling and use of nuclear weapons."[102] Thus, even though the *Shimoda* decision and the ICJ advisory opinion on the legality of nuclear weapons have both ruled that the use or threat to use nuclear weapons are violation of IHLs, the NPT mandates good faith negotiations toward disarmament, and the HRC has stated that nuclear weapons are "incompatible with respect to the right to life," as enshrined in the ICCPR, there was no specific international law that explicitly prohibited or banned nuclear weapons. A gap or lacuna in international law existed, and some of the nuclear-armed states argued that the "*Lotus* approach"—the view that anything not explicitly prohibited by international law should be permitted—should hold.[103] But that changed in 2017. The legal gap was filled when the UN voted to approve the text of a proposed international treaty to unconditionally ban nuclear weapons.

Seventy-two years after the attacks on Hiroshima and Nagasaki, the international political community finally reached the point of explicitly banning nuclear weapons, declaring them illegal under international treaty law. On July 7, 2017, at the UNGA, 122 countries voted to approve the text of a draft of the Treaty on the Prohibition of Nuclear Weapons (TPNW). The treaty "bans the use and possession of nuclear weapons as well as activities that make it possible to build and maintain them" and prohibits nations not only from using or threatening to use nuclear weapons but also from developing, testing, producing, manufacturing, transferring, or allowing these weapons to be stationed on their territory.[104] As American Ray Acheson, director of the Women's International League for Peace and Freedom's disarmament program, pithily notes, "You cannot do anything with nuclear weapons under this treaty—except get rid of them."[105] Physicians for Social Responsibility (PSR), one of the leading organizations that advocated for the treaty, shares on its website that the TPNW not only fills the legal gap by banning the use and possession of nuclear weapons but also introduces transparent verification standards; helps nuclear-armed countries (which did not participate in the drafting of the treaty) meet their disarmament obligations by providing a path to join the treaty; compensates victims of nuclear use, testing, and production; and requires countries to mitigate environmental contamination.

The focus on addressing some of the injustices of nuclear weapons was particularly important. As Austrian diplomat Alexander Kmentt points out, "The treaty's positive obligations on victim assistance and environmental remediation are the first provisions in an international treaty that recognizes and seeks to remedy this injustice."[106] In general, this historic legal effort and process of making law establishes a new international legal norm prohibiting nuclear weapons and contributes to the moral stigmatization of these indefensible weapons.

The passage of TPNW was primarily the result of the efforts of the International Campaign to Abolish Nuclear Weapons (ICAN). Officially launched in Australia in 2007, ICAN is composed of more than five hundred partner organizations in more than one hundred countries and led a global campaign to mobilize people around the world to persuade and pressure their governments (largely from the Global South) to vote for, sign, and ratify the TPNW. ICAN activists "revitalized and built a transnational network of campaigners, working to challenge the status quo, confront power, build alternative narratives around nuclear weapons, engage a new generation of activists and diplomats, and learn from those who had come before—from those who participated in the processes to ban landmines and cluster munitions."[107] The campaigners then brought their proposal for a nuclear ban to the UN and succeeded, as the General Assembly passed the treaty despite the ferocious opposition and pressure tactics of the nuclear-armed states. Due to this heroic work, ICAN was awarded the Nobel Peace Prize in 2017.

To become a binding legal instrument, TPNW needed to be ratified by fifty countries. On October 24, 2020, Honduras delivered the critical fiftieth vote for ratification, and as stipulated in the agreement, ninety days later, on January 22, 2021, the TPNW entered into force, becoming legally binding for states that have joined the treaty. As of January 2024, ninety-three countries had signed the treaty and seventy had ratified or acceded to it. American lawyer John Burroughs, senior analyst with the LCNP, notes that "in assessing the significance of the TPNW, it is important to understand how it reinforces and builds upon existing international law, notably the obligations set forth in the [ratified in] 1970 NPT and those analyzed in a 1996 Advisory Opinion of the International Court of Justice."[108]

While this ban treaty is an important advance in international law as it relates to nuclear weapons, there is a glaring problem with the TPNW. As Falk trenchantly observes, there is "a gaping hole in this newly cast net of legal prohibition," an "enormous fly in this healing ointment" of what he calls the nuclear ban treaty (NBT): "The refusal of all nine nuclear weapons states to join in the NBT process even to the legitimating extent of participating in the negotiating conference with the opportunity to express their objections and influence the outcome."[109] These states made it abundantly clear that those at the top of the geopolitical system were vehemently opposed to the entire project, even though, as the LCNP argued, "the TPNW robustly recognizes and reinforces existing international law requiring the non-use and elimination of nuclear weapons" and "applies to states whether or not they join the treaty, as the treaty's preamble recognizes."[110]

It was not surprising that the nuclear weapons powers refused to participate in the negotiations for the TPNW and adopted a posture of undisguised hostility to the proposed ban. Most of them have been in flagrant violation of Article VI of the NPT for over fifty years. As Gerson points out, the process leading to the TPNW "emerged from the righteous anger of most of the world's nations at the nuclear powers' refusal to fulfill their NPT obligation to engage in good faith negotiations for the elimination of their nuclear arsenals."[111] Given that the most powerful nations were already in breach of their solemn legal duty to disarm, they were not inclined to accept a complete legal ban on their indefensible weapons. In fact, three of the permanent members of the UN Security Council, the United States, United Kingdom, and France (all of whom yield veto power), were so angered by the nuclear ban treaty venture that they "went to the extreme of issuing a Joint Statement of denunciation," which contained a tone of "defiant assertion removing any doubt as to the abiding commitment to a nuclearized world."[112] It was a defiant assertion that they would continue to break any laws attempting to eliminate their prized nuclear weapons. No clearer evidence of the fundamental conflict in international relations between what Falk calls the geopolitical system and the juridical system can be found.[113]

Falk notes the nuclear powers argued that the TPNW "does not address the security concerns that continue to make nuclear deterrence necessary"; but he counters the claim that "coercive diplomacy" is needed to achieve global security and stability with an argument that "restorative diplomacy" (efforts to ensure a nation's security by means other than nuclear deterrence) in combination with the norms embodied in the nuclear ban treaty would achieve greater results.[114] Acheson concurs with Falk concerning the TPNW, noting that "those behind the treaty are challenging the idea that nuclear weapons provide security and thus reduce and eliminate the perceived value of nuclear weapons," adding that she believes that the treaty will "decrease economic incentives for nuclear-weapon production by cutting into financial support, and convince allies of nuclear-armed states to reject nuclear weapons in their collective security doctrines by making it a public-policy issue."[115] TPNW is an important advance in international law. Attempting to offset the power and control of those states that sit atop the geopolitical system, it democratizes the nuclear debate, filling an important legal gap and sending a clear message to the international political community. As American Robert Dodge, cochair of the Nuclear Weapons Abolition Committee of PSR, warns, "While nuclear weapons still exist, any nation that violates the [TPNW] will now be in breach of international and humanitarian law and should be considered a pariah state and ultimately on the wrong side of history."[116] From the state crime perspective advanced in this book, that nation will now be engaged in a serious criminal act.

CONCLUSION: THE PARADOX OF INTERNATIONAL LAW

This chapter has demonstrated that nuclear weapons are illegal under public international law. I have described several attempts by concerned publics to use IHL (the law of armed conflict), although it predates the rise of air power, the aerial bombing of civilians, and the existence of nuclear weapons, to both conceptualize and respond to the blameworthy harms and serious threats (state crimes) that have arisen from the existence of these deadly phenomena. The *Shimoda* decision and the advisory opinion of the ICJ both ruled that the use of or threat to use nuclear weapons would be illegal under humanitarian law. I have also described how Article VI of the NPT obligates the nuclear weapons states to enter good faith negotiations for complete nuclear disarmament and to achieve that precise result. The ICJ opinion unanimously reinforced that solemn legal obligation. Furthermore, according to the UN HRC, the threat or use of nuclear weapons would violate Article 6 of the ICCPR concerning the "right to life." The TPNW goes even further than these legal instruments and bans by law the use, threat to use, and possession of nuclear weapons and all activities related to their production and development. The international political community has spoken in a loud and clear voice: nuclear warfare is illegal and nuclear weapons are prohibited under international public law. From a criminological perspective, the making of these laws represents the first step in the development of a criminology of nuclear weapons.

But can these international legal norms assist in the prevention and control of apocalyptic nuclear crimes? Despite the existence of these laws, the nine nuclear-armed states continue to possess more than 12,500 of these terrifying weapons and threaten to use them in a variety of ways.[117] These countries, despite their professed belief in and support for international law in general, continue to engage in nuclear state crimes. This is one of the clearest illustrations of Falk's distinction between the juridical system (linking states on the basis of equality before the law) and the geopolitical system (linking dominant states on the basis of inequalities of power and wealth), or as McCoy puts it, "the stark duality of raw military power joined uneasily to international principles."[118] These geopolitical nuclear crimes reveal the *paradox of international law.*

Public international law provides a critical epistemological framework, a set of important legal standards and substantive concepts, that allows us to classify certain state actions as crime for the purpose of scientific study and bring them within the boundaries of the field of criminology. These legal concepts and categories allow us to see the atomic bombing of Japanese civilians as a "crime," identify the "victims" of Hiroshima and Nagasaki, and understand that the continued possession of and threat to use nuclear weapons are also "illegal." These laws, however, as much as they allow us to intellectually recognize the phenomenon of nuclear state crime (law on the books) and build a criminology of nuclear weapons, ultimately fail to provide social protection and legal recourse for those who are victimized by these geopolitical crimes or public accountability for the states and state officials who engage in these international criminal acts (law in action). While the existence of the public international laws described in this chapter is an impressive achievement, allowing us to conceptualize the use, threat to use, and continued possession of nuclear weapons as crimes and examine the victimization they cause, the historical record demonstrates that this juridical system has failed to prevent these geopolitical crimes from occurring or to hold the guilty parties accountable. This paradox of international law must be examined and changed if we hope to accomplish the difficult goal of abolishing nuclear weapons.

CHAPTER 3

The Use of the Atomic Bomb against Japan and the Normalization of a Geopolitical Crime

> Americans also came slowly to recognize the barbarity of World War II, especially the mass killings by bombing civilians. It was that redefinition of morality that made Hiroshima and Nagasaki possible and ushered in the atomic age in a frightening way.
> —Barton J. Bernstein, "The Atomic Bombings Reconsidered"

> Contrary to Truman's lies and the propaganda campaign, the bombings were terrorizing crimes against humanity. Hundreds of thousands of civilians, their wooden homes and their neighborhood were purposely targeted.
> —Joseph Gerson, *Empire and the Bomb*

MONDAY, APRIL 26, 1937, was a beautiful, clear day in the ancient Basque city of Guernica (Gernika) in northern Spain. It was a market day, and the town was filled with people from around the area. But these were not normal times. The Basque campaign of the Spanish Civil War was raging nearby and the rebel forces of General Francisco Franco, along with their fascist German and Italian allies, were engaged in a "new kind of warfare, a war waged against civilians."[1] At 4:40 that afternoon, when the center of Guernica was most crowded, a deadly air attack began as new modern aircraft from the German Condor Legion and the Italian Aviazione Legionaria appeared overhead and started to bomb and strafe the town. It is estimated that up to a thousand people may have been killed in the vicious attack, and much of Guernica, the symbolic capital of the Basque people, was destroyed by the "thermite rain" of the incendiary devices dropped by Nazi bombers.[2] The attack on Guernica was not the first time civilians had been bombed from the air, but as British poet Ian Patterson

51

notes, "It was the first time that a completely unmilitarised, undefended, ordinary civilian town in Europe had been subjected to this sort of devastating attack from the air."[3] The purpose of the bombing was to break the will of the Basque people and eliminate their "appetite for resistance" to Franco's Nationalist insurgents.[4]

The aerial bombing of a civilian population by an organized military force can be defined as a state crime because it violates the "long-standing and widespread" moral principle and international legal norm of "noncombatant immunity."[5] This is a foundational principle of international humanitarian law (IHL; the laws of war). The bombing of civilians has also been defined as state terrorism: systematic state violence against civilians in violation of international laws to break their morale and obtain some political objective.[6] But what also makes the bombing of Guernica in 1937 sociologically relevant is that it was labeled as "deviant" and condemned by a wide variety of social audiences worldwide at the time. As American editor and writer Tom Engelhardt points out, "The self-evident barbarism of the event—the first massively publicized bombing of a civilian population—caused international horror. It was news across the planet."[7] As Patterson has observed, "Many attacks since then, including the ones we have grown used to seeing in Iraq and the Middle East in recent years, have been on such a scale that Guernica's fate seems almost insignificant by comparison. But it's almost impossible to overestimate the outrage it caused in 1937."[8]

The global outcry over the bombing of Guernica stemmed as much from what the attack presaged as from the actual damage inflicted. As American writer Mark Kurlansky notes, "The world was horrified—outraged at the ruthless massacre of unarmed civilians but also terrified at its first glimpse of the warfare of the future."[9] From the bombing of Guernica came perhaps the most famous painting of the twentieth century, Pablo Picasso's *Guernica*. First installed in the Spanish pavilion at the Paris World's Fair in June 1937, the massive panel symbolically expresses both the horror of the world at the bombing and the act's interpretation as "criminal." According to Patterson, "Picasso's painting . . . made Guernica the most famous image of total war, and articulated the terror of it so potently that the picture has become almost synonymous with a sense of outrage and condemnation."[10] Quickly, the little town of Guernica became a cultural symbol, and the very word itself "carried an accumulation of horror at everything connected with the bombing of undefended civilian towns and homes."[11]

Two years later, on September 1, 1939, at the outset of World War II, President Franklin D. Roosevelt (FDR) quickly issued an appeal "to the

Pablo Picasso, *Guernica*, 1937. © 2024 Estate of Pablo Picasso / Artists Rights Society (ARS), New York.

Governments of France, Germany, Italy, Poland and his Britannic Majesty" concerning noncombatant immunity.[12] With the bombing of Guernica, the Japanese air attacks on the coastal cities of China, and other recent aerial assaults in mind, FDR declared,

> The ruthless bombing from the air of unfortified centers of population during the course of the hostilities which have raged in various quarters of the earth during the past few years, which has resulted in the maiming and in the death of thousands of defenseless men, women, and children, has sickened the hearts of every civilized man and woman, and has profoundly shocked the conscience of humanity.
>
> If resort is had to this form of inhuman barbarism during the period of tragic conflagration with which the world is now confronted, hundreds of thousands of innocent human beings who have no responsibility for, and who are not even remotely participating in, the hostilities which have now broken out, will lose their lives. I am therefore addressing this urgent appeal to every government which may be engaged in hostilities publicly to affirm its determination that its armed forces shall in no event, and under no circumstances, undertake the bombardment from the air of civilian populations or of unfortified cities, upon the understanding that these same rules of warfare will be scrupulously observed by all of their opponents. I request an immediate reply.[13]

As Daniel Ellsberg points out, "Roosevelt's message was not an appeal to a new standard of conduct in war. Quite the contrary, he was reaffirming the importance of what was regarded as an international norm, part of the common law of international relations, despite recent violations of it by fascist powers that had been widely and strongly condemned."[14] In response to FDR's fervent plea, all the warring nations solemnly declared their intent to uphold international law, avoid attacking civilians from the air, and bomb only military targets.

In just a few years, however, within the context of the global human catastrophe that was World War II, the terror bombing of civilian populations (often referred to as *area* or *strategic* bombing) became both commonplace and morally acceptable to many of the same political leaders and publics that had just condemned the horror of Guernica and supported Roosevelt's appeal. The wartime erosion of restraints on the state crime of bombing civilians from the air, what American historian Barton Bernstein called a "transformation of morality," was evidenced on all sides during the conflict.[15] From the Blitz of London to the bombing of Rotterdam, the firestorms of Hamburg, Dresden, and Tokyo, and finally "the most extreme and permanently traumatizing instance of state terrorism"[16]—the atomic bombings of Hiroshima and Nagasaki—the morally blameworthy harm of bombing civilians, in violation of humanitarian law and in defiance of world opinion, would become a normalized state crime.

This chapter analyzes the controversial use of atomic bombs against Japan during World War II as a form of geopolitical state crime (a process of breaking the laws of war). However, as previously noted, the atomic attacks against Hiroshima and Nagasaki need to be placed in the broader context of the widespread and illegal conventional bombing of cities and civilian populations that took place in both Europe and Asia during World War II. According to American historian Ronald Schaffer, it was the area bombing of civilians in Germany and Japan by the Allied nations during the war in particular that wrought "a revolution in the morality of warfare."[17] While the German and Italian attack on Guernica and the Japanese bombardment of civilians in China in 1937 brought forth a "chorus of outraged condemnation" from around the world that "reached unprecedentedly high levels," and despite FDR's urgent appeal in 1939, the Allied terror bombing attacks on Germany and Japan became normal and acceptable to many people by 1945.[18] This is a prime example of what American sociologist Diane Vaughan calls "the normalization of deviance."[19]

According to Vaughan, the normalization of deviance occurs when actors in an organizational setting, such as a corporation, a government agency, or a military unit, come to define their harmful deviant acts as normal and acceptable because they fit with and conform to the cultural norms of the organization within which they work. Even though their actions may violate some outside legal or moral standard (international law or just war theory in this case) and be labeled as criminal or deviant by people outside the organization, state organizational officials (presidents and generals, for example) come to deny that these actions are wrong because the officials are conforming to the cultural mandates that exist within the work group culture and social environment in which they carry out their occupational roles.

To understand why the atomic bombings of Japan took place, we must first examine how the war crime of terror bombing civilian populations in violation of the legal and moral principle of noncombatant immunity was subjected to what South African sociologist Stanley Cohen called "interpretive denial" and became "normalized" during World War II.[20] As the global conflict unfolded, social definitions and cultural mandates concerning the terror bombing of cities began to change, and the moral constraints on this practice almost completely collapsed in just a few short years of what came to be called "total war."[21] Once normalized, that is, culturally approved within military organizations and the larger political culture, this form of state terrorism, the "most barbaric style of warfare imaginable" as Engelhardt calls it,[22] would influence the decision to drop the atomic bomb, provide a political justification for this decision, be used as a defensive shield against moral challenges to the "official narrative" or "Hiroshima narrative" of why the weapon was used,[23] and then continue to characterize American war fighting into the twenty-first century.[24]

It is also important to understand that American officials acted to achieve imperial ends—the geopolitical goals of a rising empire—during the Second World War and that these state goals also influenced the decision to drop atomic bombs. Joseph Gerson describes the atomic bomb used against Japan as "an imperial hammer."[25] Thus, to further our understanding of geopolitical nuclear crimes we must also examine "power politics" as related to "the emerging Cold War."[26] The use of atomic bombs at Hiroshima and Nagasaki was influenced by the desire to use the new weapon as a "master card," a "royal straight flush" against the Soviet Union, as Secretary of War Henry L. Stimson put it,[27] and advance the more general postwar imperial goals of U.S. political and military leaders. The decision to drop "the Bomb" on Japanese cities has been examined as a form of "atomic diplomacy"[28] and described as "the first major operation of cold diplomatic war with Russia."[29] The evidence shows that the atomic attacks on Hiroshima and Nagasaki were as much shaped by power politics related to empire as they were "a military response to a fanatical foe pure and simple, although this became a staple argument in subsequent justifications."[30] Later threats to use nuclear weapons and the continued possession of these deadly devices into the twenty-first century would also be decisively shaped by these political dynamics—the Cold War and the American pursuit of empire.

The Hiroshima Narrative: Interpretive Denial and the Normalization of Terror Bombing

The basic facts concerning the atomic bombings of Hiroshima and Nagasaki are clear. On August 6, 1945, at 8:15 in the morning, the *Enola Gay*, a Superfortress B-29 bomber plane piloted by Colonel Paul Tibbets, commander of the 509th Composite Group, dropped a five-ton uranium-235 atomic weapon that exploded with a yield estimated at sixteen kilotons of

TNT above the large Shima Hospital in Hiroshima, a Japanese city of some 350,000 people. The atomic blast of "Little Boy," as the bomb was named by the U.S. military, "leveled almost the entire city."[31] Three days later, another Superfortress B-29, *Bock's Car*, piloted by Major Charles W. Sweeney, dropped a plutonium-239 bomb nicknamed "Fat Man" over Nagasaki, Japan, a city of about 270,000. Heavy cloud cover had forced the bomber crew to abandon the city of Kokura as the target, and instead the second atomic bomb exploded with the force of twenty-one kilotons over a large Catholic cathedral in the Urakami District of the harbor town at 11:02 A.M. on August 9, 1945. As Bass describes, after "an intense flash . . . a giant ball of fire rose from the scorched earth, shooting up like a pillar."[32] The death and destruction below were stunning to behold.

We will never know for certain how many people were killed in Hiroshima and Nagasaki "because the atomic weapons destroyed not only a large number of the cities' inhabitants, but much of the infrastructure that might be used in making such an assessment."[33] It is estimated that between 70,000 and 100,000 men, women, and children died in the initial blast over Hiroshima, primarily due to flash burns from the nuclear explosions, secondary blast effects (such as falling debris), and burns caused by the ensuing fires.[34] Many residents of the city would continue to die from radiation sickness caused by exposure to gamma rays emitted by the fission process and other bomb-related injuries and diseases for years. American historian John Dower puts the death toll at 130,000 to 140,000 by the end of 1945, with the total number of deaths reaching as high as 250,000 by the 1950s.[35] The atomic bomb that exploded over Nagasaki is estimated to have killed between 40,000 and 70,000 people in the initial blast. Dower calculates the number of deaths ultimately resulting from the August 9 bombing to be around 75,000 by the end of the year, with a final fatality estimate of 140,000.[36] Approximately 400,000 human beings eventually died as the result of just two bombs.

We should be careful not to reduce these morbid calculations to an intellectual exercise that we can psychologically distance ourselves from. As American historian Michael Bess argues, "This tendency toward psychological numbing is understandable and perhaps unavoidable, but we need to resist it as vigorously as we can. We must keep reminding ourselves what it really means, in practice, to speak the words 'firestorm' or 'Hiroshima.' For hidden beneath the abstraction of the words—grown customary from heavy use— lie the unimaginable cruelty and madness of what actually happened."[37] We are speaking here of what Admiral William D. Leahy, chairman of the Joint

Chiefs of Staff, called a "barbarous weapon" in late 1945.[38] The impacts of atomic bombs on flesh-and-blood human beings, flash burns from nuclear explosions, injuries from secondary blast effects, radioactive poisoning, various forms of cancer, birth defects, psychological trauma, the social stigma of victimization, and many other effects seem, in the words of Dower, "almost preternaturally malevolent" (beyond what is natural or normal).[39] And for the injured, burned, and sick survivors—the *Hibakusha*—this horrific experience became what Robert Jay Lifton called "a permanent encounter with death."[40] Thus, while for purposes of legal and criminological analysis I refer to the vast majority of the men, women, and children who were victimized by the two atomic bombings as "civilian noncombatants," we must always look beyond that legal abstraction to see the "human nuclear annihilation" and the "lived consequences" suffered by so many individual human beings from the use of these barbarous weapons.[41]

I have described how the use of the atomic bomb in 1945 has been interpreted as a violation of IHL by the *Shimoda* decision, by the 1996 World Court opinion that was declaratory of existing IHL, and by various legal scholars who have carefully studied the matter. In the aftermath of the dropping of the bombs on Japan, a few religious leaders, journalists, and public intellectuals would render much the same judgment. Although the atomic attacks are technically a form of lawbreaking (a violation of IHL), do they rise to the level of Robert Agnew's concept of crime as a morally blameworthy harm—a voluntary and intentional harm committed without excuse of justification? There was at the time, and still is today, great controversary over this question among Americans. While the gruesome facts concerning the atomic attacks against Japan in 1945 are clear, the social and historical meanings given to them vary tremendously. The political, military, moral, and legal interpretations of the atomic bombings of Hiroshima and Nagasaki are, to this day, bitterly contested. Bess has concisely summarized most of the core issues involved in these controversies with a series of basic questions concerning the decision to drop the atomic bomb:

> Was it necessary to drop the bomb in order to get the Japanese to surrender?
> Was this weapon qualitatively different from all the other weapons used during the war?
> Did the use of the bomb speed up the Japanese surrender?
> Were there plausible alternatives for achieving surrender without invading Japan or dropping the bomb?

Did the atomic bombing of Japan, by shortening the war, result in a net saving of lives?

Was the Nagasaki bomb necessary?

Was there a plausible alternative for achieving surrender with a lower loss of life, by using the bomb differently than the United States actually did?

Did the United States drop the bomb to intimidate the Soviet Union?

Did U.S. leaders rush to drop the bomb, in the hope of bringing about Japanese surrender before the Soviets could enter the Pacific War?

Was the bomb used out of racism?

Did the use of this weapon violate the basic principles of a just war?

Was the dropping of the atomic bomb justified? How to judge the morality of this act?[42]

As previously noted, it is difficult to explore these moral issues and other criminological concerns about the atomic bomb without first considering the more general phenomenon that developed among all the major airpowers during World War II, of the movement from sporadic, selective, and tactical attacks on military and military-industrial targets to "the use of airpower to destroy cities and terrorize and kill civilians."[43] The aerial bombardment of civilian populations in urban areas, variously referred to as "area bombing," "strategic bombing" or "total war," has been examined by numerous scholars.[44] Most of them concur with the assertion that, at the least, "deliberately mounting military attacks on civilian populations, in order to cause terror and indiscriminate death among them, is a moral crime."[45] Many also define these acts as *war crimes* under international law. Dess characterizes these bombings, often carried out with incendiary substances such as thermite or napalm, as "atrocities," while American historian Mark Selden and legal scholar Richard Falk both define them as acts of "state terrorism." Whatever they are called, did these military actions set the stage for the use of the atomic bomb?

The answer is yes. These scholars argue that the use of atomic weapons against Hiroshima and Nagasaki did not represent a dramatic departure from the aerial bombing of civilians in cities that preceded them. According to Selden, the atomic attacks simply "marked an additional cruel step in erasing the combatant/noncombatant distinction."[46] And as American weapons expert Joseph Cirincione points out, there is "compelling evidence that most senior officials did not see a big difference between killing civilians with fire bombs and killing them with atomic bombs. The war had brutalized everyone. The strategy of intentionally attacking civilian targets, considered beyond the pale at the beginning of the war, had become commonplace in both the European and Asian theaters. Hiroshima and Nagasaki, in this context, were the continuation of decisions reached years earlier."[47] The atomic bombings of Japan flowed from a social and political process that began almost as soon as the war itself began to escalate.

To provide a sociological account of the illegal bombing of civilians during the Second World War, the use of atomic weapons against Japan, and the normalization of these deviant state practices, I draw on the integrated framework for the study of organizational (state-corporate) crime that fellow criminologist Ray Michalowski and I have developed.[48] Our model links three levels of analysis—macro, meso, and micro—with three catalysts for action: motivation (goals), opportunity (means), and formal social control (legal sanctions). The objective was to inventory and highlight the key factors that contribute to or restrain organizational deviance at each intersection of a catalyst for action and a level of analysis. We viewed the organization as the key unit of analysis, nested within an institutional and cultural environment and engaged in social action through the decisions of individual actors who occupied key positions within the structure of the organization, and whose work-related thoughts and acts are shaped by the structure and culture of the organization. According to this schema, organizational deviance is most likely to occur when pressures for organizational goal attainment intersect with attractive and available illegitimate organizational means in the absence or neutralization of effective formal social controls.

Important conceptual additions to the model are provided by Cohen's idea of interpretive denial and Vaughan's notion of the normalization of deviance. In *States of Denial: Knowing about Atrocities and Suffering*, Cohen demonstrated how individuals, organizations, publics, political cultures, and governments—whether victims, perpetrators, or observers—frequently incorporate statements of denial into their social definitions, beliefs, knowledge, and practices in such a way that atrocities and suffering related to state crimes are not acknowledged or acted on.[49] According to Cohen, *denial* "refers to the maintenance of social worlds in which an undesirable situation (event, condition, phenomenon) is unrecognized, ignored or made to seem normal."[50] One of the categories of denial that he identifies is *interpretive* denial. With interpretive denial, the basic facts are not denied (as they are in a *literal* denial), however, "they are given a different meaning from what seems apparent to others."[51] Here, the event or the harm (in this case the atomic bombings of Japan) is socially and morally framed or reframed in such a way as to deny the state's responsibility or culpability.

Vaughan's related concept of the normalization of deviance also makes many significant contributions to the understanding of organizational deviance.[52] First, it offers a useful corrective to the tendency to view all crimes, including organizational crimes, as the result of individual rational choices; that is, calculated decisions where the costs and benefits of wrongdoing are weighed by the actors before acting. Second, it advances our sociological understanding of how organizational and political cultures narrow choices and shape social definitions of what is rational and acceptable at any given moment, and how these choices and definitions can lead to unlawful or deviant behavior on behalf of the organization. Finally, it shows how organizational culture can be the mediating factor between macro- and micro-social forces. As Vaughan points out, "Organizational settings make visible the ways that macro-institutional forces outside of organizations and occupations are joined with micro-processes, thus affecting individual decisions and actions. Organizations provide a window into culture, showing how culture mediates between institutional forces, organizational goals and processes, and individual illegality so that deviance becomes normalized in organizational settings."[53] The question is, how did these structural and organizational forces, the process of interpretive denial, and the phenomenon of the normalization of deviance operate during World War II concerning the state crime of terror bombing civilians?

ENDING THE WAR AND SAVING LIVES: THE SOCIAL CONSTRUCTION OF THE MORALITY OF U.S. GOALS

Although in 1937 there was international outrage and horror over the bombing of civilians—and at the very beginning of World War II, FDR appealed to the belligerent nations not to engage in the bombardment of civilian populations from the air—American attitudes concerning these practices would change rather quickly. Schaffer has documented that at the start of the American involvement in the war in 1942 there was considerable opposition within the U.S. Army Air Force (USAAF) to directing air attacks at primarily civilian targets.[54] This opposition was particularly strong among the leaders of the Air Corps Tactical School at Maxwell Field in Montgomery, Alabama. Labeled the "Bomber Mafia," the Air Corps faculty members were passionate advocates for high altitude, daylight, "precision" bombing of strategic, military targets.[55] The Bomber Mafia argued that, although risky, this kind of precision bombing was more effective in damaging the enemy's war-making capacity and had the additional moral virtue of causing fewer civilian casualties.

This "revolutionary" strategy, made possible by advances in the construction of aircraft and technological developments like radar and the Norden bombsight, appealed to some leaders in the USAAF because of the moral questions raised by area bombing.[56] According to Schaffer, there is evidence that during the war some generals did raise "the moral issue" and "based military decisions at least partly on moral concerns."[57] In addition to their own misgivings about the strategy of terror bombing, U.S. air generals considered that it could cause problems with Congress and the American people, "who did not appear to have the stomach for annihilating ordinary Germans."[58] Strongly disapproving of the British approach of nighttime bombing, American military officials initially agreed to a division of labor in which the USAAF would carry out the more dangerous daytime "precision bombing" against military and industrial targets, while the British Royal Air Force (RAF) would engage in "strategic or area" bombing at night, which caused far more civilian deaths. As Ellsberg observes, "At the time, many American air officers regarded what their allies the British were doing as mass murder."[59] The evidence, therefore, suggests that at the beginning of the Second World War there was little normative support within American political culture or military institutions for the illegal practice of bombing civilians.

By the end of the war, however, the normative constraints on the terror bombing of cities that seemed to be in place had almost completely collapsed. Due to various technological problems and adverse weather conditions, precision bombing raids like the ones on the Schweinfurt ball-bearing plants in Germany and the early attempts to attack Tokyo not only were unsuccessful but also resulted in "staggering losses" of planes and men.[60] The Bomber Mafia lost influence within the U.S. military. Staunch advocates of precision bombing, such as General Haywood Hansell, were replaced by officers, like General Curtis LeMay, who were willing and able to carry out the more "successful" strategy of terror bombing, despite the huge number of civilian deaths they caused.[61] With the perceived success of the area bombing approach of General Arthur Harris, commander of the RAF in Europe, and LeMay (who was in charge of the latter stages of the American air war in the Pacific) on Japan, Bernstein's concept of a "redefinition of morality" would take place.[62] As Selden also argues, "The most important way in which World War II shaped the moral and technological tenor of mass destruction was the erosion in the course of war of the stigma associated with the systematic slaughter of civilians from the air, and elimination of the constraints that for some years had restrained certain air powers from area bombing."[63] General LeMay himself later reflected on "how moral compunctions against city bombing had disintegrated in World War II as retaliation and re-retaliation led the Allies to all-out strategic air warfare whose ultimate expression was the raids on Hamburg and Tokyo and the atomic bomb attacks."[64]

One key factor in this normative transition is how the goals of the war were morally framed or socially constructed by U.S. political leaders. The primary goal of the United States and its allies during World War II, of course, was to win the war. The "precision bombing" of military and war-related industrial targets, with its attendant collateral damage, and the "area bombing" of enemy civilian populations to destroy their morale were two of the means available to achieve that ultimate end. As previously noted, area bombing came to be viewed as the more successful strategy. But by late 1944, military victory was all but assured in both the European and Pacific theaters. At this point, secondary war goals came to the forefront: ending the war now as quickly and decisively as possible and, by accomplishing those objectives, saving the lives of Allied military personnel. As Dower points out, "It is possible to see a terrible logic in the use of the [atomic] bombs that is unique to the circumstances of that moment and at the same time not peculiar at all. This logic begins with ending the war and saving American lives."[65] The majority of American political and military leaders came to believe over the course of the war that the accomplishment of these national goals necessitated a change from a sole reliance on the less effective precision bombing to an increasing use of terror bombing of enemy civilian populations, including the utilization of the newly developed atomic bomb.[66] Dower argues that during the war military leaders had become increasingly reliant on the use of "brute force"; that is, they developed a "fixation on deploying overwhelming force, as opposed to diplomatic or other less destructive alternatives, including most controversially, an unwillingness to back off from demanding Japan's unconditional surrender."[67] As the war progressed, only a few political leaders, such as Secretary of War Henry L. Stimson, openly expressed any moral or legal qualms about this increasing use of brute force, which included the terror bombing of civilians.[68] Many years later, however, General LeMay, one of the staunchest advocates for terror bombing and the general brute force strategy, confessed, "I suppose if I had lost the war, I would have been tried as a war criminal."[69] The victors, of course, rarely have to face legal accountability for wartime actions.

Some historians argue that the use of overwhelming force, specifically the strategic bombing campaigns and the use of atomic weapons, did help shorten the war somewhat, and thus did save some American lives.[70] Whether these were the only options available to end the conflict and how many lives were "saved" using the atomic bomb are matters of considerable dispute. After the atomic attacks on Japan, and in the early postwar period, President Harry Truman, Secretary of War Stimson, military leaders, and others who had participated in the decision to drop the atomic bombs engaged in a strong form of interpretive denial. They created what Lifton and American writer Greg Mitchell call an "official narrative" to justify the attacks.[71] A narrative is a story, a recitation of a series of events told in a way that renders them coherent and thereby conveys some form of social meaning. These narratives, or "social frames,"[72] may contain what some sociologists refer to as "vocabularies of motive"[73] or "techniques of neutralization."[74] The narrative is an attempt to explain or frame the motives behind a particular social action, to justify or legitimate the act, and to neutralize the guilt that might be experienced in relation to any harms that might be produced by the behavior.

According to Lifton and Mitchell, "What the Hiroshima narrative conveys is the justification, even wisdom, of our use of the atomic bomb to save lives and end the war,"[75] and thus this frame serves to deny state wrongdoing and neutralize any official guilt for violating the moral norm of noncombatant immunity and IHL. These socially constructed moral goals (a vocabulary of "good" motives) certainly did influence the decisions that were made concerning the use of atomic weapons in 1945. But the elaboration of the "official narrative" after the war also represented, in Lifton and Mitchell's terms, a "wrong turning," a justification and legitimation of the bomb that would have far-reaching consequences. They argue in *Hiroshima in America: Fifty Years of Denial* that due to this wrong turning, "instead of viewing Hiroshima as an ethical crisis and a harbinger of danger, Americans became entranced by the bomb, drawn to its destructive power."[76] This moral framing and denial of guilt would lead to additional geopolitical crimes concerning nuclear weapons in the postwar period.

The Official Narrative

The official narrative, an attempt at interpretive denial concerning the bomb, began on August 6, 1945, with President Truman's public announcement of the atomic attack on the city of Hiroshima, which he misleadingly referred to as "an important Japanese army base." As Lifton and Mitchell point out, Truman's statement concerning the bombing stressed military necessity, triumphal revenge (for Pearl Harbor), scientific and industrial achievement, the near mystical destructive power of the weapon ("it is an atomic bomb"), and American decency ("suggesting that the use of such a weapon by a decent people against an evil enemy was morally acceptable").[77] This statement contains several classic "techniques of neutralization" including the "denial or blaming of the victim" and an "appeal to higher loyalty."[78]

On the evening of August 9 (the day of the Nagasaki attack), Truman spoke directly to the American people for the first time since his return from Potsdam, repeating his false assertion that Hiroshima was a military base and stating that the bomb was dropped on a military target "because we wished in the first attack to avoid, in so far as possible, the killing of civilians."[79] Framing the decision as a "military necessity," Truman engaged in a denial of moral or legal responsibility for the harms that resulted. As in his initial announcement on August 6, the president also cited Japanese atrocities (blaming the victim) as part of the motivation for the use of the bomb, and for the first time he mentioned the goal of saving "thousands" of American lives (another appeal to higher loyalty).

In the days that followed, the official story was further developed by the U.S. military, with General Leslie R. Groves, military director of the Manhattan Project, orchestrating the narrative. Groves left nothing to chance (he did not want any of the field commanders to say the war could have been won without the bomb), hiring a respected journalist, William L. Laurence, the Pulitzer Prize–winning science reporter of the *New York Times*, to write a series of reports and dispatches from an embedded position within the Manhattan Project. Laurence's passionate support for nuclear physics in general and the atom bomb project in particular, his high journalistic reputation, and his skill as a writer made him an ideal person to tell the initial story and frame the meaning of the bomb and the new atomic age. As Lifton and Mitchell observe, "It was he, perhaps more than anyone, who set the tone for the entire era."[80]

The early efforts of the Truman administration and the U.S. military to interpret and frame the bombings of Hiroshima and Nagasaki as a positive wartime development, and to deny any hint of moral or legal concerns, did encounter some challenges. Early criticism of the official narrative came from journalists, religious leaders, public intellectuals, and the atomic scientists themselves. Some of the challengers took note of the position of international law concerning the use of these horrific weapons. A few American newspapers, quoting from Tokyo radio, offered the different and disturbing point of view that "the atomic bombing was . . . a 'crime against God and man'; not a legitimate part of war but something 'inhumane,' a cruel 'atrocity,' and a violation of international law, specifically Article 22 of the Hague Convention which outlawed attacks on defenseless civilians."[81] Conservative columnist David Lawrence harshly criticized the indiscriminate use of the atomic bomb against men, women, and children, and compiled a list of quotations concerning outlawing or protesting war against civilians that included the Hague Conventions of 1899 and 1907 and FDR's 1939 appeal. The Federal Council of Churches, atomic scientists like Hungarian refugee Leo Szilard (who had submitted a petition to the president seeking to avoid the use of the bomb against Japan), and leading American public intellectuals like Robert Hutchings, Norman Cousins, Lewis Mumford, and Dwight Macdonald (among others) all expressed grave moral concerns over the attacks on Hiroshima and Nagasaki and what they portended for the future.[82]

More challenges to the official Hiroshima narrative and its positive interpretation of the atomic bombing of Japan arose in 1946. The report of the U.S. Strategic Bombing Survey for the Pacific War, a panel of military officers and economists, surprised many Americans by condemning city bombing as "ruthless and barbaric," concluding that the Hiroshima and Nagasaki bombings did not defeat Japan and that Japanese leaders would have surrendered before the end of 1945 without an invasion, even if atomic bombs had not been dropped.[83] Many historians concur with this assessment and argue in particular that Japan would have surrendered earlier if the demand for "unconditional surrender" would have been modified and an assurance that the emperor could be retained had been offered.[84] Americans also began to find out more about the deadly effects of radioactive fallout. Although the information was slow to emerge and subject to U.S. government censorship, details about the horrible effects of nuclear radiation and the intense suffering of many of the victims in Hiroshima and Nagasaki due to radiation sickness eventually became public knowledge. Perhaps the most significant challenge to the official narrative came in 1946 from American writer John Hersey's Hiroshima (a long New Yorker article, later published as a book), which, in a dispassionate tone, allowed readers to experience the horror and trauma of the atomic bomb (including the effects of radiation) in a very direct way.[85] The book had a profound cultural impact and allowed many Americans, for the first time, to see the Japanese people and the actual victims of the atomic bombs as flesh-and-blood human beings.[86]

Despite the emergence of these "thoughtful, persistent questions about the Hiroshima decision," most moral and legal concerns about the use of atomic weapons against Japan would soon be put to rest by the publication of "a highly influential magazine article" that reasserted the official narrative "so effectively it would remain virtually unchallenged for decades."[87] The article, written by Stimson (with some important assistance) and published in *Harper's Magazine* in February 1947, is a classic example of interpretive denial. Stimson's article was initially prompted by a letter from James B. Conant, president of Harvard University, to Harvey H. Bundy, who served as an assistant to Stimson in the War Department during World War II. Conant, who headed up the National Defense Research Committee during the war and also served as a member of the Interim Committee that had advised President Truman about the use of the atomic bomb, was deeply concerned about the "drumbeat of criticism" being directed at the official narrative, which he felt "was turning public opinion against the bomb and its creators—not to mention that it was undermining Americans' belief in their leadership."[88] He was especially alarmed about Hersey's *Hiroshima* story and "the growing perception" that the atomic scientists themselves had opposed the use of the bomb before Hiroshima.[89] Bundy and Conant prevailed upon Stimson, a lifelong Republican and highly venerated public servant, to write a vigorous defense of the decision to use atomic bombs against Japan. Even though Stimson had exhibited what American historian Sean L. Malloy called "a seemingly schizophrenic attitude toward the moral concerns" involved with the bomb, and used "a tortured logic" to "sanction the use of indiscriminate force against Japanese civilians," he agreed to lend his name to the project.[90] Based on initial drafts from Bundy, General Groves, and Interim Committee secretary R. Gordon Arneson, Bundy's son McGeorge—then a junior fellow at Harvard who would later serve as the national security advisor to presidents Kennedy and Johnson—produced "a polished final product" for Stimson to work with.[91] A definitive essay written in a calm and dispassionate voice that "would serve as the basic text for historians and journalists for decades," the published article "caused a sensation nearly akin to that produced by John Hersey's *Hiroshima*."[92] The official narrative had been cemented.

In the *Harper's* article, Stimson (and his fellow drafters) presented a comprehensive overview of the Manhattan Project, described the step-by-step decision-making process concerning the use of the bomb against Hiroshima, and argued that the use of atomic weapons was "the least abhorrent choice" available to achieve the goal of ending the war as quickly as possible. He also asserted that the atomic attacks had been authorized to avoid a costly invasion of the Japanese islands, a campaign that might have been "expected to cost over a million casualties to American forces alone." As American historian J. Samuel Walker points out, "Stimson was not the first to suggest the figure of 1 million, but after his article appeared, that number, or often an embellished variation of it, became indelibly etched into the mythology of the decision to use the bomb."[93] What opposing argument could prevail against the seemingly authoritative assertions that the bomb had been the only way to end the bloody war and that its use thereby saved not just a million casualties but, as it came to be embellished, a million *American lives*?

While several historians do support the claims that the atomic attacks had been the only way to end the war short of a costly invasion of the islands of Japan and that the lives of up to a million soldiers had been saved by shortening the war and avoiding the invasion,[94] many others have challenged these assertions. Australian journalist Paul Ham, for example, refers to it as an "utter fallacy."[95] In his study, Walker argues that the bomb "was not necessary to prevent an invasion of Japan" and that it "saved the lives of a relatively small but far from inconsequential number of Americans."[96] Bernstein put the figure at "25,000 to 46,000 Americans who might have otherwise died in the invasions."[97] American writers Oliver Stone and Peter Kuznick point out that several high-ranking generals (including MacArthur and Eisenhower) and political figures (including Secretary of State James F. Byrnes) felt that the bomb was not necessary to end the war.[98] And in his massive study of air power and military coercion in war, which includes both the conventional and atomic bombing raids of World War II, American political scientist Robert Pape flatly asserts that the evidence shows this kind of "strategic bombing does not work" in any way.[99] Despite the debate among historians about the truth of the claims that the bombings "worked" by ending the war and saving lives, it is important to note that, according to the principle of noncombatant immunity found in both the just war moral tradition and the international laws of war, it is *never permissible* to target innocent civilians or noncombatants to accomplish war aims or save the lives of military combatants. Furthermore, under IHL, the use of force must not be disproportionate to the accomplishment of military objectives or indiscriminate in its harmful effects.

Ham argues that Stimson's *Harper's* article defending the use of the bomb "was profoundly flawed."[100] Malloy concurs, pointing out that it contained various "strategic omissions" and made no mention of the "behind-the-scenes moral unease" that had afflicted him and others over the issue of targeting cities and civilians.[101] The article did not address the internal controversy over the question of whether the unconditional surrender terms should be modified to allow the Japanese emperor to remain—which did eventually happen after the bombs were dropped. It did not comment on the moral questions related to targeting civilians or the failure to provide a warning to Japan. It did not discuss the issue of providing a demonstration of the power of the atomic bomb to the world before using it in combat. Furthermore, the article did not raise any of the questions concerning the relationship of the bomb to future U.S. relations with the Soviet Union (discussed more fully later in this chapter). As Malloy concludes, "In order to present the case for using the bomb in such a way as to ensure continued public support, Bundy and his fellow contributors deliberately stripped their narrative of any ambiguities that might raise troubling questions about the decision. The result was a misleading account that flattened the complex moral, diplomatic and military dilemmas surrounding the development and use of nuclear weapons into a simple binary choice pitting the bomb against a costly invasion of Japan."[102]

In the latter stages of World War II, and in the postwar Truman-Stimson Hiroshima narrative, the goals of shortening the war and saving the lives of American "boys" by avoiding an invasion of the Japanese homelands were presented as self-evidently "good" and "just." The entire conflict, of course, in a nationalistic fervor, was defined as the "Good War."[103] Defeating what was to most the obvious "evil" of Hitler and the fascists, whose own state crimes during the war were massive, exacting "just retribution" for the "sneak" attack on Pearl Harbor and other Japanese atrocities during the war, and defending freedom and democracy at home against the criminal aggression of the Axis powers were such clear moral goals that *any means necessary* to accomplish them came to be viewed as acceptable and legitimate to most American leaders and the public. In their comparative analysis of the Holocaust and Allied strategic bombing practices, American sociologist Eric Markusen and American historian David Kopf refer to this justification as the "healing-killing paradox"—the concept that "an evil means is justified in the service of a valued, noble cause."[104] Markusen and Kopf note, "Moral qualms that might be aroused by the evil nature of the means are assuaged or neutralized by a preoccupation with the worthiness of the goal to be attained by use of such means."[105] In his study of the strategic bombing campaigns of the Second World War, Schaffer makes much the same argument.[106] The end of the war, it was argued, justified the violent destructive military means used to accomplish them, even if civilian noncombatants were killed.

Thus, the social construction of the goodness and morality of the war in general, and the specific objectives of shortening the bloody conflict and saving the lives of "our boys in uniform," overwhelmed and short-circuited any attempt to critically evaluate the morality and legality of the terror bombing of the civilian populations of the "evil" enemy as a means to those taken-for-granted legitimate ends. The interpretative claims made by the Stimson article and Truman's statements can be viewed as the lynchpin of what Cohen calls a "culture of denial,"[107] a culture in this case that served to neutralize blame for the atrocities of Hiroshima and Nagasaki and legitimate the atomic attacks, and by extension all forms of terror bombing during the war, in the eyes of the American people and the world. As Cohen points out, "Cultures of denial encourage turning a collective blind eye, leaving horrors unexamined or normalized."[108] Ham concludes that "the *Harper's* article put the American mind at ease, slipped into national folklore, and the Stimsonian spell appeared to tranquillise the nation's critical faculties on the subject."[109] This was denial at its most effective power.

Writing in 1995, Lifton and Mitchell observed that this collective phenomenon of turning a blind eye—this unfolding process of denial related to Hiroshima and the moral frame put in place by Truman and Stimson—was still holding strong fifty years after the bombs were dropped. As American historian Christian Appy argues, "The tale developed to justify the bombings that led to a world in which the threat of human extinction has been a daily reality may be the most successful legitimizing narrative in our history."[110] The success of the official narrative is the major reason that Bass can conclude that Americans have not "engaged in any serious national recking with the firebombing of Japanese cities and the use of the atomic bombs."[111] That Hiroshima narrative, that moral frame, that culture of denial still shapes nuclear policy today, and it is one of the critical forces leading us to live on the edge of extinction still today.[112]

TECHNOLOGICAL IMPERATIVES
AND INSTRUMENTAL RATIONALITY

While the official narrative was most important, a second factor in the normalization of terror bombing was the way in which the destructive technologies of air power increasingly came to be the instrumental means relied on to accomplish wartime goals within U.S. political and military institutions and specific organizations such as the White House, the War Department, the Joint Chiefs, the USAAF, the Manhattan Project, and the Interim Committee. As Selden notes, in a variety of wartime organizational settings, "Technology was harnessed to the driving force of American nationalism."[113] This bureaucratic process was driven by the "scientific sweetness" of the Manhattan Project itself (wedding a powerful scientific project to the power of the state), the "technological imperative to develop and deploy ever more devastating weapons," and "the relentless techno-cratic thrust of war machinery set in motion."[114]

To realize its military goals, the United States would increasingly rely on advancements in the technologies of mass destruction (the use of brute force). The rise of American air power would serve as the technical means by which these wartime aims would be secured. The B-29 Superfortress bomber, the Norden bombsight, the napalm bomb and other incendiary devices, improved radar, and, of course, the development of the atomic bomb all made possible the greater use of aerial bombardment as a primary tool of war. Technocratic momentum within the war machine soon became a powerful organizational force that would override the consideration of appropriate political and military goals and the legality and morality of the technical means under development.

Throughout the war, a form of instrumental rationality that fixates on the most effective and efficient means to accomplish pregiven and unques-tioned ends developed within the institutions and organizations associated with military planning that led inexorably to the terror bombing of civilian populations. Organizational and bureaucratic imperatives concerning the development of technologies of mass destruction increasingly came to drive the war-planning process, and moral and legal concerns about these tech-nologies were pushed aside. As American sociologist Robert Jackall has pointed out, "The rational/technical ethos of bureaucracy transforms even those issues with grave moral import into practical concerns."[115] Thus, the instrumental rationality of the organizational form itself appears to be par-tially responsible for the state terrorism of bombing civilians. As Jackall further observed, "The very rationality which makes bureaucratic struc-tures effective administrative tools seems to erode moral consciousness."[116] Instrumental rationality contributed to the redefinition of the morality of terror bombing during World War II.

American historian Michael Sherry has produced a compelling social analysis of this rational bureaucratic process in its association with the devel-opment of American air power.[117] He calls attention to the emergence of "civilian militarism" and the organizational dynamics of what he terms "technological determinism" and "technological fanaticism." Sherry argues "that among policymakers, if not in the public at large, a technological fanaticism often governed actions, an approach to making war in which satisfaction of organizational and professional drives loomed larger than the overt passions of war."[118] Referencing Sherry's analysis, Dower notes that "the Manhattan Project provides a discrete case study of technical imperatives and technocratic momentum within this vast [military] bureaucracy—and, beyond this, an illustration of the socialization, indoctrination, and plain intellectual numbing that accompanied this."[119] Terror bombing would be one result of this bureaucratic process.

The very concept of "precision bombing," which the Bomber Mafia and other American political and military leaders clung to for much of the war, implies a faith that advances in technology allowed attacks to be carried out on military and war-related industrial targets with only minimal and unintentional "collateral damage" to civilians and noncombatants. As American historian Sahr Conway-Lanz points out, both during and after the Second World War, "many Americans tenaciously clung to the optimistic assumption that violence in war could still be used in a discriminating manner despite the increased destructiveness of weapons."[120] Buttressing this assumption was the fact that the advancing technology of air power provided a literal distancing from the people being harmed for scientists and military personnel. As Sherry has observed, "By virtue of their economic and technological superiority, Americans could act out war's destructive impulses while seeing themselves as different from their enemies . . . the intricate technology of war provided physical and psychic distance from the enemy."[121] Literal distancing, combined with bureaucratic compartmentalization and military secrecy, helped foster a killing technological fanaticism.

Within the organizational settings in which World War II military planning took place then, an instrumental rationality concerning the application of the new technological means of mass destruction using air power and the unquestionable moral goals of the war took hold. As Selden points out, "What was new was both the scale of killing made possible by the new technologies and the routinization of mass killing or state terrorism."[122] This technological fanaticism served to override and displace moral and legal concerns over the use of terror bombing within the various political and military bureaucracies charged with wartime decision making. It also provided the optimistic assumption that air attacks could be carried out in a discriminating way, as well as physical and psychological distance from the actual consequences of bombing civilian populations. Technological fanaticism, therefore, was one more factor in the dynamic social process that spawned terror bombing during war and allowed it to become normal and acceptable.

INTERNATIONAL LAW, MILITARY NECESSITY, AND THE LEGITIMATION OF TERROR BOMBING

Despite the long-standing principle of noncombatant immunity, or any of the formal legal standards found in the laws of war as they existed at the time, the final factor that influenced the normalization of terror bombing during World War II was the weakness of international law itself. The primary problem with international law in general is the lack of any effective enforcement mechanism. As chapter 2 noted, the paradox of international law is that while a plethora of laws and legal standards have been promulgated over the years (particularly regarding conduct during war), states have been unwilling to give up much sovereignty to allow for any formal controls or coercive enforcement tools to be created that may be able to effectively punish or deter violations of these standards. Absent any effective formal legal controls, the compelling drive to achieve nationalistic and imperialistic goals during the war through the effective and available means of terror bombing was not deterred by the mere existence of the legal principle of noncombatant immunity.

While no effective coercive enforcement mechanisms existed under international law at the time of actual hostilities, following the war there was the important effort to hold states and political and military leaders to account for their actions during the conflict that constituted "war crimes" broadly conceived. The International Military Tribunals at Nuremberg and Tokyo prosecuted, convicted, and then sanctioned several German and Japanese government officials for "illegal" acts they had allegedly engaged in during the war.[123] Related to the normalization of deviance thesis, however, it is important to note that the aerial bombardment of civilian populations, whether to destroy their morale or for any other purpose, was not one of the crimes prosecuted in these war crime trials. Thus, this de facto legal legitimacy conferred upon terror bombing by the postwar tribunals helped to normalize the bombing of civilians and ensure that it would be a normal and acceptable method of warfare from then on.

Alongside the failure to control terror bombing due to a lack of formal enforcement mechanisms, there is an even more fundamental way that international law legitimizes state violence and contributes to its normalization—the elastic definition of "military necessity" within IHL.[124] Through overly

broad and unchallenged conceptions of military necessity and military objectives, international law has legitimized and facilitated state practices during
war such as terror bombing. The doctrine of military necessity provides a
loophole in the law large enough to fly a Superfortress B-29 bomber through.

In several ways then IHL played a significant role in the development
and normalization of terror bombing. By the failure to create effective
mechanisms to enforce the legal standards that purport to provide immunity for noncombatants, and by the refusal of the Allies to include area
bombing as a war crime to be prosecuted by the military tribunals formed
after World War II, the international legal community helped to institu-
tionally facilitate and culturally legitimate the targeting of civilians by air
during wartime. Furthermore, the elastic definition of military necessity
that was deliberately written into the laws of war over the years has allowed
states to interpret their bombing behavior as "legal" and provided them
with a rhetorical device to assure their publics that the deaths of innocent
civilians in such attacks are regrettable but necessary to accomplish wartime
goals. Thus, terror bombing became normalized and culturally approved
within military organizations and political cultures.

"EMPIRE AND THE BOMB": IMPERIAL GOALS, POWER POLITICS, AND ATOMIC DIPLOMACY

In addition to the social, organizational, and cultural processes that led
to the interpretive denial and normalization of terror bombing during World
War II, which then influenced the decision to drop atomic bombs on Japan
in 1945, broader structural forces drove these and other U.S. geopolitical
crimes as well. The political and military leaders of an emerging American
Empire formulated imperial goals, engaged in an intense form of power politics, practiced atomic diplomacy at the end of World War II, maintained a
huge nuclear arsenal in the postwar period, and threatened to use those
weapons in various ways during the Cold War and beyond. Nuclear weapons
would play a central role in the military and political decisions that the leaders of the American Empire and its warfare state would make from 1945 on.
Furthermore, the structural forces driving the nuclear policies of the U.S.
Empire would come to be cloaked in the myths of American Exceptionalism
and shielded from public scrutiny by the normalization of the bomb that was
a result of the outcome of the "Good War" in 1945 and the official narrative
concerning the use of the atomic bomb against Japan.

In addition to the moral and political goals of ending the war quickly
and saving the lives of American soldiers through the "legitimate" use of

brute force, revisionist historians have documented that the United States shared with its adversaries certain other nationalistic and geopolitical motives. World War II "propelled the U.S. to a hegemonic position" that provided a unique opportunity for American leaders to pursue these imperial designs.[125] Enhancing the economic power and geopolitical position of the emerging American Empire became central goals of U.S. wartime policies, supporting the policy of terror bombing.[126]

As McCoy reminds us, "Empire is not an epithet but a form of global governance in which a dominant power exercises control over the destiny of others, either through direct territorial rule (colonies) or indirect influence (military, economic, and cultural)."[127] Many scholars argue that the United States has been an imperial project from its earliest years,[128] and that empire has become what American historian William Appleman Williams termed "a way of life."[129] One important dimension of empire as a way of life is that efforts at economic expansion and imperial domination (geopolitical crimes) are almost always rationalized (interpretively denied) within the broad historical and cultural narrative of American Exceptionalism[130]— the central tenet of which is "the broad faith that the United States is a unique force for good in the world, superior not only in military and economic power, but in the quality of its government and institutions, the character and morality of its people, and its way of life."[131] American historian Andrew Bacevich points out that this narrative includes the myth of the "reluctant superpower" and argues that it reigns "as the master narrative explaining (and justifying) the nation's exercise of global power."[132] American political scientist Carl Boggs argues that in the United States various myths of morality (that America is a noble, idealistic country working to do good in the world) "permeate a political culture that gives policy-makers a relatively free hand to pursue geopolitical ambitions" and commit what he calls "crimes of empire."[133] This is a powerful narrative indeed.

American historian Walter Nugent argues that the United States has created three empires during its history.[134] The first form of empire building involved continental expansion from 1782 to 1853. In this era, the foundational crimes of the country were the violent imposition of chattel slavery on kidnapped Africans and the genocide of Indigenous Americans. The second imperial era involved offshore empire building from the 1850s to 1917 that resulted in territorial acquisitions and formal colonies. As Bass points out concerning the Pacific region in particular, "In the Philippines and Guam, the United States replaced Spain to become an imperial overlord after 1898."[135] Theodore Roosevelt, soon to become vice president in early

1901, defended this "new American imperialism," arguing that "the expansion of America overseas was simply an extension of American expansion over the continent."[136] However, the United States would soon abandon, for the most part, its brief experiment with formal colonization as too economically and politically costly. "Instead of direct imperial control," Bass points out, "the United States would opt for a more indistinct hegemony, resting on a global network of alliances, trade deals, and overseas bases from Guam to Guantanamo"—a third form of empire.[137]

This third iteration of the American Empire is what Williams described as "Open Door" imperialism—a form of empire based on diplomacy among the major capitalist powers to keep foreign markets open to trade, rather than dividing the world into the closed trading blocs typical of mercantile capitalism.[138] Although it was based on considerable military might (by 1905 the U.S. Navy was second only to that of Great Britain), the strategy of controlling without owning became the basic design of American foreign policy in the twentieth century.[139] The United States became (for the most part) an "informal" empire as opposed to a formal or colonial empire. As Selden observes, "In contrast to earlier territorial empires, this took the form of new regional and global structures facilitating the exercise of American power."[140] This emerging third form of the American Empire would be the context within which the decisions of World War II and the subsequent Cold War would be made.

The Great War of 1914 to 1918 was an important watershed in the emergence of this third form of American Empire. British historian Adam Tooze argues that that war ushered in a "new order of power" in the world that featured a "new centrality" for the United States.[141] He observes that the United States emerged from the First World War "unscathed and vastly more powerful," a "novel kind of 'superstate' exercising a veto over the financial and security concerns of the other major states of the world."[142] Although American political leaders were not yet committed to the full assertion of military power at this time, they did indirectly exercise forms of economic and political power to open the world to U.S. trade and investment, which would eventually lead to the full-blown creation of the Pax Americana that still dominates the world today.

The Second World War then provided a unique opportunity for the United States to greatly expand this emerging, informal empire by confronting and defeating rival imperial powers, making a conscious decision to pursue global military supremacy, and creating new regional and global political and economic structures. First, the war in the Pacific can be viewed as a competition for imperial control of Asia. As Gerson points out, "Wartime propaganda, the post war U.S.-Japanese military alliance, and Cold War mythology have obscured the underlying continuity of twentieth and twenty-first-century U.S. foreign and military policy: expansion and maintenance of empire in the Pacific and Asia. A clash of imperial ambitions precipitated 'The Day of Infamy' at Pearl Harbor."[143] This "clash of empire against empire" necessitated the decisive defeat of Japan and the complete destruction of Japanese militarism and imperialism.[144] Some historians argue that the firebombing of Japanese cities and the use of the atomic bombs were viewed as important means (Gerson's "imperial hammer") to accomplish these geopolitical goals in addition to exacting just retribution for wartime atrocities.[145]

Second, the early course of the war in Europe convinced American officials and intellectuals not only that the United States needed to enter the conflict but that through the war and beyond it must also pursue global dominance through armed supremacy and impose world order by force. American historian Stephen Wertheim asserts that when the Nazis steamrollered France in May 1940, they "swept away the old order and with it the assumptions of American elites," and the "German conquest of France convinced U.S. foreign policy elites not only to enter the war, as historians have shown, but also to supplant Great Britain as the premier world power."[146] He argues that after the events of May and June 1940, U.S. officials and intellectuals made the monumental decision that the United States now had to "impose order by force" and "achieve global dominance" in the postwar period.[147] American foreign policy and the world order would never be the same. Although Wertheim does not mention the use of atomic bombs, his thesis that American leaders made a conscious choice in 1940 to use "the superior coercive power of the U.S. to underwrite a decent world order" strongly suggests that this critical decision significantly shaped the later determination to use atomic weapons against Japan in 1945 (even after Hitler and the rising power of fascism in Europe had been defeated).[148]

American leaders not only decided to pursue global military supremacy in the postwar period but also intended to establish economic and political dominance. As American historian Howard Zinn notes, "Before the war was over, the [Franklin Roosevelt] administration was planning the outlines of the new international economic order, based on partnership between government and business."[149] This new international economic order would enhance and expand the informal Open Door imperialism the United States had been practicing since the early years of the twentieth century. Zinn points out, "Quietly, behind the headlines in battles and bombings, American diplomats and businessmen worked hard to make sure that when the war ended, American economic power would be second to none in the world. United States business would penetrate areas that up to this time had been dominated by England. The Open Door policy of equal access would be extended from Asia to Europe, meaning that the United States intended to push England aside and move in."[150] World War II, and this new international economic order, would finally lift the United States completely out of the Great Depression and establish it as both the world's dominant military power and the economic hegemon in charge of the key institutions of global capitalism such as the International Monetary Fund (IMF), the World Bank, and the General Agreement on Tariffs and Trade (GATT). Along with these global economic institutions, the creation of the United Nations, with the veto power for the United States and other major powers, would serve to ensure American political dominance over the postwar geopolitical order as well. A larger and stronger global American Empire would emerge from the "Good War" and provide the historical context for decisions about nuclear weapons in the postwar era.

As World War II was establishing a position from which the United States could pursue a more deliberate imperial project and dominate the world, American political and military leaders were already recognizing that the Union of Soviet Socialist Republics (USSR or Soviet Union), their wartime ally, would be their chief geopolitical and ideological rival in the postwar period. The contest for power and domination between the Soviet Union and the United States that would later be called the Cold War was well underway before the "hot" war against fascism was over. American officials increasingly came to view Stalin and the Soviets as a threat to their postwar imperial designs in both Europe and East Asia, and the perception of this threat would be an important factor in the frenzy to drop the atomic bomb before the Soviet entry into the Pacific war. As Dower notes, "Those knowledgeable about the new weapon had relations with the Soviet Union in mind from an early date."[151] He points out that General Groves, director of the Manhattan Project, once casually observed, "You realize of course that the main purpose of this project is to subdue the Soviets."[152] Atomic diplomacy was underway.

Although such power politics clearly played a role in the decision to bomb Japan with atomic weapons, this political concern was not openly addressed in postwar public statements. As Boyer notes, "For all its detail and eloquence, Stimson's account of this decision-making process fell short of a full discussion of all the calculations in the minds of American policy-makers in the spring and summer of 1945. Specifically, he did not confront the question of the place of the Soviet Union in American calculations."[153] However, many historians have since argued that the decision to use the bomb was motivated more by political factors related to the perceived Soviet threat than by any purely military factors. Dower observes that "the documentary as well as anecdotal evidence that 'atomic diplomacy' extraneous to Japan per se was never far from the minds of the war planners is in any case voluminous."[154] This empirical evidence is important to examine.

The foremost scholar to address this critical issue is American historian Gar Alperovitz.[155] He presents persuasive evidence that American leaders dropped atomic weapons on Hiroshima and Nagasaki to impress Stalin with the power of the bomb and to intimidate the Soviet Union in the coming postwar contest for domination. Alperovitz argues that Japan was on the verge of surrender in the summer of 1945 and Truman and his advisors were well aware that various alternatives to using the bomb existed. These included modifying the demand for unconditional surrender, a demonstration of the power of the new atomic bomb, waiting for the Soviet entry into the Pacific war (which the Japanese feared the most), and the continuation of conventional bombing combined with a blockade.[156] Alperovitz contends that these alternatives were explored and then rejected—discarded for diplomatic and political reasons concerning the Soviet Union. After examining these facts, Alperovitz concludes that U.S. leaders decided to use this powerful new weapon on Japan to gain political leverage over the Soviets in the postwar period. To gain this political advantage over an imperial rival, the United States carried out the terror bombing of two cities using atomic weapons. Gerson, quoting Stimson, concurs, arguing that "the people of Hiroshima and Nagasaki were attacked to ensure that 'the Soviets would be more accommodating to the American point of view' in the Cold War era."[157] Atomic diplomacy was a central force behind the use of the bomb.

A related political factor that is asserted to have played a role in the decision to drop the atomic bomb was the threat of Soviet expansionism in the Far East. Once the war in Europe was over, Stalin had pledged to enter the Pacific war by attacking Manchuria, eventually driving the Japanese out of China, and perhaps becoming involved in a prospective invasion of the Japanese homelands. As Japanese historian Tsuyoshi Hasegawa points out, alarmed by the prospect of Soviet territorial gains in East Asia and a shared occupation of Japan, American leaders hoped to use the atomic bomb to end the war quickly before the Soviet Union could enter the fight and become a major player in the end game in the Pacific.[158] Gerson also notes, "By bringing the war to an immediate halt, before the Soviet Union 'joined the kill,' [U.S. officials] hoped to limit the Soviet's postwar influence in northern China, Manchuria, Korea, and possibly even in Japan, a devastated but technologically advanced nation."[159] Again, imperial rivalry, rather than military necessity, appears to have influenced the decision to bomb civilian populations with a new weapon of mass destruction.

Some historians argue that the desire to intimidate the Soviet Union (in order to influence its behavior in the postwar period) and the effort to forestall Soviet expansionism in East Asia were not the *primary* motivations for the decision to drop the atomic bomb.[160] However, these scholars do acknowledge that these two political considerations concerning the Soviet threat did play an important role in the calculations that led to the bombings of Hiroshima and Nagasaki, and thus in the deaths of tens of thousands of innocent Japanese civilians. Other historians argue more directly that "Truman decided to inaugurate the nuclear age *mainly* to impress (and surely to intimidate) the Soviets, to warn potential future competitors."[161] Dower concurs: "The perceived game was nothing less than global domination at the dawn of the nuclear age."[162] In sum, the evidence strongly suggests that power politics and atomic diplomacy also decisively shaped the decision to drop the atomic bomb.

Conclusion: Normalization, Empire, and Exceptionalism

The air attack on innocent civilians at Guernica in 1937 caused international outrage, and two years later, at the start of World War II, Franklin Roosevelt implored the belligerents to refrain from the "inhuman barbarism" of aerial bombardment and to uphold "the rules of warfare." But a "transformation of morality" occurred during the war and terror bombing became widespread, resulting in the use of atomic weapons against the cities of Hiroshima and Nagasaki. Many historians and legal scholars contend that the atomic bombing of Japan was a state or geopolitical crime—objectively illegal and criminal under IHL as it existed in 1945—because it violated the moral and legal principle of noncombatant immunity and other standards of international law in force at that time.[163] The state officials who ordered these terror attacks, which massacred innocent civilians—as Ham labels it, "deliberate civilian annihilation"[164]—could have, and should have, known that the practices they were engaged in were immoral under just war theory and illegal under the laws of war. As British philosopher A. C.

Grayling has pointed out, the bombing campaigns of World War II were "controversial" even at the time they took place, and the decision makers were "fully apprised" and even criminally aware (had "mens rea") of the moral and legal objections that were being raised about them.[165]

While Grayling is correct, it is also true that the political and military officials who approved and carried out these terror bombings did not see themselves as "criminal," nor did most of the publics they served. (Those who thought otherwise at the time, such as British pacifist and feminist Vera Brittain, were a small minority.)[166] The state officials who engaged in these objectively criminal acts also appear not to have made a calculated decision to break any laws. Bess has argued that it is particularly important to understand the human and emotional context in which the "choices under fire" of political and military leaders during World War II were made.[167] Yet while Bess is right to insist that we consider the human and emotional context within which these momentous decisions were made, Malloy makes the important point that "acknowledging the difficulties faced by the American trustees of the bomb does not, however, absolve them of responsibility for their actions."[168] We must still stive to assess their moral and legal accountability for the great harms they caused.

It is equally important from a sociological perspective to understand the broader social context—the structural, cultural, and organizational forces that shaped the decisions about terror bombing in general and the use of atomic weapons in particular. To fully grasp the erosion of the social and moral constraints against attacking civilians through the air during World War II, it is critical to understand how American political and military officials were enmeshed in a culture of denial. These leaders were conforming to cultural mandates concerning ending the war, saving American lives, and advancing national interests that were derived from the mythic idealism of American Exceptionalism. They used the technological means at their disposal within bureaucratic settings dominated by a form of instrumental rationality that erodes moral consciousness. They interpreted international law through the lens of an elastic concept of military necessity, and they were never forced to contemplate the threat of formal legal sanctions. In a few short years during the war, bombing civilians, even with a new weapon of mass destruction, had unfortunately become normalized. As Vaughan points out, "When deviance is normalized, the action is not seen as wrong by actors in that setting—thus making it important to study decision-making as situated action. It is not concealed from other members of the organization; it is, in fact, culturally approved and therefore rewarded.

Deviant actions are viewed as normal because they fit with and conform to cultural mandates of the group to which the actor belongs. So powerful can these mandates become that not following them is deserving of reproach, negative sanctions, or ostracism by other members of the group."[169] Vaughan's observations are an apt description of the social factors surrounding the decision to drop the atomic bomb.

Considerations of the morality and legality of the decision to use the atomic bomb, or of strategic bombing during World War II in general, were overwhelmed by the social construction of the morality of the "good" war and the appeal of imperial goals. To most political and military leaders, and to most of the American people, the goals of winning the war as quickly as possible, saving the lives of American boys in uniform, and exacting a just retribution on the evil German and Japanese empires were paramount and justified the use of any means, including the terror bombing and annihilation of enemy civilians. A culture of denial developed in which other important nationalistic and imperialistic goals motivating wartime decisions either were not recognized as such or were interpreted within mythic idealism— the belief, as Thomas Jefferson asserted, that the United States is an "empire for liberty"[170]—a belief that has, since the earliest days of white colonial settlement in North America, imagined every act of expansion as part of a noble "civilizing mission."[171]

The myth of American Exceptionalism has often shielded the American people from a critical examination of their history and the powerful imperial motives that so often drive U.S. foreign policy. World War II, the "Good War," only reinforced the mythic idealism at the heart of this powerful cultural narrative. In *Worshipping the Myths of World War II*, American writer Edward W. Wood Jr. argues that one of the myths of that war is the idea that "when evil lies in others, war is the means to justice."[172] In the end, the "healing-killing paradox" prevailed.[173] Americans had come to believe more strongly than ever that the fight against evil and the advancement of America's exceptional ideals justified any of the means, including excessively violent atomic means, they selected to accomplish their national goals. With its political and military dominance secured by the atomic bomb and the outcome of World War II, and justified by American Exceptionalism, "nuclear weapons had become an essential element of geopolitical power" for the United States in the postwar era.[174] A power it would threaten to use often in the coming decades.

CHAPTER 4

Crimes of Empire

COLD WAR NUCLEAR THREATS AND THE
FAILURE OF INTERNATIONAL CONTROLS

Since the late 1940s the U.S. has fought strenuously against
outlawing nuclear weapons, even as their inevitable targeting of civilian populations with mass terror renders them
both effectively illegal and immoral.
——Carl Boggs, *Origins of the Warfare State*

Since the first nuclear holocausts were inflicted on Hiroshima and Nagasaki, there has been a deadly connection
between US nuclear terrorism and the maintenance of the
US empire.   ——Joseph Gerson, *Empire and the Bomb*

ON A CHILLY September morning in 1933, as he walked
along Southampton Row near the British Museum in London, Leo Szilard
had a flash of insight that would end up making a critical contribution to
the development of the atomic bomb. The refugee Hungarian theoretical
physicist often took long walks to think about complex problems, and on
this cool, damp morning in Bloomsbury he was pondering the puzzle of
how to create and maintain a nuclear chain reaction that could release the
energy of the nucleus of an atom—an issue he had been wrestling with for
years. Szilard had recently read an account of a speech by the renowned
British physicist Ernest Rutherford, who, despite his own groundbreaking
research (with chemist Frederick Soddy) showing that certain elements such
as radium could be changed or transmuted into other elements releasing a
great amount of energy, had expressed doubt about the practical application
of such atomic energy.[1] Lord Rutherford's comment that "anyone who
looked for a source of power in the transformation of the atom was talking
moonshine," had rankled Szilard and refocused his intense concentration
on this daunting theoretical question.[2] As he stepped off the curb that

83

morning, thinking of how to respond to the challenge raised by skeptics like Rutherford, the answer finally came to him in a flash. According to Szilard's biographer, William Lanouette, the scientist recalled: "As the light changed to green and I crossed the street, it suddenly occurred to me that if we could find an element which is split by neutrons [which had been discovered by physicist James Chadwick a year earlier] and which would emit two neutrons when it absorbed one neutron, such an element, if assembled in sufficiently large mass [critical mass], could sustain a nuclear chain reaction."[3] American historian Richard Rhodes, in his Pulitzer Prize–winning account of *The Making of the Atomic Bomb*, described the fateful moment more poetically: "As he crossed the street time cracked open before him and he saw a way to the future, death into the world and all our woe, the shape of things to come."[4] Szilard had conceived the nuclear process that would make possible the construction of the atomic bomb and, with it, the potential destruction of human civilization.

This portentous contribution to the process of creating atomic weapons would later create a huge personal dilemma for Szilard. For, in addition to his intense efforts to solve the theoretical puzzle of how to release the energy of the nucleus of an atom, he also had a strong predilection for, in his words, "Saving the World."[5] After World War I, the young physicist studied and taught in Berlin, often working with his mentor and friend Albert Einstein. As the threat of fascism emerged in Germany, Szilard "hatched an abortive plan to create a small group of wise, unselfish men and women to preserve civilization from the disaster that loomed."[6] After he fled to London to escape the Nazis, Szilard worked tirelessly to help other refugee scholars find new jobs. On that momentous morning in 1933 he immediately recognized the profound and threatening implications of his insight concerning the creation of a nuclear chain reaction. Within a year, Szilard "had written a rough outline of how such a process might work," and then "filed for a patent with the British, assigned it to the British Admiralty, and urged that it be kept secret."[7] American historian Alex Wellerstein describes this act as "arguably the first instance of nuclear secrecy—even before fission [the splitting of the nucleus of an atom] was discovered and atomic bombs were technically possible."[8] Szilard would become increasingly concerned with keeping theoretical ideas about nuclear energy secret and, later, preventing the use of the powerful bomb he would help to create.

In early 1939, now living and working in the United States (in New York at Columbia University), Szilard heard the dramatic news that nuclear fission had been discovered by the German scientists Otto Hahn and Fritz Strassmann, in collaboration with the Austrian physicists Lise Meitner and Otto Frisch. He immediately realized that his "hypothetical neutron-induced chain reaction" had gone from the realm of "science fiction to possibility" if secondary neutrons were created by the process of fission.[9] If that possibility was real (and later research in the spring of 1939 confirmed the existence of secondary neutrons), Szilard wanted that fact kept secret from Hitler and the Nazis. As a Jewish refugee, he greatly feared a nuclear-armed Germany. This new discovery (which Szilard thought would bring grief to the world) had to be controlled, and he and other physicists were soon involved in the "first collective attempt for nuclear secrecy."[10] Beginning with a call for self-censorship, the scientists soon attempted to exert control over the publication process of papers involving nuclear fission. However, as Wellerstein documents, this proposed system of nuclear secrecy quickly fell apart, and this "attempt to create an ad hoc, non-state based, unenforced, international secrecy pact among scientists who viewed one another as competitors was perhaps the wildest of Szilard's many wild ideas."[11] Wild as it may have seemed at the time, Szilard's "crusade for scientific secrecy" would serve as a model for later efforts at nuclear secrecy.[12] These efforts, however, would soon shift from the scientists themselves to the control of government officials, and here, too, Szilard would play a critical role.

In July 1939, Szilard and Eugene Wigner, a fellow refugee scientist from Budapest, initiated a fateful meeting on Long Island with Albert Einstein (also by then a refugee in the United States). Concerned about the recent discovery of how the explosive chain reaction Szilard had conceived could be produced by using uranium layered with graphite and the secondary neutrons released from nuclear fission, the three alarmed scientists prepared a letter (in the name of Einstein but drafted by Szilard), which they hoped to send to a Belgian minister whom Einstein knew, with a cover letter to the U.S. State Department.[13] The scientists hoped to warn the Belgian royal family (and alert the State Department) that Nazi Germany coveted the world's largest uranium supply in the Belgian Congo and could use it to create a super weapon. Upon further reflection, Szilard had an "uneasy feeling about this approach" and contacted Dr. Alexander Sachs, a vice president of the Lehman Corporation (a large Wall Street investment bank) and a private advisor to President Franklin D. Roosevelt (FDR).[14] Recognizing the importance of the issue, Sachs promised to deliver a warning letter directly to Roosevelt.

Albert Einstein and Leo Szilard with the famous letter they wrote to President Roosevelt in 1939. Courtesy Universal History Archive / Universal Images Group via Getty Images.

Several days later, now accompanied by another Hungarian refugee, theoretical physicist Edward Teller (who would later play a critical role in the development of the hydrogen bomb), Szilard went back to Einstein's rented summer cottage, and they redrafted the letter. As Einstein's biographer Walter Isaacson notes, the world's most famous scientist, at the bequest of and in the words of his friend Szilard, "was about to tell the president of the United States that he should begin contemplating a weapon of almost unimaginable impact that could unleash the power of the atom."[15] Sachs eventually gave the warning letter, "a successful mix of the physicists' insights and concerns,"[16] to FDR personally, and after some additional delays, on January 19, 1942, President Roosevelt authorized the Manhattan Engineering District to produce an American atomic bomb. Szilard would then work on what came to be called the Manhattan Project at the Chicago Metallurgical Laboratory (Met Lab), convinced, as was Einstein, that the United States had to beat Hitler to the bomb. But as the race to create the bomb unfolded, the atomic scientists would discover, to their dismay, that power over the control of nuclear secrets would quickly shift from science to the state.

Despite his ongoing contributions to the development of atomic weapons, Szilard would also continue his efforts to "save the world." Fearing a future atomic arms race, he wrote a memo to his colleagues at the Met Lab in September 1942 that resurrected the idea of a society of righteous intellectuals "who can, by repeated discussions, make clear . . . what the existence of atomic bombs will mean from the point of view of the post-war period."[17] By the spring of 1945, the Met Lab "was in ferment, not only over the question of a postwar nuclear arms race, but over the prospective use of the atomic bomb."[18] As the German war effort was collapsing, it became clear that the American bomb was no longer needed to deter a Nazi bomb, but it could be used as an offensive weapon against Japan in the Pacific theater.

Szilard later recalled his thoughts at the time: "Initially we were strongly motivated to produce the bombs because we feared the Germans would get ahead of us and the only way to prevent them from dropping bombs on us was to have bombs in readiness ourselves. But now, with the war won, it was not clear what we were working for."[19] Szilard, Eugene Rabinowitch, and other Manhattan Project scientists in Chicago (and elsewhere) now began to work "feverishly to delay the full military use of the bomb at least until a demonstration shot could be arranged."[20] The U.S. military was strongly resistant to this idea. Frustrated, Rabinowitch even considered leaking the plan to use the bomb against Japan to the news media—"a shocking breach of security."[21] Later regretting his failure to take this drastic step, "Rabinowitch explained that if had alerted the public they would have at least known *in advance* of 'a crime' that was to be carried out in their name."[22] Szilard did take more drastic steps.

In late March, not inclined to follow any chain of command, Szilard (armed with an introductory letter from his friend Albert Einstein) requested a meeting with President Roosevelt on a secret matter. He drafted a memo ("Atomic Bombs and the Postwar Position of the United States in the World") to convince FDR that to avoid a postwar nuclear arms race with Stalin and the Soviet Union, the United States should delay the use of the bomb against Japan and set up a system for the international control of nuclear weapons. It was the first of many attempts he would make to "stop the bomb."[23] Roosevelt died in April before the meeting could be arranged, however, and so Szilard then tried to set up a meeting with the new president, Harry S. Truman. Instead of scheduling a meeting directly with the president, Truman's appointment secretary, Matthew J. Connelly, shuttled Szilard (and the Met Lab's associate director, Walter Bartky) off to meet instead with the president's newly designated secretary of state, James F. Byrnes, on May 28 at his home in Spartanburg, South Carolina. The hawk-ish Byrnes, according to Martin Sherwin, "seemed grossly ignorant about the implications of atomic energy and its diplomatic value" and was not convinced by Szilard's arguments against using the bomb against Japan.[24] He responded forcefully by noting that the use of the bomb would help justify the enormous government expenditure on the Manhattan Project and make the Russians "more manageable," a statement that "flabbergasted" Szilard.[25] As he wrote later, "I was rarely as depressed as when we left Byrnes' house and walked toward the [train] station."[26] Szilard's unauthor-ized meeting with the new Truman administration caused an uproar back at the Met Lab in Chicago and angered General Groves, the chief military administrator of the Manhattan Project, who considered it a breach of national security.

As a last-ditch effort to prevent the military use of the bomb (and pro-mote the postwar control of atomic weapons), Arthur Compton, the director of the Met Lab, appointed a Committee on Social and Political Implications of Atomic Energy. Chaired by James Franck, another refugee scientist, the committee delivered a report (written by Rabinowitch and strongly influ-enced by Szilard) on June 11, 1945, that made a forceful argument against dropping atomic bombs on Japan. But the report was ignored, and two months later Hiroshima and Nagasaki were destroyed. As American histo-rian Paul Boyer notes, although "the Franck Report had failed to prevent the obliteration of two Japanese cities . . . the impulse behind it . . . intensified in the postwar period, as several thousand scientists were drawn into intense political activity."[27] For his part, Szilard made one final personal effort to stop the bomb. In July 1945 he drew up and circulated among Manhattan Project scientists a petition addressed to President Truman, imploring him to avoid the military use of the bomb they had constructed. "I personally feel," Szilard wrote to a colleague, "that it would be a matter of importance if a large number of scientists who have worked in this field went clearly and unmistakably on record as to their opposition on moral grounds to the use of these bombs in the present phase of the war."[28] General Groves made sure that the petition never made it to President Truman. Szilard had failed in this effort to save the world from the bomb he had helped conceive on that Sep-tember morning in 1933. But he and many of his fellow atomic scientists would continue to work to ban the scourge of the powerful weapon they had just unleashed.

The dropping of atomic weapons on Japan in August 1945 was a trans-formative event in human history, and the bomb would "become the defin-ing feature of the post–World War II world."[29] After becoming aware of the death and destruction these weapons caused in Hiroshima and Nagasaki, people around the globe could now imagine how nuclear devastation could end civilization in the next war. This apocalyptic imaginary generated intense fear and altered human consciousness and culture.[30] As Jonathan Schell observed, the people of the world now had to confront the "nuclear predicament."[31] The bomb existed, and at the least the knowledge of how to create these weapons would always exist. These two facts raised critical ques-tions: Could we abolish these horrible weapons before they destroyed the world and establish the necessary international controls over nuclear energy to prevent future bombs from being built? Boyer describes how key social, cultural, and political leaders began to obsess over these and other questions related to the atomic bomb as early as August 1945.[32] And soon thereafter, led initially by many of the atomic scientists, a worldwide nuclear disarma-ment movement arose.[33] Most of the people who participated in this move-ment judged Hiroshima and Nagasaki to be "crimes against humanity," and they were determined to prevent future apocalyptic crimes related to nuclear weapons from being committed.

Having failed to prevent the military use of the bomb, many of the atomic scientists who had worked on the Manhattan Project (but certainly not all) turned their efforts to the control of the deadly weapon they had just created. They found that they now had "cultural celebrity and political influence," and they attempted to use both to "promote the cause of peace" and head off a deadly nuclear arms race.[34] Szilard marveled at the scientists' new cultural and political influence: "It is remarkable," he wrote, "that all these scientists should be listened to. But mass murders have always com-manded the attention of the public, and atomic scientists are no exception to this rule."[35] In the immediate postwar period, the atomic scientists used their new status to warn the American people about the dangers posed by the bomb, mobilize public opinion to stop the impending arms race, and influence political decision making concerning nuclear weapons. The scientists organized committees, wrote reports, lobbied government officials, developed the Federation of American Scientists (FAS), launched the *Bulletin of the Atomic Scientists*, created the iconic Doomsday Clock, advocated for the establishment of a world government, and teamed up with pacifists, World Federalists, and significant public intellectuals in a heroic effort to confront and ban the bomb and stave off a nuclear arms race.[36]

By the early 1950s, however, the scientists' movement would begin to wane. During the Manhattan Project itself, and in the early postwar period, "a significant difference of opinion had developed between top government officials on the one hand, and a circle of scientists and middle-range government officials on the other. To the official guardians of national security, the Bomb offered a splendid opportunity to bolster national military strength and to humble competing nations."[37] Due to the political decision to pursue U.S. global military supremacy in 1940 and other imperial goals within the world geopolitical system after World War II, the emergence of Cold War economic interests and anticommunist political paranoia, the normalization of the decision to use the bomb against Japan, and the influence of the cultural narrative of American Exceptionalism, the early efforts of the atomic scientists to ban the bomb would fail—and their "messianic role" would come to an end.[38] One major factor in the decline of the influence of the atomic scientists in the 1950s was the traumatizing effect of the "extraordinary American inquisition" of J. Robert Oppenheimer, the father of the atomic bomb, during the height of the "McCarthyite hysteria" in 1954 when he was stripped of his security clearance for opposing the development of the hydrogen bomb and advocating for international control of nuclear weapons.[39]

Despite McCarthyism and the trauma and public effects of Oppenheimer's ordeal, many of the scientists would remain involved in the political effort to ban the bomb and end the arms race through the continuing publication of the *Bulletin of the Atomic Scientists* and the creation of transnational antinuclear organizations such as the Pugwash Conferences on Science and World Affairs.[40] But even though a powerful world disarmament movement would later build on the early postwar work of the dissident scientists (and experience some occasional, limited successes), as the Cold War intensified the United States would continue to possess ever more destructive nuclear weapons, develop new technologies to deliver them, block any political and legal moves toward disarmament, and threaten to use these deadly devices in a variety of conflict situations in violation of international law. Despite the early work of the scientists' movement, the rise of popular protests against the bomb and radioactive fallout, and the emergence of the world disarmament movement, American political leaders, with "exhilarating visions of postwar national power,"[41] would continue to engage in numerous apocalyptic crimes related to nuclear weapons.

INTERNATIONAL CONTROL OF NUCLEAR WEAPONS

In the immediate postwar period, the nuclear predicament raised several critical questions. Would the newly created atomic weapons be controlled by the U.S. military or by a civilian political organization? Would the United States maintain its monopoly over these weapons, or would America seek to develop some form of international controls over the bomb and nuclear energy? If international controls over atomic weapons were developed, would they take place under the auspices of the nascent United Nations, or would a stronger form of world government be necessary?

The first issue that the atomic scientists' movement confronted after the war was an effort to establish military control over the bomb. In October 1945, a measure drafted by the War Department was introduced in Congress. The May-Johnson Bill called for all atomic research and development to be placed under the control of the U.S. military. As Boyer observes, "Most scientists were appalled by the measure, both for its militarization of the atom and for its stringent secrecy provisions."[42] The newly created Federation of Atomic (later American) Scientists, which saw the bill as an attempt by General Groves "to extend military power and style into the post-war period,"[43] mounted a major lobbying campaign to defeat the bill. Szilard was especially active in the political effort to block May-Johnson, alerting other scientists to the danger of military control, testifying at hearings, and personally lobbying members of Congress.

In late October the scientists appeared to score a significant victory in their campaign to prevent exclusive military control of atomic energy and development when the Senate created the Special Committee on Atomic Energy. Chaired by Connecticut senator Brien McMahon, the Special Committee provided a forum for the critics of the May-Johnson Bill and the supporters of civilian control of atomic energy. And in July 1946, with the passage of the Atomic Energy Act, the scientists seemed to have won the battle. The McMahon Act (as it was called) established a civilian Atomic Energy Commission (AEC). According to Boyer, however, it was not an unalloyed triumph, for "the much-amended act contained security provisions nearly as stringent as those of the May-Johnson bill and embedded a powerful Military Liaison Committee into the basic framework of the AEC."[44] Wellerstein also notes the shift to a greater military emphasis in the legislation despite a victory for civilian control and argues that "nuclear secrecy" was made "legally permanent and expansive" in the bill "through the unique and novel legal concept of restricted data."[45] Yet at the time, the McMahon Act appeared to be a major victory for the atomic scientists, demonstrating that "the activist scientists had made the transition to successful political lobbyists with ease."[46] Larger challenges awaited the movement.

With civilian management of the atom seemingly ensured, the next critical issue the newfound activists confronted was international control of atomic energy. As Boyer points out, "For many scientists, this was *the* cause."[47] Without strong international controls, the atomic scientists feared that a virulent nuclear arms race would develop and lead to the destruction of civilization. This critical issue arose early on during the Manhattan Project itself. The internationally famous Danish physicist Niels Bohr (a Nobel Prize winner) had been among the first to raise an alarm about the possibility of a postwar nuclear arms race between the United States and the Soviet Union. When he learned of the full extent of the Manhattan Project in 1943, Bohr traveled to the United States and became a consultant to the project. He formulated various proposals for the international control of atomic energy, which he sent to Churchill and Roosevelt in numerous memoranda and letters. Commenting on these proposals, Sherwin notes, "Simply put, Bohr believed that the development of the atomic bomb necessitated a new international order."[48] The unprecedented nature of the atomic bomb meant that it could not be monopolized by one country. Meeting with President Roosevelt in 1944, Bohr argued for openness between the Allies during both the war and the postwar period. He believed that Stalin should be informed of the Manhattan Project before the bomb was dropped and before the war ended. Soviet participation in postwar atomic energy planning should also be guaranteed. He argued that international cooperation was of the essence. As Wellerstein observes about Bohr's concern, "It was perhaps a naively idealistic goal, but his emphasis on the importance of total openness would influence many later efforts toward international control."[49] This goal would come to be championed within the Roosevelt administration as well.

Bohr's meeting with FDR spurred a conversation between the president and the influential scientist-administrator Vannevar Bush on postwar planning. Bush, the head of the Office of Scientific Research and Development (OSRD), then engaged in a long discussion about international control of atomic energy with James B. Conant (president of Harvard University), who headed the National Defense Research Committee (NDRC). Bush and

Conant, prime political architects of the Manhattan Project, then wrote several memoranda to Secretary of War Henry L. Stimson in September 1944, urging him to take some official action concerning postwar control of the atomic bomb. They asserted that the U.S. atomic advantage would be temporary, that complete secrecy was impossible, and that the failure to share information about the bomb with the world would trigger an international arms race in the postwar period. As Bush and Conant further argued, "The only way out was free exchange of information, a complete renunciation of secrecy, very similar to the idea of 'openness' that Bohr championed."[50] The approach advocated by Bohr and the scientific advisors "appealed to Stimson," and in a meeting with Bush later that September, "the secretary of war agreed that an international approach to the problem of atomic fission should be carefully studied and lamented that it had been impossible to command Roosevelt's attention on the subject."[51] Stimson himself, however, would later equivocate on the issue and fail to act decisively.

These internal efforts to spur action on the international control of atomic weapons during the war failed for several reasons. The same month that Stimson met with Bush to discuss the issue (September 1944), President Roosevelt made a secret deal with British prime minister Winston Churchill (concealed from FDR's own advisors) in which he committed the United States to keep the atomic bomb secret from the Soviet Union. As Malloy notes, "Whatever fears FDR entertained about an arms race were not enough to trump his wartime commitment" to Churchill in the "Hyde Park Aide-Memoire."[52] And despite his sympathy for the various plans for international control of atomic energy in the postwar period, Stimson failed to champion these proposals until shortly before he left office after the war. The reason for his reticence? According to Malloy, "By the end of 1944, the secretary of war had made up his mind. securing postwar concessions from the Soviet Union should take priority over the international control of atomic energy."[53] The bomb was a bargaining chip—"a royal straight flush" that could be used against Stalin.[54] Reflecting on the failures of Roosevelt and Stimson to advance the cause of international control during the war, Wellerstein also emphasizes how radical the positions of Bohr, Bush, and Conant were: "The argument was that a new technology—the atomic bomb—would require a remaking of the world. International politics and industrial practices would both have to be forever changed." Such radical ideas would not survive the politics of the times. [55]

Shortly after Franklin Roosevelt died in April 1945, Stimson (along with General Groves) met with the new president, Harry S. Truman, to inform him of the existence of (in Truman's words) "the most terrible weapon ever known in human history, one bomb of which could destroy a whole city."[56] FDR had kept his vice president in the dark about the Manhattan Project, but now President Truman would be forced to grapple with all the complex moral and legal issues concerning the atomic bomb. He, too, would be "torn between seeking a long-term international solution to the dangers of nuclear fission and the short-term diplomatic advantages that might be gained by using the bomb as a bargaining chip."[57]

As the previous chapter described, the Truman administration engaged in a form of atomic diplomacy regarding Stalin and the Soviet Union and the decision to bomb Hiroshima and Nagasaki. The Potsdam Conference in July 1945 appears to have had a decisive influence on Truman's decisions concerning these issues. The new president approached the Big Three Summit with Churchill and Stalin with some trepidation. The rough-and-tumble negotiations over the shape of postwar Europe and the path to a successful conclusion to the Pacific war would be the first major test of his diplomatic skills. But on July 16, Truman was buoyed by the news of the successful Trinity test of the atomic bomb in the desert at Alamogordo. The tough bargaining sessions at Potsdam had led the American delegation (which had started with a "generally hostile attitude toward the Russians") to conclude that "the Soviets were living up to their worst expectations."[58] But news of the successful atomic test in New Mexico was a "game changer." In Stimson's view, it was "the great equalizer"—Soviet assistance was no longer necessary and, in fact, unwelcome.[59]

Knowing that the United States now had the atomic bomb gave Truman "a greatly strengthened hand" and "a new confidence and optimism. The most powerful weapon ever created was part of his arsenal."[60] The Americans did not directly inform the Soviets about the atomic bomb (as some in the delegation desired), but Truman did "casually mention to Stalin," on July 24, "that we had a new weapon of unusual destructive force."[61] And the Potsdam Declaration at the end of the conference, which threatened Japan with "prompt and utter destruction" if it did not surrender unconditionally, excluded Stalin and the Soviet Union. In his masterful study of the origins of the arms race, Sherwin concludes, "The steady course toward a postwar atomic armaments race that Bohr had sought to alter passed several important markers at Potsdam. Not only were Soviet fears about the consequences of an American atomic bomb heightened, but on the American side, what little commitment there was among high officials for the international control of atomic energy all but vanished."[62]

The evidence shows that within both the Manhattan Project and the higher circles of the U.S. government during World War II, there were discussions and debates about not only whether to use the atomic bomb against Japan but also whether to keep the bomb a secret from the Soviets. The latter decision would negatively influence the prospects for international control of atomic energy in the postwar era, and after the use of the weapons against Hiroshima and Nagasaki, both bitterly contested debates would move into the public sphere. The normalization of "terror" bombing in general and the use of atomic bombs against Japan specifically, decisively influenced by Stimson's 1947 *Harper's Magazine* article, resolved the first of these debates. The second debate, concerning international control of nuclear weapons, would heat up in the immediate postwar period and continue in one form or another into the present. In the end, larger social and political forces related to the pursuit of empire and the emergence of the Cold War would shape U.S. decisions to continue to possess nuclear weapons and threaten to use them on numerous occasions.

For the atomic scientists, international control of atomic energy continued to be "the cause" in the early postwar era. In October 1945, more than five hundred scientists at Harvard and MIT signed a statement that "summed up a rapidly evolving consensus" concerning the issue of international control.[63] The scientists noted that other nations would soon be able to produce atomic bombs; no effective defense was possible; more bombs did not provide security; a future atomic war would destroy civilization; and thus, unprecedented international cooperation was necessary for survival. Even J. Robert Oppenheimer, who as director of the Los Alamos Laboratory had supported the use of the bomb against Japan, was now arguing for "international controls on nuclear weapons."[64] Not only that, in an August 17, 1945, letter to Henry Stimson, Oppenheimer also expressed a deep commitment to "making future wars impossible."[65] In October of that year, when the now-famous scientist tried to persuade Truman to support these views, confiding to him, "I feel I have blood on my hands," the president became "infuriated" and "ejected" him from the Oval Office.[66]

While the atomic scientists continued to express support for the international control of the bomb in "countless speeches and articles,"[67] the "atomic tragedy" of Henry Stimson came full circle. On September 21, 1945, his final day in office as secretary of war, at his last cabinet meeting, Stimson reversed course and urged President Truman to immediately approach the Soviet Union and strike a deal on the control of atomic arms. As Malloy argues, "There was no greater tragedy in [Stimson's] long career than the failure to control the use and spread of nuclear weapons in accord with his own deeply held convictions about war and morality."[68] Stimson's about-face and impassioned plea for international control of the atomic bomb fell on deaf ears, as did the appeals of Szilard, Oppenheimer, and the other atomic scientists. Secretary of State Byrnes forcefully opposed the idea, and Sherwin argues that the resolution of the Stimson-Byrnes cabinet debate that day "fixed the role of nuclear weapons in postwar diplomacy."[69] Truman was the "referee," and he "concluded the debate by supporting Byrnes."[70] The new president was not inclined to take the political risk of accepting Stimson's proposal, and neither were the rest of his cabinet members (with the exception of Henry Wallace, former vice president and then secretary of commerce). As Malloy explains, "Amid a climate of postwar atomic triumphalism and growing tensions with the Soviet Union, public, press, and congressional opinion was running strongly against Stimson's plan" (and the pleas of the atomic scientists).[71] But one major effort would still be undertaken.

The "high point" of the early postwar efforts for international control came in 1946 with the production of "A Report on the International Control of Atomic Energy," called the Acheson-Lilienthal Report,[72] which was largely written by Oppenheimer (who would later be victimized by the anticommunist crusade and unjustly labeled a security risk). He proposed a "dramatic and comprehensive plan" to create a new international agency, the Atomic Development Authority, that "would have sovereign ownership of all uranium mines, atomic power plants and laboratories."[73] Oppenheimer's plan might have won international support, but Bernard Baruch, the Wall Street financier appointed by Truman to present the American proposal to the United Nations, would reformulate and essentially "gut" the plan to make it unacceptable to Stalin.[74] Presented to the newly created United Nations Atomic Energy Commission (UNAEC) at its first meeting in June 1946, the reformulated report (now called the Baruch Plan) offered to turn over all U.S. atomic weapons to the UN, but only on the condition that other countries would pledge not to produce them and agree to an onerous inspection system. There was scathing criticism of the Baruch Plan, with some observers charging that it was deliberately designed to be rejected by the Soviets to score a propaganda victory in the early days of the Cold War. British historians Campbell Craig and Sergey Radchenko, for example, argue that the Truman administration "clearly reached the conclusion in February 1946, if not considerably earlier, that it did not want to achieve international control in any meaningful sense, and that it wanted to use the Baruch Plan as a clever means to force the Soviet Union to take the blame for its failure."[75] The political ploy worked.

The Soviet Union, in the process of developing its own atomic weapons, and fearing American domination of the proposed international authority, did indeed reject the Baruch Plan. The Soviet delegate to the UN, Andrei Gromyko, "bluntly insisted that a world moratorium on the production and use of atomic weapons must precede any agreement on international control."[76] The Soviets insisted that the United States must first eliminate its atomic weapons before a system of international controls and inspections could be put in place. Although the talks continued, "by May 1948, when the UNAEC finally expired, the international control effort launched with such optimism two years before was long since dead."[77] Wellerstein argues that international control "was always a long-shot idea," since it required "a total remaking of the international order," and concludes that "the failure of international control was not surprising; that it was briefly taken as seriously as it was is the more remarkable thing, and reflects on how unsettling the atomic bomb was to the existing order."[78] The atomic scientists, world government advocates, and the young disarmament movement had failed in their first attempt to ban the bomb. To understand more fully why their efforts failed requires a broader sociological and geopolitical lens.

IMPERIAL GOALS AND THE COLD WAR

There is strong historical evidence to support the argument that in the 1940s American leaders decided to pursue global military supremacy, achieve economic and political dominance in the postwar world through new international legal structures, and thwart Stalin's own geopolitical ambitions for the Soviet Union. As noted in the previous chapter, these imperial goals and nascent Cold War political calculations were among the most significant social forces that influenced the decision to use atomic bombs against Japan. As Sherwin observes, "Relying on the bomb to shape diplomacy and military policy was a wartime decision."[79] Following the war, these same institutional goals and political calculations also influenced U.S. decisions to ultimately reject the international control of atomic energy, to engage in a protracted arms race with the Soviet Union, to produce the super (hydrogen) bomb, to develop a powerful warfare / national security state, to threaten to use nuclear weapons in various conflict situations, and to continue to possess nuclear weapons in violation of the NPT and much later the TPNW. These state actions, most of which violate forms of public international law, can thus be characterized as "crimes of empire."[80] The foundational political-economic structure, nuclear institutional complex, and ideological justifications for these state crimes were set in place between 1940 and 1952.

The German conquest of France in May 1940 caused U.S. foreign policy elites to fundamentally rethink their assumptions about America's role in the world.[81] Although the United States was already an established imperial power, it was an informal empire as opposed to a formal or colonial one. This was what Williams characterized as "Open Door imperialism," a form of empire based primarily on diplomacy among the major capitalist powers to keep foreign markets open, a strategy of controlling economic resources and exerting political influence without direct ownership or military control.[82] But as Wertheim argues, after the fall of France to the Nazis in 1940, U.S. officials and intellectuals decided that to continue American economic and political expansion the United States now had to "impose order by force" and "achieve global dominance" in the postwar era.[83] Although Wertheim does not discuss nuclear weapons directly (an odd omission), his thesis that American leaders made a conscious choice during the 1940s to use "the superior power of the U.S. to underwrite a decent world order" implies that atomic power would play a central role in achieving global military supremacy and shaping the postwar world.[84] Williams argued that U.S. political leaders viewed the atomic bomb as a "self-starting magic lamp" as they anticipated the arrival of "their long-sought City on the Hill in the form of a *de facto* American Century embracing the globe."[85] The bomb would enhance the American Empire.

The outcome of World War II provided the United States with a position of unrivaled military, political, and economic power. And even before the war was over, American leaders were "laying the groundwork for a new postwar economic and political order."[86] As Canadian political economists Leo Panitch and Sam Gindin observe, "The American empire that emerged after World War II was the product of considerable planning."[87] Starting at Bretton Woods in 1944, new international economic structures were developed, such as the International Monetary Fund (IMF), the World Bank, and the General Agreement on Tariffs and Trade (GATT). In 1945, new political and legal international institutions were also created: the United Nations (with a veto power for the United States as a permanent member of the Security Council), the World Court, and the International Military Tribunals (at Nuremberg and Tokyo), all backed up by the new American global military supremacy. These international structures would give rise to a new form of "world organization" as "a vehicle for U.S. hegemony."[88] The new international economic structure would enhance and expand the informal, Open Door imperialism that the United States had been practicing since the turn of the century, and America's preeminent position in the emerging geopolitical and juridical systems would serve to ensure the political dominance of the United States in the new world order. American leaders already clearly understood in 1945 that the bomb could greatly enhance the prospects for their deliberate imperial project and postwar domination.

There was only one potential challenger to this larger and stronger American Empire—the Soviet Union. Although the countries were allies during the war, U.S. political and military leaders were very cognizant that Stalin's Soviet Union would be their chief rival in the postwar period. They recognized that the Soviets constituted a geopolitical and ideological threat to America's postwar imperial designs. As the previous chapter explains, the perception of this threat influenced the decision to drop the atomic bomb before a possible Soviet entry into the Pacific war, and it animated the strategic thinking of U.S. policymakers about using the bomb to forestall Soviet expansionism in the Far East. It was also hoped that atomic weapons could be used as a bargaining chip to influence Stalin's behavior after the war. This crude "atomic diplomacy" not only had a major effect on the decision to drop the bomb on Japan,[89] but it also decisively influenced both domestic (within Truman's cabinet) and world (at the UN) negotiations over the international control of atomic energy in the early postwar years. It is clear that in both settings the Truman administration had come to value the bomb as the key to America's postwar dominance—what American historian Gregg Herken called "the winning weapon."[90] In Sherwin's assessment, "The diplomacy of atomic energy came to rest during the war on a simple and dangerous assumption: that the Soviet government would surrender important geographical, political, and ideological objectives in exchange for the neutralization of the new weapon."[91] But the Russians would not surrender their objectives, and they would not cooperate with the American vision of the postwar world order. This would lead to the full eruption of the Cold War in the late 1940s, and with it a dangerous nuclear arms race between the United States and the Soviet Union.

THE EARLY COLD WAR

The Cold War was an ideological, economic, and geopolitical struggle between the United States and the Soviet Union. This epic conflict would dominate the postwar international political system for more than forty years as the two "superpowers" that emerged from World War II contested with each other for global influence. Each perceived that their national security, vital interests, and way of life were at stake in the ideological struggle between the two different political and economic systems. The Cold War can be analyzed in many ways, and there is a huge literature on the subject.[92] It is impossible to do justice to the topic here. For the purpose of developing a criminology of nuclear weapons, therefore, I focus primarily on those dimensions of the conflict that involve the production, continued possession, and threats to use these weapons that constitute violations of international law.

By any account, the bomb is at the heart of the Cold War struggle. As Sherwin reminds us, "Regardless of the myriad other forces that would shape the Soviet-American relationship—economics, ideology, geography, national ambitions, alliances—it was clear from August 6, 1945, that nuclear weapons would command the central role."[93] The fundamental issue concerning the Cold War confrontation was the nuclear threat. By the beginning of 1946 it was evident that Stalin was not intimidated by America's atomic diplomacy and would challenge, where he could, U.S. attempts to construct a new postwar imperial order. In a belligerent speech in early February, his harsh rhetoric about capitalist greed and plans to rebuild the Soviet economy alarmed many Americans. Two weeks later, George Kennan, the senior U.S. diplomat in Moscow, dispatched his "long telegram" warning of the Soviet Union's own imperial ambitions, internal tyranny, and hostility to the capitalist world. At a speech in Missouri in March, Winston Churchill, referring to the Soviet attempt to establish a buffer zone of satellite states in Eastern Europe (a buffer the Russians perceived as necessary to prevent another invasion from the west in the future), warned that an "Iron Curtain" was descending across the European continent. But as American Cold War historian Robert J. McMahon points out, it wasn't just Soviet behavior that "induced apprehension among American and British policy-makers"—it was also "the prospect that the Soviet Union might capitalize on and benefit from the socioeconomic distress and accompanying political upheavals that continued to mark the postwar world."[94] These leaders feared that those involved in radical nationalist movements and the anticolonial struggles that emerged after the war would see communism as a preferable alternative to Western capitalism. This was the ideological and political milieu within which the Baruch Plan for international control of atomic energy (intended to be unacceptable to Stalin) would be crafted, presented to the UNAEC, and rejected by the Soviets.

The Truman administration also faced domestic political challenges due to economic issues such as rising unemployment, wage demands, and labor unrest. As a result, the Republicans captured both the House and the Senate in the 1946 midterm elections for the first time since 1930. But even though Truman faced a "harsh political climate" at home and "big hurdles in Congress when it came to labor," on foreign policy issues "he was able to build a bipartisan coalition of support."[95] He was able to accomplish this by moving to the right, pledging to "contain" the Soviet threat, and attempting to reduce the appeal of communism. On March 12, 1947, President Truman delivered a forceful address to Congress in which he asserted that the United States would "support free peoples who are resisting subjugation by armed minorities or by outside pressures."[96] In announcing what came to be known as the "Truman Doctrine," the president was responding to Great Britain's decision to stop providing economic assistance to Greece and Turkey, which were both battling communist insurgencies. But the doctrine also spelled out a broader "strategy of containment," advocated for in greater detail later that year in a *Foreign Affairs* article by George Kennan (writing anonymously as "X").[97] The concept of "containment" would "guide American foreign policy for the next two decades,"[98] and atomic weapons were expected to play a central role in containing the Soviet Union.

While the Truman Doctrine was a declaration that the United States would contain the Soviet Union's perceived geopolitical advances, the Marshall Plan (announced by the new secretary of state George C. Marshall in June 1947) was intended to provide an infusion of economic aid to help rebuild Western Europe and reduce the appeal of communism in the so-called Third World. According to American historian Jill Lepore, the president "liked to say" that the Truman Doctrine and the Marshall Plan "were two halves of the same walnut."[99] In the postwar period, the Truman administration attempted to use all the tools at its disposal to blunt nationalistic and anticolonial movements, promote Open Door policies, and assist the political and economic transformation of Europe. As Bacevich concludes, "U.S. grand strategy during the Cold War required not only containing communism, but also taking active measures to open up the world politically, culturally, and above all, economically."[100] This "war" would be fought at many levels.

But it was still another American response to the Cold War that concerned the atomic scientists, the disarmament movement, and even some within the Truman administration—the advancement of the U.S. commitment to military supremacy.[101] In addition to the production of new weapons and the expansion of the armed forces, new "defense" institutions were created by the passage of the National Security Act in 1947. Among the new militarily related organizations established by this act were the Central Intelligence Agency (CIA) and the National Security Agency (NSA). The War Department was transformed into the Department of Defense (DOD)—and given its own building (the Pentagon)—and the position of the chairman of the Joint Chiefs of Staff was created. After reviewing these military developments, Lepore observes, "In this political climate, the 'one world' vision of atomic scientists, along with the idea of civilian, international control of atomic power, faded fast."[102] The Cold War was beginning to fuel the acceleration of the central role for nuclear weapons in American foreign policy, and in 1947 the *Bulletin of the Atomic Scientists* set its new Doomsday Clock at seven minutes before midnight.

Few observers expected Harry Truman to win reelection in 1948, but in a major political surprise he defeated the governor of New York, Republican Thomas Dewey, and two other candidates. The Democrats also regained control of both houses of Congress. In the late 1940s and early 1950s, President Truman would be forced to deal with a series of Cold War crises and make critical decisions concerning nuclear weapons and an emerging arms race. One crisis began in June 1948 when Stalin blocked all ground access to West Berlin. Truman responded to the Soviet blockade with the famed Berlin Airlift, flying in supplies and fuel around the clock. But in another instance of atomic diplomacy and thinking about the bomb as "the winning weapon," the president also sent sixty B-29 bombers to bases in England and a smaller number to Germany. These planes were described in government press releases as "atomic capable," although they "were probably not equipped with atomic bombs."[103] The B-29s appeared to have had little effect on Stalin, but the airlift was successful, and he would call off the Berlin Blockade in May 1949. In September of that year the Western allies would create the Federal Republic of Germany (West Germany). The Soviets interpreted this move as threatening and responded one month later by establishing the German Democratic Republic (East Germany). As McMahon notes, "Europe's Cold War lines were now clearly demarcated, the division of Germany between west and east mirroring the broader division of Europe into American-led and Soviet-led spheres."[104] The United States and its allies also created the North Atlantic Treaty Organization (NATO) in 1949, as part of a broader containment strategy.

THE HYDROGEN BOMB

Two other events in 1949 would significantly escalate the Cold War and increase the nuclear danger. In late September, President Truman announced that an atomic explosion had been detected in the Soviet Union, and while Americans were still absorbing the shock that Stalin now also had the bomb, Mao Zedong's communist forces prevailed in the Chinese civil war and the People's Republic of China (PRC) was proclaimed on October 1. The Soviet acquisition of atomic weapons dramatically changed the nature of the Cold War. It not only heralded the end of U.S. nuclear hegemony but also opened the door to a Soviet–American arms race. The fact that the Russians had been able to produce an atomic bomb only four years after Hiroshima and Nagasaki caused some to reflect on the Stimson–Byrnes debate in late 1945, when the outgoing secretary of war had argued that "the crux of the matter" was "taking advantage of 'momentary superiority' versus seeking an international arrangement that would eliminate the bomb's threat to civilization."[105] International control was the road not taken then, and now in 1949, when both countries had the bomb, that path would not be reopened. Instead, as Australian nuclear historian Joseph Siracusa notes, "The other potential path was to engage in full-scale competition and an arms race," and "for a variety of reasons, mostly derived with the Cold War mindset, the administration chose the latter course. It was a watershed moment."[106] The Doomsday Clock was ticking.

The Soviet atomic test and the "loss of China" created enormous political pressure on President Truman to take a militarized path, developing a more aggressive strategy for fighting the Cold War, approving a $319 million expansion of atomic bomb production, and deciding to move ahead with the development of a new kind of weapon, a "super" bomb.[107] This new weapon, variously referred to as a hydrogen, thermonuclear, or nuclear bomb, released energy when hydrogen atoms were fused. It was far more powerful than the fission bomb, which produced energy by splitting the heavy nucleus of an atom like uranium-235. Although the potential for building a fusion bomb was already well known to the atomic scientists, "during the winter of 1949–50 a highly classified debate had been raging in defence and scientific circles over whether to proceed with . . . the super."[108] Edward Teller, the father of the hydrogen bomb, realized that "the Soviet bomb now presented him with the perfect opportunity to push his pet project," and he lobbied hard for its development.[109] But for other scientists, like Oppenheimer, there were major concerns about the morality of this more powerful weapon and its potential impact on American–Soviet relations. The AEC's General Advisory Committee (GAC), chaired by Oppenheimer, worried about greatly extending a "policy of exterminating civilian populations," with some individual members expressing ethical objections to what they called "a weapon of genocide" and "necessarily an evil thing considered in any light."[110] The GAC recommended against a crash program to build the super bomb. Despite these grave moral concerns and this considerable internal opposition, Teller and the other Cold Warriors eventually won the political battle, and Truman decided to proceed with the development of the hydrogen bomb in January 1950. On November 1, 1952, the United States would carry out its first test of a thermonuclear device in the Pacific, and the Soviets would respond with their own H-bomb test in 1953.

The political pressure on President Truman to proceed with the super bomb and more aggressively fight the Cold War increased in the early 1950s with the discovery and public revelation of Soviet atomic spying,[111] the intensification of the anticommunist witch hunts and political paranoia of McCarthyism,[112] and the creation of "the seminal strategic doctrine of the Cold War—'United States Objectives and Programs of National Security' . . . National Security Council 68."[113] Early in his presidency, Truman tried to resist political demands to further militarize American foreign policy. According to Lepore, aides to the president said that in the late 1940s he "was unpersuaded by the growing fear of communism."[114] Truman was also initially hopeful that he could preside "over a vast demobilization of the military and the wartime industrial complex" and return the country "to the normalcy of a small standing army and hemispheric isolation."[115] He was also concerned about the cost of expanding the military and the atomic arsenal.[116] But given the rise of McCarthyism and the fact that "for months right-wing Republicans had accused the Truman administration of being soft on communism by letting China 'fall' and by not purging the 'Reds under the bed' at home,"[117] it would have been political suicide for the president not to have given the go-ahead on the H-bomb or serious consideration to National Security Council Resolution 68 (NSC-68). Then came an event that accelerated these trends and cemented in place a new national security state.

The Korean War, the National Security State, and an Arms Race

One of the most consequential results of World War II was the emergence of the phenomenon of the "warfare state" that has become entrenched in the American political structure. According to Boggs, the warfare state in the United States refers to "a broad ensemble of structures, policies, and ideologies: permanent war economy, national security state, global expansion of military bases, merger of state, corporate, and military power, an imperial presidency, the nuclear establishment, superpower ambitions."[118] While the legacies of World War II are of obvious importance to the creation of the global American empire and the intensification of the Cold War, many historians point to the Korean War as the decisive factor in the full emergence of the warfare/national security state. McMahon notes that "with uncommon unanimity, scholars have affirmed . . . the Korean War as a key turning point in the international history of the postwar era," making the United States "a world military–political power."[119]

American historian Bruce Cumings, for example, argues that the Korean conflict was the pivotal "occasion for transforming the United States into a very different country than it had ever been before . . . a country that the founding fathers would barely recognize."[120] Although President Truman had at first hoped to demobilize the military after World War II, some members of the U.S. foreign policy establishment, including the reelected president's new secretary of state, Dean Acheson, argued for a stronger national security stance: a move toward globalism, a standing army, greater military preparedness, foreign bases, and a willingness to not only "contain" Soviet communism but "roll it back" through military confrontations. This more aggressive Cold War strategy, which would require a dramatic increase in defense spending, was outlined early in 1950 in the alarmist NSC-68. As Boyer points out, this document "offered a wholly militarized vision of America's world mission earlier articulated by Woodrow Wilson and, long before that, by the New England Puritans."[121] But according to Cumings, advocates for the military escalation of the Cold War did not decisively win the political debate for this hardline policy within the Truman administration until the army of the Democratic People's Republic of Korea (DPRK) in the north crossed the thirty-eighth parallel and attacked the Republic of Korea (ROK) in the south on June 25, 1950. With the Soviet Union boycotting the Security Council, the United States and the

UN responded with a resolution in defense of the ROK, and the Korean "police action" was under way.

As Acheson later described, the Korean War was the crisis that "came along and saved us." What he meant by that, according to Cumings, was that the war "enabled the final approval of NSC-68 and the passage through Congress of a quadrupling of American defense spending."[122] Thus, it was the Korean conflict that bequeathed to the United States a large standing army, an empire of hundreds of foreign military bases, a permanent national security state at home, a gigantic Pentagon budget, and a willingness to become the policeman of the world and intervene militarily around the globe during the Cold War struggle. Cumings adds, "The indelible meaning of the Korean War for Americans was the new and unprecedented American military-industrial complex that arose in the 1950s."[123] The American imperial project and the quest for global military supremacy, already underway, now accelerated.

The full emergence of the American Empire with its "warfare" and "national security" state was a pivotal moment. This new historical social structure would lock in place the central position of nuclear weapons in U.S. foreign policy. The trajectory of wartime and early Cold War atomic tendencies would continue unopposed within the higher circles of government and the larger political culture. A strong bipartisan consensus solidified around the continued possession and use of nuclear weapons. The rise of a "nuclear-industrial complex"[124] and an ideology of "nuclearism"[125] provided a firm political and cultural foundation, an institutionalized, self-replicating social system that allowed the bomb to be used to advance the cause of "empire" from the early 1950s to the present.[126]

CONCLUSION

American state officials had used atomic bombs against Japan in 1945 and then averted international control of atomic energy in the immediate postwar period to maintain their nuclear superiority. They hoped their possession of the bomb would intimidate Stalin and make the Soviet Union "behave" during the early Cold War. In the coming years, nuclear weapons would be used to threaten "mass retaliation" against the Soviets if they planned to invade Western Europe or strike first with their bomb. And since the Truman Doctrine provided a "blank check for intervention,"[127] U.S. leaders came to rely on their stockpile of warheads to provide a "nuclear umbrella"[128] to cover postwar military interventions with conventional forces around the world to achieve imperial goals. American presidents would also begin to threaten to use nuclear weapons against opponents in specific conflict situations, "to terrorize them into negotiating on terms acceptable to the US."[129] These varied "uses" of nuclear weapons were made culturally acceptable and ideologically rationalized by the normalization of the use of the bomb during World War II and an appeal to the myths of American Exceptionalism and the reluctant superpower. In the Cold War context, they were also justified as necessary actions in the fight against global communism, thereby linking U.S. imperialism to the mythic ideal of liberation rather than one of geopolitical expansion.[130] Concerning this "interpretive denial," British historian Niall Ferguson observes that "for an empire in denial, there is really only one way to act imperially with a clear conscience, and that is to combat someone else's imperialism."[131]

Despite the protests of the atomic scientists and the disarmament movement, every president that followed Harry Truman would adhere to the basic imperial political script that had been written during World War II and in the early postwar era. Each would build on the foundation of the Cold War national security state that emerged during the Korean War. A fundamental precept of this postwar national security state was that the United States needed to rely on nuclear weapons and the willingness to threaten to use them to effect "deterrence." As Boggs points out, "The postwar evolution of atomic politics, above all for the U.S., allowed for certain normalization of nuclearism—an ideology that made its peace with the prospect of mass destruction, or total war."[132] While there are some important variations in emphasis concerning the role of nuclear weapons in American foreign policy, and differing circumstances in which, beyond deterrence, specific threats to use these weapons were made after Korea, the basic pattern was set by 1952. As Daniel Ellsberg documents, "Every president from Truman to Clinton has felt compelled at some point in his time in office—usually in great secrecy—to threaten and/or discuss with the Joint Chiefs of Staff plans and preparations for possible imminent U.S. initiation of tactical or strategic nuclear warfare, in the midst of an ongoing non-nuclear conflict or crisis."[133] The failure to establish international controls over nuclear arms in the early postwar period, which resulted in the continuing possession and buildup of these arsenals, left the door wide open for presidents to illegally "use" the weapons in this way to achieve imperial goals in conflict situations during the Cold War and beyond. This failure would take the world to the brink of nuclear Armageddon on several occasions. But it would also later foster efforts to limit or reduce nuclear arsenals through "arms control" international treaties.

CHAPTER 5

Nuclear Madness, Arms Control Treaties, and the End of the Cold War

Kennedy and Khrushchev are enemies—ideological and military adversaries—who have blundered into a confrontation that neither wanted or anticipated. Each is aware that an accident, or even a misinterpretation, can instantly ignite a nuclear exchange. Yet each feels obligated to continue to press his goals despite recognizing that nothing he can achieve is worth the consequences of a nuclear war.
—Martin J. Sherwin, *Gambling with Armageddon*

Deeply influenced by the antinuclear movement, Gorbachev waged an unremitting campaign against nuclear weapons and nuclear war that, eventually, convinced Reagan to join him in breaking with the Old Thinking and routing their conservative foes.
—Lawrence S. Wittner, *Confronting the Bomb*

I WAS BORN IN EARLY 1951, less than six years after the atomic bombs were dropped on Hiroshima and Nagasaki. I have lived my whole life under the shadow of nuclear weapons, but my perception of that danger has waxed and waned. In October 1962, during the Cuban Missile Crisis, I was acutely aware that something very important was unfolding on the global stage, but as an eleven-year-old I did not fully appreciate the fact that the world was on the brink of extermination. I recall getting out one of my favorite toys, an Erector metal construction set, and attempting to build what I imagined was a rocket launcher site like those being constructed in Cuba—blissfully unaware that in their political and military maneuvering about these real sites, world leaders were, as Martin Sherwin put it in the title of his book on the crisis, "Gambling with Armageddon."

An estimated one million protesters gathered at the United Nations and marched through the streets of Manhattan to Central Park on June 12, 1982, to call for an end to nuclear weapons. Courtesy Andy Levin / Science Source.

Flash forward almost twenty years to Saturday, June 12, 1982. On that day I laid down my one-year-old son Andrew right in the middle of Fifth Avenue, one of the most famous streets in New York City and one of its busiest—to change his diaper! Rest assured, I was not putting my young son in any danger—no angry drivers had to swerve to avoid us in the middle of the road. That's because there were no cars on New York City's main artery and most expensive shopping street that day. Fifth Avenue (along with other major streets) was closed to vehicular traffic on this Saturday to allow hundreds of thousands of people to march through Midtown Manhattan from Dag Hammarskjold Plaza near the United Nations up to the Great Lawn in Central Park to protest the nuclear arms policies of the hawkish Ronald Reagan administration and demand a "freeze" on nuclear weapons. My family had traveled to New York to join in the demonstration against the arms race and lend our support to the worldwide nuclear freeze movement. "Saving the World from Nuclear War" was the goal of the marchers that day![1]

Despite the serious nature of the threat that was being confronted, the June 12 march and rally had a festive feel. People were there to peacefully celebrate life by protesting and resisting the threat of nuclear apocalypse.

Those who were able to make it all the way to the Great Lawn in Central Park that day heard powerful speeches (from the architect of the freeze proposal, Randall Forsberg, and many others) and wonderful music provided by an all-star cast of performers. The Central Park rally in New York City and the broader nuclear freeze campaign demonstrated the power of mass protest and organized social movements. The revived global disarmament movement in the early 1980s (a form of societal reaction to state lawbreaking) not only influenced Mikhail Gorbachev and Ronald Reagan and forced the United States and the Soviet Union back to the arms control bargaining table but also played a significant role in ending the Cold War and reducing the nuclear danger at that time.[2]

This chapter advances the analysis of the commission of nuclear crimes (the breaking of laws related to nuclear weapons) and the societal reactions to these crimes from 1953 to the end of the Cold War in 1991. During the second half of the twentieth century, the United States and the Soviet Union would build vast arsenals of nuclear weapons that would combine to reach a total of sixty-five thousand warheads by 1986.[3] The ideology of "nuclearism" would continue to be normalized, and vast nuclear-industrial complexes would be built. American political leaders would make geopolitical calculations that "apocalyptic violence, when employed for noble ends (defeating Communism, fighting terror, spreading democracy) was to be valued."[4] Even though the United States and the Soviet Union came to the brink of nuclear annihilation on numerous occasions during the Cold War, and then attempted to stand back from the dark abyss by negotiating arms control agreements that limited or reduced the number of warheads and delivery vehicles each possessed, the risk of apocalyptic crimes remained.

President Eisenhower's Nuclear Buildup

Dwight Eisenhower came into office in 1953 intending to advance an even more "aggressive, coherent and anti-Communist program" than the one President Truman had pursued.[5] The Cold War fight against communism, in fact, was such a high priority for Eisenhower that he and the mainstream of the Republican Party "actually acquiesced to the core principles of the New Deal, thereby facilitating the New Deal's transition from political movement to political order."[6] But the fight against communism would not only have a huge impact on domestic social and economic policy at the time but also have a dramatic effect on the nuclear arms race. For while General Eisenhower had opposed the use of the atomic bomb against Japan in 1945 and outgoing President Eisenhower would warn about the undue influence

of the "military-industrial complex" in his farewell address in 1961, Ike's
Cold War anticommunism would still cause his administration to preside
over "the greatest buildup of military capacity in US history,"[7] resulting in
thousands of new nuclear warheads being added to the American arsenal
(more than twenty thousand by 1961). As Martin Sherwin observes, although
Eisenhower "recognized that nuclear war was irrational," he came to the
point where he accepted the idea that these deadly devices were "the most
cost-effective and efficient means of reinforcing American objectives" during the Cold War, and he eventually asserted that the atomic bomb should be
considered "as simply another weapon in our arsenal."[8] American historian
Daniel Sjursen also points out that to "lower defense expenditures and balance the budget," Eisenhower "decreased America's reliance on conventional
ground forces and expanded the nation's nuclear arsenal and capabilities."[9]
With his "New Look" initiative, which was designed to "massively retali-
ate" against any conventional Soviet aggression with a first use of nuclear
arms, Eisenhower "confirmed his determination to normalize nuclear weapons."[10] This was part of the madness of nuclearism.

The Eisenhower administration's more aggressive anticommunist foreign
policy, nuclear weapons buildup, and New Look initiative were spearheaded
by the powerful secretary of state John Foster Dulles and his brother, Allen,
who ran the Central Intelligence Agency from 1953 to 1961. The Dulles
brothers were "preeminent Cold Warriors" who took a "ruthlessly confrontational view of the world" and dismissed the possibility of "peaceful coexistence" or accommodation with the Soviet Union.[11] As a result of their
zealous anticommunism, their fervent support for U.S. corporate expansion
and free enterprise, their strong belief in American Exceptionalism, and
their missionary Christianity, they pursued "reckless adventures"[12] such as
covert CIA interventions to thwart Third World nationalism (Iran, 1953;
Guatemala, 1954) and a rapid buildup of nuclear weapons with a first-strike
capability. The Dulles brothers greatly augmented the Cold War paradigm
in the 1950s and promoted the fears it aroused (of Soviet expansionism,
internal communist subversion, and nuclear war). As American journalist
Stephen Kinzer concludes in his revealing book *The Brothers*, "They did as
much as anyone to shape America's confrontation with the Soviet Union.
Their actions helped set off some of the world's most profound long-term
crises."[13] The brothers accelerated the nuclear madness of the postwar period.

President Eisenhower was a full partner with the Dulles brothers in pros-
ecuting these more aggressive Cold War policies. Armed with the recently
developed super (hydrogen) bomb, the Eisenhower administration made a

"radical shift" by proclaiming in its New Look initiative that "nuclear weapons were America's first line of defense."[14] Rather than fighting expensive, hard-to-win land wars, the United States would now rely on the bomb for defense. This new policy mandated "a strong military posture, with emphasis on the capability of inflicting massive retaliatory damage by offensive [nuclear] striking power."[15] In support of this policy, Eisenhower would build up the Strategic Air Command (SAC) with its heavy bombers, now under the command of General Curtis LeMay, who had led the bombing campaign in the Pacific theater at the end of World War II; develop intercontinental ballistic missiles (ICBMs) and submarine-launched ballistic missiles (SLBMs); and deploy tactical and medium-range nuclear missiles to American bases in Europe and Asia.[16] Not even the death of Stalin in March 1953, and fresh opportunities to ease the tensions of the Cold War with the new "reformist Soviet leader Nikita Khrushchev,"[17] caused President Eisenhower and the Dulles brothers to reassess their hardline foreign policy and its reliance on nuclear weapons.

Not only did Eisenhower preside over a huge buildup of military capacity and initiate a radical shift in U.S. nuclear strategy, but he also threatened to use nuclear weapons in several specific conflict situations. Korea, where the war had bogged down into a quagmire, was one example. President Eisenhower, who had inherited the so-called police action from Truman, was determined to end the war as quickly as possible. Concerning "the mess in Korea," President Truman himself had once shocked the world by blurting out, "There has always been active consideration of [the use of the atomic bomb]."[18] According to his memoirs, as Eisenhower struggled to figure out a way to extract the United States from the Korean conflict, he too contemplated the use of nuclear weapons.[19] As criminologist David Kauzlarich and I have explained, "The availability of atomic weapons, the experience of their dramatic effect in ending World War II, and the rational instrumental logic characteristic of most organizational structures led the Eisenhower administration to consider the use of atomic bombs as the most effective and efficient means to end the war."[20] For various reasons that we explored (world public opinion foremost among them), President Eisenhower eventually decided not to use atomic weapons during the war but to "threaten" their use as a way to decisively influence peace negotiations and end the conflict.[21]

Korea was the first time the Eisenhower administration threatened to use nuclear weapons to address a specific political conflict, but it would not be the last. In 1954, when the French garrison at Dien Bien Phu in Vietnam was under siege by Ho Chi Minh's nationalist forces, Secretary of State

Dulles offered the foreign minister of France several tactical nuclear weapons to use.[22] In August 1958, a confrontation developed between Communist China and the United States in the Taiwan Strait when Mao began shelling the islands of Quemoy and Matsu, claimed by Chinese nationalist forces under General Chiang Kai-shek. Eisenhower responded by putting the U.S. military "on full alert," rushing a "formidable naval armada" to the strait, and authorizing "the dispatch of additional nuclear equipped forces to the region."[23] And as Daniel Ellsberg later revealed with the release of a still-classified document in 2021, the Eisenhower administration had also drawn up plans to carry out nuclear strikes on mainland China, exposing just how dangerous that crisis had been.[24] These nuclear threats set a pattern for future American presidents to follow. As Gerson and Ellsberg have documented,[25] threats to use nuclear weapons like those made by Eisenhower on Korea, Vietnam, and China have occurred on more than twenty-five occasions since World War II in an attempt to impose a global American imperial order and to provide a "nuclear shield" or "umbrella of U.S. power."[26] This nuclear shield covers the use of conventional forces and makes them, in the words of former Secretary of Defense Harold Brown, more "meaningful instruments of military and political power."[27] Nuclear weapons can be used without being exploded.

Like President Truman, Eisenhower was also confronted with worldwide pressure to head off the Cold War arms race with the Soviet Union and develop a plan for international control of nuclear weapons. Bertrand Russell, the famous British philosopher, had begun to speak out about the danger of nuclear war and issued a statement in 1955 (signed by Albert Einstein) that called for an international conference of scientists "to appraise the perils that have arisen as a result of the development of weapons of mass destruction."[28] The Russell-Einstein Manifesto, as it came to be called, would lead two years later to the founding of the Pugwash Conferences on Science and World Affairs (held in Pugwash, Nova Scotia) with the renowned Polish and British atomic scientist Joseph Rotblat as its president.[29] The original transnational antinuclear movement organization, Pugwash "brought together U.S. and Soviet scientists for direct private discussions" and sponsored "major conferences, special symposia, study groups, and other informal groupings."[30] Leo Szilard, still trying to save the world from the bomb he helped develop, was also working to "create new forums for arms control, such as the Pugwash Conferences."[31]

Despite the pressure from Pugwash and other transnational antinuclear movement organizations, President Eisenhower was resistant to any agreement to control nuclear weapons that might interfere with his planning for a major nuclear buildup.[32] In place of an arms control proposal he did not really want to make, Eisenhower instead created the Atoms for Peace program, which called for a new International Atomic Energy Agency to explore peaceful uses of atomic energy. The Atoms for Peace proposal appeared to offer a positive solution to the nuclear predicament, but as Schell noted, "building up nuclear power and cutting back on nuclear weapons were not the same."[33] At the time, however, in the midst of the Cold War, the good faith of the Atoms for Peace proposal was taken for granted and Eisenhower was lauded for seeking "peace."[34] The reality was far different, for under the more aggressive anticommunist foreign policy of Eisenhower and the Dulles brothers, the U.S. nuclear arsenal grew from about twelve hundred weapons in 1954 (when the New Look initiative was announced) to well over twenty thousand weapons by 1961—an "insane accumulation" according to American journalist James Carroll.[35] It was also during the Eisenhower administration, at the height of the McCarthyite communist witch hunt in 1954, that the most famous Manhattan Project scientist— J. Robert Oppenheimer—became the "most prominent victim" of the anticommunist hysteria when the Atomic Energy Commission revoked his security clearance and humiliated him, primarily due to his resistance to early work on the hydrogen bomb and his support for international control of nuclear weapons.[36] Oppenheimer's ordeal was vividly brought to the big screen in an award-winning movie (*Oppenheimer*) released in 2023 by British American filmmaker Christopher Nolan.

JFK and the Cuban Missile Crisis

Despite Eisenhower's massive nuclear buildup, during the 1960 presidential campaign John F. Kennedy (JFK) accused the Republican administration of allowing a dangerous "missile gap" to develop between the United States and the Soviet Union—a claim that was not true.[37] Norwegian historian Odd Arne Westad argues that Kennedy "used the fictitious 'gap' to illustrate his willingness to get one over on the Soviets in a competition for global power."[38] As president, JFK took a belligerent approach to the Soviet Union (particularly over the division of Berlin) and Fidel Castro's Cuba (the Bay of Pigs fiasco occurred on his watch). With his willingness to add more missiles and bombers to the nuclear arsenal (as demanded by the military) and his inability to rein in the "nuclear war planners" like the young Daniel Ellsberg—busy developing a Single Integrated Operational Plan (SIOP) for a first strike attack that could kill 275 to 325 million people—President Kennedy continued to fight the Cold War within the structures laid out by the National Security Strategy (NSS) that had emerged in the early 1950s.[39] Boggs asserts that "by the 1960s the NSS—and of course the warfare state itself—had become a self-replicating behemoth, an institutionalized fixture within American society."[40] Operating within this institutional and imperial framework, Kennedy found himself on the brink of a catastrophic nuclear war in October 1962 when the Soviet Union installed nuclear missiles in Cuba.

The Cuban Missile Crisis was the closest the world has ever come to what C. Wright Mills called "World War III."[41] In his definitive analysis of the crisis, Sherwin observes that a nuclear apocalypse was avoided only due to, in the words of former Secretary of State Dean Acheson, "plain dumb luck."[42] While much of Sherwin's analysis focuses on the thirteen days of the crisis, October 16 to 28, he argues that it is critical to "historicize" the event by placing it in its larger context—the seventeen years between August 1945 and October 1962.[43] Mills's bold assertion that "the immediate cause of World War III is the military preparation of it" is aptly demonstrated by these Cold War moves and countermoves of the late 1940s and 1950s, which led up to the near-miss of the Cuban Missile Crisis.[44]

President Kennedy, the Cold Warrior, was praised for his handling of the crisis: for resisting the advice of the military and some of his civilian advisors to bomb and invade Cuba, for instead implementing a naval blockade, and for eventually listening to the advice of his UN ambassador Adlai Stevenson (whom he greatly disliked) to follow a path of negotiations during the short time provided by the blockade. And at the end of the thirteenth day, the world got "lucky," and a last-minute deal avoided what would have been the greatest crime in human history—an all-out nuclear war.

While JFK was lionized for "forcing" the Soviets to "back down," avoiding Armageddon, Sherwin rightly points out that, despite finding a way out of the crisis, "the president chose to risk a war with the Soviet Union even though neither he nor his secretary of defense believed that Khrushchev's missiles altered the balance of nuclear power or seriously endangered the United States."[45] This is an illustration of what Mills called the "crackpot realism" of the "power elite" whose decisions were shaped by a bureaucratic state military apparatus and the enlargement and international centralization of power.[46] State officials like Kennedy and Khrushchev, operating in the historical context of the Cold War conflict between two superpowers, pursuing geopolitical goals within centralized internal power structures with new technological means (hydrogen bombs, ICBMs, tactical missiles, U2 surveillance aircraft), and unencumbered by restrains and controls within a weak international political community came close to annihilating the world. In the moment, each understood that they were on the brink of Armageddon, yet as Sherwin observes in the epigram to this chapter, "each [felt] obliged to continue to press his goals despite recognizing that nothing he [could] achieve [was] worth the consequences of a nuclear war."[47] As long as nations continue to possess these apocalyptic weapons, historical and structural forces will push their leaders to play nuclear roulette with the lives of millions. As Sherwin concludes, "The real lesson of the Cuban missile crisis—the lesson that is consistently resisted because it marginalizes the value of nuclear weapons—is that nuclear armaments create the perils they are deployed to prevent, but are of little use in resolving them."[48] Disarmament is the only way out of the nuclear dilemma—or else state officials, afflicted with "crackpot realism," will always be "Gambling with Armageddon."

Chastened by the Cuban nuclear crisis, President Kennedy then "sought a way out of the Cold War altogether—at least a way out of the aspect of the Cold War that threatened global annihilation."[49] On June 10, 1963, he gave a powerful speech at American University outlining a vision for world peace. International reaction to the speech was positive, and it "spurred Khrushchev to take up Kennedy's challenge" to reduce tensions, halt the arms race, and work toward a just and genuine peace.[50] On June 20, the United States and the Soviet Union agreed to set up a "hotline" between the offices of their two leaders, attempting to avoid the more cumbersome communication process that had hindered negotiations during the Cuban Missile Crisis. Later that year, after much back and forth for almost a decade following the Soviet Union's first proposal of a comprehensive nuclear test ban in 1955 and the initiation of a unilateral moratorium by the Soviets in 1958, the two countries signed the Partial Test Ban Treaty (PTBT), which outlawed tests of nuclear weapons in the atmosphere. This treaty, while not banning all tests, nevertheless was the "first significant agreement of the nuclear age."[51] These limited but positive moves were also influenced by a revitalized international disarmament movement, led by the transnational Pugwash Conferences, the British Campaign for Nuclear Disarmament, and the Committee for a Sane Nuclear Policy in the United States. According to Wittner, this global movement made a "dramatic advance" and reached "high tide" between 1958 and 1965, causing popular resistance to the bomb to grow "to unprecedented proportions" around the world.[52]

Given President Kennedy's moves in the aftermath of the Cuban Missile Crisis—his visionary peace speech at American University, his signing of the PTBT, his increasing recognition that the United States and the Soviets had reached an era of nuclear stalemate—coupled with the dramatic advance of the international disarmament movement, we are left to wonder what other initiatives he might have pursued had he lived to serve a second term. As noted in chapter 2, the events of 1963 had created enough political space for JFK to seriously consider the Irish proposal for a global treaty to stop the proliferation of nuclear weapons, and after Kennedy's assassination, President Lyndon B. Johnson (LBJ) continued to push for the adoption of this Non-Proliferation Treaty (NPT) at the UN. Confronted by the first Chinese nuclear test in 1964, Johnson had to choose between a strategy of "preventive war" to stop such proliferation or support its "functional equivalent," an international "nonproliferation agreement." LBJ decided "to oppose all proliferation, and to do so by negotiation."[53] Those negotiations eventually produced the NPT, "a Rosetta Stone of the second nuclear age, when the world transitioned from organized anarchy to provisional order."[54] The treaty, which was initially signed in 1968 and entered into force in 1970, is regarded as "the diplomatic crown jewel" of Lyndon Johnson's presidency.[55] At the signing ceremony, Johnson called the NPT "the most important international agreement since the beginning of the nuclear age."[56] And despite President Richard Nixon's anticommunism and Cold War reservations, he then signed the official treaty in March 1970 after Senate ratification. While Jonathan Hunt has criticized the nuclear club for setting up "a two-tier postcolonial hierarchy" through the NPT, a hierarchy that would allow the nuclear powers to later respond to "ambiguous nuclear threats" with military actions that "supersede the UN Charter's ban on wars of choice," the treaty's Article VI obligation for disarmament was a critical advance at the time and has been used ever since as a legal mechanism to press the nuclear club to discard their warheads.[57]

President Johnson's "Great Society" domestic agenda and the increasing resistance to his escalation of the Vietnam War dominated his time in the White House. And while his "terror bombing" campaign against North Vietnam (Operation Rolling Thunder) is considered a war crime,[58] and there was considerable discussion within the military and among his advisors about the possibility of using nuclear weapons in Vietnam, Johnson himself did not seriously contemplate nuclear attacks against the North Vietnamese.[59] Richard Nixon, on the other hand, would not only threaten to use the bomb in Vietnam but also paradoxically engage in détente with the Soviet Union and open the door to negotiations for important arms control agreements.

President Nixon, the "Madman" Threat, and Détente

From a criminological perspective, the most significant action President Nixon took was to engage in the geopolitical state crime of threatening to use nuclear weapons in Vietnam. Like Dwight Eisenhower, Nixon inherited an unpopular land war in Asia and sought to extricate the United States from that bloody conflict. During the presidential campaign of 1968 he outlined his infamous "madman theory" to his confidant and future chief of staff, H. R. Haldeman.[60] Nixon wanted his people to get word to the North Vietnamese that he was a communist-obsessed "madman" who could not be controlled when he was angry and would likely use nuclear weapons against them if they didn't come to terms to end the war. Nixon firmly believed that Eisenhower's nuclear threats against North Korea and China had "worked" and had resolved those conflicts in favor of the United States. Thus, in an attempt to force the North Vietnamese to end the war in 1969, he issued his "November Ultimatum," with the expectation that Ho Chi Minh would be in Paris within two days begging for peace.[61] That did not happen. President Nixon's threat to use nuclear weapons against North Vietnam failed, but that failure would not deter him or other presidents from using this kind of "nuclear diplomacy" again in the future in an attempt to achieve geopolitical and imperial goals.

While Nixon threatened to illegally use nuclear weapons to end the Vietnam War, the staunch anticommunist warrior would also surprisingly advance the cause of arms control through his policy of "détente"—the easing of hostile or strained relations. In his inaugural address in 1969, President Nixon proposed "a new era of negotiation" in which the United States and the Soviet Union would work together "to reduce the burden of arms" and build a "structure of peace."[62] McMahon argues that the concept of détente came to serve "as a convenient shorthand for the more stable and cooperative relationship" between the two superpowers that characterized the international politics of the late 1960s and most of the 1970s.[63] Détente did not end up creating that new structure of peace Nixon spoke of, but it did allow both sides to manage the Cold War in such a way as to reduce the risk of accidental nuclear war and limit the costly and destabilizing arms race. An "essential prerequisite" for this new "cooperative relationship," according to McMahon, was the fact that by the late 1960s the Soviet Union had achieved "relative parity with the United States in strategic nuclear weapons."[64] Official recognition of Soviet parity had occurred in September 1967 when then–Secretary of Defense Robert McNamara "formally replaced" the Eisenhower policy of massive retaliation, acknowledging the new situation of "assured destruction," which was later given the ironic acronym MAD when the word "mutually" was added to the concept.[65]

Recognizing the significance of nuclear parity and struggling with the economic challenge of funding both its Great Society programs and the costly war in Vietnam, the Johnson administration was open to the idea of arms control negotiations with the Soviets. In 1967, President Johnson indicated his intention to negotiate an arms control deal with the Soviet Union by meeting with Soviet premier Alexei Kosygin in Glassboro, New Jersey. The following year, Johnson signed the NPT and hoped to travel to the Soviet Union to "open the first serious negotiations between the two powers over nuclear arms and delivery systems."[66] But he eventually canceled the trip after the Soviet invasion of Czechoslovakia following the 1968 Prague Spring protests. Then, LBJ's shocking decision not to run again (forced in great part by mounting protests against the Vietnam War) and the narrow outcome of the 1968 election left the issue of nuclear arms control in the hands of that anticommunist "madman," Richard Nixon.

President Nixon's surprising embrace of the policy of détente would eventually bear fruit concerning arms control. Nixon and his national security advisor, Henry Kissinger, "worried that the United States had become dangerously overextended globally," stretching its resources too thin, and they were "determined to implement" a new "recalibrated Cold War strategy."[67] That strategy was détente, and in October 1969 the Nixon administration committed the United States to negotiations with the Soviet Union on the Strategic Arms Limitation Treaty (SALT). In May 1971, the two sides made significant progress on the treaty, and the following May, President Nixon traveled to Moscow to meet with Soviet premier Leonid Brezhnev. This momentous trip had been preceded by Nixon's even more dramatic and historic visit to China in February 1972. That pioneering trip to China may have helped "loosen the logjam" with Moscow, and in May of that year Nixon and Brezhnev signed "a series of agreements on economics, social cooperation, and above all, arms control."[68] One accord limited each side to the deployment of two missile defense systems (anti-ballistic missiles or ABMs), and in another interim agreement with a duration of five years, the existing numbers of ICBMs and SLBMs were frozen. However, the deal did not prohibit the multiple warheads carried on the recently developed multiple independently targetable reentry vehicles (MIRVs) or restrict long-range bombers. The result was a slight advantage for the Soviets in missiles, while the U.S. "maintained a marked superiority in total, deliverable nuclear warheads."[69] But as the Swedish disarmament minister Alva Myrdal pointed out, the SALT accord did not dismantle a single warhead, leading her to denounce "the game of disarmament" being played by the United States and the Soviet Union.[70]

Although it did not reduce the number of nuclear warheads, the SALT agreement (like the NPT before it) still had great symbolic and political significance, and it did ease some of the Cold War tensions between the two superpowers. But as McMahon notes, the accords did not "dispel all suspicions" or "prevent later massive strategic misunderstandings," and they "certainly did not halt the arms race."[71] Jonathan Schell argues that while the NPT and SALT "were manifestations of the same underlying turn toward treaties as the . . . means of reducing nuclear danger," during this time neither the United States nor the Soviet Union "expressed the slightest serious interest in actually fulfilling the terms of Article VI [of the NPT] by surrendering their own nuclear arms. On the contrary, they rejected abolition as utopian."[72] Both countries would continue to possess great quantities of nuclear weapons in violation of international law.

The SALT and ABM accords did help Nixon win reelection in 1972, but his administration was bogged down by efforts to finally end the Vietnam War and soon embroiled in the Watergate scandal that would eventually force the president to resign in disgrace in 1974. Although negotiations for a SALT II agreement were underway in late 1972, future progress on arms control would depend on Nixon's successors. President Gerald R. Ford met with Brezhnev at Vladivostok in November 1974, and the two leaders established principles relating to reductions in ICBMs, SLBMs, long-range bombers, and MIRVs. However, they could not finalize the pact, and the negotiations for a SALT II agreement fell to a new president, who was "a zealot about nuclear weapons."[73]

THE DILEMMAS OF PRESIDENT JIMMY CARTER

In the wake of the Watergate scandal and President Ford's pardon of Richard Nixon for any crimes committed during that sordid affair, Jimmy Carter came to the White House in 1977 as an outsider who promised to bring about major change. The former governor of Georgia was a devout Christian with a strong moral vision who saw himself as a peacemaker. More than any other president in the postwar era, Carter had an "instinctive revulsion toward nuclear weapons."[74] He pledged to realign American foreign policy with the country's professed values of freedom and human rights.

He believed that the United States needed to overcome its "inordinate" and "unreasoned" fear of communism, a fear that had distorted U.S. foreign policy throughout the Cold War era.[75] A former naval officer, President Carter was "determined to end the arms race with the Soviet Union," and having served as a protégé to Admiral Hyman Rickover (the architect of the nuclear submarine program), he "knew more about nuclear weapons than any of his predecessors."[76] During the campaign of 1976, candidate Carter pledged "to cut the defense budget and to wipe the moral blight of nuclear weapons from the face of the earth"[77]—goals he would not be able to achieve.

Despite his revulsion toward nuclear weapons and his determination to end the arms race, Carter was paradoxically transformed into a Cold Warrior during his presidency—approving the deployment of intermediate missiles to Europe, authorizing a new experimental ICBM system, and declaring a distinctive foreign policy doctrine that had the potential to lead to the use of military force (including nuclear weapons) over the issue of Middle Eastern oil. The tragedy of his time in office is that certain geopolitical events, forms of ideological resistance, and domestic power politics came together in a way that "pushed Carter to embrace a more hawkish Cold War approach and to move away from the values of human rights he championed early in his presidency."[78] President Carter's conversion, in a few short years, into a Cold Warrior who deployed and threatened to use nuclear weapons demonstrates how larger structural and cultural forces can shape the actions of people who occupy official positions within an organizational entity (such as the presidency) and overwhelm even the most committed individual moral vision.

What were some of the larger social forces that impacted Carter and his administration? First, senior military officers within the Pentagon viewed President Carter with suspicion. They were alarmed at his advocacy for "minimal deterrence" (the idea that the Soviets could be deterred with only one or two hundred missiles), his support for a ban on all nuclear testing, and his proposed cuts in military spending.[79] The Pentagon's powerful organizational resistance to Carter's goals represented a huge political obstacle. The new administration was also roiled with internal bureaucratic and ideological clashes over foreign policy among the hawkish national security advisor Zbigniew Brzezinski, the staid secretary of state Cyrus Vance, and the liberal U.S. ambassador to the United Nations Andrew Young. But the most significant factors that thwarted Carter's efforts to change American foreign policy and eliminate nuclear weapons were strong right-wing criticism and organized political resistance at home, and a series of challenging and disruptive geopolitical events abroad.

Even before Carter entered the White House, a group of conservative anticommunists, opposed to the arms control efforts of the Johnson, Nixon, and Ford administrations, began to attack the very concept of détente itself. These ideologues pushed hard for a "Second Cold War."[80] The Cold War, of course, had not disappeared from American life and political discourse despite the improved U.S.–Soviet relationship represented by Nixon's détente. The "painstakingly formulated" arms control agreements of the 1970s had not ended the conflict but did represent "attempts to manage tensions and move the superpowers away from the brink of nuclear war arrived at under Kennedy and Khrushchev in 1962."[81] For the "diehard" Cold Warriors, however, only strategic nuclear superiority was acceptable in the face-off with the Soviet Union.[82]

The right-wing hawks opposed to détente and arms control included several prominent atomic scientists, such as physicists Frederick Seitz, Edward Teller, and Robert Jastrow. These strident anticommunists regarded the idea of peaceful coexistence with the Soviet Union as "morally repugnant, believing that the Soviets would use disarmament to achieve military superiority and conquer the West."[83] During the 1970s, wealthy right-wing individuals created various "think tanks," such as the Heritage Foundation, the Hudson Institute, and the George C. Marshall Institute, to advance their conservative policy agenda. As American historians Naomi Oreskes and Erik Conway conclude, "These organizations and their allies in Congress fostered an assault on détente. By the end of the decade, they had destroyed the idea of peaceful coexistence, justifying a major new arms buildup during the Reagan years."[84] They were also successful in pushing Jimmy Carter to the right.

One strategy of the opponents of détente was to question the official assessments of the Central Intelligence Agency concerning the Soviet nuclear threat. The hawks claimed, with little evidence, "that the Soviet Union was seeking superiority over the United States and preparing to fight and win a nuclear war."[85] In 1976, during the last year of the Ford administration, these critics convinced George H. W. Bush, then director of the CIA, to undertake an "independent" analysis of Soviet capabilities and intentions. The idea of an independent assessment was promoted by the president's Foreign Intelligence Advisory Board, which included extreme hawks like Teller who wanted the CIA to issue "the most alarming statement possible" concerning the Soviet threat in order to undercut détente and arms control.[86] Bush appointed three review panels within the CIA to carry out an assessment of the Soviet Union's offensive and defensive nuclear capabilities as well as its strategic objectives. Dubbed "Team B," the panels consisted entirely of Cold War "hawks who already believed that the CIA was underplaying the Soviet threat."[87] Thus, it was no surprise that Team B came back with an alarming report that concluded the Soviets were using détente to advance their true goal of global hegemony. The report contained very little factual evidence yet still promoted the deployment of new nuclear weapons systems and greater anti-ballistic defense measures on the part of the United States.

The alarmist, fact-free Team B report was leaked during the presidential campaign in 1976, to little effect. But just days after Carter defeated Ford in the election, "a relic of the 1950s 'red scare' was resurrected" when the Committee on the Present Danger was formed, including four members from Team B.[88] One of the most prominent members of Team B involved in the creation of the anticommunist committee was Paul Nitz, the author of the seminal document NSC-68 and "one of the original architects of American Cold War foreign policy in the Truman administration."[89] The Committee on the Present Danger would spend the next four years criticizing Carter's proposals, organizing political opposition to his goals, and attempting to push U.S. foreign policy far to the right. During the campaign, Carter not only had supported ending the arms race but also had promised to "re-inject morals and a concern for human rights into America's tarnished, post-Vietnam foreign policy,"[90] a promise that enraged the Cold War hawks and engendered fierce resistance to every foreign policy initiative he pursued.

In addition to organized right-wing opposition from groups like the Committee on the Present Danger, the new president also encountered a series of events on the global stage that would work to undercut his efforts to eliminate nuclear weapons. The first geopolitical issue Carter encountered concerned medium-range nuclear missiles in Europe. In the mid-1970s, the Soviet Union had deployed the new SS-20 missile in Eastern Europe. The SS-20 was mobile, carried three MIRV warheads, and could strike targets in Western Europe. NATO had no intermediate missiles of its own that could respond to the alleged threat posed by the SS-20. In October 1977, West German chancellor Helmut Schmidt, who had serious concerns about Carter, "lit the fuse of a political bomb" by declaring that the "principle of parity" (equal levels of nuclear arms between East and West) must apply to all weapons, "not just those based in the United States and the Soviet Union."[91] NATO leaders demanded that the United States deploy to

Western Europe two new weapons under development as a counterweight to the SS-20: the ground-launched Cruise Missile and a new medium-range ballistic missile, the Pershing II.

Cold War hawks pressured Carter to deploy the new weapons, and within the administration "the technical and strategic debates went on for weeks . . . with little sign of resolution."[92] Then, political controversy over another new proposed weapon, the enhanced radiation warhead, would end the debates and lead to the deployment of the so-called Euromissiles. Dubbed the "neutron bomb," the enhanced radiation warhead was denounced by critics as "the ultimate capitalist weapon"—killing people while sparring property.[93] After much domestic debate and back-and-forth discussions with NATO, President Carter canceled the neutron bomb project (which he detested) in early April 1978. But in response to the resulting political furor, the administration approved a plan to build and deploy to Europe 464 ground-launched Cruise Missiles and 108 Pershing IIs. As Kaplan notes, "This wouldn't be the last time Carter was forced to approve nuclear weapons that he abhorred for the sake of politics he found distasteful."[94]

President Carter also stumbled early on in his dealings with the Soviet Union, "pursuing contradictory goals and sending the Soviets conflicting signals."[95] His attempt to seek more radical cuts in nuclear weapons arsenals delayed the signing of the formal SALT II treaty (aligning with the Vladivostok principles and limiting each superpower to 2,250 nuclear launchers) until June 1979, when he was in a much weaker political position with Congress.[96] By then the Soviet Union had also undercut Carter's domestic support with a series of provocative moves (such as placing the new intermediate-range missiles in Eastern Europe). The "alarmist" Committee on the Present Danger criticized Carter's "cult of appeasement" and "sought to increase bellicosity toward the Soviet Union," weakening support for SALT II in the Senate. [97] Furthermore, the Joint Chiefs of Staff refused to endorse the arms agreement (effectively killing it) unless President Carter agreed to fully fund a new ICBM called the MX (short for Missile Experimental). As Kaplan points out, "The explicit mission of the MX [was to maintain America's first strike capability in an era when the Soviets were building more ICBMs."[98] To try to save the treaty, Carter was forced to accept this trade-off. Paradoxically, like other presidents both before and after him, to advance arms control, he was compelled to accept a destabilizing weapon system he opposed.

Despite the contradictory political trade-off, the SALT II treaty would have likely been rejected anyway, but two other geopolitical shocks in late

1979 delivered the knockout punches. The Iranian hostage crisis of November (following the Islamic Revolution that overthrew the U.S.-installed government of Shah Mohammad Reza Pahlavi in January of that year) and the Soviet Union's invasion of Afghanistan in December alarmed Americans, imperiled the Carter presidency heading into an election year, and doomed SALT II. Only days after the Soviet invasion, President Carter withdrew the treaty and took several punitive measures toward Moscow. Détente was dead, and the "Cold War was back—with a vengeance."[99] Not only did these geopolitical events kill SALT II and reignite the Cold War, they hastened Carter's transformation into a Cold Warrior. As the Soviets advanced in Afghanistan and the humiliating Iran hostage crisis dragged on amid intense media coverage, the president tried to rebut the impression that he was weak, was ineffectual, and lacked a strong foreign policy.

On January 23, 1980, Carter seized the opportunity presented by the State of the Union Address to unveil a new forceful military policy that would eventually put the country on the path to direct military intervention in the Middle East. As Andrew Bacevich points out, Carter, "who just months before had earnestly sought to persuade Americans to shake their addiction to oil now decried . . . the possibility of outsiders preventing Americans from getting their daily fix."[100] In what came to be known as the "Carter Doctrine," the president proclaimed, "Let our position be absolutely clear. An attempt by any outside force to gain control of the Persian Gulf region will be regarded as an assault on the vital interests of the United States of America, and such an assault will be repelled by *any means necessary, including military force.*"[101] This was a major change in policy with enormous implications. From 1945 on, the United States had relied on other countries like Saudi Arabia, Iran under the shah, and its client state in Israel to provide the political stability (and military might) in the region that would guarantee its "vital interests" (the free flow of oil foremost among them). But now Carter declared that the United States would be taking on the military burden itself, at least as far as access to oil in the Middle East was concerned. As Bacevich notes, "Implementing the Carter Doctrine implied the conversion of the Persian Gulf into an informal American protectorate. Defending the region meant policing it."[102] And just like the defense of Western Europe, this policing would take place under the nuclear umbrella.

Carter then took a concrete step toward implementation of this policy by ordering the creation of the Rapid Deployment Joint Task Force (RDJTF), a military command center that was capable of quickly injecting

U.S. troops into the Greater Middle East during a crisis situation.[103] The stage was set for more direct military intervention in the Persian Gulf region to protect American access to and control of oil. Although Bacevich convincingly argues that the Carter Doctrine "initiated the War for the Greater Middle East by tying the American way of life to control of the Persian Gulf" and its oil, the declaration itself had little immediate impact.[104] Despite the stronger foreign policy stance and the creation of the RDJTF, Carter still lost the 1980 election to Ronald Reagan. And despite Reagan's more hawkish foreign policy, the full military implications of the Carter Doctrine for the Middle East would not be realized until the 1990s with the Persian Gulf Wars. But as he took office in 1981, the new president stood ready to vigorously prosecute a revived Cold War and pursue another buildup of nuclear weapons in defiance of international law and the legal obligation to disarm.

PRESIDENT REAGAN, THE ESCALATION OF THE COLD WAR, AND THE NUCLEAR FREEZE MOVEMENT

Ronald Reagan was a transformational president. One critical transformation concerned domestic economic and social policy as his administration helped lead the United States away from the state-centered "New Deal Order" created by Franklin Roosevelt and then cemented in the anti-government "Neoliberal Order" that prized free-market principles above all else.[105] Within a decade, this neoliberal ideology would also come to have a huge impact globally following the fall of communism, which "opened a large part of the world—the former Soviet Union and Eastern Europe in particular—to capitalist penetration."[106] The free-market shock therapy enshrined in the neoliberal order that rose to dominance during the Reagan era would be one factor that undermined the prospects for nuclear disarmament after the end of the Cold War.

With regard to U.S. foreign policy and nuclear weapons, there was also another "Reagan Revolution" that led to a new Cold War, a renewed arms race, and an increased threat of nuclear war.[107] During the 1980 election campaign, Reagan had "encouraged what looked like a reckless, nuclear brinksmanship with the Soviets."[108] As president, his "inflammatory rhetoric" and hawkish "peace through strength" approach to foreign affairs amplified tensions with the "evil empire" of the Soviet Union and expanded the nuclear arsenal.[109] This belligerent stance also generated a backlash, a massive revival of the worldwide antinuclear movement.[110] The Reagan administration would work hard to contain the impact of the resurrected peace and disarmament movement and the influential calls for a "freeze" on nuclear weapons, but the grassroots protests and efforts of antinuclear "cultural activists" would have a significant effect on the president, leading to yet another major transformation.[111] During his second term, President Reagan the hawk would, paradoxically, bring the country back to the arms control table and, in cooperation with a dynamic new Soviet leader, Mikhail Gorbachev, negotiate a treaty that would drastically reduce intermediate nuclear weapons.

Although President Carter had embraced the process of détente and sought to advance human rights and eliminate nuclear weapons, Reagan, on the other hand, had long opposed détente and came to office in 1981 determined to take an even "more adversarial stand against the Soviet Union" and pursue a "massive military buildup"—political actions that would heat up the Cold War to even more "dangerous levels."[112] Reagan had been a member of the anticommunist Committee on the Present Danger, and he placed thirty-two other members of that committee in important positions within his administration. As Kaplan notes, "Reagan entered the White House with an entourage bent not merely on deterring and containing the Soviet Union but on weakening and rolling back its empire."[113] In effect, Reagan's election transformed the 1976 Team B into the new Team A, a group of advisors whose "views became the basis for Reagan's confrontational foreign policy during his first term in office, and, most famously, his decision to pursue the Strategic Defense Initiative (SDI)— better known as Star Wars."[114] Tragically, Reagan's obsession with the SDI would later kill the best opportunity to completely eliminate nuclear weapons that the world has ever had.

The Reagan team came into office determined to reverse the reductions in military spending that were the result of détente and the ending of the Vietnam War. Their "mission" was to "rearm America," and to accomplish this goal they carried out "a vast expansion of the defense budget."[115] From 1981 to 1989, defense spending climbed from $157.5 billion to $303.6 billion a year—which, measured as a percentage of gross national product, represented a significant increase from 5.7 percent to 7.4 percent.[116] According to McMahon, "It was the largest peacetime arms build-up in US history," and it "represented a bid to re-establish US strategic superiority—a status that Reagan and many fellow conservatives had never been willing to surrender in the first place."[117] In addition to this "massive military buildup," the Reagan administration attempted to "fight Communism" with "an aggressive new policy of interventionism through proxy wars," particularly in Central America.[118]

In October 1981, President Reagan signed a new National Security Decision Directive (NSDD-13), which was to provide guidance for the use of nuclear weapons. As Kaplan notes, "NSDD-13 stated, up front, that, if deterrence failed and nuclear war erupted, 'the United States and its allies must prevail'—must win."[119] Reagan also authorized the deployment of the Pershing II and ground-launched Cruise Missiles to Western Europe, a move that was very "unpopular" on the continent.[120] With the Reagan administration's overheated anticommunist rhetoric and its provocative military policies, the Cold War conflict "seemed to take on a new and more dangerous dimension."[121] Fears of nuclear war and apocalyptic destruction resurfaced. The *Bulletin of the Atomic Scientists* moved the Doomsday Clock to four minutes to midnight in 1982.

These fears would revitalize the peace and disarmament movement that had first emerged in the early years of the Cold War. That movement, according to Boyer, had been in a "Big Sleep" from the period after the Cuban Missile Crisis through the era of détente in the 1970s.[122] But now, with a new Cold War heating up and glib talk of fighting and surviving a nuclear war coming from the Reagan administration, millions of people around the world again mobilized against nuclear weapons. As Wittner notes, during the 1980s, "peace and disarmament groups burgeoned into mass movements of unprecedented size and intensity."[123] One specific issue that animated this new surge of activism was the prospective deployment of those new intermediate-range missiles in Western Europe. Across the continent, millions of people joined mass protest rallies against the deployment of the Euromissiles in the fall of 1981. When President Reagan visited France and West Germany in June 1982, "he was greeted with more mass demonstrations."[124] Back home, Reagan faced an escalating "political problem" as well, "where growing public consciousness about the danger of nuclear war gave rise to the largest peace coalition since the Vietnam war."[125] This consciousness was being raised in part by what American historian William Knoblauch calls "fear books"—antinuclear nonfiction books that "rallied Americans to the disarmament cause and helped to galvanize huge protests."[126] Two of the most important of these books were *The Fate of the Earth* by Jonathan Schell and *Nuclear War: What's in It for You?* by the antinuclear group Ground Zero.[127]

The revival of the global nuclear disarmament movement was presaged in the late 1970s by organized resistance to nuclear power. As Wittner points

out, "Opposition to nuclear power plants spurred disarmament activism."[128]
The Soviet invasion of Afghanistan in 1979, the announcement of the Carter Doctrine—"threatening the use of nuclear arms if the Soviet Union
should attempt to move beyond Afghanistan to dominate the Persian Gulf
and its oil reserves"[129]—and then, most importantly, the Reagan administration's reignition of the Cold War all contributed to the resurgence of
public concern with the nuclear threat in the early 1980s. Reagan's "belli-
cose rhetoric rang like an alarm bell, setting off a vast antinuclear campaign" that reinvigorated existing peace and disarmament groups and
generated new organizations committed to the resistance of nuclear weapons.[130] The British Campaign for Nuclear Disarmament (CND), the National
Committee for a Sane Nuclear Policy (SANE), Mobilization for Survival,
Physicians for Social Responsibility (PSR), and the International Physicians
for the Prevention of Nuclear War (IPPNW) were just a few of the more
prominent groups involved in this transnational campaign.

One of the most influential responses to the escalation of nuclear danger in the late 1970s and early 1980s came from the Nuclear Weapons Freeze
Campaign. In the spring of 1980, Randall Forsberg, a defense and disarmament researcher, issued a "Call to Halt the Nuclear Arms Race."[131] Forsberg's "call" demanded an immediate bilateral Soviet–American "freeze on
testing, production, and further deployment of nuclear weapons." According to American historian Vincent J. Intondi, "The freeze campaign . . .
was breathtakingly simple and profoundly significant in its political implications."[132] And as Wittner points out, "Determined to halt the nuclear
arms race, most U.S. peace organizations united behind the idea of a Nuclear
Freeze."[133] The Nuclear Weapons Freeze Campaign generated enormous
popular support as well and soon came to threaten the Reagan administration's arms buildup. Freeze resolutions were introduced before a wide range
of church groups, professional associations, and civic organizations, including city councils and state legislatures.

The Central Park protest that my family and I attended on June 12,
1982, was largely inspired by Forsberg's call for a nuclear weapons freeze.
Organized to coincide with the UN Second Special Session on Disarmament, which had started earlier that week, the New York City march and
rally drew more than one million people. According to Schell, "It was not
only the largest antinuclear demonstration but the largest political demonstration of any description in American history."[134] The event was sponsored by a large coalition of peace and social justice organizations, and the
organizing group, the June 12th Rally Committee, selected the theme

"Freeze the Arms Race—Shift the Budget to Human Needs." Although numerous conflicts and divisions occurred during the planning process,[135] the march and rally ended up involving an intergenerational, interracial, gender-inclusive crowd with strong union participation. With its diversity, it looked like the famous "Rainbow Coalition" that American civil rights activist Reverend Jesse Jackson was organizing at that time.

The peaceful and joyous rally of June 12 and the Nuclear Weapons Freeze movement it boosted had a serious political impact in 1982 and beyond. That fall, freeze resolutions passed in eight out of nine states where they had been introduced and (in watered-down versions) in both the U.S. House and Senate. By November 1983, "the freeze had been endorsed by more than 370 city councils, 71 county councils, and by one or both houses of 23 state legislatures."[136] As Schell points out, "It is a matter of public record that the movement powerfully undercut support for Reagan's nuclear buildup."[137] The revived disarmament movement in general would later influence President Reagan to enter into nuclear arms negotiations with the Soviet Union. Wittner argues that "with protest against nuclear weapons sweeping around the world, the antinuclear campaign became the largest, most dynamic movement of modern times."[138] And some contend that the movement has borne fruit far into the future as well. Looking back more than thirty years later, Intondi observes, "Perhaps the true legacy of the June 12th rally [and the freeze campaign it supported] is the recent success of ICAN and the passage of the Nuclear Weapons Ban Treaty at the United Nations."[139]

The societal reaction to the perceived nuclear crimes of the Reagan administration also involved several other groups of "antinuclear cultural activists."[140] In addition to the authors of the antinuclear fear books, Knoblauch analyzes the impact of the scientists who warned about the danger of "nuclear winter" and the filmmakers who produced apocalyptic dramas like *The Day After.* Popular American scientist Carl Sagan, a professor of astronomy and space sciences at Cornell University and the cowriter and narrator of the award-winning PBS television series *Cosmos,* introduced the term *nuclear winter* to the public in October 1983. According to Sagan, even a small nuclear exchange would throw a huge cloud of dust up into the atmosphere, which would then block sunlight and plunge the earth into darkness and freezing temperatures. The climatic effects of a nuclear war, Sagan warned, would generate a global environmental disaster among many other severe forms of destruction. Knoblauch notes that the concept and theory of nuclear winter was "a product of an emerging global ecological consciousness," and it helped renew the kind of "Cold War scientific activism" that the early atomic scientists had engaged in.[141] Many historians have analyzed Sagan's public campaign to alert the world community to the threat of nuclear winter, the pushback and criticism he and the other activist scientists received from the Reagan administration and certain right-wing scientists and think tanks, and the public impact of the crusade.[142] And while the controversy would fade by the end of the decade, there is strong evidence that during the mid-1980s the scientific dispute over nuclear winter increased public consciousness about nuclear danger and put political pressure on the Reagan administration to reconsider its nuclear weapons policies. For Sagan, the political conclusions to be drawn from the science were clear: "The arms race was pointless, and the only logical way to proceed was with 'safe and verifiable reductions' . . . in global nuclear arms."[143] A conclusion that Ronald Reagan at first resisted.

Since the dawn of the nuclear era, films have also played a major role in the creation of an anti–Cold War culture.[144] Early on, important movies like *On the Beach* and *Dr. Strangelove* had significant social impact and helped generate antinuclear public attitudes. In the 1980s, filmmakers again had a huge effect as antinuclear cultural activists. Among numerous antinuclear films at the time, the movie with the greatest impact was ABC's *The Day After*, a made-for-television "apocalyptic drama" that aired on November 20, 1983, and became "a nation-wide media event."[145] The film aired at a time of heightened Cold War tensions that year following Reagan's announcement of the SDI in March, his speech labeling the Soviet Union an "evil empire" and the nuclear freeze "a dangerous fraud" that same month, and worldwide anger over the shooting down of a civilian Korean airliner (mistaken for a U.S. reconnaissance plane) by the Soviet Union after the plane crossed over into Soviet airspace in September.

The plot of *The Day After* focuses on the survivors of a nuclear exchange in Lawrence, Kansas, as they deal with the traumatic effects of the immediate attack, deadly radiation poisoning, and the chaos of societal collapse. The powerful film, with its realistic portrayal of the horrors of nuclear war, was viewed by more than one hundred million people, making it "one of the most-watched media events of the 1980s."[146] Canadian historian Andrew Hunt contends that *The Day After* had a "seismic, paradigm-shifting impact" and that "it is impossible to overstate, or exaggerate, the influence and significance of *The Day After*."[147] For not only did the film raise the consciousness of the American people about nuclear danger and further generate antinuclear attitudes around the globe, it also had a deep effect on

President Reagan and would later play an important role in motivating his efforts to negotiate arms control agreements in his second term.[148]

REAGAN, GORBACHEV, AND THE END OF THE COLD WAR

As the election year of 1984 dawned, the Reagan administration was still hard at work in its ongoing effort to contain what it considered the damaging political impacts of the nuclear freeze movement, the scientific warnings about nuclear winter, and antinuclear films like *The Day After.* The administration decided to soften its rhetoric and modify its hardline military stance. With an effective public relations campaign stressing that the president was not a warmonger but rather believed in "peace through strength" as a better means to avoid war, and with an emphasis on the "protective shield" that would be provided by the SDI and make Americans safe, the Reagan administration was able to successfully blunt the political impact of the peace and disarmament movement. With the nuclear weapons issue contained, and running a campaign "that stressed an optimistic, patriotic theme of *Morning in America*,"[149] Reagan was able to easily win reelection over the Democratic candidate Walter Mondale. The peace movement was dismayed. Yet during his second term, President Reagan, the anticommunist hawk, would engage in "a surprising reversal of course. Abandoning his early stance of confrontation, Reagan suddenly turned in earnest to negotiation."[150] What accounts for this major change?

Several historians argue that despite his public image of being a Cold War hawk or even a warmonger, deep down Reagan "was also a fervent opponent of nuclear weapons" and believed that the policy of deterrence based on MAD (mutually assured destruction) was indeed a form of "madness."[151] Kaplan asserts that Reagan "detested nuclear weapons and, as passionately as Jimmy Carter, wanted to see them abolished"—a fact his aides sought to keep hidden.[152] In a 1982 interview, President Reagan had even alluded to reducing, "if not totally eliminating the nuclear weapons, the threat to the world."[153] These beliefs appear to have been reinforced by two dramatic events in November 1983. The broadcast of the movie *The Day After* had a major impact on the president. Knoblauch reports that, according to Reagan's diary, the film "drove home the horrors of nuclear war to the president in ways that grassroots demonstrations could not."[154] That same month, Reagan was also shaken to discover that a Soviet misinterpretation of a NATO military exercise called Able Archer as an actual attack almost led to an accidental nuclear war. This near disaster gave the president a greater appreciation of "the security dilemma that faced the Soviet Union" and "made him more receptive to the initiatives" that would be introduced later by a new Soviet leader.[155] But one of the most important factors in Reagan's surprising change of course was the overall influence of the world disarmament movement. As Andrew Hunt argues, the important role of the antinuclear movement in bringing about this "great reversal" in Reagan should not be overlooked: "Years of hard work and obstacles lay ahead, but a great reversal was under way, and the antinuclear movement—in all of its grassroots and cultural manifestations—helped pave the way for that shift."[156] A dramatic change in leadership within the Soviet Union in 1985 then produced a willing partner for advancing this shift and producing significant results.

The turnaround in Reagan's policies on arms control in his second term started slowly. Even though the Soviets had accepted a U.S. proposal for a new negotiating framework at the UN in late 1984, instability within the Kremlin prevented any progress in the negotiations. Leonid Brezhnev had died in November 1982, and his successor, Yuri Andropov, passed away in February 1984. His replacement, Konstantin Chernenko, died in March 1985. Then in a surprising move, a much younger, more reform-oriented politician emerged as the new Soviet leader (general secretary of the Communist Party). "More cosmopolitan than his predecessors," fifty-four-year-old Mikhail Gorbachev "represented a new generation of Soviet leadership" and pushed for "transformative new policies."[157] Recognizing the deep economic problems of the Soviet Union and how the crushing burden of military spending limited efforts at reform, Gorbachev pursued policies of *perestroika* (economic and social restructuring) and *glasnost* (political openness). Most importantly, the new Soviet leader was determined to end the nuclear arms race. As American historian Matthew Evangelista points out, the "strong normative commitments" of Gorbachev and his foreign minister, Eduard Shevardnadze, to arms control were "shaped in part by their interaction with the transnational disarmament movement, particularly its representatives among Soviet and Western scientists and physicians."[158] Gorbachev's rise to power, and his principled opposition to nuclear weapons, opened the door for the resumption of serious arms control negotiations between the United States and the Soviet Union and was a crucial turning point on the road that led to a major arms control agreement and eventually to the end of the Cold War itself.

Reagan and Gorbachev met five times during Reagan's final term in office, developed a close personal relationship, and came very near to completely abolishing nuclear weapons at one meeting. And while that radical goal was not realized, the two leaders still ended up signing a significant arms control treaty. As a result of their meetings, Soviet–American relations were transformed and Cold War tensions were relaxed. Reagan and Gorbachev first met at Geneva in November 1985, a "get acquainted summit" that "produced little of substance."[159] But the two leaders developed a good rapport and Gorbachev was able to persuade Reagan to agree to the inclusion of the statement, "A nuclear war cannot be won and must never be fought," in the summit's final report—"a rebuke of Reagan's national security directive, NSDD-13."[160] Importantly, the statement also gave official recognition to "the uselessness of the bomb for war."[161] Geneva set the stage for what was to come, an ongoing process of dialogue and negotiation that would eventually lead to concrete results.

As Gorbachev attempted to implement his new policies of perestroika and glasnost in 1986, he realized that he sorely needed an arms control treaty to ease international tensions and overcome domestic political opposition to his radical measures.[162] In January, he had issued a call for a nuclear-free world (which horrified some anticommunist U.S. officials), and in September he requested a quick meeting with President Reagan to advance the stalled negotiations.[163] Reagan agreed to another summit, and the two men met in Reykjavik, Iceland, over the weekend of October 11–12. Intense negotiations concerning several dramatic proposals ensued, with Gorbachev suggesting at one point that they eliminate all strategic offensive weapons. In an amazing development, the two leaders appeared to be on the verge of actually eliminating all nuclear weapons over ten years. Complete abolition was on the table, and both men were serious. As Wolverton points out, "Reagan and Gorbachev almost agreed on something that for forty years previously had been unthinkable: complete and mutual nuclear disarmament."[164] But Gorbachev's opposition to the SDI, and Reagan's insistence on continuing research on the initiative (now a pet project of the military-industrial complex in the United States), "led the Soviet leader to withdraw the breathtaking proposals he had placed on the table."[165] The summit came to a "tragic close" without an agreement.[166] In a lament over the lost opportunity for abolition, Kaplan notes, "It was a tragicomic denouement to ten hours of substantive conversation, in which the leaders of the two superpowers came so close to ending the nuclear arms race, obstructed only by their fantasies and fears—Reagan's fantasies, Gorbachev's fears—about a high-tech super-dome that hadn't yet been conceived, much less developed, tested, built, or deployed."[167] The unnecessary impasse over the "Star Wars" fantasy derailed one of world's best chances to be rid of the nuclear threat.

But all was not lost. The rapport and goodwill that had been built up between the two leaders remained. Gorbachev also came away from Reykjavik convinced that the United States "had no intention of launching a first strike against the Soviet Union."[168] His scientific and political advisors finally convinced him that SDI was an unworkable fantasy that would never be deployed. Additionally, in November 1986, the Republicans lost control of the U.S. Senate, further weakening political support and funding for the initiative. Thus, with the advice and encouragement of various trusted "transnational actors," Gorbachev decided to "unlink" the SDI from the negotiations over intermediate-range missiles.[169] With the unlinking of Star Wars from the negotiation process, rapid progress was made on an Intermediate Nuclear Forces (INF) Treaty. In December 1987, Gorbachev traveled to Washington, where he and President Reagan signed the accord. The INF Treaty called for the elimination of all ground-launched nuclear missiles (1,846 Soviet and 846 U.S. weapons) within three years.[170] As Wolverton points out, "For the first time an entire category of nuclear weapons had been abolished. It may not have been total disarmament, but it was an encouraging step in that direction."[171] To the surprise of many, Reagan and Gorbachev had achieved a major arms control agreement. Even more dramatic events would soon follow.

In the spring of 1988, Reagan, the former Cold War hawk, made a trip to Moscow. It was a testament not only to the transformation of the man but to "the ongoing transformation of Soviet-American relations—and the Cold War."[172] Gorbachev made another visit to the United States in December of that year, meeting one last time with Reagan, holding discussions with president-elect George H. W. Bush, and delivering a major speech at the UN, where he announced "that the Soviet Union would no longer follow the Brezhnev Doctrine of intervention in the Communist bloc and would allow each satellite state to determine its own path."[173] Gorbachev then withdrew 50,000 troops from Eastern Europe (part of an overall 500,000 reduction of Soviet military forces). Following this dramatic move, popular democratic revolutions already underway in Eastern Europe intensified and began to sweep communist regimes out of power across the region in 1989. The Berlin Wall, that powerful symbol of the Cold War, came down in November. As McMahon observes, "The demolition of the Berlin Wall and the concomitant implosion not just of Eastern Europe's communist governments but of the entire Warsaw Pact alliance system meant the end of the Cold War."[174] Germany was reunited the following year and accepted into NATO. With this epochal event, the Cold War was rapidly moving toward a dramatic conclusion.

With major changes taking place internally in the Soviet Union and sweeping across Eastern Europe, Gorbachev found himself even more embattled at home. When his advocacy for the policies of glasnost and perestroika "triggered unexpected consequences" such as "the eruption of secessionist nationalisms and popular democracy in both the Soviet republics and Soviet satellite colonies in Eastern Europe—Gorbachev repeatedly declined to curb reform or to unleash repression."[175] This was a significant departure from his predecessors. And on top of dealing with domestic political opposition that came at him from all sides, he also had to develop a relationship with a new American president.

G. H. W. Bush had been Reagan's vice president for eight years. He was a more cautious politician and early on showed "a seeming reluctance to pick up quickly where the Reagan administration had left off."[176] Early in 1989, President Bush called for a "policy review" of U.S.–Soviet relations, which Gorbachev privately referred to as "the pause."[177] But despite the slow start, the two leaders eventually developed a rapport and became good friends. Meeting in Malta in December 1989, Bush and Gorbachev resumed the stalled negotiations on the Strategic Arms Reduction Treaty (START I) that had begun during Reagan's second term. The logjam over the treaty was finally broken when Gorbachev, despite the opposition of hardliners at home, agreed to "unlink" START from the SDI, just as he had done with the INF Treaty earlier.[178] President Bush, despite his lingering Cold War "qualms" about the agreement, traveled to Moscow in July 1991 for the signing of START I.[179] Unlike previous arms control measures, which had only limited the growth of weapons, "START required both the United States and the USSR to actually reduce their arsenals to approximately six thousand nuclear warheads and sixteen hundred delivery vehicles (missiles and aircraft) each."[180] Peace activists hoped this was a major step toward eventual complete disarmament.

Then, to the surprise of many, the Soviet Union disintegrated. Gorbachev's attempt at restructuring the system, Boris Yeltsin's political challenge to his rule, the impact of the popular democratic revolutions that swept across Eastern Europe, the fall of the Berlin Wall, the reunification of Germany, and the dissolution of the Warsaw Pact had roiled politics in the Soviet Union during the previous two years. One month after the signing of START I, hardliners launched a coup against Gorbachev. While neither

Yeltsin nor the Soviet military supported the coup and Gorbachev was soon returned to power, the Communist Party, "to which he still pledged fealty, was kaput."[181] Gorbachev resigned in December 1991, and the Soviet Union ceased to exist. A commonwealth of independent states replaced it, with Yeltsin, the president of the democratic Russian Republic, taking Gorbachev's place in the Kremlin. The collapse of the Soviet Union brought the Cold War to a definite conclusion. As Westad pointed out, "There was no country left to challenge the United States globally in the name of a radically different ideology."[182] But he goes on to note that "conflicts and tensions that had grown from the Cold War would remain, as would its nightmarish weapons and curbed strategies."[183] The Cold War had ended, but what about the nuclear danger?

CONCLUDING QUESTIONS

With the Cold War over, what would now happen to those "nightmarish weapons"? In a post–Cold War world, would the United States need to continue to possess nuclear devices? Who would they be targeted at? And why? An opportunity for complete disarmament seemed to have arrived. Would it be seized or squandered? If nuclear weapons were abolished, how would the international community resolve conflicts and tensions in a future world without them? The end of the Cold War raised these and many other questions. They were not easy to answer.

CHAPTER 6

After the Cold War

LOST OPPORTUNITIES FOR DISARMAMENT, NUCLEAR NONPROLIFERATION BY FORCE, AND THE PRAGUE PROMISE

From 1990 on, the general model of a "rogue state" ruled by an "outlaw regime" armed with chemical and nuclear weapons became the standard currency of national security discourse.

—Michael Klare, *Rogue States and Nuclear Outlaws*

Policymakers should heed the lessons of transnational relations during the Cold War and not squander the opportunity to cultivate a peaceful and democratic Russia as a full member of the international community.

—Matthew Evangelista, *Unarmed Forces*

And so the nuclear arsenals of the Cold War, instead of withering away with the disappearance of that conflict, were delivered intact, like a package from a deceased sender, into the new age, though now lacking the benefit of new justifications—or, for that matter, of new opposition.

—Jonathan Schell, *The Unfinished Twentieth Century*

JUST TEN WEEKS after taking office in 2009, President Barack Obama traveled to the Czech Republic, where he delivered a major speech on April 5 in Hradcany Square near the Prague Castle. At an open-air rally on a beautiful spring day, the new American president made a dramatic announcement: "As the only nuclear power to have used a nuclear weapon, the United States has a moral responsibility to act. We cannot succeed in this endeavor alone, but we can lead it, we can start it. So today, I state clearly and with conviction America's commitment to seek the peace and security of a world without nuclear weapons."[1] It was a stunning statement. While the world disarmament movement had long advocated for the

President Barack Obama delivers his first major speech, stating a commitment to seek the peace and security of a world without nuclear weapons in front of thousands in Prague, Czech Republic, April 5, 2009. Courtesy Barack Obama Presidential Library.

abolition of nuclear weapons, no American president had ever committed the United States to seek a world without these deadly weapons in such a forthright way. Joseph Siracusa points out, "As president of the remaining superpower [Obama] bestowed upon the notion of eliminating nuclear weaponry a particularly significant blessing that drew worldwide attention and approval."[2] This vision of a world with zero nuclear weapons generated great "hope" for "change" (two of candidate Obama's campaign themes) concerning the global threat posed by the nuclear danger.

According to Fred Kaplan, President Obama's grand "Prague Promise" was influenced by several significant factors.[3] First, Obama had written a thesis on nuclear disarmament as an undergraduate student at Columbia University. Second, after being elected to the U.S. Senate in 2004, Obama was appointed to the Foreign Affairs Committee, where he developed a close relationship with the chair of the committee, moderate Republican Richard Lugar. According to Kaplan, "Lugar had developed a passion for keeping loose nukes locked up," and in 1992 he was a cosponsor (with Sam Nunn) of legislation that provided financial assistance to Russia and other former Soviet republics to safely store or destroy nuclear weapons.[4] Lugar served as a mentor to the young senator from Illinois, and in August 2005 he and Obama went on a weeklong tour of nuclear, chemical, and biological weapons sites in the former Soviet republics. Third, shortly before Obama announced his candidacy for president, an op-ed appeared in the *Wall Street Journal* calling for "A World Free of Nuclear Weapons."[5] Written by four former U.S. government officials (dubbed the "Four Horsemen"), who were highly respected within the national security establishment, the intent of the article "was to lend theatrical urgency to a series of risk-reducing steps that they viewed as practical for the short term."[6] Candidate Obama viewed the op-ed, which garnered a lot of attention within the national security world, "as legitimizing his own ideas, which might have been dismissed as starry-eyed if he'd expressed them prior to its publication."[7] Obama later incorporated a commitment to starting down the long road toward eliminating nuclear weapons into an important campaign speech, and after he was elected, he decided to make that critical issue the focus of his speech in Prague.

President Obama also asserted at Prague that in the short term the United States would work collaboratively with other nations to contain the spread of nuclear weapons, reduce the number of preexisting warheads, secure nuclear materials, and encourage other nations to do the same.[8] Then, by articulating concrete steps by which to achieve these policy goals, Obama outlined in the speech a hopeful agenda for reducing the role of nuclear weapons internationally in the near term. First, the president asserted, to reduce the number of warheads in the stockpiles of both the United States and Russia, he intended to negotiate a legally binding new Strategic Arms Reduction Treaty (New START) with Russia. Second, Obama pledged to "strengthen the nuclear Non-Proliferation Treaty (NPT) as a basis for cooperation."[9] He also advocated for the ratification of the Comprehensive Test Ban Treaty (CTBT) and the creation of a new treaty to prohibit the production of fissile materials. Fourth, to ensure compliance with international treaties, the president also stressed the necessity of strong sanctions for nations that refused to cooperate: "Rules must be binding. Violations must be punished. Words must mean something."[10] Finally, President Obama declared that in the post–Cold War era, the most "immediate and extreme threat to global security" is the possibility of terrorist groups acquiring nuclear weapons.[11] In light of the new threat posed by nonstate actors seeking to obtain such weapons, securing nuclear materials was also a high priority. To address this threat, Obama announced that the United States would hold a Global Summit on Nuclear Security within the year.

Despite his commitment to reducing the U.S. reliance on nuclear weapons for national security and setting out this hopeful agenda for the short term, President Obama nevertheless quickly conceded in his speech that the grand goal of nuclear disarmament was a long-term objective and would not likely be reached within his lifetime. Dedicated abolitionists would quickly point out that this concession "fails utterly to appreciate the magnitude and immediacy of the nuclear peril."[12] Then, casting even further doubt onto the possibility of complete nuclear abolition, Obama made it clear that "as long as these weapons exist, the United States will maintain a safe, secure and effective arsenal to deter any adversary, and guarantee that defense to our allies."[13] Leaving aside these critical caveats, which were extremely disappointing to nuclear abolitionists, the president's Prague speech still seemed to clearly indicate a marked departure from the reckless nuclear policies of the previous administration. Critics within the disarmament movement, however, were quick to demand that Obama's promising rhetoric now be matched by decisive actions toward nuclear abolition.[14]

But those decisive actions did not follow, for political and economic reasons I analyze below. Most importantly, Obama would eventually give in to what American researcher and author Christian Sorensen calls "the modernization scam,"[15] part of a paradox that would expand and enhance the nuclear arsenal, not eliminate it. But the larger question here is, twenty years after the Cold War had ended, why did an American president still have to even promise to "seek" a world without nuclear weapons? Why hadn't the United States sought nuclear abolition after the Berlin Wall came down and then the Soviet threat ceased to exist? After the Soviet Union collapsed in late 1991, replaced by a friendly Russian Federation, why was nuclear deterrence still needed? Why did state crimes of political omission concerning the possession and threat to use nuclear weapons continue after the Cold War was over? Why hadn't American leaders taken advantage of what Jonathan Schell called the "Gift of Time" and used that gift to "rid the species for good of nuclear danger"?[16]

THE GIFT OF TIME: THE OPPORTUNITY FOR DISARMAMENT

Considering a renewed Cold War in the twenty-first century more generally, and the 2022 Russian invasion of Ukraine specifically, it is disheartening to go back and read Schell's prophetic words from the late twentieth century in *The Gift of Time: The Case for Abolishing Nuclear Weapons Now*: "History has handed us a political windfall. Why do we refuse to spend it? Political assets, unlike financial ones, are not apt to increase over time. If not made use of, they can, in an instant of crisis or war, evaporate."[17] And evaporate they have! After the Russian invasion of Ukraine in particular, a new nuclear danger is now upon us, one danger among many that might have been averted had we seized the gift of time at the end of the Cold War and taken advantage of the opportunities it presented to abolish nuclear weapons and realize what was called the "peace dividend"—a substantial "reduction in military spending and the possible redistribution of federal funds to other national priorities."[18] A great crime of political omission occurred in the first two decades after the Cold War, and the enormity of that state crime cannot be overstated.

In the twenty years prior to President Obama's Prague Promise, the United States failed to take advantage of the opportunities to end the nuclear menace provided by the end of Cold War hostilities. And now, more than fifteen years after Obama pledged to seek a world free of nuclear weapons, why have we still not made any progress toward that critical goal? Why does the United States (and eight other countries currently) continue to possess, modernize, expand, and threaten to use these apocalyptic weapons? How and why was the gift of time squandered?

At the time, the demise of the Cold War appeared to provide an unprecedented opportunity to abolish nuclear weapons and stop nuclear state crimes. The ending of the dangerous ideological and political struggle that had gone on for more than forty years between the "Free World" and Soviet communism, and the emerging friendship between the United States and the new Russian Federation, should have made it possible to finally accomplish the peace movement's long sought-after goal of nuclear disarmament. "Abolition is the great threshold," wrote Schell. "It is the logical and necessary destination because only abolition gets us out of the zone of mass slaughter, both as perpetrators and victims."[19] Can we, he wondered, take advantage of this gift of time provided by the end of the Cold War to cross this threshold. Or, Schell ominously asked, has a "deep moral revolution" occurred that leads us to regard "threats of mass destruction as normal"? He added, "Can we still remember that to destroy hundreds of millions of human beings is an atrocity beyond all history?"[20] The task, of course, as Schell well recognized, was immense. But still, history had provided the world with a great gift, and he declared, "If we use the gift properly and rid the species for good of the nuclear danger, we will secure the greatest of time's gifts, assurance of a human future."[21]

But the gift was squandered; the opportunity was lost! Nuclear disarmament did not occur, and the peace dividend of reduced military spending did not materialize. Corporate and political elites in the United States linked to the military-industrial-petroleum complex did not acquiesce to the reduction of their profits and power that would have resulted from such a radical realignment of American imperial policy. In what Schell later characterized as "a top-level abdication," the first three U.S. presidential administrations of the post–Cold War era—Bush I, Clinton, Bush II—all failed to take advantage of the gift of time.[22] Instead, supported by the war industry and the Pentagon, all three took steps to ensure that nuclear weapons (illegal to possess or use under international law) would remain a central component of American defense strategy—"a normal instrument of national policy."[23] These omissions and decisions were apocalyptic state crimes.

To be fair, all three of these presidents did engage in arms control negotiations, entered into agreements (not all of which took effect), or issued nuclear directives that did reduce the overall stockpile of nuclear weapons. As Cirincione points out, "By 2006, the U.S. arsenal had been cut to approximately 9,900 warheads; the Russians to about 16,000."[24] At that time, the global nuclear stockpile was the lowest it had been since 1962, and it was expected to continue to shrink (as it has to the current level of roughly 12,500 warheads).[25] Without a doubt, these reductions were important. But there was never any serious consideration given to approaching or crossing the critical threshold of abolition, and thousands of destructive nuclear weapons remained at the ready. Despite ongoing arms control negotiations with their new Russian friends, American officials in this critical era not only continued to aim their weapons at targets within Russia but also promoted economic (neoliberal shock therapy) and geopolitical (NATO expansion) policies that would eventually lead to a renewed Cold War in the twenty-first century. These presidential administrations also worked hard in the early post–Cold War years to fill in what Senator Sam Nunn had called the "threat blank" caused by the demise of the Soviet Union.[26] They created a new imperial policy that maintained U.S. military dominance, retained a major role for nuclear weapons (and the enormous profits they generated for the war industry), and attempted to achieve nonproliferation by military force.

President George H. W. Bush, the Rogue Doctrine, and Desert Storm

The Cold War ended during the administration of President George H. W. Bush. While Bush claimed undue credit for bringing the long conflict to a conclusion, in the view of some historians he did make "an indispensable contribution" to ending that long geopolitical struggle "by exercising restraint and refraining from pushing the Soviet government too hard, thus never giving Moscow a pretext to reverse course."[27] Despite a slow start, Bush developed a good relationship with Mikhail Gorbachev, conducted a successful summit with him at Malta in 1989, and traveled to Moscow in July 1991 to sign the first Strategic Arms Reduction Treaty (START) that had been initiated under President Reagan. In September of that year, President Bush also announced that the United States was taking a series of unilateral steps that he said would "make the world a less dangerous place than ever before in the nuclear age."[28] Strategic Air Command (SAC) bombers were ordered to stand down from their twenty-four-hour alert status, and tactical nuclear weapons were removed from numerous naval vessels and aircraft. On October 5, Gorbachev reciprocated with similar tactical weapons withdrawals and dealerting directives. In his 1992 State of the Union Address, Bush went further and "announced the withdrawal of all short-range nuclear weapons from Europe and South Korea."[29] Following the collapse of the Soviet Union in late 1991, the new Russian government reaffirmed its commitment to arms reduction when president Boris Yeltsin "expanded on former Soviet president Gorbachev's reduction in tactical nuclear weapons."[30] The post–Cold War era appeared to be off to a good start.

These welcome moves reduced the deployed nonstrategic stockpiles on both sides by thousands of warheads. Strategic arsenals were also reduced. The 1992 Cooperative Threat Reduction (CTR) program, sponsored by U.S. senators Nunn and Lugar, provided $400 million to Russia for weapons destruction and security in the former Soviet Union and its republics, and was credited with eventually deactivating or destroying thousands of warheads and launchers and establishing verifiable safeguards against the proliferation of nuclear weapons.[31] And before leaving office, President Bush also entered into negotiations with President Yeltsin on the START II treaty (signed in January 1993)—an agreement that Cirincione called "the most sweeping arms reductions pact in history."[32] This accord would have limited the deployed nuclear forces of both sides to be no higher that 3,500 warheads and prohibited land-based ICBMS from carrying more than one warhead.

While both countries eventually ratified the START II treaty, it never took effect due to Russian demands that the United States not move ahead with the Strategic Defense Initiative (missile defense system), demands that American officials during Bill Clinton's first term were unfortunately not willing to accept. As Kaplan explains, "By this time, support for SDI had hardened as a shibboleth among Republicans and some hawkish Democrats as well."[33] This reckless stance—based on political ideology and fantasy, not science—meant that the nuclear arms race was not over, and a great obstacle blocked the path to disarmament. But it was not only the blind faith in the SDI program that presented an obstacle to the goal of abolition. The United States also continued with the policy of nuclear deterrence, still aiming warheads at targets in Russia even as it attempted to negotiate reductions in these weapons. As Schell points out, "This continuation—this doing nothing—constituted one of the most important decisions of the nuclear age. It quietly set a standard for the post–Cold War period."[34]

On top of the ideological fixation with missile "defense" and the critical nondecision that maintained the policy of nuclear deterrence, two major campaigns undertaken by the first Bush administration would also undermine efforts toward nuclear disarmament and end up cementing a central role for nuclear weapons in U.S. defense policy going forward. One was the development of what Michael Klare called the "Rogue Doctrine," and the other was the Persian Gulf War of 1991 (called Operation Desert Storm by the Pentagon), which confirmed the utility of the new doctrine for the American power elite.[35] The Rogue Doctrine successfully filled in the glaring "threat blank" caused by the demise of the Soviet Union, provided a new general military strategy for the post–Cold War era, and outlined a possible new role for nuclear weapons to play in the pursuit of American imperial geopolitical goals. It provided another answer to what Schell called "the momentous question" of whom, if anyone, to target with these weapons now that the Soviet threat had been removed.[36] What is strange about this debate is that, as noted previously, U.S. nuclear weapons continued to be aimed at targets in the new Russian Federation, even as policymakers recognized that the Soviet threat no longer existed. Still, the external threat blank caused by the end of the Cold War posed a fundamental political dilemma for the vested interests of the U.S. Empire and the institutions of the military-industrial complex—what Carl Boggs calls "the nuclear-industrial complex."[37] The fact that there was no longer a recognizable enemy to confront threatened the bureaucratic power of the Pentagon, the geopolitical goals of American state officials seeking to extend U.S. imperial domination, and the corporate profits of military contractors in the nuclear-industrial complex. The threat blank had to be filled to protect these vested institutional interests.

The abrupt end of the Cold War had shocked and alarmed American military leaders. As Klare observes, "Not only did it deprive them of an enemy against which to train and equip their forces, but it also eradicated the mental map that hitherto had explained world events and governed U.S. policymaking."[38] In the early post–Cold War era, public support for the Pentagon diminished, its bloated budget came under the microscope, and expectations for some kind of peace dividend put the military on the defensive. But eventually, the Joint Chiefs of Staff, under the leadership of its chairman, General Colin Powell, was able "to develop an alternative strategic outlook based on non-Soviet threats to U.S. security."[39] The Pentagon began to develop policies to fill "the high-level explanatory void in Washington," and most of them "had something to do with preventing the proliferation of nuclear arms and other weapons of mass destruction."[40] The threat blank left by the disintegration of the Soviet Union was soon filled by an emerging class of regional Third World powers—which Klare would dub "Rogue States and Nuclear Outlaws."[41]

According to the Pentagon, these Third World powers had large military forces, sought to dominate the weaker states in their region, and were accused of seeking nuclear weapons and other weapons of mass destruction (WMDs). In a "post–Cold War assessment of possible approaches to nuclear strategy," the Joint Strategic Target Planning Advisory Group called for the targeting of "every reasonable adversary" and also developed a "rationale for targeting Third World powers with nuclear weapons."[42] As Schell points out, as a result of various military planning efforts like this, "The idea that new targets for nuclear weapons might be discovered in the third world began to take root."[43] By seeking to deter these rogue states and nuclear outlaws, the United States would be able to remain a "global superpower," maintain a large military budget (despite the calls for a peace dividend), and prevent the "horizonal proliferation" of nuclear, biological, and chemical weapons.[44] With the development of the Pentagon's Rogue Doctrine (also known as the New Strategy or the Regional Defense Strategy), "classical strategic policy and nonproliferation policy began to merge."[45]

The targets of U.S. nuclear arms expanded, therefore, to include not just those in Russia but now "rogue states" that might be seeking WMDs as well. American military might, and perhaps its nuclear arsenal, would now be "used" to stop the spread of nuclear weapons to Third World regional powers. To many political leaders around the world this new radical counterproliferation role assigned to U.S. nuclear weapons appeared to cement a nuclear double standard: the United States (and a few other powerful countries) could possess large numbers of nuclear warheads, but Third World countries could not even aspire to one. This "nuclear hypocrisy" or "nuclear apartheid" is a major impediment to the legally obligated pursuit of disarmament.[46]

Almost as soon as the Rogue Doctrine was developed, the Bush administration had an opportunity to put the doctrine to a test. On August 2, 1990, Middle Eastern power Iraq, under the leadership of Saddam Hussein, invaded, occupied, and annexed its neighbor Kuwait. In January 1991, the United States responded to the Iraqi invasion with a military campaign dubbed Operation Desert Storm. This military operation to drive Hussein out of Kuwait was not only a test of the Rogue Doctrine but also an early component of what Andrew Bacevich calls "America's War for the Greater Middle East."[47] This was an expansive imperial war whose initial focus, at least, was on access to and control over foreign petroleum. To understand Operation Desert Storm more fully, some additional historical context is necessary.

In the post–World War II period, a key geopolitical concern of the U.S. Empire, in addition to thwarting independent nationalism in the Third World and fighting the Cold War against the Soviet Union, was gaining access to and control over the vast supplies of petroleum and natural gas in the Greater Middle East. Not only was the global capitalist system "fueled and lubricated by oil,"[48] it was also "a resource so vital to American prosperity that access to it must be protected at any cost, including the use of military force."[49] The availability of cheap petroleum became a critical national security issue and would eventually lead to direct military intervention in the Middle East, what Bacevich and others refer to as "blood for oil."[50]

Operation Desert Storm represented the first major implementation of the "Carter Doctrine," laid out in 1980 by President Jimmy Carter, which stated that any attempt by outside forces to gain control of the Persian Gulf region would be regarded as an assault on the vital interests (read oil) of the United States and be repelled by any means necessary, including military force. The military operation against Hussein's Iraq in 1991 would ratchet up American imperial involvement in the region and set in motion social and political forces that would produce more warfare and devastating long-term consequences.

After the 1979 Islamic Revolution in Iran, the United States viewed Hussein as a regional strongman who might provide a geopolitical bulwark against the Iranian mullahs. President Reagan had even provided support to

Iraq during its bloody and expensive war with Iran in the 1980s. That war left Baghdad deeply in debt to its small neighbor Kuwait, and when the Kuwaiti government refused to forgive the debt, Hussein began to eye the country's rich oil fields to solve his financial problems. President Bush and his administration struggled at first to develop a coherent policy toward Iraq, perhaps signaling to Hussein that it would not be concerned with any military move he might make against his neighbor. But when the Iraqi army invaded Kuwait, the White House quickly concluded that "Iraq posed an indisputable threat to America's interests in the Gulf."[51] Bush was particularly concerned about the "threat" Iraq posed to the oil fields and safety of Saudi Arabia, and he cited America's energy needs and dependence on Saudi oil as major justifications for his decision to use military force to drive Hussein from Kuwait.

As Operation Desert Storm got underway in early 1991, importantly aided by "unprecedented collaboration" between Gorbachev and Bush it should be noted,[52] the U.S. administration offered additional rationales for military intervention such as the need to liberate Kuwait, deter international aggression, and eliminate Iraq's WMDs. The issue of Iraq's nuclear capabilities was a particularly important concern to raise. Some American officials claimed that the Iraqis were only months away from acquiring nuclear weapons. These officials conveniently ignored the fact that any progress Iraq had made with its nuclear weapons program occurred while the United States was supporting Hussein, and given their inside knowledge of the state of that program, the U.S. military was not really concerned about any Iraqi nuclear threat as it undertook Operation Desert Storm.[53] Thus, as Klare later concluded, "The record makes it clear, though, that the president and his senior associates initially viewed the invasion of Kuwait through the lens of the Carter Doctrine; as a threat to Saudi Arabia and the free flow of oil from the Gulf."[54] The fact that it could also serve as a test of the Rogue Doctrine to eliminate WMDs was an additional and welcome benefit.

Operation Desert Storm appeared to be a complete and decisive victory. U.S. forces quickly ejected the Iraqi invaders from Kuwait and restored the emir to his throne. President Bush, however, decided not to pursue the Iraqi army all the way back to Baghdad—and Hussein, despite losing the war, would survive in power for the time. Bacevich concludes, "Viewed as 'a war for oil,' which indeed it was, Desert Storm produced a satisfactory yet imperfect outcome."[55] However, "from the perspective of the U.S. military establishment, Operation Desert Storm represented a remarkable success."[56]

The war was a resounding success because it confirmed the Rogue Doctrine: a significant regional power, a rogue state seeking WMDs, had been defeated on the battlefield, and this victory demonstrated the worth of the new general military strategy that had been developed to fill the threat blank created by the end of the Cold War. Thus, the impact of the victorious war was felt not only in the Middle East and its vast oilfields but also back at home. As Klare observes, "For the Department of Defense, success was now at hand—not only on the battlefields of the Persian Gulf, but on the funding battlefields in Congress, the publicity battlefields in the mass media, the research and development battlefields of industrial America, and on the most important of all battlefields, the public mind."[57] The threat blank had been successfully filled. A new strategic template had been created for all future wars in the post–Cold War period. The peace dividend had been averted.

This confirmation of the Rogue Doctrine not only served the bureaucratic interests of the Pentagon and the imperial geopolitical goals of American state officials but also protected the profits of the major weapons contractors. The state-corporate crime literature and the history of the American Empire both point to the importance of understanding the interrelationships between economic and political factors—the deep structural relations between corporations and the state. It is the dialectical relationship between private business interests (including defense industry corporations) and the American political system (including the institution of the military) that generates the production of nuclear arms. Major weapons contractors like Lockheed Martin, Raytheon, Boeing, General Dynamics, and Northrop Grumman take advantage of what American economist Seymour Melman called "Pentagon capitalism" and the larger drive for imperial domination by the American Empire to reap tremendous profits.[58] Not only does this war industry operate on the basis of corporate greed, but the weapons contractors within the industry also engage in specific deviant actions (corporate crimes) such as price gouging, outright fraud, wasteful practices, mismanagement, and the production of cost overruns.[59] Yet the Pentagon rarely sanctions these organizational crimes, and "the cost of coddling contractors" is enormously high.[60] This state facilitation of corporate crime by Congress adds billions to the Pentagon budget each year. Klare argues that one of the planned goals in the development of the Rogue Doctrine was to "ensure a need for continued acquisition of new, high-tech weapons systems, thus preserving a significant portion of the military-industrial apparatus built up during the Cold War era."[61] Thus, the confirmation of the doctrine by Desert Storm kept this permanent war economy, this nuclear-industrial complex, firmly in place.

An analysis of the development of the Rogue Doctrine, and the political support provided to it by Operation Desert Storm, also provides empirical confirmation of the treadmill of destruction (ToD) theory in sociology. This theory offers a perspective on the relationship between the state, its military institution, the capitalist economy, and the environment. ToD theory argues that there is a distinct expansionary dynamic associated with war and militarism rooted in the state and its geopolitical interests, which, while related, cannot be reduced solely to capitalism and its "treadmill" of economic production.[62] This theoretical approach was developed to "recast the environmental sociology literature by specifying the scope conditions under which a 'treadmill of production' and a 'treadmill of destruction' are applicable."[63]

Treadmill of production (ToP) theory is a macrostructural sociological perspective that argues that the climate crisis and other forms of ecological destruction are rooted intrinsically in the political economy of capitalism.[64] ToP focuses on the system imperative of economic growth and the enduring conflict between the capitalist mode of production and protection of the environment. The theory contends that the drive for endless growth and ever greater profits leads to increasing levels of environmental degradation. ToP theorists argue that there is an inherent and deadly contradiction between the political economy of global capitalism and ecological health.[65] Human economic systems—particularly capitalism with its expansionary logic—extract natural resources and transform them through a production process that interferes with the organization of ecological systems and results in ecosystem disruption and ecological disorganization.

While the ToP perspective explains the accelerating impact of society on ecological conditions due to economic factors such as capitalist competition, the quest for profits, and the search for increased market share,[66] ToD theory points to a different underlying logic: the military as a social structure and the imperatives of militarism. As American sociologists Gregory Hooks and Chad L. Smith explain, "The 'treadmill of destruction' draws attention to a distinct expansionary dynamic that also generates additions to and withdrawals from the environment . . . expansionary dynamics associated with war and militarism; geopolitical competition and arms races."[67] This theory helps us understand distinctive forms of state crime related to the military institution. As American sociologists Brett Clark and Andrew K. Jorgenson note, "The treadmill of destruction perspective within sociology makes an important contribution highlighting how the expansionary practices of the military produce a system that is highly resource consumptive and waste generating—not to mention it creates distinctive forms of environmental inequality."[68]

While I concur that ToD theory provides important insights that further substantiate the Pentagon's environmental crimes, I would also emphasize again that the state-corporate crime literature, the history of the global American Empire, and a political economy analysis point to the importance of understanding the interrelationships between economic and political factors, the deep structural relations between corporations and the state and its institutions. Private military contractors—through lucrative corporate campaign contributions, political lobbying, the hiring of former defense and military officials, and the promotion of a militarist ideology—exert enormous influence over spending decisions concerning the Pentagon. The Rogue Doctrine was not developed in a vacuum. Sorensen analyzes how this process operates within the "war industry" with regard to the production of nuclear weapons, arguing that the current effort to modernize the U.S. nuclear arsenal is a costly "scam" and a form of state-facilitated "theft."[69] To say nothing of the fact that the modernization and continued production of these weapons is also a violation of international laws that could have cataclysmic effects in the future. The presence of this powerful military-industrial-congressional complex continues to represent a major obstacle to the reduction of the military budget and the path to disarmament.

PRESIDENT CLINTON, THE NUCLEAR POSTURE REVIEW, AND ROGUES

Despite his role in helping to end the Cold War, his close relationships with Russian leaders Gorbachev and Yeltsin, his efforts to negotiate two START agreements, and the military success of Operation Desert Storm, George H. W. Bush was defeated in his reelection bid in 1992 by the former governor of Arkansas, William Jefferson Clinton. The "sharp and painful recession" of the early 1990s, his violation of a pledge not to raise taxes, and the impact of Ross Perot's third-party candidacy weakened Bush's electoral prospects.[70] With the Cold War over, foreign affairs had become a more distant concern for the American people than the economy and other domestic problems. Bill Clinton campaigned hard on economic issues and eked out a narrow victory. As American historians Glenda Elizabeth Gilmore and Thomas J. Sugrue point out, Clinton was "the most prominent member of the Democratic Leadership Council (DLC), a group of insurgent

Democrats . . . who argued that . . . the party needed to move rightward on civil rights, foreign policy, and especially economic policy."[71] And as president, Clinton did move to the right on all these issues, "and much of his agenda amounted to a continuation of work begun by Reagan and Bush."[72] Clinton would become America's "neoliberal president par excellence" by more fully implementing the neoliberal economic policies his predecessors had initiated.[73]

Defense policy, however, was not Clinton's strong suit, and his primary campaign mantra was, "It's the economy, stupid."[74] Not only did Clinton enter the White House focusing primarily on domestic concerns and "caring little about foreign policy,"[75] he also showed "no interest in America's nuclear arsenal."[76] Like Bush before him, Clinton was guilty of a critical abdication as he failed to coherently address the questions of what nuclear weapons were for in a post–Soviet Union world. As Australian nuclear activist Helen Caldicott put it, under Clinton, "the opportunity for nuclear disarmament was tragically lost."[77] Schell points out that during President Clinton's two terms in office, "Cold War arsenals sailed on undisturbed into the post–Cold War era—still made up of a triad of submarines, aircraft, and land-based missiles, still on hair-trigger alert, still ready to fire at an instant's notice after mere warning of attack, still prone to accidental use, and still capable of destroying the United States and the [former] Soviet Union dozens of times over."[78] Like President Bush, President Clinton also squandered the gift of time, and his administration too was guilty of the state crime of political omission concerning nuclear disarmament.

Despite his lack of interest in foreign affairs, Clinton would be forced to deal with a host of foreign policy crises and critical issues during his two terms in office. In practice, the Clinton administration's foreign policy was also generally consistent with that of the previous administration. President Clinton shared Bush's views of America as a global leader that should use its economic and military power to ensure openness and integration in the world economic system.[79] In this sense, Clinton-era foreign policy remained consistent with the Open Door system of informal imperialism practiced by the United States since the beginning of the twentieth century, stressing global economic integration through free trade and democracy.[80] Thus, with regard to Russia, President Clinton actively supported the neoliberal economic shock therapy that was being promoted and implemented by Western economists in the republics of the former Soviet Union.

The fall of communism had opened Russia and Eastern Europe to capitalist penetration. As American historian Gary Gerstle points out, "After

1991, capitalists and capital poured into Eastern Europe, along with pha-
lanxes of economists from the West, many of them preaching free market
shock therapy as the best way to implant capitalist principles quickly
and powerfully."[81] Within formerly state-controlled economies, natural
resources and state-owned industries were suddenly privatized, free markets
imposed, deregulation accomplished, individualism promoted, and social
services and public supports slashed. These neoliberal economic polices
led to "the near-collapse" of the Russian economy in the 1990s, "with a
65 percent drop in GDP and a reduction in male life expectancy from
65 to 58. It also created a new class of 'oligarchs': politically connected businessmen who became extraordinarily wealthy through a corrupt process of
acquiring state assets."[82] This economic suffering and growing inequality
would create political instability in Russia, Ukraine, and other parts of
Eastern Europe, which presented obstacles to arms control negotiations and
opened new sources of geopolitical conflict in the future.

Concerning general military strategy, nuclear weapons policy, and arms
control negotiations, the Clinton administration also had similarities to the
Bush team—adopting a form of the Rogue Doctrine, maintaining a nuclear
posture that differed little from the late Cold War policies of his predecessors,
attempting (mostly unsuccessfully) to negotiate and ratify various Strategic
Arms Reduction Treaties, and developing a policy of counterproliferation
by force in dealing with "rogue" states. While these approaches did little to
advance the cause of disarmament, Clinton's most disastrous foreign policy
decision as it affected Russia was his effort at the "enlargement" of the
NATO military alliance by absorbing former Warsaw Pact members and
encroaching eastward toward the Russian border.

Bush administration officials and other Western leaders had made informal promises to Mikhail Gorbachev in 1990 and 1991 that NATO would
not expand toward Russia's borders (a major concern of both Yeltsin and
Gorbachev). In a February 9, 1990, meeting, U.S. secretary of state James
Baker made a famous "not one inch eastward" promise to Gorbachev, and
that same year a State Department memorandum "advised that it was not in
the best interests of NATO or the United States to grant NATO membership
to Eastern European states."[83] The Clinton administration, however, came
to view NATO expansion as a positive foreign policy move. Following the
deployment of Russian troops into Chechnya in December 1994, Central
and Eastern European governments began to pressure President Clinton to
allow them to join the military alliance. Within NATO itself, pressure was
also building "to begin inviting the former Warsaw Pact members to join the

organization as a means of containing Russian expansion, despite the fact that verbal exchanges between Mikhail Gorbachev and the administration of President Bush (including the president himself) precluded any such expansion."[84] It was clear to the West that the enlargement of NATO eastward would be viewed by Russian leaders as a provocation.

But President Clinton was warming to the idea. He thought that NATO expansion would "strengthen European security, as well as Euro-American hegemony" and "prevent France and Germany from developing the EU [European Union] into a truly independent economic and diplomatic power to balance the unipolar dominance of the United States in the post–Cold War world."[85] Clinton also thought the enlargement of NATO would burnish his foreign policy credentials for the 1996 reelection campaign. But the plan to expand NATO eastward was met with withering criticism from fifty foreign policy experts, who labeled it as a policy error of "historic proportions" and condemnation from George Kennan, the architect of the "containment policy" in the early years of the Cold War, who branded the idea a "tragic mistake."[86] Nevertheless, the door to NATO expansion was open, and George W. Bush and Barack Obama would follow Clinton through that door with tragic consequences for the prospect of nuclear disarmament.

At the start of his first term, President Clinton appointed Representative Les Aspin as his secretary of defense. Aspin had served on the House Armed Services Committee, had developed considerable expertise on military affairs, and had also been highly critical of the Pentagon in the past. In early 1993, Secretary Aspin ordered a comprehensive assessment of the Department of Defense's (DOD) programs and policies. According to a DOD news release, this "start-from-scratch" assessment, known as the "Bottom-Up Review," was intended "to reshape defense policy for the post–Cold War, post–Soviet Union World" that the new administration found itself in.[87] Aspin was hoping to initiate a wide-ranging debate over U.S. military strategy, the size and orientation of its forces, its budget, and its war fighting capabilities, just as Colin Powell and the Joint Chiefs of Staff had done in the previous administration. But the Clinton DOD found that Powell's "New Strategy" had altered the terms of the debate "in favor of some version of the Rogue Doctrine."[88] When the results of the Bottom-Up Review were made public in September 1993, it became clear how much the assessment had been shaped by the concepts of that earlier doctrine when the report emphasized the need to contain "rogue leaders set on regional domination through military aggression while simultaneously pursing nuclear, biological, and chemical weapons capabilities."[89] And over the next seven years, the

Clinton administration would struggle mightily to deal with what it considered "rogue states" in Iraq, North Korea, and the Balkans.

One critical issue that, surprisingly, was not explicitly addressed in the Bottom-Up Review was the role of nuclear weapons in U.S. military strategy. Throughout the Cold War these weapons at been at the center of America's defense policy, but now with that struggle over and former Soviet warheads being transferred to Russia (from Ukraine, Kazakhstan, and Belarus), stored, dismantled, or taken off alert status, a much smaller U.S. arsenal could be envisioned. Abolitionists like Schell pressed the case that disarmament itself should be pursued and given the highest priority. When Clinton became president, the total number of U.S. warheads had already declined to 18,500.[90] Further reductions were expected with the implementation of the START I and II treaties. Given the changed geopolitical situation, what function did any remaining nuclear weapons serve? Where would these warheads be targeted? At Russia, at China, at rogue states and nuclear outlaws for the purpose of counterproliferation? To try to answer these important questions, Secretary Aspin announced in the fall of 1993 that the DOD would conduct a comprehensive review of U.S. nuclear policy. Called the Nuclear Posture Review (NPR), this assessment was to answer the important question of why the United States still needed nuclear weapons.

From the point of view of the abolitionists and the world disarmament movement, the Clinton NPR was a major failure. As Schell observed, "Continuing in the tradition of nondecision begun by Truman at the time of the Hiroshima bombing, the administration sidestepped its own question."[91] Neither the president nor his top foreign policy officials—Secretary of Defense Aspin, Secretary of State Warren Christopher, or National Security Advisor Anthony Lake—became seriously involved in the review, which was left to lower-tier DOD bureaucrats and military officers. One of those officials, Assistant Secretary of Defense Ashton Carter, proposed an agreement with Russia to take both strategic arsenals off of hair-trigger alert and also suggested a modification to the U.S. "launch on warning" policy, which dictated that the president order a retaliatory response merely upon reports that Soviet missiles had been launched.[92] Carter also had publicly committed to shifting U.S. defense policy from a reliance on nuclear weapons to deter aggression to a conventional military force that could counter any attacks on allied targets in Europe or elsewhere. As Ritter notes, however, "This vision was in direct opposition to the views of America's military leadership, which continued to see U.S. nuclear weapons as an essential element of national security."[93] Without strong leadership from the top of the administration, the Pentagon stepped in and "chewed up" even the minimal proposals that lower-level bureaucrats like Carter were advancing during the review.[94]

The Clinton NPR was released in September 1994. It stated that America would "lead but hedge" regarding nuclear weapons, meaning that the U.S. would lead by pursing significant arms control negotiations but hedge by continuing to maintain a large nuclear arsenal in case Russia might become an enemy again. According to the review, the "TRIAD structure" of the arsenal (bombers, submarine-launched missiles, and intercontinental ballistic missiles) would be retained intact.[95] Disarmament advocates were appalled. Klare observed that the NPR rejected the "argument that, with the Cold War over, the United States can dispense with nuclear weapons (or, at the very least, radically reduce their number)," with Clinton administration officials insisting that "a robust nuclear capacity is needed to cope with unspecified future threats."[96] As Schell later argued, "This formulation in effect erased the collapse of the Soviet Union as an event worthy of major response in the nuclear field. With or without a global antagonist, nuclear policy and the arsenal that supported it would remain essentially unchanged."[97] In a speech on national security in July 1994, President Clinton clearly endorsed the principal conclusions of the soon to be released NPR by stating, "We will retain strategic nuclear forces sufficient to deter any future hostile leadership with access to strategic nuclear forces from acting against our vital interests . . . we will continue to maintain nuclear forces of sufficient size and capability to hold at risk a broad range of assets valued by such political and military leaders."[98] By supporting the Pentagon-shaped NPR and the retention of the nuclear arsenal, Clinton was squandering the gift of time, failing to seize the opportunities provided by the end of the Cold War to abolish nuclear weapons, and violating the United States' clear legal obligation under Article VI of the Non-Proliferation Treaty of 1968 to pursue nuclear disarmament.

Concerning arms control negotiations, the Clinton administration did try to push the slow-moving Strategic Arms Reduction Treaty process forward. START I (signed by Bush and Gorbachev in July 1991) would enter into force on December 5, 1994, after the issues surrounding the transfer and/or elimination of the strategic nuclear weapons that had been based in Belarus, Ukraine, and Kazakhstan (a process set up by the Lisbon Protocol of 1992) had finally been resolved.[99] With this problem solved, serious negotiations on START II could resume. Signed by Presidents Bush and Yeltsin in January 1993, the START II treaty was still awaiting ratification by both countries, slowed by concerns over the U.S. missile defense program. Although President Clinton had announced the termination of Reagan's "Star Wars" program (the SDI) in July 1993, his order "only cut the space-based portion of the massive missile defense effort. Ground-based missile defense was still part of the U.S. strategic future."[100] Clinton met with President Yeltsin in Moscow on January 14, 1994, to resolve the remaining issues concerning START I, and during those negotiations tried to allay Russian fears about the U.S. missile defense program. But even after the U.S. Senate finally ratified START II in January 1996, the Russian Parliament refused to act based on concerns about both missile defense and the American-led NATO military intervention in the civil war then raging in the Balkans.

Even though START II was still unresolved, President Clinton pushed forward on the issue of nuclear testing and a proposed CTBT. President Bush had announced a unilateral moratorium on nuclear weapons testing in October 1992. Clinton twice extended the moratorium, and then, after attending a Nuclear Safety Summit in Moscow in April 1996, finally signed the CTBT on September 24, 1996—as did the leaders of Russia, France, China, and the United Kingdom, "committing these declared nuclear weapons states to never again test nuclear weapons."[101] However, Republican opposition to Clinton's arms control policies were building in the U.S. Senate. In January 1997, Republican senators introduced the National Missile Defense Act, which threatened to further derail START II. Despite this Republican pressure, Clinton and Yeltsin met again in March 1997 in Helsinki, where they "agreed to immediately begin negotiations on a START-3, designed to limit each side to 2,000 to 2,500 deployed strategic warheads by the end of 2007, following Russian ratification of START-2."[102] To facilitate the ratification of START II by the Russian Parliament, Clinton tried to work out the differences between the two countries over missile defense. While this effort was ongoing, he sent the CTBT to the Senate for ratification in September 1997.

In accordance with the guiding terms of the NPR, while the Clinton administration was trying to "lead" on these various arms control agreements, it also continued to "hedge" on issues concerning the maintenance of the nuclear arsenal and the targeting of nuclear weapons. The same month that the administration sent the CTBT to the Senate for ratification, it also released its new guidelines for the targeting of U.S. nuclear weapons. Presidential Decision Directive 60 (PDD-60), "The U.S. Strategic Nuclear Doctrine," directed the Pentagon to move away from the Reagan strategy of using nuclear weapons to "prevail" in nuclear warfare and back to a more classic deterrence posture. As Ritter points out, while the United States "would no longer plan to fight a protracted nuclear war . . . PDD-60 did retain established targets inside Russia, reflecting the opinion of many in the Clinton administration that despite all that had transpired since the fall of the Soviet Union, Russia still represented the major nuclear threat to the United States."[103] Notwithstanding its efforts to negotiate and/or ratify the various START agreements and the CTBT, with the NPR and the PDD-60, the Clinton administration failed to advance the cause of disarmament. Still trapped in the structure of the post–World War II national security state and the culture of nuclearism, the administration failed to seize the opportunity provided by the changed geopolitical situation after the Cold War to rid the world of the nuclear threat.

Clinton's efforts at arms control also ended in abject failure. In October 1999, the U.S. Senate voted against ratification of the CTBT, "sending the Clinton administration a shocking political defeat and setting back the issue of arms control around the world."[104] In the late 1990s, the administration engaged in numerous military actions in Iraq and the Balkans that strained American–Russian relations and also set back discussions on revising the Anti-Ballistic Missile Treaty and developing a START III agreement. Then, on July 23, 1999, President Clinton signed the Missile Defense Act, further straining relations with President Yeltsin and Russia over this contentious issue. And when Clinton demanded that Russia stop its aerial bombardment of civilians during the Chechen conflict that November, Yeltsin angrily replied that Clinton had "forgotten that Russia has a full arsenal of nuclear weapons."[105] Following Yeltsin's unexpected resignation in late December 1999, Vladimir Putin was elected president of Russia on March 26, 2000. Putin, a former KGB agent, then surprisingly delivered a ratified START II agreement in April and met with Clinton in June and September that year to reaffirm existing arms control treaties and continue work toward START III. But START II would never enter into force because the U.S. Senate rejected a 1997 protocol to the treaty concerning missile defense (that had been signed by Clinton and Yeltsin) and several ABM Treaty amendments as well. Clinton would leave office in January 2001, and attempts at negotiating START III were eventually abandoned.

Not only did the Clinton administration maintain the U.S. nuclear arsenal despite the end of the Cold War and fail to deliver any significant arms control agreement with Russia, but it also facilitated the development of a policy of counterproliferation by force through its dealings with "rogue states" like Iraq and North Korea. Clinton inherited and then continued the Bush administration policy of containment in Iraq after Operation Desert Storm. And, regarding Saddam Hussein, the Clinton administration pursued a policy of "containment plus regime change,"[106] keeping the United States still effectively at war with Iraq. Clinton also continued the comprehensive economic sanctions, despite their devastating human costs, that had been imposed on the country by the Bush administration following the 1991 war, pursued low-level warfare against Iraq in the form of unauthorized "no fly zones," and used the UN Special Commission (UNSCOM) WMD inspections process as a way of spying on the Iraqi military.[107] In December 1998, after another in a series of minor confrontations with Hussein, the United States ordered the UN weapons inspectors out of the country and then launched a four-day bombing campaign (code named Operation Desert Fox). As Ritter observes, the aerial bombardment was "ostensibly designed to degrade Iraqi WMD programs kept hidden from UN inspectors, but in reality [it was] a final effort to remove Saddam Hussein from power."[108] But the bombing campaign also lent support to the Rogue Doctrine and the emerging argument that the best way to stop the proliferation of nuclear weapons to rogue states was through the use of military force.

The Clinton administration was also compelled to deal with a crisis in North Korea, another alleged "rogue state," over its nascent nuclear weapons program. In 1992, the International Atomic Energy Agency (IAEA) discovered evidence of an attempt by North Korea to divert plutonium from a civilian nuclear power reactor, which could then be used to create a nuclear weapon. This was a violation of the Nuclear Non-Proliferation Treaty (NPT) that North Korea was a signatory to in 1985. In response to the IAEA report, the North Korean government under Chairman Kim Il-sung refused further inspections (required under the NPT) and threatened to become the first country to withdraw from the nonproliferation accord. The international community was suddenly faced with the emerging threat of a nuclear-armed North Korea. In early 1993, the Clinton administration responded by securing a UN Security Council resolution that would impose sanctions on North Korea if it did not allow the international inspectors to remain. Furthermore, as Schell reports, "At this moment of high tension, the Clinton administration gave serious consideration to a preemptive military attack, called the Osirak option (after Israel's attack on Iraq's nuclear reactor at Osirak in 1981), on North Korea's nuclear facilities."[109] President Clinton was presented with various military options to consider, and "strategies to remove the existing regime from power were also discussed."[110] The revolutionary policy of nonproliferation by preemptive military force and regime change was seriously being contemplated by an American president.

But the 1993 Korean nuclear crisis (the first of many to come) was temporarily resolved without resort to military violence due to the diplomatic efforts of former president Jimmy Carter, who traveled to North Korea in June and spent three days negotiating with Pyongyang's leaders. As a result of these discussions, which went well beyond what the Clinton administration had initially authorized Carter to pursue, a twelve-point agreement emerged in which Kim Il-sung agreed to stop reprocessing plutonium and allowed the international inspectors to remain.[111] In October, after lengthy and contentious negotiations, the United States and North Korea signed an accord called the Agreed Framework, which contained many of the provisions Carter had outlined in the June agreement. In exchange for fuel oil, two light-water nuclear reactors (allowed under the NPT), and a pledge to move forward toward the normalization of political and economic relations, North Korea "renewed its commitment to the Non-Proliferation Treaty and locked up the reactor's fuel rods."[112] In one of its rare foreign policy accomplishments, the Clinton administration continued to have a good relationship with Kim Il-sung's son and successor Kim Jong-il, and more diplomatic progress seemed possible with this particular "rogue state." But Clinton's successor would both unravel the relationship with North Korea and put into action the radical policy of nonproliferation by preemptive military force and regime change by invading and occupying Iraq.

PRESIDENT GEORGE W. BUSH, THE NEOCONS, AND NUCLEAR PREEMPTION

In December 2000, the U.S. Supreme Court stopped the process of counting votes in Florida and awarded the state's Electoral College votes, and thus the presidency, to George W. Bush (even though Bush had lost the popular vote to Al Gore by more than a half-million ballots). The administration of the second President Bush would go on to be one of the most lawless in American history, engaging in a veritable state crime wave. By invading Iraq in 2003, with a deceitful claim that the purpose was to prevent the proliferation of nuclear weapons and other WMDs, the Bush administration violated the UN Charter and engaged in an illegal war of aggression—what the Nuremberg Tribunal had called the "Supreme International Crime."[113] The Bush administration also committed a variety of war crimes (violations of international humanitarian law) during the brutal occupation that followed, including torture (in violation of the 1949 Geneva

Conventions and the 1984 UN Convention Against Torture)—state crimes that resulted in the deaths of hundreds of thousands of Iraqis.[114]

Other consequential crimes that the George W. Bush administration engaged in were the failure to take any serious actions to reduce carbon emissions and reduce global warming and the intentional abdication of its moral and legal responsibility to pursue and achieve nuclear disarmament.[115] With regard to nuclear weapons, the second Bush administration not only failed to take advantage of the gift of time but also "swept aside forty years of superpower arms control," giving itself in this realm "what it perhaps valued most in every area of foreign policy, a completely free hand, unconstrained by alliances or treaty obligations."[116] Then it contemplated using that freedom illegally to launch nuclear weapons first, preemptively, in a variety of military situations.[117] And to make matters worse, the Bush administration also encouraged neoliberal shock therapy for Russia, Iraq, and other places, while supporting the continued expansion of NATO, despite Russian protests.[118]

The foreign policy, general military strategy, and specific approach to nuclear weapons of the George W. Bush administration cannot be understood without first analyzing the impact of the "neoconservative" ideology and political movement. The term *neoconservative* (often abridged as *neocon*) was first used by the American democratic socialist leader Michael Harrington in the early 1970s to describe a group of political figures and intellectuals who had been his comrades in the U.S. Socialist Party but were now moving politically to the right. Many of this original neoconservative group had been associated with the Henry "Scoop" Jackson wing of the Democratic Party, but in reaction to the cultural liberalism and anti–Vietnam War stance associated with the 1972 Democratic presidential candidate George McGovern, they moved to the right, eventually joining the Republican Party.[119]

Many neoconservatives affiliated with the Reagan administration, often providing intellectual justification for that administration's early policies of military growth and rollback of, rather than coexistence with, the Soviet Union. While the first generation of neoconservatives also addressed economic and cultural issues, their primary foreign policy goal was confronting what they claimed to be the globe-girdling threat of the Soviet Union's "evil empire." As the Soviet Union began to unravel, neocons in the administration of George H. W. Bush began forcefully promoting an aggressive post-Soviet neo-imperialism. Their first concern, shared by many within the military-industrial complex, was to stave off cuts in the military budget in response to the weakened Soviet threat and popular expectations for a peace dividend.

Independent of General Colin Powell's efforts to develop a new military strategy, Secretary of Defense Dick Cheney had also attempted to fill the "threat blank" vacated by the Soviet Union. In 1992, aides to Secretary Cheney, supervised by neocons Paul Wolfowitz and I. Lewis (Scooter) Libby, prepared a draft document titled "Defense Planning Guidance" (DPG), a classified, internal Pentagon policy statement used to guide military officials in the planning process. The draft 1992 DPG provided a first look at the emerging post–Cold War neoconservative imperialist agenda. As American investigative reporter David Armstrong noted, the DPG "depicted a world dominated by the United States, which would maintain its superpower status through a combination of positive guidance and overwhelming military might. The image was one of a heavily armed City on a Hill."[120] It was a vision of a new American Empire for the post–Cold War world.

The draft DPG stated that the first objective of U.S. defense policy should be to prevent the reemergence of a new rival. It also endorsed the use of preemptive military force to achieve its goal. The document called for the United States to maintain a substantial arsenal of nuclear weapons and to develop a missile defense shield. The DPG was a clear statement of the neoconservative vision of unilateral use of military supremacy to defend American interests anywhere in the world, including protecting U.S. access to vital raw materials such as Persian Gulf oil.[121] But the aggressive tone of the DPG generated a firestorm of criticism when a draft was leaked to the press. President George H. W. Bush and Secretary Cheney quickly distanced themselves from the document and ordered a less obviously imperialist version prepared. But the positions taken in the draft would be resurrected in the George W. Bush administration.

The surprisingly rapid collapse of the Soviet Union in the early 1990s revealed that the neocons had been wrong on almost every issue concerning the Soviet threat. Consequently, neoconservatism lost much of its legitimacy as a mainstream political ideology, and these early neocons would eventually find themselves in political exile as part of a far-right wing of the Republican Party. The election of President Clinton removed the neocons from positions within the U.S. government but not from policy debates. From the sidelines, they generated a steady stream of books, articles, reports, and op-ed pieces to influence the direction of American foreign policy. In 1995, second-generation neoconservative William Kristol founded the right-wing magazine *Weekly Standard*, which quickly became a major outlet for neocon thinking. Many of the neoconservatives also joined well-funded conservative think tanks to advocate for their agenda.

Throughout the Clinton years, the neocons opined about new threats to American security, continually calling for greater use of U.S. military power to address them.[122] One persistent theme in their writings was the need to eliminate Saddam Hussein's government from Iraq, consolidate American power in the Middle East, and change the political culture of the region.[123] Neoconservatives subjected the Clinton administration to a steady barrage of foreign policy criticism, particularly with respect to Clinton's handling of Iraq and the Middle East in general. In early 1998, the Project for a New American Century (PNAC), a key neoconservative think tank, released an open letter to President Clinton urging him to forcefully remove Hussein from power.[124] In September 2000, PNAC issued a report titled "Rebuilding America's Defenses: Strategy, Forces and Resources for a New Century." This report resurrected the core ideas of the controversial draft DPG of 1992.[125] The report called for massive increases in military spending, the expansion of U.S. military bases, and the establishment of client states supportive of American economic and political interests. The imperial goals of the neocons were clear. What they lacked was the opportunity to implement these goals. Two unanticipated events gave them the opportunity to do so.

The first occurred with the U.S. Supreme Court decision that awarded the presidency to George W. Bush in December 2000. During the younger Bush's two terms in office, America's use of preemptive military force as a counterproliferation policy received a huge boost, arms control agreements were gutted, and the nuclear hypocrisy of the United States was exacerbated. These outcomes were due, in part, to the fact that more than twenty neoconservative and hardline nationalists were given high-ranking positions within the new administration.[126] These policymakers disdained international law and believed that the U.S. Empire should take advantage of the "unipolar moment"[127] created by the end of the Cold War to use American military power to advance the geopolitical and economic interests and cultural ideals of the United States around the world.[128] The neoconservatives and hard-core nationalists who eventually came to dominate foreign policy within the second Bush administration were strong advocates of U.S. nuclear supremacy and believed that nuclear weapons could play an important role in achieving America's imperial foreign policy goals.

President George W. Bush himself came to this conclusion following the second major unanticipated event—the terror attacks of September 11,

2001. After this traumatic event, not only did Bush launch a "War on Terrorism" and order the illegal invasion of Iraq in 2003,[129] he also "embarked on a series of initiatives that would constitute a full-scale transformation of the nation's nuclear policies."[130] In this effort, the Bush administration engaged in various actions that could be defined as state crimes related to nuclear weapons.

From the very beginning, the second Bush administration compounded the historical state crimes of the United States related to nuclear weapons in two ways. First, the administration issued a series of documents and statements that were aggressively militaristic in their content and served to transform American strategic nuclear policies in a way that increased the probability that the United States would, in the future, once again make a conscious decision to intentionally use nuclear weapons.[131] As Ritter points out, through the NPR of 2001, National Security Presidential Directive 14 (NSPD-14), "Nuclear War Planning Guidance," and the publication of a new Single Integrated Operational Plan (SIOP-03), the new Bush administration was "integrating nuclear weapons into the military response profile in a manner not seen since the early days of the Reagan administration," and he concluded, "Rather than heading away from the edge of the nuclear abyss, the administration was taking a giant step forward toward making the horror of nuclear weapons employment not only a possibility but a reality."[132] The nuclear danger was increasing again.

Second, because the neocons within the administration sought global domination and "nuclear primacy"[133] and believed that military force (including the use or threat to use nuclear weapons) was the key to achieving these geopolitical goals, they also violated the legal obligation to disarm by (1) putting forth elaborate plans to modernize and expand the American nuclear arsenal;[134] (2) subverting the 2005 NPT Review Conference;[135] and (3) making a series of decisions that "tore at the web of arms control treaties that had grown up over four decades" and threatened Russian security.[136]

The most revolutionary and clearly illegal policy the Bush administration advocated, in the 2002 "National Security Strategy of the United States," was the overthrow of regimes by military force that were suspected of attempting to acquire WMDs (biological and chemical weapons as well as nuclear arms). The "Bush Doctrine" as it came to be called, of stopping proliferation through the unilateral, preventive use of military force to overthrow the governments of offending states, was a radical corollary to the Rogue Doctrine and the militarization of nonproliferation that had already been undertaken by the Clinton administration. As Cirincione puts it, "The new strategy sought the elimination of regimes rather than weapons, in the belief that the U.S. could determine which countries were responsible enough to have nuclear weapons and which ones were not."[137] The doctrine would be put into effect with the illegal invasion and military occupation of Iraq in 2003 (falsely alleged to have WMDs) and subsequently used to threaten "a preemptive nuclear attack" against Iran to prevent that country from attempting to acquire a nuclear weapon.[138] Schell described the revolutionary nature of this policy: "Never before had the United States—or any country—proposed that military action should be the means for solving the world's proliferation problem."[139]

As the threat to attack Iran shows, the Bush Doctrine not only threatened the use of preemptive conventional military force but also threatened nuclear preemption. The administration's NPR of December 2001 specifically raised the possibility of using American nuclear weapons to preempt a chemical or biological attack. In 2002, National Security Presidential Directive 17 (NSPD-17), "National Strategy to Combat Weapons of Mass Destruction," also "specifically authorized preemptive nuclear first strikes if U.S. intelligence could conclude that specific targets might contain chemical, biological or nuclear weapons."[140] The creation of a new military command (Global Strike), a new nuclear war fighting operations plan (OPLAN 8022), and the 2005 release of the Pentagon's "Doctrine for Joint Nuclear Operations" all provide additional documentation that the Bush administration envisioned and planned for the illegal first use of nuclear weapons in a variety of situations.[141]

There was one glaring contradiction to the Bush Doctrine regarding proliferation—North Korea. The Bush administration was certainly concerned about an impending uranium enrichment program in North Korea, and the president labeled the country as a member of the "axis of evil" in his 2002 State of the Union Address (along with Iran and Iraq). But in reaction to North Korea's attempt to obtain nuclear weapons, the administration's main response was to withdraw from the Agreed Framework that had been negotiated by Bill Clinton and refuse to sit down and talk with Pyongyang—regarding negotiations as "an act of appeasement."[142] The Agreed Framework had already been unraveling (with the United States reneging on some of its promises and with North Korea's enrichment program), and Kim Jong-il decided to one-up the Bush administration and take the more drastic step of withdrawing from the NPT in January 2003. President Bush reacted to this escalation by sending fighter jets and bombers to Guam, but it was a feeble gesture with no follow-through. In early 2003, the U.S. military was preparing to invade Iraq (which did not have WMDs) and chose to ignore North Korea (which was on the verge of joining the nuclear club). Given all the focus on Iraq in terms of material and political support, Bush could do little to respond to North Korea. As Kaplan put it, "In short, Bush took no military action because he couldn't. And he took no diplomatic action because he didn't want to."[143] On October 9, 2006, North Korea set off its first underground nuclear explosion. Many more would follow.

Since the Bush administration envisioned and planned for the intentional use or threat to use nuclear weapons (illegal under international law) to prevent the acquisition of WMDs by certain "rogue" states (even though it took no action against North Korea), and it strongly objected to the imposition of any international legal controls over the United States,[144] it never had any intention of complying with the legal obligation to negotiate and achieve nuclear disarmament as required by Article VI of the NPT (a state crime). Not only did the administration have no intention of complying with this obligation, but it also engaged in a series of actions to undermine the NPT. First, rather than planning for disarmament, the administration undertook an effort to rebuild the U.S. nuclear weapons production infrastructure. As Daley observes, "The idea was both to modernize existing nuclear weapons production facilities and to construct new ones, enabling the United States to mass-produce new nuclear weapons for the first time since the end of the cold war."[145] The Bush administration also took aim at various treaties it believed would restrict U.S. actions regarding the possession and use of nuclear weapons. The neoconservatives and hard-core nationalists who occupied important positions within the administration had long expressed their contempt for international law and arms control and nonproliferation treaties. As Cirincione notes, "Many officials in the Bush administration believed that the entire process of negotiating and implementing nonproliferation treaties was both unnecessary and harmful to U.S. national security interests."[146] Therefore, it was not surprising that upon taking office President Bush declined to revive the CTBT and in December 2001 announced the United States' withdrawal from the Anti-Ballistic Missile Treaty.

The Bush administration's most significant violation of the solemn legal obligation to disarm, however, occurred in 2005 when the administration undermined the NPT Review Conference, resulting in "the biggest failure in the history of this treaty."[147] The previous 2000 Review Conference had agreed on thirteen practical steps for the systematic and progressive effort to implement Article VI of NPT that imposes a legal duty on the nuclear weapons states to negotiate in good faith and conclude complete nuclear disarmament. Bush officials rejected the 2000 agreement, which had been endorsed by the Clinton administration, a move that angered many of the other delegations and poisoned the atmosphere for the remainder of the conference. The Bush administration refused to make any concessions to strengthen the treaty or take any moves toward disarmament negotiations, and the conference ended without coming to an agreement on any statement. Harald Muller, director of the Peace Research Institute in Frankfurt, Germany, argues that throughout the process the Bush administration showed its clear disdain for multilateralism and international law and that the decisive responsibility for the failure of the conference rested with the United States.[148]

The Bush administration also stoked Russian fears by withdrawing from the ABM treaty (which President Putin referred to as the "cornerstone" of arms control) and endorsing the eastern expansion of NATO. In a June 2001 tour of Europe, which included several stops in Eastern Europe, President Bush made it clear that NATO expansion "was no longer a question of whether but a question of when," stating that "Russia should not fear the expansion of freedom-loving people toward her borders."[149] While Putin and Bush had a friendly relationship with each other, the Russian president made it clear at their meeting in Genoa in July 2001 that his country had great concerns about both the issue of missile defense and the enlargement of NATO. But as Ritter notes, "The Bush administration shrugged off the Russian protests as largely irrelevant, since in their view Russia was not in a position economically or militarily to challenge the United States."[150] Russian concerns increased even more when NATO extended invitations to more Eastern European countries (Bulgaria, Slovakia, and Slovenia) and the Baltic states, while also taking on a more militaristic stance by providing some support for the U.S. invasions of Afghanistan (2002) and Iraq (2003). But it was not until 2007, at the Munich Security Conference, that Putin began to "publicly challenge NATO expansion and call for a more inclusive international security framework that should include Russia and China."[151] The Russian leader did not see the world order as unipolar.

Bush did manage to sign one formal arms control agreement with Russia, the Strategic Offensive Reductions Treaty (SORT), also known as the Moscow Treaty. Presidents Bush and Putin signed SORT in Moscow on May 24, 2002. The two sides agreed to deploy not more than 1,700 to 2,200 strategic warheads by the end of 2012. But the agreement did not restrict the number of delivery vehicles that could be retained or require the destruction of a single warhead. The Bush administration claimed that it had reduced the operational warheads in the U.S. arsenal to 2,200, but the pact allowed another 2,400 warheads to be held in reserve, ready to be returned to service in a matter of weeks. As Ritter charged, "It appeared that the Bush administration was using arms control as a cover for maintaining a larger, more robust nuclear capability than publicly advertised."[152] Other critics pointed out that "the treaty totals less than 500 words, repudiates key arms-control principles and achievements, eschews predictability, and compounds the proliferation dangers from Russia's unsecured nuclear weapons complex."[153] With the weak SORT agreement, its decision to withdraw from the ABM treaty, its support for NATO expansion, its opposition to the CTBT, its inability to devise a successor agreement before START I expired, its failure to negotiate with North Korea, and its lies about Saddam Hussein's alleged WMDs leading to the illegal invasion of Iraq in 2003, the actions of the Bush administration "resulted in the virtual destruction of the framework of disarmament and nonproliferation that was supposed to enhance U.S. and world security in the post–Cold War era."[154] The George W. Bush presidency did more to squander the gift of time than any other administration, leaving in its wake a plethora of state nuclear crimes.

AFTER PRAGUE: NEW START, MODERNIZATION, AND PRESIDENT OBAMA'S PARADOX

After his grand Prague pledge to seek a world without nuclear weapons, President Obama would take a variety of steps to move the United States in that direction. The most important step he would take was to sign a New START agreement with Russia in 2010 that limited deployed warheads to 1,550. But to get the new treaty ratified by the Senate, Obama would have to make a deal with key Republican senators that would eventually commit the United States to spend more than a trillion dollars over thirty years to "modernize" and then expand the nuclear weapons arsenal. This modernization decision would undermine his Prague Promise and prevent him from making any real progress in reducing the nuclear threat. President Obama would be able to nibble around the edges of U.S. nuclear policy to make some changes to Bush-era policies, negotiate a nuclear deal with Iran, and reinvigorate the debate over a no-first-use pledge, but in the end he too would fail to make any significant difference in the continued possession and threat to use nuclear weapons by the United States.

After Prague, the first indication of where the Obama administration might go with its nuclear weapons policy was revealed in early April 2010, when it released the now congressionally mandated U.S. NPR. Compared to the NPR of the previous administration that expanded the role of nuclear weapons and the conditions under which they could be used, the Obama NPR significantly reduced the reliance on nuclear weapons in the national security strategy of the United States.[155] Taking into account the geopolitical changes in the world since the end of the Cold War, including the disastrous 2003 invasion of Iraq, the Obama NPR stressed that the fundamental role of nuclear weapons is one of deterrence rather than preventive use, and accordingly restricted the conditions under which these weapons could be used. The 2010 NPR also stated that the United States would no longer conduct nuclear testing and would not develop new nuclear warheads, as had been done under the Bush administration. Furthermore, under President Bush the distinction between chemical, biological, and nuclear weapons had been blurred, therefore ignoring the globally catastrophic consequences of nuclear weapons. The Obama NPR, however, reasserted the distinction, recognizing the unique and devastating nature of nuclear weapons.[156]

During the review process there was a heated debate within the Obama national security team over the question of whether to declare a policy of "no-first-use" in the NPR, a pledge that the United States would never be the first to use nuclear weapons in any conflict. As Kaplan notes, "This would mark a reversal of American policy dating back to the dawn of the nuclear age."[157] Every president in the post–World War II era had asserted a right to respond to any conventional attack on the United States or its allies with nuclear weapons, especially a Soviet attack on NATO countries in Western Europe. According to Kaplan, "This was the essence of 'extended deterrence' and the 'nuclear umbrella'; it was the centerpiece of America's treaty obligations, especially to the allies in NATO."[158] President Obama, firmly opposed to any first use of nuclear weapons, wanted to include the pledge in the NPR to signal to the world (and his own generals) that he really did mean what he said in Prague—that the United States was going to reduce its reliance on these weapons. Facing stiff internal resistance from the national security state, Obama eventually compromised on the issue. The final report committed the United States to no longer using or threatening to use nuclear weapons against states that are signatories to the NPT and are abiding by their treaty obligations. However, this "negative security assurance" (as the NPR called it) was not extended to countries that are not part of the NPT or are not in compliance with the treaty, most notably Iran and North Korea at that time. Nonetheless, the limited prohibition on first use in the 2010 NPR represented a beginning step toward ending the American state crime of threatening to use nuclear weapons.

But in the larger picture, this commitment was only a baby step toward achieving the grand goal of "a world without nuclear weapons." It did little to advance the cause of nuclear abolition. Furthermore, continuing to privilege deterrence as the fundamental role of nuclear weapons still necessitated that the arsenal be maintained, secured, and sustained. To strike a balance between maintaining weapons while working to reduce them, the Obama NPR further advocated for a reliable Stockpile Management Program to extend the life of existing nuclear weapons. While the Obama administration argued that such a program to lengthen the life of current nuclear weapons would thus reduce the development of new ones (a position that the president would be forced to backtrack on later), it more importantly illustrates that the deterrent role of nuclear weapons functions as a convenient justification for the continued possession of and threat to use them.

Perhaps the most important achievement of President Obama's first term was to change the tone of the conversation concerning foreign policy in general and nuclear weapons in particular. The Prague speech and other early foreign policy addresses were intended to create the space to solve problems related to international peace and security. Prague not only laid out a shining long-range vision of a world free of nuclear weapons but also created the atmosphere that would allow progress to be made on numerous concrete issues related to arms control and nonproliferation. Related to this change in tone was Obama's determination to reengage the world to restore the practice of diplomacy. The essence of President Obama's early foreign policy was to forge "a new relationship with the world based on mutual interest and mutual respect."[159] After the aggressive unilateralism and disdain for international forums that characterized the Bush years, Obama's strategy was to "reinvigorate international organizations and establish breathing room for progress across a broad front."[160] This effort was perhaps the key reason why Obama was awarded the Nobel Peace Prize in 2009.

This change in tone and the restoration of diplomatic engagement led to at least one concrete positive result early on—the signing of a New START treaty with Russia that succeeded the 1991 pact between the two countries. Presidents Obama and Dmitry Medvedev signed the accord on April 8, 2010. The treaty made modest progress by committing each country to reducing their arsenals by 30 percent before 2017. Moreover, the treaty stipulated that each country was to limit their deployed warheads to

1,550 as well as capping the number of delivery vehicles (such as missiles, submarines, and bombers) at 800. In addition to reduction quotas, the treaty also called for the continuation of weapons inspections for both counties to ensure those goals would be reached.

Following Bush administration policies that resembled those of the Cold War era, some informed observers claimed that the New START treaty constituted "the resetting of an important button."[161] Yet while the reductions by both countries were welcome, many argued that they did not go far enough in moving toward nuclear disarmament and the Prague Promise. As Schell pointed out, "After all, the limit *on* the 1,550 is also a permission *for* the 1,550. The arrangement indefinitely leaves intact the essential fact that the United States and Russia are poised to blow each other up many times over, as if the cold war had never ended."[162] On top of this problem, an even more serious setback to the Prague vision arose during the effort to get the treaty ratified in the U.S. Senate.

In addition to the maintenance of such a large nuclear arsenal, the Obama administration also made a contradictory concession aimed at garnering congressional support for the treaty. Powerful Republican senators, such as Jon Kyl and Mitch McConnell, threatened to vote against the ratification of the treaty unless Obama promised to support lavish additions to the nuclear budget. The Republicans had gained six seats in the Senate as the result of the 2010 midterm elections and threatened to block the treaty without major concessions on the president's part. Republicans supported the war industry's claim that "a massive overhaul of the U.S. nuclear weapons complex" was needed, justifying it as "rebuilding a crumbling nuclear weapons infrastructure."[163] To save the treaty, Obama gave in and pledged to spend $180 billion over the next ten years to upgrade and modernize the nuclear weapons complex.[164] The administration also made a controversial commitment to a limited missile defense program. After these concessions were extracted, the U.S. Senate ratified the New START accord on December 22, 2010, by a vote of 71–26. As Kaplan concluded, "Obama got the nuclear arms treaty. Kyl got a down payment on the next round of the nuclear arms race."[165] More demands from the nuclear-industrial complex would follow.

After he signed New START in early April 2010, President Obama hoped to foster even more global cooperation on critical nuclear weapons issues. The following week, leaders from forty-seven countries converged on Washington, D.C., for a Nuclear Security Summit. Although this summit had little to do with the administration's position on the U.S. nuclear arsenal, it was one more sign of Obama's concern with the overall issue of nuclear weapons. The announced goal of the summit was to evaluate the threat of nuclear terrorism and establish a plan of action for the next four years.

Then in May, the NPT Review Conference was held in New York. After the Bush administration's undermining of the 2005 Review Conference, participant states in the monthlong 2010 conference were under a great deal of pressure to reach consensus and reaffirm the three pillars of the NPT: nonproliferation, disarmament, and peaceful nuclear energy. Wrought with compromise and contention, the Final Document produced in the last hours of the conference set out a concrete twenty-two-point Action Plan on nuclear disarmament, security assurances, fissile materials, nuclear testing, and other measures in support of disarmament. Moreover, the Final Document also stressed the essential role of the CTBT and the need for signatories, including the United States, to ratify the treaty. However, dashing the hopes of non–nuclear weapons states (NNWS) for a 2025 deadline for total elimination of nuclear weapons, the nuclear weapons states (NWS) agreed only to a more diluted commitment to "accelerate concrete progress" toward nuclear disarmament and to report back on advancement in 2014, a year before the next scheduled review.[166] Thus, while the 2010 Review Conference did little to move the international political community toward a world without nuclear weapons as envisioned by Obama in Prague, the Final Document did reaffirm past NPT commitments, which was sorely needed in light of the failures of the 2005 Review Conference.

After the New START treaty was finally ratified by the Senate, President Obama hoped to engage in further arms control negotiations with Russia. However, Moscow chose not to participate in further bilateral negotiations. Again, it was the U.S. fixation on missile defense and political resistance to discuss any limits to such a system that blocked new talks.[167] Russia was also demanding a multilateral negotiation involving other nuclear powers such as China and France. In 2012, there was also a significant change in Russian leadership. Vladimir Putin, who as prime minister had never completely relinquished control to President Medvedev in 2008, was elected president again. As Kaplan reports, "Putin began reversing some of Medvedev's more accommodating policies," and "he began rebuilding the military and modernizing his nuclear missiles."[168] And while Obama and Putin would work together to try to resolve the crisis over alleged chemical weapons use in Syria and facilitate a nuclear weapons deal in Iran—the Joint Comprehensive Plan of Action or JCPOA—their "nascent cooperation" would be "undermined by events in Ukraine in 2014."[169] Putin's annexation of Crimea and U.S. support for the 2014 coup in Ukraine along with NATO expansion would spark a new Cold War and set Russia, Ukraine, and its Western allies on the path to a frightening hot war that would revive the nuclear danger in 2022.

In May 2016, as President Obama's second term was winding down, he traveled to Japan to visit the site where the ominous nuclear age had begun in 1945—the first American president to ever do so. In Hiroshima, as a bookend to the speech he gave in Prague at the beginning of his presidency, Obama repeated his call for the elimination of nuclear weapons. In graceful, soaring rhetoric, he implored the global community to "change our mindset about war itself," to seek "peaceful cooperation and not violent conflict," and to "define our nations not by our capacity to destroy, but by what we can build."[170] The elegant speech moved American author John Feffer to ruefully conclude that "Obama's approach to nukes will be his most significant legacy—as well as his most salient failure."[171] From Prague to Hiroshima, he argued, Obama's clear, consistent, and forceful call for a world free of nuclear weapons, and some of his policy accomplishments to that end (like the JCPOA with Iran), constitute his most enduring and significant legacy. But, in addition to these positives, Feffer notes, we must also consider his salient failures—Obama's paradox—the decisions and political omissions that leave us still facing apocalyptic nuclear danger today.[172]

Obama's failures include the inability to follow up the New START accord with any other arms control agreement with Russia. Furthermore, after the administration conducted a review of the U.S. strategic war plan (the Single Integrated Operational Plan or SIOP) and concluded that security requirements "would allow" reductions "by up to one-third" from the limits that were set in the New START, it took no action.[173] In the follow-up Nuclear Employment Strategy, unveiled in June 2013 and based on a previous classified document, the Obama administration decided that there would be no such unilateral cut. As Kaplan points out, "in its recitation of the core principles of nuclear deterrence and nuclear warfighting, the document was much the same as those produced by previous administrations."[174] Not only would all three legs of the triad be maintained, but U.S. nuclear weapons would be "modernized" following President Obama's deal with Senate Republicans to secure ratification of the New START. Obama then confounded this disastrous decision during his second term by once again bowing to Republican Party and war industry pressure and authorizing yet another plan to modernize, and expand with new weapons, the American nuclear arsenal.[175]

Despite Obama's Prague Promise and his eloquent rhetoric in Hiroshima, the United States under his administration would continue to possess thousands of nuclear weapons in violation of Article VI of the NPT. Not only would the United States continue to possess these indefensible weapons, but it would also spend billions of dollars to modernize and expand them. This was President Obama's Nuclear Paradox. His promising rhetoric was undercut by harsh political and ideological realities. Trapped in the institutions and culture of the American Empire, its goals of military supremacy and geopolitical domination, its national security state, its nuclear-industrial complex, and its culture of exceptionalism and nuclearism, Obama—despite his personal vision and commitment to abolishing nuclear weapons—was unable to alter these historical social structures and reverse the crimes of the American nuclear state.

CHAPTER 7

Current Apocalyptic Threats, the American Empire, and a Pathway to the Abolition of Nuclear Weapons

Can our social imagination, our governing institutions, and our political courage catch up with our ever-accelerating scientific and technological prowess? Nowhere is that challenge presented more starkly, nowhere are the stakes conceivably higher, than in the challenge of abolishing nuclear weapons, and saving ourselves from nuclear apocalypse.
—Tad Daley, *Apocalypse Never*

And abolition alone can, by ending the nuclear double standard, stop proliferation and make effective the existing bans on other weapons of mass destruction. The logic of abolition is the real alternative to the logic of empire.
—Jonathan Schell, *The Unconquerable World*

THIS BOOK HAS analyzed the making of international laws related to nuclear weapons, the breaking of these laws by the United States and other nuclear powers, and various efforts to create social and political controls in response to these state crimes. In my attempt to develop a criminology of nuclear weapons I have drawn on the scholarship of international law experts, historians, and social scientists, presenting the abundant empirical evidence and incisive theoretical analyses they have produced. The conclusions of these scholars are stark and clear:

1. nuclear weapons pose an existential threat to human civilization;
2. the use of, threat to use, and continued possession of these deadly devices are illegal under international law; and
3. these apocalyptic weapons must be abolished by the international political community.

While I have made every effort to incorporate and synthesize the most recent and up-to-date scholarship on these critical issues and offer a contemporary criminological analysis based on this extensive theory and research, the conclusions are not new. These are the same conclusions I arrived at in the early 1980s when I first examined the literature on nuclear weapons.

After the birth of my first child in 1980, concerned with his future, I became alarmed by the belligerent rhetoric and nuclear arms buildup of the Reagan administration that intensified Cold War tensions and escalated the risk of nuclear war. In response to the confrontational and warmongering approach of President Ronald Reagan to the Soviet Union, I began to study the nuclear weapons issue and became active in the disarmament movement. Influenced by the Catholic peace movement in general, the specific Plowshares nonviolent civil disobedience actions of the Berrigan brothers (Daniel and Philip) and their colleagues, and the rising nuclear freeze campaign, my wife and I (along with our young son) attended the massive anti–nuclear weapons rally and march in New York City on June 12, 1982. I came back from New York determined to continue to study and be active on this critical issue.

Then in September 1982, I attended two inspiring presentations that had a huge impact on my evolution into a scholar-activist on the nuclear weapons issue. At the Society for the Study of Social Problems meeting in San Francisco, I attended a lecture by the Pentagon Papers whistleblower Daniel Ellsberg, now speaking out against the nuclear threat (which he continued to do until his death in 2023). After listening to the passionate and eloquent Ellsberg, I wrote in my personal journal that I needed "to renew my commitment to nuclear disarmament." My transition into a scholar-activist concerning the nuclear danger accelerated when I attended a conference on "The Prevention of Nuclear War" at Western Michigan University (WMU), which featured a keynote address by the famed psychiatrist and public intellectual Robert Jay Lifton. I was very moved by Lifton's inspirational presentation, and I wrote in my journal the next day that I saw him "as somewhat of a role model—a dedicated social scientist writing, teaching, and speaking out on this critical political issue. With a little more preparation," I noted optimistically, "I, too, could speak out about nuclear weapons from a critical sociological perspective."

In his section of the influential book *Indefensible Weapons: The Political and Psychological Case Against Nuclearism* (written with international law scholar Richard Falk), Lifton observes, "In order to relinquish a stance of immobilization—or the various combinations of resignation, cynicism, and waiting for the bomb—each person seems to have to cross a certain line, on the other side of which is some degree of commitment in one's life toward combatting the nuclear threat."[1] By beginning to study the legal, political, and historical literature on nuclear weapons, attending the march and rally in New York City, listening to the encouraging messages of Ellsberg and Lifton, and becoming active in the local nuclear freeze campaign, I crossed that line in 1982. The following year, I became the chief organizer of "Celebrate Life: A Week of Education and Action to Prevent Nuclear War" held at WMU. I invited one of my heroes, Senator George McGovern, to be the keynote speaker, and the former presidential candidate offered an eloquent and forceful address. The "Celebrate Life" committee also organized local lectures, discussion groups, a film series, and a march from the WMU campus to Bronson Park in downtown Kalamazoo for a rally at the end of the week. We raised thousands of dollars to support the week of education and action, and with the money left over established a chapter of United Campuses to Prevent Nuclear War (UCAM), an offshoot of the Union of Concerned Scientists. The WMU UCAM would continue to organize anti–nuclear weapons protests and educational activities for many years.

In addition to this anti–nuclear weapons activism, I also began to write and publish academic journal articles and books about the sociology and criminology of nuclear weapons. With my friend Sam Marullo (then a professor of sociology at Cleveland State University, later at Georgetown University), I coedited a special feature on "The Sociology of Nuclear Threat" in 1985 for the *Sociological Quarterly*. Sam and I also wrote the lead article for the special feature "Toward a Sociology of Nuclear Weapons."[2] In that article, we reviewed previous sociological work on nuclear weapons, outlined some topics ripe for investigation on the issue, and offered a general call for sociological theory and research on the nuclear threat. Responding to this call for scholarship on nuclear weapons issues, one of my graduate students at the time, David Kauzlarich (now professor of sociology at the University of North Carolina at Greensboro), and I wrote several journal articles and an academic book, *Crimes of the American Nuclear State*, on some of these topics.[3] In these scholarly works, Kauzlarich and I used international law as the legal framework for bringing state actions related to nuclear weapons within the boundaries of criminology, and we later analyzed the criminological implications of the opinion of the International Court of Justice on the illegality of nuclear weapons in a subsequent journal article.[4]

By "crossing the line" and engaging in these significant projects related to the nuclear threat, my fellow activists and academic colleagues and I felt, to use Professor Lifton's words, a new sense of "shared power" and the "possibility" of bringing about "collective change." We found these protest activities and our scholarship to be life-affirming. As Lifton expressed it, "While confronting massive death is irreducibly grim, we find ourselves more in touch with what we care most about in life—with love, sensuality, creative realization, and the capacity for life projects that have meaning and satisfaction for us. We find ourselves in no way on a death trip, but rather responding to a call for personal and professional actions and commitments on behalf of that wonderous and fragile entity we know as human life."[5]

Not only did we find anti–nuclear weapons work to be life-affirming and emotionally satisfying, we seemed to be having a real political impact as well. The nuclear freeze movement played a significant role in pushing the hawkish President Reagan to the negotiating table, and with the signing of the INF treaty in 1987 by Reagan and Gorbachev, international tensions eased. Then, to the surprise of many activists and political observers, the Soviet Union disintegrated and the Cold War ended in 1991. The World Court ruling on the illegality of nuclear weapons in 1996—confirming the conclusions of many legal scholars—and the steady drawdown of nuclear weapons stockpiles in the 1990s created a sense among disarmament activists and many in the international political community that the nuclear danger was gone. The world appeared to breathe a sigh of relief, and by the end of the twentieth century the nuclear threat as a critical issue would fade from public consciousness. It was at this point that Jonathan Schell would argue that the gift of time had arrived,[6] and the abolition of nuclear weapons seemed like a real possibility.

But as this book has documented, the gift of time was squandered and nuclear disarmament did not occur. The nuclear danger remained, even though it mostly lurked below the level of popular consciousness. After writing a book about the existential threat of climate change in 2020, I decided to return to the other major apocalyptic threat—the critical issue of the nuclear danger. And as I read the more recent literature, I found that, in general, not much had changed. Even today, after the Russian invasion of Ukraine and Putin's repeated nuclear threats, the possibility of nuclear war does not make the top ten list of the American public's biggest fears.[7] Nuclear weapons, now being modernized and expanded, still pose an existential threat to human civilization. The use of, threat to use, and continued possession of these deadly devices are still illegal under international law and have now been completely banned with the entry into force of the Treaty on the Prohibition of Nuclear Weapons. The Doomsday Clock still exists and has now moved closer to midnight than ever before, especially with the new nuclear danger created by the war in Ukraine. And it is still the case that the overriding conclusion of disarmament activists and legal scholars alike is that these apocalyptic weapons must be abolished by the international political community. Most importantly, "a global grassroots movement calling for nuclear restraint and human survival" is still deemed critical if the world is to achieve the abolition of nuclear weapons and survive.[8]

But the large-scale political movement to abolish these indefensible weapons, which has ebbed and flowed since 1945, must do more than just win what Falk calls the "legitimacy wars."[9] The disarmament movement has been able to repeatedly win these wars and seize the moral high ground, but its strategies and tactics of nonviolent resistance, while winning some partial political and legal victories along the way, have not prevailed in convincing or forcing the nuclear states to give up their weapons. A stronger global movement, one that is capable of bringing about structural change at the international level, is necessary. As Falk has pointed out, "In effect, the vertical dimension of world order needs to become subject to the discipline of international criminal law for the sake of human wellbeing, and ICL needs to be expanded to include Geopolitical Crimes."[10]

And going beyond international criminal law, Falk also argues that we need to "consider the case for the transformation of world order so as to achieve a just, democratic, and effective form of global governance."[11] He refers to this form of world order as "humane global governance," adding "the word 'humane' so as to give attention to the importance of developing desirable types of order and stress the pervasive relevance of ethics and human rights in designing global reforms."[12] But Falk concludes, "The possibility of a humane form of global governance is dependent on democratizing participation and accountability, as well as transcending nationalism and statism, which means a form of global governance that is post-Westphalian, privileging people over market and state, which is to say, the emergence of a new structure and normative mandate for world order."[13] Abolishing nuclear weapons depends on achieving the visionary future Professor Falk proposes. But before we address that great challenge and describe some concrete steps the international community could take to move toward that critical goal, it is important to first acknowledge and describe the current nuclear dangers that the world faces.

CURRENT APOCALYPTIC THREATS

The most significant apocalyptic threat confronting the world today is the fact that the nine nuclear weapons states continue to possess roughly 12,500 warheads and threaten to use them either for the sake of general "deterrence" or in specific conflict situations—such as the war in Ukraine. As the Federation of American Scientists points out in a report on the "Status of World Nuclear Forces" (updated March 28, 2023), of these 12,500 warheads, the United States and Russia combined "possess approximately 89 percent of the world's total inventory of nuclear weapons, and 86 percent of the stockpiled warheads available for use by the military."[14] The other seven nuclear-armed states each possess no more than a few hundred nuclear weapons for "national security," although, according to the FAS, "many of these states are increasing their nuclear stockpiles."[15] But the biggest offenders continue to be the United States and Russia, and I primarily focus on them.

The "Nuclear Notebook," which is researched and written by Hans M. Kristensen, director of the Nuclear Information Project with the Federation of American Scientists—along with senior research associates Matt Korda and Eliana Reynolds—is published occasionally in the *Bulletin of the Atomic Scientists* to provide a current assessment of the number of nuclear weapons held by the two major powers. Kristensen and Korda report that "at the beginning of 2023, the United States Department of Defense maintained an estimated stockpile of approximately 3,708 nuclear warheads for delivery by ballistic missiles and aircraft."[16] They point out that most of these warheads (1,938) are not deployed but are stored for potential upload onto these delivery vehicles as needed. Kristensen and Korda estimate that approximately 1,770 warheads in the stockpile are currently "deployed" (1,370 on ballistic missiles and 300 at strategic bomber bases), with "an additional 100 tactical bombs deployed at air bases in Europe."[17] The other warheads in the stockpile "are in storage as a so-called hedge against technical or geopolitical surprises."[18] In addition to the DOD stockpile, another 1,536 warheads (intact but retired and waiting dismantlement) are stored by the Department of Energy. According to the "Nuclear Notebook," this adds up to a total U.S. inventory of 5,244 warheads in 2023.[19]

On the other hand, according to Kristensen, Korda, and Reynolds, "Russia has a stockpile of approximately 4,489 nuclear warheads assigned for use by long-range strategic launchers and shorter-range tactical forces."[20] Of this total stockpile, approximately 1,674 strategic warheads are deployed—834 on land-based ballistic missiles, 640 on submarine-launched

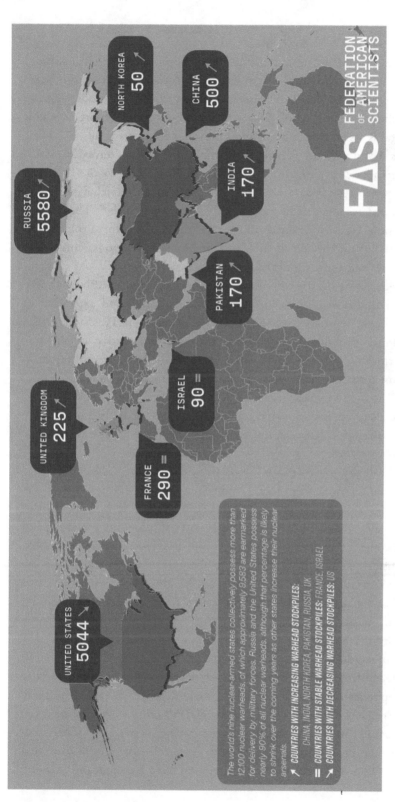

Hans M. Kristensen, Matt Korda, Eliana Johns, and Mackenzie Knight, "Estimated Global Nuclear Warhead Inventories, 2024." Courtesy Federation of American Scientists. Note: Numbers show estimated total nuclear warhead inventories, which include stockpiled warheads for use by military forces, warheads held in reserve, and retired warheads in queue for dismantlement. Of the 9,583 warheads in global military stockpiles, about 3,880 are deployed on ballistic missiles and at bomber bases. Approximately 2,000 warheads on ballistic missiles are on alert and can be launched on short notice.

ballistic missiles (SLBMs), and 200 at heavy bomber bases.[21] In addition, Russia has 999 strategic warheads and 1,816 nonstrategic warheads in storage, with another 1,400 retired, but still largely intact, warheads awaiting dismantlement. According to a 2023 "Nuclear Notebook" report, this adds up to a total Russian inventory of approximately 5,889 warheads.[22] Adding in China's 410 warheads, France's 290, the United Kingdom's 225, Pakistan's 170, India's 164, Israel's 90, and North Korea's 30 to the U.S. and Russian arsenals, the Federation of American Scientists concludes that the nine nuclear states together possess roughly 12,500 warheads.[23] The continued possession of these weapons, in violation of the Nuclear Non-Proliferation Treaty (NPT) and the Treaty to Prohibit Nuclear Weapons, constitutes both a state crime and an apocalyptic threat.

The existential risk that these weapons pose is heightened by a variety of political factors and social forces: the modernization and expansion of nuclear arsenals; tensions between the United States and Russia (over the war in Ukraine and other issues); the increasingly competitive and antagonistic relationship between the United States and China; an authoritarian and unconstitutional chain of command concerning the weapons; the possibility of the use of nuclear weapons by either rogue states or nonstate terrorists; the chance of nuclear warfare by accident, miscalculation, or mistake; and finally, the nexus between nuclear weapons and the climate crisis.

MODERNIZATION AND EXPANSION

As if the continued existence of the current nuclear arsenals of the United States and Russia did not pose enough of an apocalyptic threat, there are major efforts underway in both states to modernize and expand their stockpiles of nuclear weapons. As the previous chapter described, under political pressure from hawkish neoconservative ideologues and the nuclear-industrial complex, both George W. Bush and Barack Obama advanced costly plans to overhaul and rebuild the U.S. nuclear weapons production infrastructure. Rather than take advantage of the gift of time provided by the end of the Cold War to move toward disarmament, the Bush administration, in pursuit of imperial goals, aggressively attempted to modernize existing nuclear weapons facilities and build new ones.[24] And to garner Republican support in the U.S. Senate for the New START treaty in 2010, President Obama pledged to spend $180 billion over the next ten years to upgrade and modernize the nuclear weapons complex.[25] Then during his second term, Obama further undermined his Prague Promise of a world free of nuclear weapons by again giving in to Republican Party and war industry pressure and authorizing yet another disastrous and even more costly plan to modernize and expand the American nuclear arsenal.[26]

These efforts at modernization and expansion of the American nuclear arsenal continued under both Donald Trump and Joe Biden. The Trump administration announced in 2018 that it intended to replace or rebuild all three legs of the U.S. strategic triad—intercontinental ballistic missiles (ICBMs), SLBMs, and long-range bombers—at an estimated total cost of $1.7 trillion. In a statement to the House Armed Services Committee on February 6, 2018, Secretary of Defense Jim Mattis wrote that "to remain effective . . . we must *recapitalize our Cold War legacy nuclear deterrent forces*, continuing a modernization program initiated during the previous administration."[27] In a companion move in 2019, the administration then withdrew from the Intermediate Nuclear Forces (INF) Treaty that had been negotiated by Ronald Reagan and Mikhail Gorbachev in 1987. As Klare explained, "Refurbishing the nuclear arsenal and exiting arms-control agreements are all part of a White House effort to restore the coercive power of the U.S. stockpile."[28] The Trump administration's specific plans for overhauling America's nuclear weapons infrastructure were laid out in its 2018 Nuclear Posture Review (NPR). Since the administration viewed nuclear arms as "the ultimate tool of national power," a refurbished arsenal was necessary to "allow the United States to threaten and intimidate countries that either lack such weapons or rely on the US for its 'nuclear umbrella'—as do most NATO powers and Japan."[29] Such imperial beliefs and actions concerning the bomb on the part of powerful state officials represent a clear apocalyptic threat.

While the Biden administration adopted a far less belligerent tone, it too continued the modernization and expansion programs of previous U.S. administrations. In a major disappointment for abolitionists and arms control advocates, the administration's 2022 NPR "supports retention of a triad and continued investments in all existing major modernization programs including land-based, sea-based, air-based, command and control, and some supplemental capabilities."[30] These investments will be quite costly. In a January 2023 update, the Center for Arms Control and Non-Proliferation reports that the United States "plans to spend up to $1.5 trillion over 30 years to overhaul its nuclear arsenal by rebuilding each leg of the nuclear triad and its accompanying infrastructure."[31] The Pentagon justifies the nuclear modernization plans as a necessary response to the activities of Russia and China, both of which are also engaged in modernization and expansion programs, and perhaps assisting each other in these efforts.[32] Unlike the Trump NPR of 2018, the Biden NPR of 2022 put a renewed emphasis on arms control, nonproliferation, and risk reduction. It should also be noted that the Biden administration was able to negotiate an extension of the New START treaty with Russia until 2026, although this came before the Russian invasion of Ukraine and the diplomatic disruptions it caused.

In the final analysis, however, President Biden's nuclear policy was a huge disappointment to disarmament experts and activists. As Lisbeth Gronlund, research affiliate with the Department of Nuclear Science and Engineering at MIT, asserted, "This NPR is a repudiation of Obama's pledge to seek the peace and security of a world without nuclear weapons. It is shocking that President Biden signed off on this document."[33] While the general appeal of President Obama's Prague Promise remains, the fact is that every president in the twenty-first century has supported some form of nuclear modernization, including Obama. Whether to advance an imperial agenda of domination, engage in an arms race with Russia and China, respond to political pressure from the military-industrial complex, or express an ideological belief related to nuclearism, this support has been strong and consistent. The result is the exact opposite of abolition. Instead of getting rid of the weapons, as required under international law, not only do nuclear arsenals remain available for use, but their killing power is also dramatically enhanced due to revolutionary new technologies that increase targeting capability.[34] As Daniel Ellsberg and Norman Solomon insist, concerning plans to build new ground-based ICBMs, "to avoid Armageddon, don't modernize missiles—eliminate them."[35] Modernization of any kind only heightens the nuclear danger.

Tensions between the United States and Russia

Tensions between the United States and Russia (most recently over the war in Ukraine) also heighten the nuclear danger. By 2024, as the bloody conflict grinded on, many informed observers argued that the longer this war continues, the greater the nuclear risk grows. The nuclear danger caused by the Russian invasion of Ukraine was highlighted in early 2023 by the *Bulletin of the Atomic Scientists* when it moved its Doomsday Clock ahead ten more seconds to ninety seconds before midnight (nuclear apocalypse), the closest the clock has ever been to "global catastrophe." As noted in chapter 1, the *Bulletin* moved the hands forward "largely (though not exclusively) because of the mounting dangers of the war in Ukraine."[36] Calling Putin's thinly veiled threats to use tactical nuclear weapons in the war "a terrible risk," the *Bulletin* warned, "The possibility that the conflict could spin out of anyone's control remains high."[37] In January 2024, the *Bulletin* kept the clock at ninety seconds before midnight, but in its Doomsday Clock Statement declared that "our decision should not be taken as a sign that the international security situation has eased."[38]

Tensions between the United States and Russia over Ukraine have also threatened the New START (Strategic Arms Reduction Treaty). The treaty was extended by both countries in 2021 but then suspended by Putin in 2023 in response to the sanctions imposed on Russia following the invasion of Ukraine. This important treaty is the last remaining nuclear weapons agreement between the two countries and is set to expire in 2026. A continuation of war in Ukraine threatens the renewal of New START.

The threat of the use of tactical nuclear weapons in Ukraine, and the fear that it could spiral into a terminal nuclear exchange between the major powers, led to increasing calls for a ceasefire, de-escalatory talks, and some form of negotiated settlement.[39] However, as of August 2024, no serious peace negotiations were underway. On the contrary, the United States seemed determined to use the war to weaken the Russian military and perhaps achieve some sort of "victory."[40] Again, the fear is that the longer the war drags on, the more likely it is to spin out of control and lead to the catastrophic use of nuclear weapons. As the editors of *The Nation* argued, "The sooner this war can be brought to an end, the better for the entire world."[41] At the time of this writing in the summer of 2024, it is impossible to predict what will happen regarding the war in Ukraine. But it is clear that this war and continuing tensions between the United States and Russia over the conflict and related issues like NATO expansion pose an apocalyptic threat that must be addressed and resolved in some form. Aside from the specific dangers posed by the hostilities in Ukraine, Benjamin and Davies point to a larger critical issue overriding the conflict, noting that, however the war in Ukraine eventually ends, "it has underlined the continuing imperative for nuclear disarmament, and no amount of residual hostility can be allowed to prevent the resumption of serious international efforts to forever ban nuclear weapons from the face of the Earth."[42] Indeed, these indefensible and illegal weapons must be abolished.

The Relationship between the United States and China

While the escalating hostility between the United States and Russia represents an apocalyptic threat, the increasingly competitive and confrontational relationship between the United States and the People's Republic of

China (PRC) has also increased the nuclear danger. In the late twentieth and early twenty-first centuries, China emerged as a "rising power" with a "fundamental transformation" of its economy and an "extraordinary record of growth."[43] Alfred McCoy has described how the PRC has executed a farsighted geopolitical strategy to increasingly gain control of Eurasia, resulting in the erosion of America's global power.[44] Concerning the future of the world order, he argues that, "at present, China is the sole state to have most (but not all) of the requisites to become a new global hegemon."[45] Writing in 2021, McCoy predicted that as U.S. global power continues to decline, a Chinese "world system" will emerge to replace the current American world order.[46] Even though reports of serious economic troubles in China began to surface in 2023,[47] the country remains a superpower and a major player on the geopolitical stage.

U.S. political elites and intelligence analysts have long been aware of the geopolitical challenge that China poses to the imperial dominance of the United States and the current American world order.[48] Shortly after the Russian invasion of Ukraine, U.S. secretary of state Antony Blinken gave a speech in which he claimed that "the foundations of the international order are under serious and sustained challenge"; but rather than dwell on Vladimir Putin, who Blinken did argue was "a clear and present danger," the secretary quickly pivoted to China, "the only country with both the intent to reshape the international order and, increasingly, the economic, diplomatic, military, and technological power to do it."[49] The Biden administration's 2022 National Security Strategy also declared that while Russia was still a dangerous threat to American security, China is now "the only competitor to the U.S." on the global stage.[50] And as China's global power and influence rises, U.S. officials have become increasingly antagonistic in their rhetoric and actions toward the PRC, suggesting that a "New Cold War with China—a period of intense hostility and competition falling just short of armed conflict—has started."[51] Since China is also a major nuclear power, this is an ominous development that constitutes an additional apocalyptic threat.

While the United States has grave concerns about China's human rights abuses, and with many of its trade and energy policies, American political leaders have also become increasingly alarmed about the perceived threat that China's growing military power poses to U.S. security. These geopolitical concerns led President Obama to make a notable "pivot to Asia" in his foreign policy. As McCoy observes, "Well before China's military prowess was so pronounced, President Obama broke with Washington's consensus about a benign Beijing and developed a deft geopolitical strategy to counter China's rise—a pivot of strategic military forces to Asia and a twelve-nation trade pact, the Trans-Pacific Partnership, that was designed to drain Beijing's Eurasian infrastructure of its commercial lifeblood."[52] As China's global power and economic influence continued to rise, Donald Trump declared a "trade war" with the PRC in 2018 and his hard-right foreign policy team used increasingly hostile rhetoric to describe China's People's Liberation Army (PLA) and its nuclear weapons programs.[53] President Biden has continued the tough U.S. line on China's human rights abuses, regional expansionism, and military buildup, announcing the establishment of a Pentagon Task Force on China in 2021.[54] Concerning the so-called encirclement or containment policy being directed at China, Klare argues that "the Biden administration, like the Trump administration before it, has no intention of allowing the PRC to achieve parity with the United States on the world stage . . . and is prepared to employ every means, including military force, to prevent his from happening."[55] A new Cold War seems to have emerged indeed.

It is important to note that China's possession of nuclear weapons (now estimated at roughly 500 warheads by the FAS in 2024),[56] and its current modernization and expansion efforts are also illegal under international law and should be condemned by the world community. As a 2021 *Washington Post* editorial noted, "China is rising as a nuclear power" and "its ambitions warrant global attention."[57] The *Post* cites a Pentagon report that "asserts China may possess up to 700 deliverable nuclear warheads by 2027" and "likely intends to have at least 1,000 by 2030."[58] A recent *New York Times* article also asserts that China is "on track to massively expand its nuclear arsenal," declaring that soon there will be "3 nuclear superpowers, rather than 2," and that this fact will "usher in a new strategic era."[59] As this new Cold War intensifies, these developments are cause for concern.

However, Klare also points out that the Pentagon repeatedly "inflates the Chinese nuclear threat" in an effort "to extract budget increases from Congress."[60] As he reports, in 2021 the Department of Defense focused almost entirely on the military threat posed by the PRC. He goes on to explain, "Sensing that a majority in Congress—Democrats as well as Republicans—are keen to display their determination to blunt China's rise, senior officials are largely framing the military budget around preparation for a possible conflict with that country."[61] Michael Swaine, an analyst with the Quincy Institute for Responsible Statecraft, concurs with Klare, arguing that "threat inflation is a major problem in evaluating

China's military capabilities and the military security-related intentions of China's leadership," adding that American government and media assessments "often employ inadequate, distorted, or incorrect evidence, use grossly hyperbolic language, display sloppy or illogical thinking, or rely on broad-brush assertions that seem to derive more from narrow political, ideological, or emotional impulses than from any objective search for the truth."[62] These exaggerated Pentagon assessments never consider the possibility that China's military buildup may be a realistic and defensive move against what its leaders perceive to be aggressive and imperial actions on the part of the United States. Reflecting on these inflated military assessments, Gerson points out, "There are alternatives to the nationally self-defeating and toxic China threat discourse in Washington, and to fueling an extremely dangerous nuclear arms race with China that could end with nuclear winter and the extermination of nearly all life as we know."[63] But peaceful, common security and diplomatic alternatives to what are perceived as aggressive PRC geopolitical policies are rarely considered by America's imperial elites.

The major risk of a military confrontation between China and the United States would most likely arise over a Chinese effort to take control of Taiwan (established as the Republic of China in 1949 after the Communist takeover of China) and a U.S. military defense of the island. The top leadership of the PRC has long been committed to reunification with Taiwan under its "One China Principle." The question is whether that reunification will come about through peaceful means or through an invasion and warfare. In every major address, President Xi Jinping repeats the "mantra" that China is prepared to "employ force as a last resort to ensure Taiwan's unification with the mainland," while maintaining that the PRC "will continue to strive for peaceful reunification with the greatest sincerity and utmost effort."[64] The "China hawks" in the Pentagon and in Congress argue that a Chinese invasion of Taiwan is "imminent" and that the U.S. military needs to be prepared to defend the island. Klare casts doubt on this prediction and asserts that despite PRC threats and military maneuvering, and today's "frenzied Washington environment—concluding that an invasion is not likely under current circumstances is all too reasonable."[65] Still, despite no formal policy, the United States appears to be firmly committed to coming to the defense of Taiwan should any invasion occur, and President Biden seemed to openly embrace that position, stating bluntly in answer to a question at a 2021 CNN "town hall," "Yes, we have a commitment to do that."[66] Such a commitment, formal or informal, could result in a military conflict with China and, in the worst-case scenario, become a "nuclear flashpoint."[67]

An Authoritarian Chain of Command— "Thermonuclear Monarchy"

In addition to great power competitions, another significant and recurrent threat related to the continued existence of nuclear weapons is that the decision whether to use these apocalyptic weapons is under the authoritarian control of a very small number of state officials who occupy the highest positions in the nuclear chain of command. This "thermonuclear monarchy," as American essayist Elaine Scarry calls it, "enables a tiny number of people (one, fifty-three, or two hundred twelve) to annihilate millions of people."[68] The fate of the earth ultimately rests on the decision-making ability and emotional and mental stability of a few human beings (such as the presidents of the United States, Russia, and China) and the accurate flow of critical information and competent advice they receive from the military command and control systems they head.

The gravest decision in human history, the decision to press the "nuclear button," is structurally designed to be an authoritarian exercise of power and cannot be made democratically. As American political theorist Langdon Winner has argued, "The atom bomb is an inherently political artifact . . . its lethal properties demand that it be controlled by a centralized, rigidly hierarchical chain of command closed to all influences that might make its workings unpredictable. The internal social system of the bomb must be authoritarian; there is no other way."[69] This structural political reality concerning nuclear weapons is described by Scarry as "a specific and severe form of monarchy because it places the national defense wholly outside the social contract."[70] Thermonuclear monarchy is not only an undemocratic use of military power but also dangerous and immoral. No political leader (no matter how sane and moral), no government (no matter how democratic), no military command (no matter how logical and efficient) has the moral or legal right to use or threaten to use weapons that will annihilate human civilization. Scarry asserts that "thermonuclear monarchy is more grave, more dark, more dangerous than any tyranny that has ever operated on earth."[71] The authoritarian social system of the bomb represents another criminal apocalyptic threat.

While thermonuclear monarchy is a dangerous hallmark of an authoritarian society such as Putin's Russia, it also afflicts the more democratic American system. Within the United States, it was the Manhattan Project and the subsequent use of the atomic bomb against Japan in 1945 that transformed the nation's history, undermined its Constitution, and created what American historian Garry Wills calls an "American Monarch."[72] According to Wills, the development of the bomb under conditions of secrecy and military control, the high level and secretive decision to use it at Hiroshima and Nagasaki, and the continuing possession and threat to use nuclear weapons following the war have altered American history and created what he describes as "Bomb Power."[73] These political and military events redefined the presidency by diminishing the role of Congress, concentrating extreme power in the executive branch, expanding the conception of the role of the commander in chief, promoting the rise of the national security state, and changing the interpretation of the Constitution. As Wills concludes, these historical forces "have moved toward a concentration of power in the presidency, far from the design of the framers of the Constitution, who were determined not to have a monarch like the king they had just rebelled against."[74] The nation's founding document and the political system it created have been illegally transformed by the bomb.

The rise of thermonuclear monarchy in the United States is primarily the result of a significant change in how the Constitution is interpreted, an altered meaning of this political touchstone that illegally allows for the authoritarian control of nuclear weapons by the president as a transformed commander in chief. The U.S. Constitution requires a congressional declaration of war before military action can be commenced. As Scarry notes, Article I, Section 8, Clause 11 "stipulates that the full House and Senate together (the full assembly of representatives) are obligated to oversee the country's entry into war."[75] Once Congress decides that the nation should go to war, then, and only then, does the president become the "commander in chief" of the U.S. military to execute the declared war.

The fact that since World War II Congress has derogated its constitutional responsibility to declare war, and allowed by default a new and expanded conception of the role of the president as commander in chief, does not make it legal. The Constitution is clear—no one person has the power to take the country to war. Any decision to use military force, including the use of nuclear weapons, by the president of the United States without the required declaration of war would violate the law of the land. As Scarry points out, "The observation that presidential first use [of nuclear weapons] violates the constitutional requirement for a congressional declaration of war has been made not only by scholars, religious leaders, congressional plaintiffs, and dissident intellectuals, but also by those at the center of executive power"—for example, "President Eisenhower."[76] But this severe constitutional breach, and the resulting thermonuclear monarchy it created, has become normalized within American political culture and accepted by much of the public. This unconstitutional authoritarian social system related to the decision to go to war poses a grave nuclear risk and must be challenged and changed.

An unlawful and undemocratic thermonuclear monarchy is bad enough when the president is emotionally stable and psychologically sound. It becomes extremely dangerous when the chief executive is unstable and psychologically unfit. This frightful situation arose in 2017 when Donald Trump, considered by many psychiatrists and mental health experts to be dangerously disordered, became president of the United States. Two groups of experts on psychopathology published books of essays that attempted to assess specifically whether Trump was psychologically fit to command the U.S. nuclear arsenal.[77] The answer both groups gave was an emphatic no! These mental health experts felt they had a duty to warn the public that Trump was dangerously unfit and posed an imminent risk of harm related to his control of nuclear weapons. The two groups assessed Trump to be erratic, impulsive, reckless, in cognitive decline, and a predatory narcissist with an attachment for falsehoods. In their expert opinions, the new president was found to be a psychologically disordered man who, unfortunately, now held "a nuclear gun to the world's head."[78] As Cirincione put it, "The greatest danger to America is her Commander in Chief."[79] However, historian Ruth Ben-Ghiat, following Winner's view of the bomb as a political artifact, argued that in her view it was "the history of authoritarianism" that provided "the best framework for understanding Trump's words and actions."[80]

Whether it was due to Trump's psychopathology or his authoritarian bent, his control of the nuclear button generated much "extinction anxiety" among psychiatrists, historians, and nuclear experts in the early years of his term in office.[81] And, having survived Trump's term in office from 2017 to 2021, these analysts are now alarmed at the potential for a second Trump presidency in 2025. As journalist Annie Jacobsen, author of *Nuclear War: A Scenario*, has trenchantly observed (with regard to Donald Trump), "You would want to have a commander-in-chief who is of sound mind, who is fully in control of his mental capacity, who is not volatile, who is not subject to anger."[82] According to the experts, Trump is not psychologically fit to have his finger on the nuclear button. And long term, we need to eliminate the possibility of thermonuclear monarchy itself by abolishing nuclear weapons.

ROGUE STATES, TERRORISTS, AND THE
POSSIBILITY OF MISTAKE

The nuclear danger also includes so-called rogue states that either have (North Korea) or aspire to develop (Iran) nuclear weapons, nonstate actors who might acquire a nuclear device and use it as an act of political terrorism, and the possibility of the accidental use of nuclear weapons by mistake or miscalculation. While all three of these problems pose grave risks, I do not provide an extended analysis of any of them, as the focus of this book is on the state nuclear crimes of the major powers in the geopolitical system. Less powerful states are labeled "rogues" by the major nuclear powers and primarily seek nuclear weapons in response to the weapons and threatening actions of those powers. Terrorist groups are nonstate actors who seek political leverage or revenge in conflicts with powerful states. And while it is the major nuclear powers who are most likely to use their weapons accidentally—American journalist Eric Schlosser points out that "the United States has narrowly avoided a long series of nuclear disasters"[83]—the mistakes or miscalculations that might lead to such a dangerous occurrence would not generally involve direct criminal intent. What unites all three of these potential nuclear threats, however, is that they are possible only due to the continued possession of nuclear weapons by the major powers and could be eliminated by the adherence of these states to the Treaty on the Prohibition of Nuclear Weapons and the abolition of these dangerous devices.

THE NEXUS BETWEEN NUCLEAR WEAPONS
AND CLIMATE CHANGE

Finally, one other critical dimension of the current apocalyptic threats posed by the continuing possession and threat to use nuclear weapons is the linkage of these dangerous weapons with disruptive climate change. The potential for nuclear war and the climate crisis are the two key existential dangers of our time. These two dangers have much in common, and the nexus between them is often ignored.[84] These "apocalyptic twins," as Lifton calls them, represent the "merging of world-ending threats" and should be considered together.[85] We must be concerned with both of these apocalyptic crimes, not only because each is a blameworthy harm that poses an existential threat to the survival of humanity in its own right, but also because they intersect with and intensify the risks of each other in various ways.

Climate Disruptions Make Nuclear War More Likely

One potential interconnection between the nuclear threat and the climate crisis is that climate disruptions may lead to the use of nuclear weapons. Criminologists have long been concerned about the possible relationship between global warming and various forms of criminality,[86] but none of them have explicitly addressed the possibility that these harmful social and political relationships may also result in the use of nuclear weapons.

One scholar who has explored this connection is Michael Klare, who contends that, "all things being equal, rising temperatures will increase the likelihood of nuclear war, largely because climate change will heighten the risk of social stress, the decay of nation-states, and armed violence in general."[87] He points out that the U.S. military is very concerned about the national security threat posed by climate change and concludes, "In the worst-case scenarios, the major powers will fight over water and other vital resources, producing new global rifts and potentially involving the United States in full-scale wars with nuclear-armed belligerents."[88] Klare points to the potential for great power clashes in the melting Arctic region (between the United States and its allies and Russia) and in the Himalayan Watershed where Pakistan and India, or China and India, could conceivably fight over climate-related reductions in vital water supplies. He is not alone in this concern. A recent report from the World Future Council also concluded that "conflicts induced by climate change could contribute to global insecurity, which, in turn, could enhance the chance of a nuclear weapon being used."[89] And in addition to resource wars, Klare also points to the possibility that several nuclear-armed states (Pakistan, India, and China) could break apart as a consequence of climate change: "In a world constantly poised for nuclear war while facing widespread state decay from climate disruption, these twin threats would intermingle and intensify each other."[90] As serious as this interconnection is, it is not the only risk of the nuclear-climate nexus.

The Use of Nuclear Weapons Would Cause Climatic Catastrophe

Not only do climate disruptions increase the possibility that nuclear weapons could be used in situations of violent conflict, the use of these weapons would in turn produce catastrophic climatic conditions such as "nuclear winter." As noted in chapter 5, Carl Sagan argued that even a small nuclear exchange would throw a huge cloud of black sooty smoke (from the burning of cities and industrial facilities) up into the atmosphere, which would then block sunlight and plunge the earth into darkness and freezing temperatures with catastrophic consequences for human civilization. The climatic effects of a nuclear war, Sagan warned, would generate a global climate modification and environmental disaster in addition to all the other severe forms of destruction it would cause. A major study has recently confirmed that there would indeed be catastrophic climatic disruptions caused by even limited nuclear warfare. Writing in *Nature Food*, a team of scientists estimated that due to "soot injection" caused by nuclear weapons detonations, "more than 2 billion could die from nuclear war between India and Pakistan, and more than 5 billion could die from a war between the United States and Russia."[91] More than any other phenomenon, the threat of nuclear winter unites the two apocalyptic crimes. As Lifton argues, "What has been insufficiently understood is the extent to which nuclear winter would bring the apocalyptic twins together to create a single, malignant, world-encompassing, climate-based annihilation of our habitat and its capacity to sustain human life."[92]

William Knoblauch notes that the concept and theory of nuclear winter was "a product of an emerging global ecological consciousness" in the 1970s and 1980s, and it helped to renew the kind of "Cold War scientific activism" that the early atomic scientists had engaged in.[93] What was new about the theoretical prediction of nuclear winter "was that a single term that brought climate change and nuclear weapons together resonated within a growing and multifaceted scientific community by linking pressing cold war issues to worries over the planet's environmental future and stimulated a vigorous debate."[94] That debate would spur disarmament and climate activism, but it would also foster the development of efforts at socially organized denial of both nuclear winter and anthropogenic climate change.

Socially Organized Denial of the Twin Threats

The critique of the concept of nuclear winter would eventually intertwine with and influence the debate over the climate crisis. Both of these twin threats would be subjected to socially organized denialist efforts, with the denial of nuclear winter later influencing the denial of global warming. As Jill Lepore notes, "The most prominent critics of the science of nuclear winter would go on to become the most prominent critics of the science of climate change."[95] The political campaign waged against one would set the stage for the later political campaign against the other.

Socially organized denial involves coordinated efforts to undermine or block the dissemination of scientific research findings that threaten specific economic, political, or ideological interests. These efforts are generally organized and/or carried out by corporate executives within capitalist business organizations, state officials embedded in governmental institutions, or cultural workers in civil society groups. These political actors provide money and other material resources, social meanings and cultural ideas, and "research" staff to counter scientific claims that threaten their interests and seek to bring about societal changes that would disadvantage their social positions. Well financed and ideologically cohesive think tanks, foundations, and media organizations carry out most of the denialist efforts. Scientific research on both nuclear winter and climate change has been the target of socially organized denial and the propaganda it produces. And as Lepore concludes, "The debate over nuclear winter . . . established the themes and battle lines of the debate over climate change, which would rage well into the twenty-first century, long after the Cold War had ended."[96] Furthermore, both of these debates provided a shield for crimes of political omission by state officials.

State Crimes of Political Omission

Both the continued possession of nuclear weapons (with their potential use) and the human-caused climate crisis can be analyzed as state crimes of political omission. As noted in chapter 1, a number of criminologists have previously conceptualized the failure of states to prevent or control blame-worthy harms that they have a moral and legal responsibility to address as a form of state crime. In an earlier work I analyzed the "politics of predatory delay" with regard to climate policy in the United States by examining the relationships of the Ronald Reagan, George H. W. Bush, Bill Clinton, George W. Bush, Barack Obama, and Donald Trump presidential administrations with Congress, political parties, and administrative agencies within the government. I found that all of them, to one degree or another, failed to act to reduce carbon emissions and mitigate the climate crisis.[97] In chapters 4 to 6 of this book, I conducted a similar analysis of all U.S. presidential administrations during the nuclear age. Following the dropping of the atomic bombs on Japan in 1945, every American president has also failed to develop international controls over nuclear weapons and has refused to disarm as required by international law. As with the mitigation of climate harms, the American state has also engaged in political crimes of omission with regard to the nuclear danger as well.

State-Facilitated Corporate Crimes

Another important dimension shared by the crime of the continuing possession of nuclear weapons and climate crimes (continued extraction of fossil fuels and emissions of greenhouse gases) is that both can be analyzed as "state-facilitated" corporate crimes. The general concept of state-corporate crime refers to serious blameworthy harms that result from the interaction of political and economic organizations. The concept and theory of state-corporate crime seeks to break through the conceptual wall between economic crimes and political crimes in order to create a new lens through which criminology can analyze how serious illegal acts and profound social injuries often emerge from intersections of economic and political power.

Ray Michalowski and I have distinguished between "state-initiated corporate crime" and "state-facilitated corporate crime."[98] State-initiated corporate crimes involve organizational harms committed by corporations under contract to a government agency and at the direction of, or with the tacit approval of, that state agency. State-facilitated corporate crimes occur when government institutions fail to regulate or restrain harms committed by business organizations either because of direct collusion or due to shared goals whose attainment would be blocked by aggressive state regulation. Both the continued production of nuclear weapons and the generation of ecological harms that fuel the climate crisis can be analyzed as state-facilitated corporate crimes utilizing the treadmill of destruction and treadmill of production theoretical approaches discussed in chapter 6.

Geopolitical Crimes of Empire

Following Falk, I argue that state crimes related to climate change and nuclear weapons can also both be characterized as geopolitical crimes that take place in the context of the drive for American Empire.[99] In Carbon Criminals, Climate Crimes, I examined the interrelated state crimes of U.S. military interventions to gain access to and control over oil, Pentagon greenhouse gas emissions that result from these wars and other operations, and the choice of a militarized form of adaptation to climate disruption as "climate crimes of empire."[100] These state harms are climate crimes that can best be understood within the context of the development of the post–World War II global U.S. Empire, the normalization of a culture of militarism within American society, and the resulting creation of the treadmill of destruction as a concomitant to the operation of the treadmill of production / high-carbon system.[101]

This book has argued that the use of, threat to use, and continued possession of nuclear weapons are also geopolitical crimes of empire. There is strong historical evidence to support the argument that in the 1940s American leaders decided to pursue global military supremacy, achieve economic and political dominance in the postwar world through new international legal structures, and thwart Stalin's own geopolitical ambitions for the Soviet Union. As chapter 3 argues, imperial goals and nascent Cold War political calculations were among the most significant social forces that influenced the decision to use atomic bombs against Japan. The full emergence of the American Empire in the 1950s with its "warfare" and "national security" state was a pivotal moment. This new historical social structure would lock in place the central position of nuclear weapons in U.S. foreign policy. The trajectory of wartime and early Cold War atomic tendencies would continue unopposed within the higher circles of government and the larger political culture. A strong bipartisan consensus solidified around the continued possession and use of nuclear weapons. The rise of a "nuclear-industrial complex"[102] and an ideology of "nuclearism"[103] provided a firm political and cultural foundation, an institutionalized, self-replicating social system that allowed "the bomb" to be used to advance the cause of "empire" from the early 1950s to the present.[104] Every American president that followed Harry Truman would adhere to the basic imperial political script that had been written during World War II and in the early postwar era.

International Law and International Agreements

A final connection between the twin apocalyptic crimes is that both must be dealt with through global cooperation."[105] According to Falk, "The two greatest world order challenges of a structural character over the course of the past 75 years have been first, nuclear weaponry and, more recently, global climate change."[106] Both the threat of nuclear war and the climate crisis need to be addressed through international law and international agreements crafted by the UN and other international bodies. As Noam Chomsky has argued, we face a stark choice between "internationalism and extinction."[107] Not only must carbon emissions be drastically reduced, nuclear weapons must also be abolished. But is there a viable pathway to abolition? Can the international community really cooperate to achieve this strategic goal?

Toward the Abolition of Nuclear Weapons

The socio-political analysis I have presented leads me to conclude that nuclear weapons are illegal and the only way to prevent the apocalyptic crime of nuclear warfare is to abolish these dangerous devices. This section assesses the prospects for nuclear abolition and outlines a potential pathway toward that goal—some intermediate steps the international political community could take toward turning back the hands of the Doomsday Clock and ultimately ridding the world of the scourge of nuclear weapons. To repeat Jonathan Schell's admonition, "Abolition is the great threshold. It is the logical and necessary destination because only abolition gets us out of the zone of mass slaughter, both as perpetrators and victims."[108]

Abolishing nuclear weapons is an extremely challenging goal. Many political observers think that abolition is a utopian objective, a fantasy, a pipe *dream*. But I disagree. Nuclear abolition, while it will be enormously difficult to achieve, is indeed possible if the organizational pressure that has been generated over the years by the disarmament movement, and the political will that has been building recently in the international political community, can be more effectively mobilized and focused on the nuclear states to achieve this end. On the ninth annual "International Day for the Total Elimination of Nuclear Weapons" in 2022, United Nations secretary-general António Guterres stated, "We reject the claim that nuclear disarmament is some impossible utopian dream. Eliminating these devices of death is not only possible, it is necessary."[109] What the disarmament movement and the international political community need to do, according to Schell, "is to turn abolition from a far-off goal into an active organizing principle that gives direction to everything that is done in the nuclear arena—in other words, a strategic goal."[110] Many international organizations, such as the Nobel Peace Prize–winning ICAN (International Campaign to Abolish Nuclear Weapons), are already hard at work on this great challenge.

While achieving the strategic goal of nuclear abolition is indeed a daunting challenge, Japanese prime minister Fumio Kishida (who is from Hiroshima) has argued that "giving up is not an option . . . I believe that we must take every realistic measure toward a world without nuclear weapons, step by step, however difficult the path may be."[111] I agree. Abolishing nuclear weapons will require the major powers in the geopolitical system to be forced by intense political pressure from the disarmament movement and the juridical system to take many very difficult but necessary and achievable intermediate steps. These steps down the path to abolition (discussed more fully below) include (but are not limited to): (1) reducing tensions between the United States and Russia (perhaps through a negotiated settlement over the war in Ukraine and a resolution of issues concerning NATO's expansion to the east) and restoring some form of strategic stability dialogue and cooperation between the two great powers; (2) through that dialogue and cooperation, restarting and extending the arms control regime to continue to reduce the number of existing weapons through negotiated agreements like the New START (which must include China and its growing stockpile of nuclear weapons); (3) as part of this arms control process, enacting a ban on the modernization and expansion of current nuclear arsenals; (4) reforming the United Nations to make it a more democratic and effective body by weakening the hierarchical geopolitical system and empowering the more egalitarian juridical system; (5) making real progress on the implementation of Article VI of the NPT, which requires disarmament ; and finally and most importantly (6) convincing the nuclear states to join the Treaty on the Prohibition of Nuclear Weapons (TPNW) and then using the "architecture of zero"[112] the treaty has created to rid the world of the existing weapons and build safeguards against their recrudescence.

All of these steps are hard. All face significant structural and political obstacles at both the local and global levels. All require building greater international dialogue, trust, and cooperation. All require the participation of, and organized grassroots political pressure from, international social movements. Almost none of the required social and political forces necessary to accomplish these steps are currently in place. There are powerful structural reasons for disarmament activists to feel discouraged about making progress and moving down this path.

One major reason for discouragement, I argue, is that all these intermediate steps toward the eventual abolition of nuclear weapons require the United States to take a strong leadership role—a role the United States is not currently playing. Only the United States has the power and position in the current hierarchical geopolitical system to take the lead and achieve these steps toward disarmament (the same goes for mitigating carbon emissions and adapting to the climate crisis). On the eve of a G-7 Summit in Hiroshima in May 2023, Hiroshima mayor Kazumi Matsui argued that the president of the United States should present "some concrete strategies or measures" toward nuclear disarmament, for "if President Biden makes the first step in that direction from here, then the world will change."[113] I think he is right to highlight the pivotal role of the United States.

Despite a recent decline in American power, the United States remains the pivotal nation and the central nuclear power. The United States created the atomic bomb; used it against Japan in 1945; foiled efforts at the international control of nuclear weapons during the early Cold War; created a new, rules-based international order in the postwar era (that it dominated); developed the hydrogen bomb; built a colossal nuclear arsenal; threatened to use these weapons in numerous conflict situations; constructed a culture of nuclearism within its political system; and created an arms control regime that, while reducing the number of warheads, did not eliminate them and thus, to this day, still maintains thousands of nuclear weapons, some of which are being modernized, with plans to expand the arsenal even more. Given this dreadful history, this political centrality related to nuclear weapons, the United States not only has the greatest ability to act to reduce the nuclear danger but also has the greatest moral and legal responsibility to lead the way to, as Obama promised, a world without nuclear weapons. Russia and China must act as well—"At the highest levels, these three countries need to take responsibility for the existential danger the world now faces"[114]—but American leadership is primary and indispensable in moving the world toward nuclear abolition.

As this book has documented, the United States—the only nation to have ever used atomic weapons—has continually refused to take the necessary actions to achieve disarmament. American political leaders have repeatedly shirked their moral and legal responsibility to bring about that future. As Andrew Bacevich argues, "The monumental arrogance and ignorance prevailing in the inner circles of power have led Americans to misapprehend their place in the global order."[115] The United States has refused to fulfill its solemn legal obligation under the NPT to disarm. It has refused to sign the Treaty on the Prohibition of Nuclear Weapons. It has refused to take a no-first-strike pledge. The United States fails to do these important things primarily because of structural forces that block such actions. The American state functions to serve the interests of neoliberal capitalism and to secure the political hegemony (dominance) of the United States in the geopolitical system.

U.S. political leaders, operating within the confines of the historical social structure of the American Empire—with its capitalist institutions and neoliberal ideology, its goals of military supremacy and geopolitical domination, its national security state, its nuclear-industrial complex, its culture of nuclearism—have acted with "reckless irresponsibility" since the end of the Cold War and seem incapable of taking the steps necessary to reduce the nuclear danger and move toward the ultimate goal of abolition.[116] As American political scientist Chalmers Johnson noted in the title of his last book, "Dismantling the Empire" is "America's Last Best Hope."[117] It may be the last best hope for a world free of nuclear weapons as well. For, unless the American Empire is challenged by a strong domestic social movement and powerful pressure from the international political community, nuclear weapons will not be abolished and the apocalyptic threat will remain. That is the harsh political reality we face. And, at the moment, there seems to be no apparent path to changing these powerful structural forces. As Bacevich notes, "In order to conceive of and implement a responsible approach to statecraft, Americans will have to think anew. The need for them to do so could hardly be more urgent."[118] But what new thinking is needed to reduce the nuclear danger and move toward the abolition of nuclear weapons?

If, somehow, grassroots political pressure and structural changes freed the United States of the strictures of its national security state, its pursuit of imperial domination, the influence of its military-industrial complex, and a resurgent Cold War ideology, it could exercise a strong positive leadership role (often proclaimed in the mythic tenets of American Exceptionalism). If the United States would in fact dismantle the historical social structure of empire (an exceeding difficult task to be sure), it could then take steps that would move the world down the path toward the abolition of nuclear weapons. The first step that responsible American leaders, liberated from the constraints of "imperial ambitions,"[119] could take in that journey would be to significantly reduce tensions with Russia (starting by negotiating a peace settlement in Ukraine and resolving the issues concerning NATO expansion). As Anatol Lieven of the Quincy Institute argues, an "honest accounting" of history is required of both the United States and Russia—both need to acknowledge their imperial "crimes" and work to bring about "a lasting peace in Ukraine."[120] Confronting this history and reducing these tensions and conflicts may then restore some form of international dialogue and cooperation that will be essential to moving the larger abolition project forward.

If the conditions for broader forms of international diplomacy and discussion are restored (a new form of détente perhaps), a less imperial America would then need to take the lead and resurrect and push forward an arms control regime that can further reduce the number of deployed warheads. A U.S. government truly interested in advancing peace and disarmament, not imperial domination, would resume the "Strategic Stability Dialogue"—high-level talks "to devise steps for reducing the risk of nuclear escalation"[121]—quickly agree to extend the New START agreement with

Russia, and then press for a new and stronger treaty that cuts nuclear weapons even more drastically. The spirit of the Reagan–Gorbachev negotiations of the 1980s could serve as an inspiration for these discussions. If a Cold War hawk like Ronald Reagan could successfully negotiate an important arms control deal with the Soviet Union, then why can't current American leaders do the same with Russia? Putin is not Gorbachev, of course. He is an international bully. But he is not completely irrational, and American presidents have successfully negotiated with him in the past. Responsible statecraft requires that you negotiate with leaders with whom you may have geopolitical differences.

A new arms reduction accord would have to include the PRC as well. That will be difficult to navigate. The Chinese will resist being pulled into any such agreement as it modernizes and expands its nuclear arsenal. But if the United States is genuinely concerned with achieving arms control and eventual disarmament, rather than scoring points in some great power competition, it will need to make some compromises in order to reach an agreement with both Russia and China. And importantly, such an accord would also have to severely restrict the efforts of all states to modernize their nuclear arsenals. As the cliché goes, when in a hole, the first thing to do is stop digging. Halting the modernization efforts of all the nuclear powers is paramount if the world is to move toward abolition.

While advancing the arms control regime involves negotiations among the major players in the geopolitical system, moving toward the abolition of nuclear weapons requires the participation and cooperation of the larger international political community. To maximize this participation, the juridical system must be strengthened. Thus, it is imperative to reform the United Nations, in particular the Security Council. Earlier chapters have analyzed elements of what I call the "paradox" of international law—that while important substantive laws and legal standards have been promulgated over the years to regulate the conduct of states during war, the more powerful states have been unwilling to give up enough sovereignty to allow for any formal procedural controls or coercive enforcement tools to be created that could effectively punish or deter violations of these standards. Absent any effective formal legal controls, the compelling drive to achieve geopolitical goals during the course of relations between states through the threat to use nuclear weapons has not been deterred by the mere existence of the substantive legal principle of noncombatant immunity or the requirement to engage in good faith negotiations to achieve nuclear disarmament. The absence of enforcement efforts, this immunity and impunity for the great powers, has resulted in the legitimation of state violence, and coupled with the elastic concept of military necessity, leads to geopolitical crimes by these powers.

The paradox of international law is also due to the flawed structure of the United Nations Security Council. As Falk points out, the UN embodies the "structural dualism" of the intersecting juridical and geopolitical systems operative in international relations.[122] The fatal flaw that pervades world order is the fact that the five permanent members of the Security Council hold the veto power, which prevents the council from taking enforcement actions that the great powers, particularly the United States, do not want to be taken. The geopolitical system, therefore, can block the enforcement of laws created within the elements of the juridical system (such as the General Assembly, the International Court of Justice, or the International Criminal Court). According to American historian Paul Kennedy, this is the "giant conundrum" of the United Nations: "Everyone agrees that the present structure is flawed; but a consensus on how to fix it remains out of reach."[123] Fixes that would restrict the power and control of the permanent members of the council, the nations that compose Falk's geopolitical system, have been rejected or not even considered. But if the United States was somehow freed from the structural constraints of empire, it could take the lead to bring about the necessary institutional and democratic reforms of the Security Council system.

After all, it was the United States that took the lead to create a new rules-based world order after World War II. The UN Charter, which codified important aspects of public international law, the creation of the Security Council to enforce the charter, and the development of the International Court of Justice (World Court) to resolve disputes between nation-states, imperfect as they were and distorted by Cold War politics, all represented steps in the direction of greater accountability for states and their leaders with regard to violations of public international law. When combined with the four Geneva Conventions of 1949 and other postwar legal efforts, this American-led vision of a new liberal, rules-based international system was placed before the international political community.[124] It had significant support and appeared to have great potential even as the Cold War deepened.

But the creation of that international legal order was undermined by the undemocratic structure of the Security Council. As noted, it is the veto power that prevents the council from being able to take the necessary enforcement actions when the major powers are involved in geopolitical state crimes such as wars of aggression (the United States against Iraq,

Russia against Ukraine), war crimes (the bombing of civilians and torture), or, our primary concern here, the continued possession of and threat to use nuclear weapons. Schell argues that the "marginalization" of the UN was caused in large part by the "onset of the nuclear age," which occurred right at the birth of the organization.[125] While Kennedy is a strong defender of the United Nations overall, he acknowledges the consequences of this marginalization, this great flaw—here, commenting on the inability of the UN to prevent the illegal U.S. invasion of Iraq in 2003: "But the blunt fact was that a Great Power, indeed the strongest nation of all, could not be constrained from unilateral action by international organization and opinion; it therefore could do things that other, lesser powers could not, a further confirmation that not all member states were equal—as if they ever had been."[126] The same point could be made about the illegal Russian invasion of Ukraine.

Given this structural dualism, the United Nations will never be able to block geopolitical crimes by a determined great power unless the veto power is eliminated. Abolishing the veto power of the permanent members of the Security Council would strengthen the juridical system, weaken the geopolitical system, and empower the General Assembly. And the hope is that these structural changes to the UN system would open the door for the enforcement of existing international laws. But these changes can happen only if the United States, shorn of imperial ambitions, exercises a strong leadership role in the democratization of the UN. The grim political reality is that, in the current international climate, none of the great powers are likely to accept this diminishment of their power or sovereignty any time soon. The United States would have to exercise exceptional political leadership to accomplish this change, leadership that it is not currently inclined to undertake, no matter which political party is in power.

The final steps in the difficult climb toward nuclear abolition would involve the utilization of the two most powerful existing disarmament treaties—the NPT and the Treaty on the Prohibition of Nuclear Weapons. If the United States were no longer seeking political hegemony in the geopolitical system, it could take the lead in implementing Article VI of the NPT—which legally obligates the nuclear powers to reduce their arsenals and pursue complete disarmament. Both the United States and Russia (the Soviet Union) signed the NPT in 1968, but since then, both have continually violated their pledge to achieve nuclear disarmament and undermined the treaty review process. In recent years, both have sabotaged NPT Review Conferences, the meetings that take place every five years in an international effort to implement the terms of the agreement. As chapter 6 documented, the neoconservatives in the George W. Bush administration, opposed to international accords and attempting to advance their imperial designs, subverted the 2005 conference. They refused to make any concessions to strengthen the treaty or take any moves toward disarmament negotiations, and the conference ended without coming to an agreement on any statement. In 2010, the Obama administration tried to repair some of the damage the Bush team did to the NPT regime, but in the end did not do enough to advance the process. Then in 2015, the conference again failed to produce an outcome document. The 2022 Review Conference (delayed due to COVID-19) also ended in failure, when Russia would not agree to the draft outcome document because of provisions related to Ukrainian control of the Zaporizhzhia nuclear power plant. Even so, the draft outcome document still did not specify any pathway to implementing Article VI. Despite more than fifty years of failure, the hope is that with some resolution of the Ukrainian war, restored international cooperation, a strengthened juridical system, and a U.S. commitment to achieve disarmament and not imperial designs, such a pathway might open up.

If an NPT Review Conference could overcome the structural obstacles imposed by the geopolitical system and make substantial progress toward implementing Article VI—that is, could take concrete steps toward achieving disarmament—it might induce the nuclear powers to make the next critical move toward the abolition of nuclear weapons by joining the 2017 Treaty on the Prohibition of Nuclear Weapons. This is the most important and difficult step to achieve of all. The TPNW is complementary with the NPT. As Austrian diplomat Alexander Kmentt points out, as "a multilateral effort by the international community to make concrete progress on nuclear disarmament . . . the TPNW is an important reinforcement of the nuclear disarmament and nonproliferation regime" represented by the NPT.[127] He goes on to note that "a comprehensive legal prohibition of nuclear weapons is an essential element of the future full implementation of the NPT disarmament obligation. As such, the TPNW is legally, structurally, and logically an effective mechanism to implement Article VI."[128] If the United States, Russia, and China—already signatories to the NPT—would also sign on to the TPNW, it would represent a giant step toward the abolition of nuclear weapons. It would be the beginning of the end of nuclear weapons. This critical issue has already been raised in the U.S. Congress. House Resolution 77–Embracing the goals and provisions of the Treaty on the Prohibition of Nuclear Weapons was introduced by Representative

James P. McGovern (D-MA-2) in January 2023 at the start of the 118th Congress, but it has generated little support.

If the nuclear states, the major powers within the geopolitical system, would join this important treaty, then the specific steps laid out in the Vienna Declaration and Action Plan—a document unanimously adopted at the First Meeting of States Parties to the Treaty on the Prohibition of Nuclear Weapons in June 2022—could be accomplished. At that point abolition would no longer be a utopian dream but a very realistic strategic goal that could be achieved within a decade. As the Vienna Declaration concluded, "In the face of the catastrophic risks posed by nuclear weapons and in the interest of the very survival of humanity. . . . We will not rest until the last state has joined the Treaty, the last warhead has been dismantled and destroyed and nuclear weapons have been totally eliminated from the Earth."[129] Abolition is the strategic goal, and the TPNW offers the critical means to that end. But structural barriers block the path forward. Can the nuclear powers be forced to take that critical step?

TURNING BACK THE DOOMSDAY CLOCK: THE CRITICAL ROLE OF SOCIAL MOVEMENTS

This book concludes that the dismantlement of nuclear warheads depends in large part on the dismantlement of the American Empire. As Ritter points out, there is no realistic possibility that nuclear abolition can be achieved as long as "the national security strategy" of the United States is "based on global dominance, which has been and continues to be the case."[130] The evidence is quite clear that American political leaders going back to World War II have pursued the goal of a U.S.-controlled postwar world order, and the possession of nuclear weapons has played a large role in that pursuit. Concerning these state officials, Boggs asserts, "The Bomb would go a long way toward securing their long-term economic and geopolitical agendas, starting with the capacity to dominate worldwide financial and industrial markets."[131] In the postwar period, the use of atomic bombs against Japan would become "normalized" and a culture of "nuclearism" would develop during the Cold War. During this era, the phrase "American imperialism" became "commonplace around the world" as a way to describe the economic and geopolitical policies of the United States, but back home, "it was rejected by mainstream and official opinion as a left-wing libel."[132] Socialized into postwar American political culture and operating within the imperial assumptions and goals of the national security state, U.S. presidents and their advisors came to accept the view that "global dominance was the best and probably the sole path to safety for the United States."[133] And while some of them, like Ronald Reagan, Barack Obama, and the "Four Horsemen" (Shultz, Perry, Kissinger, and Nunn),[134] could intellectually conceive of "a world without nuclear weapons," none of them as state officials in charge of nuclear arsenals could break free of the cultural and institutional constraints of empire to take the necessary actions toward abolition.

The critical question is whether current or future political leaders can escape the confines of the historical social structure of the American Empire, engage in new thinking, exercise their power and influence to lead the international community to take the intermediate steps outlined above, and succeed in the quest to abolish nuclear weapons. We have to be realistic; these are very difficult goals to achieve. Even the beginning steps of reducing tensions with Russia and restoring the arms control regime will be hard to take in the current political climate. It will take organized grassroots social and political pressure from outside of the geopolitical system and the American government to challenge empire and make any progress toward nuclear abolition. A powerful global social movement is needed to end imperial domination by the United States and abolish nuclear weapons. We can look to history to see that some past social movements, facing what appeared to be insurmountable obstacles, persevered and won important victories—the American movement to abolish slavery, the efforts to end the Vietnam War, the worldwide campaign to end apartheid in South Africa, and the peaceful revolutions that led to the fall of the Berlin Wall, the dissolution of the Soviet Union, and the end of the Cold War. The world disarmament movement, by repeatedly "confronting the Bomb,"[135] has also achieved some major goals—the Limited Test Ban Treaty of 1963, the reduction of warheads through the arms control regime of the late twentieth century, and the passage of the Treaty on the Prohibition of Nuclear Weapons in 2017. A special mention can also be made of the Nuclear Weapons Freeze movement of the 1980s, which forced Reagan and Gorbachev to the negotiating table, where they came excruciatingly close to eliminating all nuclear weapons.

However difficult, a more powerful political movement to challenge empire and abolish nuclear weapons must be built, within both the international political community and the United States. As the *New York Times* asserted in a headline on March 7, 2024, "It's Time to Protest Nuclear War Again." The article, by Opinion Editor Kathleen Kingsbury, previewed a special series on nuclear weapons and the threat of nuclear war titled "At the Brink," which was subsequently published in the Sunday Opinion section of the *Times* on March 10. In her introduction, Kingsbury noted that the series would "explore where the present dangers lie in the next arms race and what can be done to make the world safer." Part of the answer to that question, she observed, was hearing the demands of "a vocal constituency."[136] But as journalist Jim Carrier asked a few months later, "where is the protest?"[137]

As Carrier and many others point out, turning back the Doomsday Clock will require a large-scale, integrated, progressive social movement that can mobilize people around the world. The existing world nuclear disarmament movement must be strengthened. As Carrier notes, despite the movement's up-and-down history, the building blocks for a more integrated effort to organize, educate, and lobby around the issue of nuclear abolition are there. Many excellent organizations are working to abolish nuclear weapons at the international level: ICAN, the *Bulletin of the Atomic Scientists*, Back from the Brink, the Arms Control Association, International Physicians for the Prevention of Nuclear War, the Ploughshares Fund, the Union of Concerned Scientists, and Global Zero (to mention only a few). These organizations need to find a way to better coordinate and integrate their efforts, and they need many more material resources than they currently have.

These groups also need to join forces with the international climate crisis movement to more effectively deal with the twin apocalyptic threats. As Michael Klare has observed,

> What is essential and still largely missing is a recognition that climate and peace activism must be linked if the twin perils of global warming and nuclear war are to be overcome. People must understand that it will be very difficult to slow global warming unless the nuclear arms race is also slowed—and, likewise, that the risk of nuclear war will grow as long as nuclear armed states are threatened by climate disruptions. Only by uniting our efforts toward climate and nuclear sanity in a joint campaign for human survival will it be possible to triumph over these destructive forces.[138]

Klare is absolutely right that this kind of linkage is necessary to build a more powerful, progressive, political movement to confront and control these apocalyptic crimes. However, as he also points out, recognition of this necessity is currently missing and the linkage will be difficult to build. The climate movement has not been generally inclined to challenge U.S. imperial domination.

Linkages with other social movement groups like CODEPINK, Black Lives Matter, environmental justice organizations, and other peace groups working to reduce worldwide military spending would also help to create a more large-scale, integrated, and powerful political movement to challenge empire, abolish nuclear weapons, address the climate crisis, and promote social solidarity. As American sociologist Heather Gautney argues, such an integrated movement will "require moving past the prevailing tendency of social movements to silo themselves according to particular causes, ideologies, and identities and instead develop extensive and sustained organizing programs aimed at promoting universal freedom and genuine social solidarity."[139] Civil disobedience along the lines of the famous Plowshares Actions of the Berrigan brothers and their allies will also be necessary.[140] As Swedish scholar of human ecology Andreas Malm suggests with regard to the climate movement, more militant protest actions may be important to challenge American imperial domination and nuclear state criminals.[141] And activists also need to keep in mind that building an effective antinuclear movement often requires overcoming a strong, socially constructed fear of the other and powerful sentiments of nationalism. As American political theorist Wendy Brown points out, the work of great German sociologist Max Weber on politics "reminds us that rational argument and compelling evidence by itself does not counter popular fears and frustrations, attachments and yearnings. Rather, the task of those invested in a more just and sustainable order is to kindle and educate desire for such an order and to build that *desire* into a worldview and viable political project."[142] Countering fear and nationalism, building an abolitionist worldview and political project, and creating a desire for a more peaceful world will be important to the success of a future world nuclear disarmament movement.

An integrated, progressive political movement to challenge empire, abolish nuclear weapons, and address the climate crisis is more advanced at the international level than within the United States. Denials of the nuclear threat, U.S. imperialism, and the climate threat are deeply embedded in American political culture. Nuclearism, militarism, nationalism, and increasingly fascism are likewise strong social forces within U.S. society. The current governmental structure, the military–industrial complex, and the political climate in the United States are not conducive to organized efforts to dismantle the American Empire and advocate for nuclear abolition. The Republican Party, always more hawkish and belligerent on foreign policy, has become ever more extremist, regressive, and authoritarian, especially in the age of Trump.[143] The Democratic Party, with some progressive exceptions, is meek, timid, and conformist on issues related to the military, always fearful of the accusation that they are "weak on defense."[144] The obscenely large Pentagon budget (including billions of dollars for nuclear weapons) always passes with huge bipartisan support. The current prospects for building a social movement to challenge empire, militarism, or nuclearism in this political environment seem dismal. Still, there are many dedicated organizations working to educate and organize the American people to resist these trends and advance the cause of peace and disarmament (the American Friends Service Committee, the National Priorities Project, and CODEPINK are a few groups doing this important work).

Challenging empire and abolishing nuclear weapons will require a long and difficult political struggle. As Weber wrote, "Politics is a strong and slow boring of hard boards. It takes both passion and perspective."[145] My hope is that the criminology of nuclear weapons presented in this book not only offers a scholarly contribution to our understanding of the crimes of the powerful, but also serves as a form of public criminology that makes a small contribution to the hard work of building that larger, integrated, progressive, political movement for nuclear abolition (and climate justice as well). According to sociologist Michael Burawoy, public sociology (criminology) involves bringing the discipline "into a conversation with publics, understood as people who are themselves involved in a conversation,"[146] in this case about nuclear weapons and state crime. The content of these conversations will be quite varied but would in some form be a dialogue about the moral and political implications of criminological research findings and theoretical explanations concerning nuclear state crimes. My hope is that a public criminology of nuclear weapons can help create political or "deliberative frames" that can orient debate and/or produce progressive political action on the nuclear danger we face.[147] Difficult as it will be, all of us must do what we can to abolish these illegal weapons and prevent the greatest crime in human history from occurring—the crime of a nuclear apocalypse.

Notes

Foreword

1. Statista, "Hypothetical Lethal Radius from Ground Zero of an Air Burst Nuclear Explosion by Bomb Strength" (2024), https://www.statista.com/statistics/1369316/nuclear-bomb-lethal-radii-by-shelter-type-and-bomb-size/.
2. Gar Alperovitz, *The Decision to Use the Atomic Bomb and the Architecture of an American Myth* (New York: Knopf, 1995); Robert Jay Lifton and Greg Mitchell, *Hiroshima in America: Fifty Years of Denial* (New York: Grosset/Putnam, 1995).
3. Robert F. Kennedy, "Address by President John F. Kennedy to the UN General Assembly" (1961; U.S. State Department Archive), https://2009-2017.state.gov/p/io/potusunga/207241.htm#:~:text=Every%20man%2C%20woman%20and%20child,abolished%20before%20they%20abolish%.
4. Margaret Mead, *Learning to Live in One World* (unpublished autobiographical manuscript, 1945), Library of Congress, Manuscript Division, https://www.loc.gov/exhibits/mead/oneworld-learn.html.
5. David Ropeik, "The Rise of Nuclear Fear—How We Learned to Fear the Radiation," *Scientific American*, June 15, 2012, https://blogs.scientificamerican.com/guest-blog/the-rise-of-nuclear-fear-how-we-learned-to-fear-the-bomb/#:~:text=The%201950s%20saw%20an%20explosion,We%20built%20fallout%20shelters; T. W. Smith, "A Report: Nuclear Anxiety," *Public Opinion Quarterly* 52 (1988): 557–575.
6. Dani Blum, "'Worry Burnout' Is Real," *New York Times*, December 16, 2021, https://www.nytimes.com/2021/12/16/well/worry-burnout-covid.html; Michael Klare, "Surviving an Era of Pervasive Nuclear Instability: A Call for Grassroots Activism," *The Nation*, February 12, 2024, https://www.thenation.com/article/world/surviving-an-era-of-pervasive-nuclear-instability/.
7. Daniel Immerwahr, "Forgetting the Apocalypse: Why Our Nuclear Fears Faded—and Why That's Dangerous," *The Guardian*, May 12, 2022, https://www.theguardian.com/world/2022/may/12/forgetting-the-apocalypse-why-our-nuclear-fears-faded-and-why-thats-dangerous.
8. Robert Jay Lifton, "Looking Back at the Decision to Drop Atomic Bombs on Hiroshima and Nagasaki," *National Public Radio, Fresh Air*, August 11, 2023, https://www.npr.org/2023/08/11/1193189051/looking-back-at-the-decision-to-drop-atomic-bombs-on-hiroshima-and-nagasaki.
9. Nuclear Threat Initiative (NTI), "The Dangers Are Real" (2024), https://www.nti.org/area/nuclear/#:~:text=We%20have%20entered%20a%20new,device%20being%20used%20is%20rising.
10. Anton Troianovski, "Putin Says West Risks Nuclear Conflict if It Intervenes More in Ukraine," *New York Times*, February 29, 2024, https://www.nytimes.com/2024/02/29/world/europe/putin-speech-ukraine-nuclear-conflict.html.

11. Andrey Kalikh, "Today, the Forgotten Fear of Nuclear War Is Being Reborn—and We Have No Popular Movement Against It," *Open Democracy*, June 6, 2018, https://www.opendemocracy.net/en/odr/the-dream-of-a-nuclear-free-world-has-never-been-further-away/.

12. Raymond J. Michalowski, *Order, Law, and Crime: An Introduction to Criminology* (New York: Random House, 1985).

13. David Friedrichs, "Rethinking the Criminology of Crimes of States: Monumental, Mundane, Mislabeled and Miscalculated Crimes," *International Journal of Crime, Justice and Social Democracy* 4, no. 4 (2015): 106–115.

14. Raffaele Garofalo, *Criminology: The Study of Crime, Its Causes and Methods of Control* (Boston: Little, Brown, 1885/1914), 59.

15. Maurice Parmalee, *Criminology* (New York: Macmillan, 1918).

16. Edwin H. Sutherland, *Criminology* (Philadelphia, J.B. Lippincott, 1924); Thorsten Sellin, *Culture, Conflict and Crime* (New York: Social Science Research Council, 1938).

17. Edwin H. Sutherland, "White Collar Criminality," *American Sociological Review* 5 (1940): 1–12.

18. Paul Tappan, "Who Is the Criminal?," *American Sociological Review* 12 (1947): 96–102.

19. Marshall Clinard, *The Black Market: A Study of White-Collar Crime* (New York: Holt, Rinehart, 1952); Donald Cressy, *Other People's Money—A Study in the Social Psychology of Embezzlement* (Glencoe, IL: Free Press, 1953).

20. Mark Gaylord and John Galliher, *The Criminology of Edwin Sutherland* (New Brunswick, NJ: Transaction, 1988).

21. Edwin Sutherland, *White Collar Crime* (New York: Dryden Press, 1949).

22. Ronald C. Kramer, "Corporate Criminality: The Development of an Idea," in *Corporations as Criminal*, ed. Ellen Hochstedler (Beverly Hills, CA: Sage, 1984), 13.

23. Edwin Gross, "Organizational Crime: A Theoretical Perspective," in *Studies in Symbolic Interactionism*, ed. Norman K. Denzin (Greenwich, CT: JAI, 1978), 55–85; David Ermann and Richard Lundman, *Corporate and Governmental Deviance* (New York: Oxford University Press, 1978); Ronald C. Kramer, "Corporate Crime: An Organizational Perspective," in *White Collar and Economic Crime*, ed. Peter Wickman and Timothy Daily (Lexington, MA: D.C. Heath, 1982), 75–94; Diane Vaughan, *Controlling Unlawful Organizational Behavior* (Chicago: University of Chicago Press, 1985).

24. Stephen Box, *Power, Crime, and Mystification* (New York: Tavistock, 1983).

25. Clifford Geertz, *The Interpretation of Cultures: Selected Essays by Clifford Geertz* (New York: Basic Books, 1973).

26. Karl Marx and Friedrich Engels, *The German Ideology*, pt. 1 (New York: International, 2001), 64.

27. Charles Taylor, "Modern Social Imaginaries," *Public Culture* 14, no. 1 (2002): 91–124.

28. Thomas Kuhn, *The Structure of Scientific Revolutions* (Chicago: University of Chicago Press, 1962).

29. Émile Durkheim, *The Rules of Sociological Method*, trans. W. D. Halls (1895; New York: Free Press, 1982), 50.

30. Max Weber, *Economy and Society: An Outline of Interpretative Sociology*, vol. 1 (New York: Bedminster Press, 1968).

31. Johnathan Eig, *King: A Life* (New York: Farrar, Straus and Giroux, 2023).

32. Betty Friedan, *The Feminine Mystique* (New York: Norton and Norton, 1963).

33. Todd Gitlin, *The Sixties: Years of Hope, Days of Rage* (New York: Penguin/Random House, 1993); Mark Kurlansky, *1968: The Year That Rocked the World* (New York: Random House, 2004); Christopher Strain, *The Long Sixties: America, 1955–1973* (New York: Wiley, 2016).

34. Ellen Schrecker, *No Ivory Tower: McCarthyism and the Universities* (New York: Oxford University Press, 1986).

35. Gary Gerstle, *The Rise and Fall of the Neoliberal Order: America and the World in the Free Market Era* (New York: Oxford University Press, 2022).

36. Kramer, "Corporate Crime"; Ronald C. Kramer, "A Prolegomenon to the Study of Corporate Violence," *Humanity and Society* 7 (May 1983): 149–178; Kramer, "Corporate Criminality."

37. Ronald C. Kramer and Sam Marullo, "Toward a Sociology of Nuclear Weapons," *Sociological Quarterly* 26, no. 3 (1985): 277–292; David Kauzlarich, Ronald C. Kramer, and Brian Smith, "Toward the Study of Governmental Crime: Nuclear Weapons, Foreign Intervention, and International Law," *Humanity and Society* 16, no. 4 (1992): 543–563.

38. William J. Chambliss, "State-Organized Crime—The American Society of Criminology, 1988 Presidential Address," *Criminology* 27 (1989): 184.

39. Raymond J. Michalowski and Ronald C. Kramer, "The Space between Laws: The Problem of Corporate Crime in a Transnational Context," *Social Problems* 34, no. 1 (February 1987): 34–53.

40. John Galliher, *Criminology: Human Rights, Criminal Law, and Crime* (Englewood Cliffs, NJ: Prentice Hall, 1989).

41. Herman Schwendinger and Julia Schwendinger, "Defenders of Order or Guardians of Human Rights?," *Issues in Criminology* 5, no. 2 (1970): 145.

42. William Blackstone, *A Discourse on the Study of the Law: Being an Introductory Lecture, Read in the Public Schools* (Oxford: Clarendon, 1758).

43. Oliver Wendell Holmes Jr., *The Common Law*, rev. ed. (Mineola, NY: Dover, 1991).

44. H. L. Mencken, *Prejudices: Second Series* (London: Johnathan Cape, 1920).

45. Ellen Meiksins Wood, *The Origin of Capitalism: A Longer View* (London: Verso, 2017).

46. Hugh Thomas, *The Slave Trade: The Story of the Atlantic Slave Trade, 1440–1870* (New York: Simon & Schuster, 1999).

47. Gordon Mingay, *Parliamentary Enclosure in England: An Introduction to Its Causes, Incidence and Impact, 1750–1850* (London: Routledge, 2014).

48. James Boyle, "Fencing Off Ideas: Enclosure and the Disappearance of the Public Domain," *Daedalus* 131 (2002): 13–25.

49. Manisha Sinha, *The Slave's Cause: A History of Abolition* (New Haven, CT: Yale University Press, 2016).

CHAPTER 1 "IT IS 90 SECONDS TO MIDNIGHT"

Epigraph 1: Richard Falk, "Non-proliferation Treaty Illusions and International Lawlessness," in *At the Nuclear Precipice: Catastrophe or Transformation?*, ed. Richard Falk and David Krieger (New York: Palgrave Macmillan, 2008), 39–47, 43.

Epigraph 2: Tad Daley, *Apocalypse Never: Forging the Path to a Nuclear Weapon-Free World* (New Brunswick, NJ: Rutgers University Press, 2010), 236.

1. Christian Sorensen, *Understanding the War Industry* (Atlanta: Clarity Press, 2020), 314.

2. Paul Boyer, *By the Bomb's Early Light: American Thought and Culture at the Dawn of the Atomic Age* (New York: Pantheon Books, 1985; reissued by University of North Carolina Press, 1994), 70.

3. Lawrence S. Wittner, *Confronting the Bomb: A Short History of the World Nuclear Disarmament Movement* (Stanford, CA: Stanford University Press, 2009), 3.

4. Boyer, *By the Bomb's Early Light*, 49.
5. Robert Jay Lifton, *The Climate Swerve: Reflections on Mind, Hope, and Survival* (New York: New Press, 2017), 52.
6. Robert K. Elder and J. C. Gabel, *The Doomsday Clock at 75* (Los Angeles: Hat & Beard Press, 2022), 18.
7. Elder and Gabel, 222.
8. John Mecklin, ed., "'It Is 100 Seconds to Midnight': 2020 Doomsday Clock Statement," *Bulletin of the Atomic Scientists*, January 23, 2020, 3.
9. Mecklin, 3.
10. Noam Chomsky and Robert Pollin, *Climate Crisis and the Global Green New Deal* (London: Verso, 2020), 2.
11. Elder and Gabel, *Doomsday Clock at 75*, 15.
12. Mecklin, "'It Is 100 Seconds to Midnight,'" 7–8.
13. John Mecklin, ed., "'This Is Your COVID Wake-Up Call: It Is 100 Seconds to Midnight': 2021 Doomsday Clock Statement," *Bulletin of the Atomic Scientists*, January 27, 2021, 3.
14. Mecklin, "'This is Your COVID Wake-Up Call,'" 3.
15. John Mecklin, ed, "'At Doom's Doorstep: It Is 100 Seconds to Midnight'—2022 Doomsday Clock Statement," *Bulletin of the Atomic Scientists*, January 20, 2022, 3.
16. Philippe Sands, *Lawless World* (New York: Penguin, 2005), 4.
17. Medea Benjamin and Nicolas J. S. Davies, *War in Ukraine: Making Sense of a Senseless Conflict* (New York: OR Books, 2022), 18.
18. Arms Control Association, "Russia's War on Ukraine and the Risk of Nuclear Escalation," *Arms Control Association Issue Briefs* 14, no. 3 (February 28, 2022): 1.
19. Dan Sabbagh, "Russia to Station Tactical Nuclear Weapons in Belarus," *Guardian*, March 25, 2023, https://www.theguardian.com/world/2023/mar/25/russia -to-station-tactical-nuclear-weapons-in-belarus?fbclid=IwAR0Tue-C50fcmx _-Owohw7owHMlcZpGdj-8QCy5I8Tlflxs6e9oMY8cAhVQ.
20. Michael Klare, "Ukraine's Nuclear Flashpoints: How to Avoid Armageddon in the New Nuclear Era," *The Nation*, April 20, 2022, 1, https://www.thenation .com/article/world/ukraine-nuclear-war/.
21. Klare, 2.
22. Agence France-Presse, "World 'One Miscalculation Away from Nuclear Anni-hilation,' UN Chief Says," *Guardian*, August 1, 2022, 1, https://www .theguardian.com/world/2022/aug/02/world-one-miscalculation-away-from -nuclear-annihilation-un-chief-says.
23. Robert Jay Lifton and Richard Falk, *Indefensible Weapons: The Political and Psychological Case Against Nuclearism* (New York: Basic Books, 1982).
24. John Mecklin, ed., "'A Time of Unprecedented Danger: It Is 90 Seconds to Midnight': 2023 Doomsday Clock Statement," *Bulletin of the Atomic Scientists*, January 24, 2023, 2.
25. Mecklin, 2.
26. Linda McQuaiq, "Western Leaders Don't Want Us to Worry about Nuclear War, But We Should," *Toronto Star*, June 29, 2023, https://www.thestar.com /opinion/contributors/2023/06/29/western-leaders-dont-want-us-to-worry -about-nuclear-war-but-we-should.html.
27. John Mecklin, ed., "'A Moment of Historic Danger: It Is *Still* 90 Seconds to Midnight': 2024 Doomsday Clock Statement," *Bulletin of the Atomic Scientists*, January 23, 2024, 1. The *New York Times* Opinion Page editors agreed in early 2024 that we are "At the Brink," with a powerful series on the nuclear danger. See W. J. Hennigan, "How We Returned to the Brink," *New York Times,* Sunday Opinion (March 10, 2024, 5).

28. Mecklin, "'It Is 100 Seconds to Midnight,'" 8.
29. Mecklin, "'At Doom's Doorstep,'" 3.
30. Jon Kelvey, "Does the Doomsday Clock Actually Mean Anything? Experts Weigh In," *Inverse*, January 29, 2023, 9, http://www.inverse.com/science/is-the-doomsday-clock-legit.
31. Lifton, *Climate Swerve*, 17.
32. Ronald C. Kramer, *Carbon Criminals, Climate Crimes* (New Brunswick, NJ: Rutgers University Press, 2020).
33. William J. Chambliss, "State-Organized Crime—The American Society of Criminology, 1988 Presidential Address," *Criminology* 27 (1989): 183–208, 184.
34. David O. Friedrichs, *Trusted Criminals: White Collar Crime in Contemporary Society*, 3rd ed. (Belmont, CA: Thomson/Wadsworth, 2010), 140.
35. Gregg Barak, ed., *Crimes by the Capitalist State: An Introduction to State Criminality* (Albany: State University of New York Press, 1991); David Kauzlarich, Christopher Mullins, and Rick Matthews, "A Complicity Continuum of State Crime," *Contemporary Justice Review* 6 (2003): 241–254; Rob Watts, *States of Violence and the Civilising Process: On Criminology and State Crime* (London: Palgrave Macmillan, 2016).
36. Watts, *States of Violence*, 10.
37. C. Wright Mills, "The Structure of Power in American Society," in *Power, Politics and People: The Collected Essays of C. Wright Mills*, ed. Irving Louis Horowitz (New York: Oxford University Press, 1963), 23–38, 23.
38. C. Wright Mills, *The Power Elite* (New York: Oxford University Press, 1956), 4.
39. Steven Lukes, *Power: A Radical View*, 2nd ed. (Houndmills, UK: Palgrave Macmillan, 2005).
40. E. E. Schattschneider, *The Semi-sovereign People: A Realist's View of Democracy in America* (New York: Holt, Rinehart & Winston, 1960); Peter Bachrach and Morton S. Baratz, *Power and Poverty: Theory and Practice* (New York: Oxford University Press, 1970); Harvey Molotch, "Oil in Santa Barbara and Power in America," *Sociological Inquiry* 40 (1970): 131–144.
41. Falk, "Non-proliferation Treaty Illusions," 43, emphasis original.
42. Friedrichs, *Trusted Criminals*; David Friedrichs, "Toward a Prospective Criminology of State Crime," in *State Crime in the Global Age*, ed. William Chambliss, Raymond Michalowski, and Ronald C. Kramer (Cullompton: Willan, 2010), 67–80; David Friedrichs, "The Nuclear Arms Issue and the Field of Criminal Justice," *Justice Professional* 1 (1985): 5–9; Richard Harding, "Nuclear Energy and the Destiny of Mankind—Some Criminological Perspectives," *Australian and New Zealand Journal of Criminology* 16 (1983): 81–92; David Kauzlarich and Ronald C. Kramer, *Crimes of the American Nuclear State: At Home and Abroad* (Boston: Northeastern University Press, 1998).
43. Friedrichs, *Trusted Criminals*, 132.
44. Friedrichs, "Toward a Prospective Criminology of State Crime," 77.
45. Friedrichs, 78.
46. David Kauzlarich and Ronald C. Kramer, "State-Corporate Crime in the US Nuclear Weapons Production Complex," *Journal of Human Justice* 5 (1993): 4–28; David Kauzlarich and Ronald C. Kramer, "The Nuclear Terrorist State," *Peace Review* 7 (1995): 333–337; Kauzlarich and Kramer, *Crimes of the American Nuclear State*; Ronald C. Kramer and Elizabeth A. Bradshaw, "US State Crimes Related to Nuclear Weapons: Is There Hope for Change in the Obama Administration?," *International Journal of Comparative and Applied Criminal Justice* 35 (2011): 243–259; Ronald C. Kramer and David Kauzlarich, "Nuclear Weapons, International Law, and the Normalization of State Crime," in *State Crime:*

Current Perspectives, ed. Dawn Rothe and Christopher Mullins (New Brunswick, NJ: Rutgers University Press, 2011), 68–93; Ronald C. Kramer and David Kauzlarich, "The Opinion of the International Court of Justice on the Use of Nuclear Weapons: Implications for Criminology," *Contemporary Justice Review* 2 (1999): 395–413; Ross McGarry and Sandra Walklate, *A Criminology of War* (Bristol, UK: Bristol University Press, 2019).

47. Edwin H. Sutherland, *Principles of Criminology*, 3rd ed. (Chicago: J.B. Lippincott, 1939), 1.

48. Lesley M. M. Blume, *Fallout: The Hiroshima Cover-Up and the Reporter Who Revealed It to the World* (New York: Simon & Schuster, 2020), 188.

49. Lifton and Falk, *Indefensible Weapons*; Robert Jay Lifton, *Witness to an Extreme Century: A Memoir* (New York: Free Press, 2011).

50. McGarry and Walklate, *Criminology of War*, 97.

51. Daley, *Apocalypse Never*, 233.

52. Jonathan Schell, *The Seventh Decade: The New Shape of Nuclear Danger* (New York: Metropolitan Books, 2007), 3.

53. Lifton, *Climate Swerve*, 17.

54. Robert Heilbroner, *An Inquiry into the Human Prospect* (New York: Norton, 1974).

55. Robert Jensen, *We Are All Apocalyptic Now: On the Responsibilities of Teaching, Preaching, Writing, and Speaking Out* (Scotts Valley, CA: CreateSpace, 2013), 9.

56. Daley, *Apocalypse Never*.

57. John Somerville, "Human Rights, Ethics and Nuclear War," *Peace Research* 14 (1982): 2.

58. Jonathan Schell, *The Abolition* (New York: Knopf, 1984).

59. Jonathan Schell, *The Fate of the Earth* (New York: Knopf, 1982), 1.

60. Mark Wolverton, *Nuclear Weapons* (Cambridge, MA: MIT Press, 2022), 11. Journalist Annie Jacobsen makes a similar point in her recent book, *Nuclear War: A Scenario* (New York: Dutton, 2024).

61. Friedrichs, *Trusted Criminals*, 9.

62. Robert Agnew, *Toward a Unified Criminology: Integrating Assumptions about Crime, People, and Society* (New York: New York University Press, 2011).

63. Agnew, 38.

64. Friedrichs, "Toward a Prospective Criminology of State Crime."

65. Agnew, *Toward a Unified Criminology*, 43.

66. Chambliss, "State-Organized Crime"; Chambliss, Michalowski, and Kramer, *State Crime in the Global Age*; William J. Chambliss and Chris Moloney, eds., *State Crime*, vols. 1–4 (London: Routledge, 2015).

67. Richard Falk, "Geopolitical Crimes: A Preliminary Jurisprudential Proposal," *State Crime* 8, no. 1 (2019): 5–18.

68. Falk, 5.

69. Falk, 6.

70. Falk, 10.

71. Falk, 13.

72. Robert Reiner, *Crime: The Mystery of the Common-Sense Concept* (Cambridge: Polity, 2016), 5.

73. Carl Boggs, *Origins of the Warfare State: World War II and the Transformation of American Politics* (New York: Routledge, 2017).

74. Donald R. Taft, "Punishment of War Criminals," *American Sociological Review* 11 (1946): 444.

75. David Kauzlarich, Ronald C. Kramer, and Brian Smith, "Toward the Study of Governmental Crime: Nuclear Weapons, Foreign Intervention, and International

Law," *Humanity and Society* 16, no. 4 (1992): 543–563; Kauzlarich and Kramer, *Crimes of the American Nuclear State*; Ronald C. Kramer, Raymond J. Michalowski, and Dawn L. Rothe, "The Supreme International Crime: How the U.S. War in Iraq Threatens the Rule of Law," *Social Justice* 32 (2005): 52–81; Agnew, *Toward a Unified Criminology*; Ronald C. Kramer and Amanda Marie Smith, "Death Flies Down: The Bombing of Civilians and the Paradox of International Law," in *Towards a Victimology of State Crime*, ed. Dawn Rothe and Dave Kauzlarich (London: Routledge, 2014), 100–130; Kramer, Michalowski, and Rothe, "Supreme International Crime."

76. William J. Chambliss, "Commentary," *Society for the Study of Social Problems (SSSP) Newsletter* 26 (1995): 9.

77. Stanley Cohen, *States of Denial: Knowing about Atrocities and Suffering* (Cambridge: Polity, 2001).

78. Diane Vaughan, *The Challenger Launch Decision: Risky Technology, Culture, and Deviance at NASA* (Chicago: University of Chicago Press, 1996).

79. Ian Patterson, *Guernica and Total War* (Cambridge, MA: Harvard University Press, 2007).

80. Alfred W. McCoy, *To Govern the Globe: World Orders and Catastrophic Change* (Chicago: Haymarket Books, 2021).

81. John W. Dower, *Cultures of War: Pearl Harbor/Hiroshima/9-11/Iraq* (New York: Norton, 2010).

82. Gar Alperovitz, *Atomic Diplomacy: Hiroshima and Potsdam: The Use of the Atomic Bomb and the American Confrontation with Soviet Power* (New York: Simon & Schuster, 1965).

83. Studs Terkel, *The "Good War": An Oral History of World War Two* (New York: Pantheon, 1984); Elizabeth D. Samet, *Looking for the Good War: American Amnesia and the Violent Pursuit of Happiness* (New York: Farrar, Straus and Giroux, 2021).

84. Martin J. Sherwin, *Gambling with Armageddon: Nuclear Roulette from Hiroshima to the Cuban Missile Crisis* (New York: Knopf, 2020).

85. Shane J. Maddock, *Nuclear Apartheid: The Quest for American Atomic Supremacy from World War II to the Present* (Chapel Hill: University of North Carolina Press, 2010), 1.

86. Lifton and Falk, *Indefensible Weapons*, 191.

87. Lifton, *Witness to an Extreme Century*, 347.

88. Mike Savage, *The Return of Inequality: Social Change and the Weight of the Past* (Cambridge, MA: Harvard University Press, 2021).

89. Joseph Gerson, *Empire and the Bomb: How the U.S. Uses Nuclear Weapons to Dominate the World* (London: Pluto Press, 2007), 2.

90. Gerson, 1.

91. Daniel Ellsberg, *The Doomsday Machine: Confessions of a Nuclear War Planner* (New York: Bloomsbury, 2017), 319–323.

92. Lifton and Falk, *Indefensible Weapons*, ix.

93. Jonathan Schell, "Reaching Zero," *Nation* 290 (April 19, 2010): 16–17.

94. Jonathan Schell, *The Gift of Time: The Case for Abolishing Nuclear Weapons Now* (New York: Metropolitan Books, 1998).

95. Michael Klare, *Rogue States and Nuclear Outlaws: America's Search for a New Foreign Policy* (New York: Hill & Wang, 1995).

96. Schell, *Seventh Decade*.

97. Wright Robin, "The New Nuclear Reality," *New Yorker*, April 23, 2022, https://www.newyorker.com/news/daily-comment/the-new-nuclear-reality.

98. Schell, "Reaching Zero," 17.

CHAPTER 2   NUCLEAR WARFARE IS ILLEGAL

Epigraph 1: Lawyers Committee on Nuclear Policy, *Statement on the Illegality of Nuclear Warfare*, rev. ed. (New York, 1990), 2.

Epigraph 2: Richard Falk, "Nuclear Weapons, War, and the Discipline of International Law," in *At the Nuclear Precipice: Catastrophe or Transformation?*, ed. Richard Falk and David Krieger (New York: Palgrave Macmillan, 2008), 225–233, 225.

Epigraph 3: Robert Dodge, "Nuclear Weapons Banned—Illegal at Last," *Common Dreams*, October 26, 2020, 1, https://www.commondreams.org/views/2020/10/26/nuclear-weapons-banned-illegal-last.

1. John Fabian Witt, *Lincoln's Code: The Laws of War in American History* (New York: Free Press, 2012), 2.
2. Witt, 2.
3. Samuel Moyn, *Humane: How the United States Abandoned Peace and Reinvented War* (New York: Farrar, Straus and Giroux, 2021), 30.
4. Alexander Orakhelashvili, *Akehurst's Modern Introduction to International Law*, 8th ed. (London: Routledge, 2019), 1.
5. Anders Henriksen, *International Law* (Oxford: Oxford University Press, 2017), 2.
6. Robert Agnew, *Toward a Unified Criminology: Integrating Assumptions about Crime, People, and Society* (New York: New York University Press, 2011), 31.
7. Orakhelashvili, *Akehurst's Modern Introduction to International Law*.
8. Henriksen, *International Law*, 3.
9. Orakhelashvili, *Akehurst's Modern Introduction to International Law*, 2.
10. Henriksen, *International Law*, 5.
11. Moyn, *Humane*, 26.
12. William Slomanson, *Fundamental Perspectives on International Law*, 4th ed. (Belmont, CA: Thomson/West, 2003), 485.
13. Adam Tooze, *The Deluge: The Great War, America and the Remaking of the Global Order, 1916–1931* (New York: Viking, 2014).
14. James Terry, "The Evolving Law of Aerial Warfare," *Air University Review*, November–December 1975, 1–16.
15. David Swanson, *When the World Outlawed War* (Charlottesville, VA: David Swanson, 2011).
16. Philippe Sands, *Lawless World* (New York: Penguin, 2005), 8.
17. Sands, 10.
18. Walter Kalin and Jorg Kunzli, *The Law of International Human Rights Protection*, 2nd ed. (Oxford: Oxford University Press, 2019), 30–31.
19. Gary J. Bass, *Judgment at Tokyo: World War II on Trial and the Making of Modern Asia* (New York: Knopf, 2023), 528.
20. Ronald C. Slye and Beth Van Schaack, *International Criminal Law: The Essentials* (New York: Aspen, 2009), 3.
21. Bruce Broomhall, *International Justice and the International Criminal Court: Between Sovereignty and the Rule of Law* (Oxford: Oxford University Press, 2003), 14.
22. Antonio Cassese, *International Criminal Law* (Oxford: Oxford University Press, 2003); Slye and Van Schaack, *International Criminal Law*.
23. Louis Henkin, *International Law: Politics and Values* (Dordrecht: Martinus Nijhoff, 1995), 111.
24. Steven R. Ratner and Jason S. Abrams, *Accountability for Human Rights Atrocities in International Law: Beyond the Nuremberg Legacy*, 2nd ed. (Oxford: Oxford University Press, 2001).

25. Broomhall, *International Justice and the International Criminal Court*; Dawn L. Rothe and Christopher W. Mullins, *Symbolic Gestures and the Generation of Global Social Control: The International Criminal Court* (Lanham, MD: Rowman & Littlefield, 2006).

26. Orakhelashvili, *Akehurst's Modern Introduction to International Law*, 4, emphasis added.

27. Yuki Tanaka and Richard Falk, "The Atomic Bombing, the Tokyo War Crimes Tribunal and the Shimoda Case: Lessons for Anti-Nuclear Legal Movements," *Asia-Pacific Journal* 7, no. 3 (2009).

28. Richard Falk, "The Shimoda Case: A Legal Appraisal of the Atomic Attacks upon Hiroshima and Nagasaki," *American Journal of International Law* 59 (1965): 759–793, 776.

29. Falk, 770.

30. Lawyers Committee on Nuclear Policy, *Statement on the Illegality of Nuclear Warfare*, 18, emphasis original.

31. Richard Falk, "Non-proliferation Treaty Illusions and International Lawlessness," in Falk and Krieger, *At the Nuclear Precipice*, 39–47, 43, emphasis added.

32. Francis Boyle, *The Criminality of Nuclear Deterrence: Could the U.S. War on Terrorism Go Nuclear?* (Atlanta: Clarity Press, 2002).

33. Boyle, 73.

34. Francis Boyle, *The Future of International Law and American Foreign Policy* (Ardsley-on-Hudson, NY: Transnational, 1989); Boyle, *Criminality of Nuclear Deterrence*; Richard Falk, "Towards a Legal Regime for Nuclear Weapons," *McGill Law Journal* 28 (1983): 519–541; Richard Falk, "Is Nuclear Policy a War Crime?," *Human Rights* 11 (1983): 18–55; Falk, "Non-proliferation Treaty Illusions"; Burns Weston, "Nuclear Weapons and International Law: Prolegomenon to General Illegality," *New York Law School Journal of International and Comparative Law* 4 (1983): 227–256; Elliott Meyrowitz, *Prohibition of Nuclear Weapons: The Relevance of International Law* (Dobbs Ferry, NY: Transnational, 1990); Lawyers Committee on Nuclear Policy, *Statement on the Illegality of Nuclear Warfare*.

35. Lawyers Committee on Nuclear Policy, *Statement on the Illegality of Nuclear Warfare*, 8.

36. Laurence Boisson de Chazournes and Philippe Sands, eds., *International Law, the International Court of Justice and Nuclear Weapons* (Cambridge: Cambridge University Press, 1999), 2.

37. Ann Fagan Ginger, ed., *Nuclear Weapons Are Illegal: The Historic Opinion of the World Court and How It Will Be Enforced* (New York: Apex Press, 1998), 1.

38. International Court of Justice (ICJ), *The Legality of the Threat or Use of Nuclear Weapons (Request for Advisory Opinion Submitted by the General Assembly of the United Nations)* (General List no. 95, Advisory Opinion of 8 July 1996), para. 105 (2) E.

39. Kate Dewes and Robert Green, "The World Court Project: How a Citizen Network Can Influence the United Nations," in Ginger, *Nuclear Weapons Are Illegal*, 473–492.

40. Roger Clark, "The Case Against the Bomb: Marshall Islands, Samoa, and the Solomon Islands in the International Court of Justice—Introduction," in *The Case Against the Bomb*, ed. Roger S. Clark and Madeleine Sann (Camden, NJ: Rutgers University School of Law, 1996), 1–35.

41. Clark, 4.

42. Clark, 4.

43. Ginger, *Nuclear Weapons Are Illegal*, 36–37.

44. Boisson de Chazournes and Sands, *International Law*, 6.

45. Kevin Sanders, "Nuclear Weapons on Trial: The People Versus the Bomb," *War and Peace Digest* 3 (1995): 1.

46. ICJ, *Legality of the Threat or Use of Nuclear Weapons*, para. 22.
47. ICJ, para. 34.
48. ICJ, para. 36.
49. ICJ, para. 105.
50. M. J. Matheson, "The Opinion of the International Court of Justice on the Threat or Use of Nuclear Weapons," *American Journal of International Law* 91, no. 3 (1997): 417–435.
51. P. H. F. Bekker, "Legality of the Threat or Use of Nuclear Weapons," *American Journal of International Law* 91, no. 1 (1997): 126–138.
52. ICJ, *Legality of the Threat or Use of Nuclear Weapons*, para. 95.
53. ICJ, para. 105 (2) E.
54. ICJ, para. 105 (2) E, emphasis added.
55. Richard Falk, "Nuclear Weapons, International Law and the World Court: A Historic Encounter," *American Journal of International Law* 91, no. 1 (1997): 68.
56. Robert. H. Jackson, "Foreword," in *The Nuremberg Trial and Aggressive War*, by Sheldon Glueck (New York: Knopf, 1946), xii.
57. Boyle, *Criminality of Nuclear Deterrence*, 71–72.
58. Lawyers Committee on Nuclear Policy, *Statement on the Illegality of Nuclear Warfare*, 19.
59. Boyle, *Criminality of Nuclear Deterrence*, 74.
60. Hans Blix, *Why Nuclear Disarmament Matters* (Cambridge, MA: MIT Press, 2008), 44.
61. Jonathan R. Hunt, *The Nuclear Club: How America and the World Policed the Atom from Hiroshima to Vietnam* (Stanford, CA: Stanford University Press, 2022), 3.
62. Hunt, 3.
63. Falk, "Nuclear Weapons," 231.
64. Jonathan Schell, *The Seventh Decade: The New Shape of Nuclear Danger* (New York: Metropolitan Books, 2007), 35.
65. Schell, 34.
66. Schell, 36.
67. Sean L. Malloy, *Atomic Tragedy: Henry L. Stimson and the Decision to Use the Bomb Against Japan* (Ithaca, NY: Cornell University Press, 2008).
68. Fred Kaplan, *The Bomb: Presidents, Generals, and the Secret History of Nuclear War* (New York: Simon & Schuster, 2020).
69. Ray Acheson, *Banning the Bomb, Smashing the Patriarchy* (Lanham, MD: Rowman & Littlefield, 2021), 52.
70. Martin J. Sherwin, *Gambling with Armageddon: Nuclear Roulette from Hiroshima to the Cuban Missile Crisis* (New York: Knopf, 2020).
71. Joseph Cirincione, *Bomb Scare: The History and Future of Nuclear Weapons* (New York: Columbia University Press, 2007), 29.
72. Blix, *Why Nuclear Disarmament Matters*, 55.
73. Acheson, *Banning the Bomb*, 53.
74. Hunt, *Nuclear Club*, 3.
75. Hunt, *Nuclear Club*, 5.
76. Cirincione, *Bomb Scare*, 31.
77. Article VI of the Nuclear Non-Proliferation Treaty.
78. ICJ, *Legality of the Threat or Use of Nuclear Weapons*, para. 105 (2) F.
79. Falk, "Nuclear Weapons," 66–67.
80. Boyle, *Criminality of Nuclear Deterrence*, 192.
81. Micheline Ishay, *The History of Human Rights: From Ancient Times to the Globalization Era* (Berkeley: University of California Press, 2004).
82. Ishay, 3.

83. Judith Blau and Alberto Moncada, *Human Rights: A Primer* (Boulder, CO: Paradigm, 2009); Mary Ann Glendon, *A World Made New: Eleanor Roosevelt and the Universal Declaration of Human Rights* (New York: Random House, 2001); Akira Iriye, Petra Goedde, and William Hitchcock, eds., *The Human Rights Revolution: An International History* (London: Oxford University Press, 2012).

84. Stuart Casey-Maslen, "The Use of Nuclear Weapons and Human Rights," *International Review of the Red Cross* 97 (2015): 663.

85. Akira Iriye and Petra Goedde, "Introduction: Human Rights as History," in Iriye, Goedde, and Hitchcock, *Human Rights Revolution*, 3–24, 4.

86. Johannes Morsink, *The Universal Declaration of Human Rights: Origins, Drafting and Intent* (Philadelphia: University of Pennsylvania Press, 1999), xii.

87. Judith Blau and Alberto Moncada, "It Ought to Be a Crime: Criminalizing Human Rights Violations," *Sociological Forum* 22 (2007): 364–371.

88. Hannah Kohn, "Nuclear Weapons and the Human Right to Life" (presentation, World Peace Congress, Barcelona, October 16, 2021), https://www.lcnp.org.

89. Daniel Rietiker, "Threat and Use of Nuclear Weapons Contrary to Right to Life, Says UN Human Rights Committee" (Association of Swiss Lawyers for Nuclear Disarmament, November 7, 2018), 2, https://safna.org/2018/11/07/threat-and-use-of-nuclear-weapons-contrary-to-right-to-life-says-un-human-rights-committee/.

90. Rietiker, 2.

91. Human Rights Committee, "General Comment No. 36, Article 6: Right to Life" (United Nations, International Covenant on Civil and Political Rights, 2018), 14, emphasis added.

92. Casey-Maslen, "Use of Nuclear Weapons," 680.

93. Rietiker, "Threat and Use of Nuclear Weapons," 7.

94. Blau and Moncada, "It Ought to Be a Crime," 370.

95. Joachim J. Savelsberg, *Crime and Human Rights: Criminology of Genocide and Atrocities* (Thousand Oaks, CA: Sage, 2010), 1.

96. Gregg Barak, "Towards an Integrated Study of International Crimes and State-Corporate Criminality: A Reciprocal Approach to Gross Human Rights Violations," in *Supranational Criminology: Towards a Criminology of International Crimes*, ed. Alette Smeulers and Roelof Haveman (Antwerp: Intersentia, 2008), 51–76.

97. Caroline Lambert, Sharon Pickering, and Christine Alder, *Critical Chatter: Women and Human Rights in South East Asia* (Durham, NC: Carolina Academic Press, 2003); Diane Otto, "Rethinking the Universality of 'Human Rights' Law," *Columbia Human Rights Law Review* 29 (1997): 1–46.

98. Eric Hobsbawm, *The Age of Extremes: A History of the World, 1914–1991* (New York: Vintage, 1996); Arundhati Roy, *Public Power in the Age of Empire* (New York: Seven Stories Press, 2004).

99. Jack Donnelly, "In Defense of the Universal Declaration Model," in *International Human Rights in the 21st Century: Protecting the Rights of Groups*, ed. Gene Lyons and James Mayall (New York: Rowman & Littlefield, 2003), 20–48; Glendon, *World Made New*; William Schultz, *Tainted Legacy: 9/11 and the Ruin of Human Rights* (New York: Nation Books, 2003); Henry J. Steiner and Phillip Alston, *International Human Rights in Context: Law, Politics, Morals* (Oxford: Oxford University Press, 2000).

100. Agnew, *Toward a Unified Criminology*, 24.

101. ICJ, *Legality of the Threat or Use of Nuclear Weapons*, para. 105.

102. Blix, *Why Nuclear Disarmament Matters*, 42.

103. Boisson de Chazournes and Sands, *International Law*, 2.

104. Ira Hefland, "Ban the Bomb—Before Our Luck Runs Out," *The Progressive*, June/July 2019, 20.
105. Acheson, *Banning the Bomb*, 2.
106. Alexander Kmentt, "The Ban Treaty, Two Years After: A Ray of Hope for Nuclear Disarmament," *Bulletin of the Atomic Scientists*, January 23, 2023, 2, https://thebulletin.org/2023/01/the-ban-treaty-two-years-after-a-ray-of-hope-for-nuclear-disarmament/.
107. Acheson, *Banning the Bomb*, 7.
108. John Burroughs, "Building Blocks for Nuclear Ban Treaty: NPT and Advisory Opinion of the International Court of Justice," Inter Press Service News Agency, November 2, 2020, 1, http://www.ipsnews.net/2020/11/building-blocks-nuclear-ban-treaty-npt-advisory-opinion-international-court-justice/.
109. Richard Falk, "Challenging Nuclearism: The Nuclear Ban Treaty Assessed," *Asia-Pacific Journal* 15 (2017): 2.
110. Lawyers Committee on Nuclear Policy, "Statement of Lawyers Committee on Nuclear Policy and Western States Legal Foundation on the Imminent Entry into Force of the Treaty on the Prohibition of Nuclear Weapons" (October 24, 2020), 1, http://lcnp.org/StatementimminentEIFTPNWfin2.pdf.
111. Joseph Gerson, "Pessimism of the Intellect, Optimism of the Will: Building on the Nuclear Weapon Ban Treaty," *Common Dreams*, September 17, 2019, 1, https://portside.org/2019-09-17/pessimism-intellect-optimism-will-building-nuclear-weapon-ban-treaty.
112. Falk, "Challenging Nuclearism," 2.
113. Richard Falk, "Geopolitical Crimes: A Preliminary Jurisprudential Proposal," *State Crime* 8, no. 1 (2019): 5–18.
114. Falk, "Challenging Nuclearism," 2.
115. Ray Acheson, "How Prohibiting Nuclear Weapons Changed the World," *The Nation*, July 6, 2018, 6, https://www.thenation.com/article/archive/prohibiting-nuclear-weapons-changed-world/.
116. Robert Dodge, "A Nuclear Weapons Ban Treaty—Rx for Survival," *Common Dreams*, July 8, 2017, 1, https://www.commondreams.org/views/2017/07/08/nuclear-weapons-ban-treaty-rx-survival.
117. Hans M. Kristensen, Matt Korda, and Eliana Reynolds, "Status of World Nuclear Forces" (Federation of American Scientists, last updated March 28, 2023), https://fas.org/issues/nuclear-weapons/status-world-nuclear-forces/.
118. Alfred W. McCoy, *To Govern the Globe: World Orders and Catastrophic Change* (Chicago: Haymarket Books, 2021), 195.

CHAPTER 3   THE USE OF THE ATOMIC BOMB AGAINST JAPAN AND THE NORMALIZATION OF A GEOPOLITICAL CRIME

Epigraph 1: Barton J. Bernstein, "The Atomic Bombings Reconsidered," *Foreign Affairs* 74 (1995): 151.

Epigraph 2: Joseph Gerson, *Empire and the Bomb: How the U.S. Uses Nuclear Weapons to Dominate the World* (London: Pluto Press, 2007), 39.

1. Mark Kurlansky, *The Basque History of the World* (New York: Penguin, 1999), 197.
2. Ian Patterson, *Guernica and Total War* (Cambridge, MA: Harvard University Press, 2007).
3. Patterson, 17.
4. Helen Graham, *The Spanish Civil War: A Very Short Introduction* (Oxford: Oxford University Press, 2005), 71.

5. Sahr Conway-Lanz, *Collateral Damage: Americans, Noncombatant Immunity, and Atrocity after World War II* (New York: Routledge, 2006), 2.

6. Mark Selden and Alvin Y. So, "Introduction: War and State Terrorism," in *War and State Terrorism: The United States, Japan, and the Asia-Pacific in the Long Twentieth Century,* ed. Selden and So (Lanham, MD: Rowman & Littlefield, 2004), 1–18, 6.

7. Tom Engelhardt, *The World According to TomDispatch: America in the New Age of Empire* (London: Verso, 2008), 2.

8. Patterson, *Guernica and Total War,* 38.

9. Kurlansky, *Basque History of the World,* 200.

10. Patterson, *Guernica and Total War,* 2.

11. Patterson, 34.

12. John W. Dower, *Cultures of War: Pearl Harbor/Hiroshima/9-11/Iraq* (New York: Norton, 2010), 159.

13. Dower, 159–160.

14. Daniel Ellsberg, *The Doomsday Machine: Confessions of a Nuclear War Planner* (New York: Bloomsbury, 2017), 236.

15. Bernstein, "Atomic Bombings Reconsidered," 136.

16. Richard Falk, "State Terror versus Humanitarian Law," in Selden and So, *War and State Terrorism,* 41–61, 45.

17. Ronald Schaffer, *Wings of Judgment: American Bombing in World War II* (New York: Oxford University Press, 1985), 3.

18. Michael Bess, *Choices under Fire: Moral Dimensions of World War II* (New York: Knopf, 2006), 90.

19. Diane Vaughan, *The Challenger Launch Decision: Risky Technology, Culture, and Deviance at NASA* (Chicago: University of Chicago Press, 1996); Diane Vaughan, "Beyond Macro- and Micro-Levels of Analysis, Organizations, and the Cultural Fix," in *International Handbook of White-Collar and Corporate Crime,* ed. Henry Pontell and Gil Geis (New York: Springer, 2007), 3–24.

20. Stanley Cohen, *States of Denial: Knowing about Atrocities and Suffering* (Cambridge: Polity, 2001).

21. Eric Markusen and David Kopf, *The Holocaust and Strategic Bombing: Genocide and Total War in the Twentieth Century* (Boulder, CO: Westview, 1995); Conway-Lanz, *Collateral Damage*; Patterson, *Guernica and Total War.*

22. Engelhardt, *World According to TomDispatch,* 161.

23. Robert Jay Lifton and Greg Mitchell, *Hiroshima in America: Fifty Years of Denial* (New York: Grosset/Putnam, 1995); Greg Mitchell, *The Beginning or the End: How Hollywood—and America—Learned to Stop Worrying and Love the Bomb* (New York: New Press, 2020).

24. Gerson, *Empire and the Bomb*; Mark Selden, "A Forgotten Holocaust: U.S. Bombing Strategy, the Destruction of Japanese Cities and the American Way of War from the Pacific War to Iraq," in *Bombing Civilians: A Twentieth-Century History,* ed. Yuki Tanaka and Marilyn Young (New York: New Press, 2009), 77–96.

25. Gerson, *Empire and the Bomb,* 13.

26. Dower, *Cultures of War.*

27. Sean L. Malloy, *Atomic Tragedy: Henry L. Stimson and the Decision to Use the Bomb Against Japan* (Ithaca, NY: Cornell University Press, 2008).

28. Gar Alperovitz, *Atomic Diplomacy: Hiroshima and Potsdam: The Use of the Atomic Bomb and the American Confrontation with Soviet Power* (New York: Simon & Schuster, 1965).

29. P. M. S. Blackett, *Fear, War, and the Bomb: Military and Political Consequences of Atomic Energy* (New York: Whittlesey House, 1948), 139.

30. Dower, *Cultures of War*, 241.
31. Garry J. Bass, *Judgment at Tokyo: World War II on Trial and the Making of Modern Asia* (New York: Knopf, 2023), 78.
32. Bass, 81.
33. Bass, 201.
34. Dower, *Cultures of War*, 202.
35. Dower, 199.
36. Dower, 199.
37. Bess, *Choices under Fire*, 203.
38. Carl Boggs, *Origins of the Warfare State: World War II and the Transformation of American Politics* (New York: Routledge, 2017), 103.
39. Dower, *Cultures of War*, 205.
40. Robert Jay Lifton and Richard Falk, *Indefensible Weapons: The Political and Psychological Case Against Nuclearism* (New York: Basic Books, 1982), 3.
41. Ross McGarry and Sandra Walklate, *A Criminology of War* (Bristol, UK: Bristol University Press, 2019).
42. Bess, *Choices under Fire*, 198.
43. Mark Selden, "The United States and Japan in Twentieth Century Asian Wars," in Selden and So, *War and State Terrorism*, 19–40, 30.
44. Schaffer, *Wings of Judgment*; Ronald Schaffer, "The Bombing Campaigns in World War II: The European Theater," in Tanaka and Young, *Bombing Civilians*, 30–45; Michael Sherry, "The United States and Strategic Bombing: From Prophecy to Memory," in Tanaka and Young, *Bombing Civilians*, 175–190; Michael Sherry, *In the Shadow of War: The United States since the 1930s* (New Haven, CT: Yale University Press, 1995); Michael Sherry, *The Rise of American Air Power: The Creation of Armageddon* (New Haven, CT: Yale University Press, 1987); Robert A. Pape, *Bombing to Win: Air Power and Coercion in War* (Ithaca, NY: Cornell University Press, 1996); Sven Lindquist, *A History of Bombing* (New York: New Press, 2001); Falk, "State Terror versus Humanitarian Law"; Selden, "United States and Japan"; Mark Selden, "A Forgotten Holocaust: U.S. Bombing Strategy, the Destruction of Japanese Cities and the American Way of War from the Pacific War to Iraq," in Tanaka and Young, *Bombing Civilians*, 77–96; Bess, *Choices under Fire*; Conway-Lanz, *Collateral Damage*; A. C. Grayling, *Among the Dead Cities: The History and Moral Legacy of the WW II Bombing of Civilians in Germany and Japan* (New York: Walker, 2006); Tanaka and Young, *Bombing Civilians*.
45. Grayling, *Among the Dead Cities*, 4.
46. Selden, "United States and Japan," 30.
47. Joseph Cirincione, *Bomb Scare: The History and Future of Nuclear Weapons* (New York: Columbia University Press, 2007), 13.
48. Raymond Michalowski and Ronald C. Kramer, eds., *State-Corporate Crime: Wrongdoing at the Intersection of Business and Government* (New Brunswick, NJ: Rutgers University Press, 2006).
49. Cohen, *States of Denial*.
50. Cohen, 51.
51. Cohen, 7.
52. Vaughan, *Challenger Launch Decision*.
53. Vaughan, "Beyond Macro- and Micro-Levels of Analysis," 4.
54. Schaffer, *Wings of Judgment*; Schaffer, "Bombing Campaigns in World War II."
55. Malcolm Gladwell, *The Bomber Mafia: A Dream, a Temptation, and the Longest Night of the Second World War* (New York: Little, Brown, 2021).
56. Gladwell.
57. Schaffer, *Wings of Judgment*, xi.

58. Schaffer, "Bombing Campaigns in World War II," 36.
59. Ellsberg, *Doomsday Machine*, 251.
60. Gladwell, *Bomber Mafia*.
61. Gladwell.
62. Bernstein, "Atomic Bombings Reconsidered," 151.
63. Selden, "Forgotten Holocaust," 87.
64. Quoted in Schaffer, *Wings of Judgment*, 217.
65. Dower, *Cultures of War*, 22.
66. Schaffer, *Wings of Judgment*; Bernstein, "Atomic Bombings Reconsidered"; J. Samuel Walker, *Prompt and Utter Destruction: Truman and the Use of Atomic Bombs Against Japan*, rev. ed. (Chapel Hill: University of North Carolina Press, 2004); Paul Ham, *Hiroshima Nagasaki: The Real Story of the Atomic Bombings and Their Aftermath* (New York: Thomas Dunne Books, 2014).
67. Dower, *Cultures of War*, 22.
68. Malloy, *Atomic Tragedy*.
69. Bass, *Judgment at Tokyo*, 10. See also Dower, *Cultures of War*, 196.
70. Bess, *Choices under Fire*; Walker, *Prompt and Utter Destruction*.
71. Lifton and Mitchell, *Hiroshima in America*, xvi.
72. Erving Goffman, *Frame Analysis: An Essay on the Organization of Experience* (New York: Harper & Row, 1974).
73. C. Wright Mills, "Situated Actions and Vocabularies of Motive," *American Sociological Review* 5 (1940): 904–913; David Friedrichs, *Trusted Criminals: White Collar Crime in Contemporary Society*, 3rd ed. (Belmont, CA: Thomson/Wadsworth, 2010).
74. Gresham M. Sykes and David Matza, "Techniques of Neutralization: A Theory of Delinquency," *American Sociological Review* 22 (1957): 664–670; Stuart L. Hills, ed., *Corporate Violence: Injury and Death for Profit* (Totowa, NJ: Rowman & Littlefield, 1987).
75. Lifton and Mitchell, *Hiroshima in America*, xvi.
76. Lifton and Mitchell, xvii.
77. Lifton and Mitchell, 6–7.
78. Sykes and Matza, "Techniques of Neutralization," 668–669.
79. Lifton and Mitchell, *Hiroshima in America*, 27.
80. Lifton and Mitchell, 12.
81. Lifton and Mitchell, 25.
82. Paul Boyer, *By the Bomb's Early Light: American Thought and Culture at the Dawn of the Atomic Age* (New York: Pantheon Books, 1985; reissued by University of North Carolina Press, 1994); Lifton and Mitchell, *Hiroshima in America*.
83. Walker, *Prompt and Utter Destruction*; Ellsberg, *Doomsday Machine*; Fred Kaplan, *The Bomb: Presidents, Generals, and the Secret History of Nuclear War* (New York: Simon & Schuster, 2020).
84. Malloy, *Atomic Tragedy*.
85. Lesley M. M. Blume, *Fallout: The Hiroshima Cover-Up and the Reporter Who Revealed It to the World* (New York: Simon & Schuster, 2020).
86. Boyer, *By the Bomb's Early Light*.
87. Lifton and Mitchell, *Hiroshima in America*, 9.
88. Blume, *Fallout*, 148.
89. Lifton and Mitchell, *Hiroshima in America*, 94.
90. Malloy, *Atomic Tragedy*, 118–119.
91. Malloy, 159.
92. Lifton and Mitchell, *Hiroshima in America*, 103, 107.
93. Walker, *Prompt and Utter Destruction*, 103.
94. Richard B. Frank, *Downfall: The End of the Imperial Japanese Empire* (New York: Random House, 1999); Robert P. Newman, *Truman and the Hiroshima Cult*

(East Lansing: Michigan State University Press, 1995). Also see Michael Kort, *The Columbia Guide to Hiroshima and the Bomb* (New York: Columbia University Press, 2007), for an overview of the controversy.

95. Ham, *Hiroshima Nagasaki*, 510.
96. Walker, *Prompt and Utter Destruction*, 109.
97. Bernstein, "Atomic Bombings Reconsidered," 149.
98. Oliver Stone and Peter Kuznick, *The Untold History of the United States* (New York: Gallery Books, 2012).
99. Pape, *Bombing to Win*, 314.
100. Ham, *Hiroshima Nagasaki*, 471.
101. Malloy, *Atomic Tragedy*, 166–167.
102. Malloy, 163.
103. Studs Terkel, *The "Good War": An Oral History of World War Two* (New York: Pantheon, 1984); Edward W. Wood Jr., *Worshipping the Myths of World War II: Reflections on America's Dedication to War* (Washington, DC: Potomac Books, 2006).
104. Markusen and Kopf, *Holocaust and Strategic Bombing*, 195.
105. Markusen and Kopf, 195.
106. Schaffer, *Wings of Judgment*.
107. Cohen, *States of Denial*.
108. Cohen, 101.
109. Ham, *Hiroshima Nagasaki*, 471.
110. Christian G. Appy, "Our Merciful Ending to the Good War: Or How Patriotism Means Never Having to Say You're Sorry," *Guernica*, August 5, 2015, 2, https://www.guernicamag.com/christian-appy-our-merciful-ending-to-the-good-war/.
111. Bass, *Judgment at Tokyo*, 29.
112. Mitchell, *Beginning or the End*.
113. Selden, "Forgotten Holocaust," 87.
114. Dower, *Cultures of War*, 252.
115. Robert Jackall, "Crime in the Suites," *Contemporary Sociology* 9 (1980): 355.
116. Jackall, 356.
117. Sherry, *Rise of American Air Power*; Sherry, *In the Shadow of War*; Sherry, "United States and Strategic Bombing."
118. Sherry, *Rise of American Air Power*, xi.
119. Dower, *Cultures of War*, 263.
120. Conway-Lanz, *Collateral Damage*, 19.
121. Sherry, *In the Shadow of War*, 81.
122. Selden, "Forgotten Holocaust," 87.
123. Bass, *Judgment at Tokyo*.
124. Chris Jochnick and Roger Normand, "The Legitimation of Violence: A Critical History of the Laws of War," *Harvard International Law Journal* 35 (1994): 89.
125. Selden, "Forgotten Holocaust," 91.
126. Howard Zinn, *A People's History of the United States: 1492–Present* (New York: HarperCollins, 1980); Gerson, *Empire and the Bomb*; Leo Panitch and Sam Gindin, *The Making of Global Capitalism: The Political Economy of American Empire* (London: Verso, 2012); Boggs, *Origins of the Warfare State*.
127. Alfred W. McCoy, *In the Shadows of the American Century: The Rise and Decline of U.S. Global Power* (Chicago: Haymarket Books, 2017), 40.
128. Fred Anderson and Andrew Cayton, *The Dominion of War: Empire and Liberty in North America, 1500–2000* (New York: Penguin, 2005); Andrew J. Bacevich, *American Empire: The Realities and Consequences of U.S. Diplomacy* (Cambridge, MA: Harvard University Press, 2002); Charles A. Beard, *The Open Door at Home: A Trial Philosophy of National Interest* (New York: Macmillan, 1935); Charles A.

Beard and Mary Beard, *The Rise of American Civilization* (New York: Macmillan, 1930); Niall Ferguson, *Colossus: The Price of America's Empire* (New York: Penguin, 2004); Gerson, *Empire and the Bomb*; Steven Hahn, *A Nation without Borders: The United States and Its World in an Age of Civil Wars, 1830–1910* (New York: Viking, 2016); Richard H. Immerman, *Empire for Liberty: A History of American Imperialism from Benjamin Franklin to Paul Wolfowitz* (Princeton, NJ: Princeton University Press, 2010); Daniel Immerwahr, *How to Hide an Empire: A History of the Greater United States* (New York: Farrar, Straus and Giroux, 2019); Sidney Lens, *The Forging of the American Empire: From the Revolution to Vietnam: A History of U.S. Imperialism* (New York: Thomas Y. Crowell, 1971); Walter Nugent, *Habits of Empire: A History of American Expansion* (New York: Knopf, 2008).

129. William Appleman Williams, *Empire as Way of Life* (New York: Oxford University Press, 1980).

130. Christian G. Appy, *American Reckoning: The Vietnam War and Our National Identity* (New York: Viking, 2015); John Dower, *The Violent American Century: War and Terror since World War II* (Chicago: Haymarket Books, 2017); Andrew Fiala, *The Just War Myth: The Moral Illusions of War* (Lanham, MD: Rowman & Littlefield, 2008); Godfrey Hodgson, *The Myth of American Exceptionalism* (New Haven, CT: Yale University Press, 2009); H. H. Koh, "Foreword: On American Exceptionalism," *Stanford Law Review* 55 (2003): 1479–1527.

131. Appy, *American Reckoning*, xiii.

132. Bacevich, *American Empire*, 8.

133. Carl Boggs, *The Crimes of Empire: Rogue Superpower and World Domination* (London: Pluto Press, 2010).

134. Nugent, *Habits of Empire*.

135. Bass, *Judgment at Tokyo*, 19.

136. John R. Judis, *The Folly of Empire: What George W. Bush Could Have Learned from Theodore Roosevelt and Woodrow Wilson* (New York: Scribner, 2004), 61.

137. Bass, *Judgment at Tokyo*, 20.

138. William Appleman Williams, *The Tragedy of American Diplomacy* (1959; New York: Norton, 1988).

139. Williams.

140. Selden, "Forgotten Holocaust," 91.

141. Adam Tooze, *The Deluge: The Great War, America and the Remaking of the Global Order, 1916–1931* (New York: Viking, 2014), 6–7.

142. Tooze, 6.

143. Gerson, *Empire and the Bomb*, 43.

144. Bass, *Judgment at Tokyo*, 18.

145. Zinn, *People's History*; Boggs, *Origins of the Warfare State*.

146. Stephen Wertheim, *Tomorrow, the World: The Birth of U.S. Global Supremacy* (Cambridge, MA: Belknap, 2020), 10.

147. Wertheim, 3–4.

148. Wertheim, 7.

149. Zinn, *People's History*, 414.

150. Zinn, 413.

151. Dower, *Cultures of War*, 241.

152. Dower, 245.

153. Boyer, *By the Bomb's Early Light*, 191.

154. Dower, *Cultures of War*, 245.

155. Alperovitz, *Atomic Diplomacy*; Gar Alperovitz, *The Decision to Use the Atomic Bomb and the Architecture of an American Myth* (New York: Knopf, 1995).

156. Bernstein, "Atomic Bombings Reconsidered"; Dower, *Cultures of War*.

157. Gerson, *Empire and the Bomb*, 40.

158. Tsuyoshi Hasegawa, *Racing the Enemy: Stalin, Truman, and the Surrender of Japan* (Cambridge, MA: Belknap, 2005).
159. Gerson, *Empire and the Bomb*, 40.
160. Bess, *Choices under Fire*; Kort, *Columbia Guide to Hiroshima*; Walker, *Prompt and Utter Destruction*.
161. Boggs, *Origins of the Warfare State*, 103, emphasis added.
162. Dower, *Cultures of War*, 248.
163. Zinn, *People's History*; Lifton and Mitchell, *Hiroshima in America*; Francis Boyle, *The Criminality of Nuclear Deterrence: Could the U.S. War on Terrorism Go Nuclear?* (Atlanta: Clarity Press, 2002); Falk, "State Terror versus Humanitarian Law"; Gerson, *Empire and the Bomb*; Dower, *Cultures of War*; Boggs, *Origins of the Warfare State*.
164. Ham, *Hiroshima Nagasaki*, 510.
165. Grayling, *Among the Dead Cities*, 207–208.
166. Vera Brittain, *Seed of Chaos* (London: New Vision Press, 1944).
167. Bess, *Choices under Fire*, 202.
168. Malloy, *Atomic Tragedy*, 175.
169. Vaughan, "Beyond Macro- and Micro-Levels of Analysis," 12.
170. Immerman, *Empire for Liberty*.
171. A. G. Hopkins, "Lessons of 'Civilizing Missions' Are Mostly Unlearned," *New York Times*, March 23, 2003, https://www.nytimes.com/2003/03/23/week inreview/lessons-of-civilizing-missions-are-mostly-unlearned.html.
172. Wood, *Worshipping the Myths of World War II*, 143.
173. Markusen and Kopf, *Holocaust and Strategic Bombing*, 195.
174. Alfred W. McCoy, *To Govern the Globe: World Orders and Catastrophic Change* (Chicago: Haymarket Books, 2021), 213.

CHAPTER 4   CRIMES OF EMPIRE

Epigraph 1: Carl Boggs, *Origins of the Warfare State: World War II and the Transformation of American Politics* (New York: Routledge, 2017), 105.

Epigraph 2: Joseph Gerson, *Empire and the Bomb: How the U.S. Uses Nuclear Weapons to Dominate the World* (London: Pluto Press, 2007), 1.

1. Mark Wolverton, *Nuclear Weapons* (Cambridge, MA: MIT Press, 2022).
2. William Lanouette, *Genius in the Shadows: A Biography of Leo Szilard, the Man Behind the Bomb* (New York: Skyhorse, 2013), 137.
3. Lanouette, 138.
4. Richard Rhodes, *The Making of the Atomic Bomb* (New York: Simon & Schuster, 1986), 13.
5. Lawrence S. Wittner, *Confronting the Bomb: A Short History of the World Nuclear Disarmament Movement* (Stanford, CA: Stanford University Press, 2009).
6. Wittner, 1.
7. Alex Wellerstein, *Restricted Data: The History of Nuclear Secrecy in the United States* (Chicago: University of Chicago Press, 2021), 18.
8. Wellerstein, 18.
9. Wellerstein, 19.
10. Wellerstein, 19.
11. Wellerstein, 26.
12. Lanouette, *Genius in the Shadows*, 196.
13. Walter Isaacson, *Einstein: His Life and Universe* (New York: Simon & Schuster, 2007).
14. Lanouette, *Genius in the Shadows*, 206–207.

15. Isaacson, *Einstein*, 473.
16. Lanouette, *Genius in the Shadows*, 211.
17. Wittner, *Confronting the Bomb*, 3.
18. Wittner, 4.
19. Lanouette, *Genius in the Shadows*, 266–267.
20. Paul Boyer, *By the Bomb's Early Light: American Thought and Culture at the Dawn of the Atomic Age* (New York: Pantheon Books, 1985; reissued by University of North Carolina Press, 1994), 50.
21. Robert Jay Lifton and Greg Mitchell, *Hiroshima in America: Fifty Years of Denial* (New York: Grosset/Putnam, 1995), 249.
22. Lifton and Mitchell, 249, emphasis original.
23. Lanouette, *Genius in the Shadows*, 266.
24. Martin Sherwin, *A World Destroyed: Hiroshima and the Origins of the Arms Race* (1975; New York: Vintage, 1987), 205.
25. Lanouette, *Genius in the Shadows*, 272.
26. Lanouette, 273.
27. Boyer, *By the Bomb's Early Light*, 50.
28. Lanouette, *Genius in the Shadows*, 277.
29. Joseph M. Siracusa, *Nuclear Weapons: A Very Short Introduction*, 3rd ed. (Oxford: Oxford University Press, 2020), 25.
30. Boyer, *By the Bomb's Early Light*.
31. Jonathan Schell, *The Seventh Decade: The New Shape of Nuclear Danger* (New York: Metropolitan Books, 2007), 35.
32. Boyer, *By the Bomb's Early Light*.
33. Wittner, *Confronting the Bomb*.
34. Boyer, *By the Bomb's Early Light*, 61.
35. Boyer, 61.
36. Boyer.
37. Wittner, *Confronting the Bomb*, 8.
38. Kai Bird and Martin J. Sherwin, *American Prometheus: The Triumph and Tragedy of J. Robert Oppenheimer* (New York: Knopf, 2005), 249.
39. Bird and Sherwin, 487–488.
40. Matthew Evangelista, *Unarmed Forces: The Transnational Movement to End the Cold War* (Ithaca, NY: Cornell University Press, 1999).
41. Wittner, *Confronting the Bomb*, 7.
42. Boyer, *By the Bomb's Early Light*, 51.
43. Wellerstein, *Restricted Data*, 148.
44. Boyer, *By the Bomb's Early Light*, 52.
45. Wellerstein, *Restricted Data*, 157–158.
46. Boyer, *By the Bomb's Early Light*, 52.
47. Boyer, 52, emphasis original.
48. Sherwin, *World Destroyed*, 94.
49. Wellerstein, *Restricted Data*, 137.
50. Wellerstein, 139.
51. Sean L. Malloy, *Atomic Tragedy: Henry L. Stimson and the Decision to Use the Bomb Against Japan* (Ithaca, NY: Cornell University Press, 2008), 80.
52. Malloy, 79.
53. Malloy, 84.
54. Malloy, 111.
55. Wellerstein, *Restricted Data*, 2021: 139.
56. Malloy, *Atomic Tragedy*, 93.
57. Malloy, 95.
58. Sherwin, *World Destroyed*, 226.

59. Martin J. Sherwin, *Gambling with Armageddon: Nuclear Roulette from Hiroshima to the Cuban Missile Crisis* (New York: Knopf, 2020), 52.
60. Chris Wallace and Mitch Weiss, *Countdown 1945: The Extraordinary Story of the Atomic Bomb and 116 Days That Changed the World* (New York: Avid Reader Press, 2020), 137.
61. Sherwin, *World Destroyed*, 227.
62. Sherwin, 227–228.
63. Boyer, *By the Bomb's Early Light*, 52.
64. Paul Ham, *Hiroshima Nagasaki: The Real Story of the Atomic Bombings and Their Aftermath* (New York: Thomas Dunne Books, 2014), 463.
65. J. Robert Oppenheimer, "Letter from J. R. Oppenheimer to Henry Stimson," *Teaching American History*, August 17, 1945, 3, https://teachingamericanhistory .org/document/letter-to-secretary-of-war-henry-stimson/.
66. Ham, *Hiroshima Nagasaki*, 463.
67. Boyer, *By the Bomb's Early Light*, 52.
68. Malloy, *Atomic Tragedy*, 145.
69. Sherwin, *Gambling with Armageddon*, 65.
70. Sherwin, 65.
71. Malloy, *Atomic Tragedy*, 153.
72. Boyer, *By the Bomb's Early Light*, 53.
73. Bird and Sherwin, *American Prometheus*, 341–342.
74. Bird and Sherwin, 343.
75. Campbell Craig and Sergey Radchenko, *The Atomic Bomb and the Origins of the Cold War* (New Haven, CT: Yale University Press, 2008), 131.
76. Boyer, *By the Bomb's Early Light*, 56.
77. Boyer, 56.
78. Wellerstein, *Restricted Data*, 175.
79. Sherwin, *Gambling with Armageddon*, 4.
80. Carl Boggs, *The Crimes of Empire: Rogue Superpower and World Domination* (London: Pluto Press, 2010); Ronald C. Kramer, *Carbon Criminals, Climate Crimes* (New Brunswick, NJ: Rutgers University Press, 2020).
81. Stephen Wertheim, *Tomorrow, the World: The Birth of U.S. Global Supremacy* (Cambridge, MA: Belknap, 2020).
82. William Appleman Williams, *The Tragedy of American Diplomacy* (1959; New York: Norton, 1988).
83. Wertheim, *Tomorrow, the World*, 3–4.
84. Wertheim, 7.
85. Quoted in Andrew J. Bacevich, *American Empire: The Realities and Consequences of U.S. Diplomacy* (Cambridge, MA: Harvard University Press, 2002), 27.
86. Glenda Elizabeth Gilmore and Thomas J. Sugrue, *These United States: A Nation in the Making, 1890 to the Present* (New York: Norton, 2015), 289.
87. Leo Panitch and Sam Gindin, *The Making of Global Capitalism: The Political Economy of American Empire* (London: Verso, 2012), 72.
88. Wertheim, *Tomorrow, the World*, 12.
89. Gar Alperovitz, *Atomic Diplomacy: Hiroshima and Potsdam: The Use of the Atomic Bomb and the American Confrontation with Soviet Power* (New York: Simon & Schuster, 1965); Gar Alperovitz, *The Decision to Use the Atomic Bomb and the Architecture of an American Myth* (New York: Knopf, 1995).
90. Gregg Herken, *The Winning Weapon: The Atomic Bomb in the Cold War* (Princeton, NJ: Princeton University Press, 1988).
91. Sherwin, *World Destroyed*, 237.

92. Robert J. McMahon and Thomas G. Paterson, eds., *The Origins of the Cold War*, 4th ed. (Boston: Houghton Mifflin, 1999); Odd Arne Westad, *The Cold War: A World History* (New York: Basic Books, 2017).

93. Sherwin, *Gambling with Armageddon*, 34.

94. Robert J. McMahon, *The Cold War: A Very Short Introduction* (Oxford: Oxford University Press, 2003), 27.

95. Gilmore and Sugrue, *These United States*, 305.

96. Jill Lepore, *These Truths: A History of the United States* (New York: Norton, 2018), 537.

97. George Kennan (under the pseudonym X), "The Sources of Soviet Conduct," *Foreign Affairs* 25 (July 1947): 566–582.

98. Gilmore and Sugrue, *These United States*, 307.

99. Lepore, *These Truths*, 338.

100. Bacevich, *American Empire*, 4.

101. Wertheim, *Tomorrow, the World*; Lepore, *These Truths*.

102. Lepore, *These Truths*, 538.

103. Herken, *Winning Weapon*, 259.

104. McMahon, *Cold War*, 32.

105. Sherwin, *Gambling with Armageddon*, 67.

106. Joseph M. Siracusa, *Nuclear Weapons: A Very Short Introduction* (Oxford: Oxford University Press, 2008), 53.

107. Herken, *Winning Weapon*.

108. Siracusa, *Nuclear Weapons*, 54.

109. Wolverton, *Nuclear Weapons*, 76.

110. Herken, *Winning Weapon*, 307.

111. Craig and Radchenko, *Atomic Bomb*.

112. Ellen Schrecker, *Many Are the Crimes: McCarthyism in America* (Boston: Little, Brown, 1998); Albert Fried, *McCarthyism: The Great American Red Scare: A Documentary History* (New York: Oxford University Press, 1997); David Reynolds, *America, Empire of Liberty: A New History of the United States* (New York: Basic Books, 2009); Gilmore and Sugrue, *These United States*; Lepore, *These Truths*.

113. Sherwin, *Gambling with Armageddon*, 71.

114. Lepore, *These Truths*, 537.

115. Bruce Cumings, *The Korean War: A History* (New York: Modern Library, 2010), 213.

116. Herken, *Winning Weapon*, 254.

117. Reynolds, *America, Empire of Liberty*, 323.

110. Boggs, *Origins of the Warfare State*, 3.

119. McMahon, *Cold War*, 51.

120. Cumings, *Korean War*, 207.

121. Boyer, *By the Bomb's Early Light*, 108.

122. Cumings, *Korean War*, 210.

123. Cumings, 211.

124. Boggs, *Origins of the Warfare State*.

125. Robert Jay Lifton and Richard Falk, *Indefensible Weapons: The Political and Psychological Case Against Nuclearism* (New York: Basic Books, 1982).

126. Gerson, *Empire and the Bomb*.

127. Bacevich, *American Empire*, 228.

128. Noam Chomsky, *The Umbrella of U.S. Power: The Universal Declaration of Human Rights and the Contradictions of U.S. Policy* (New York: Seven Stories Press, 1999).

129. Gerson, *Empire and the Bomb*, 2.

130. Chalmers Johnson, *The Sorrows of Empire: Militarism, Secrecy, and the End of the Republic* (New York: Metropolitan Books, 2004).
131. Niall Ferguson, *Colossus: The Price of America's Empire* (New York: Penguin, 2004), 78.
132. Boggs, *Origins of the Warfare State*, 110.
133. Daniel Ellsberg, *The Doomsday Machine: Confessions of a Nuclear War Planner* (New York: Bloomsbury, 2017), 319.

CHAPTER 5   NUCLEAR MADNESS, ARMS CONTROL TREATIES, AND THE END OF THE COLD WAR

Epigraph 1: Martin J. Sherwin, *Gambling with Armageddon: Nuclear Roulette from Hiroshima to the Cuban Missile Crisis* (New York: Knopf, 2020), 9.

Epigraph 2: Lawrence S. Wittner, *Confronting the Bomb: A Short History of the World Nuclear Disarmament Movement* (Stanford, CA: Stanford University Press, 2009), 177.

1. Vincent J. Intondi, *Saving the World from Nuclear War: The June 12, 1982, Disarmament Rally and Beyond* (Baltimore: Johns Hopkins University Press, 2023).
2. Wittner, *Confronting the Bomb*.
3. Joseph Cirincione, *Bomb Scare: The History and Future of Nuclear Weapons* (New York: Columbia University Press, 2007), 43.
4. Carl Boggs, *Origins of the Warfare State: World War II and the Transformation of American Politics* (New York: Routledge, 2017), 110.
5. Sherwin, *Gambling with Armageddon*, 77.
6. Gary Gerstle, *The Rise and Fall of the Neoliberal Order: America and the World in the Free Market Era* (New York: Oxford University Press, 2022), 38.
7. Odd Arne Westad, *The Cold War: A World History* (New York: Basic Books, 2017), 287.
8. Sherwin, *Gambling with Armageddon*, 79–81.
9. Daniel A. Sjursen, *A True History of the United States: Indigenous Genocide, Racialized Slavery, Hyper-Capitalism, Militarist Imperialism, and Other Overlooked Aspects of American Exceptionalism* (Lebanon, NH: Truth to Power, 2021), 436–437.
10. Sherwin, *Gambling with Armageddon*, 80–81.
11. Stephen Kinzer, *The Brothers: John Foster Dulles, Allen Dulles, and Their Secret World War* (New York: St. Martin's Griffin, 2013), 313.
12. Kinzer, 314.
13. Kinzer, 312.
14. Sherwin, *Gambling with Armageddon*, 79.
15. Sherwin, 81.
16. Westad, *Cold War*.
17. Matthew Evangelista, *Unarmed Forces: The Transnational Movement to End the Cold War* (Ithaca, NY: Cornell University Press, 1999), 40.
18. David Reynolds, *America, Empire of Liberty: A New History of the United States* (New York: Basic Books, 2009), 325.
19. Daniel Ellsberg, *The Doomsday Machine: Confessions of a Nuclear War Planner* (New York: Bloomsbury, 2017), 317.
20. David Kauzlarich and Ronald C. Kramer, *Crimes of the American Nuclear State: At Home and Abroad* (Boston: Northeastern University Press, 1998), 63–64.
21. Kauzlarich and Kramer, *Crimes of the American Nuclear State*, 64.
22. Ellsberg, *Doomsday Machine*; Sjursen, *True History of the United States*.
23. Robert J. McMahon, *The Cold War: A Very Short Introduction* (Oxford: Oxford University Press, 2003), 79–80.

24. Charlie Savage, "Risk of Nuclear War over Taiwan in 1958 Said to Be Greater Than Publicly Known," *New York Times*, November 3, 2021, https://www.nytimes.com/2021/05/22/us/politics/nuclear-war-risk-1958-us-china.html.

25. Joseph Gerson, *Empire and the Bomb: How the U.S. Uses Nuclear Weapons to Dominate the World* (London: Pluto Press, 2007); Ellsberg, *Doomsday Machine*.

26. Noam Chomsky, *World Orders Old and New* (New York: Columbia University Press, 1994); Noam Chomsky, *The Umbrella of U.S. Power: The Universal Declaration of Human Rights and the Contradictions of U.S. Policy* (New York: Seven Stories Press, 1999).

27. Gerson, *Empire and the Bomb*, 2.

28. Evangelista, *Unarmed Forces*, 31.

29. Evangelista, 3.

30. Evangelista, 32.

31. William Lanouette, *Genius in the Shadows: A Biography of Leo Szilard, the Man Behind the Bomb* (New York: Skyhorse, 2013), 323.

32. Jonathan Schell, *The Seventh Decade: The New Shape of Nuclear Danger* (New York: Metropolitan Books, 2007).

33. Schell, 38.

34. Schell, 38.

35. Quoted in Sherwin, *Gambling with Armageddon*, 85.

36. Kai Bird and Martin J. Sherwin, *American Prometheus: The Triumph and Tragedy of J. Robert Oppenheimer* (New York: Knopf, 2005), 548.

37. Ellsberg, *Doomsday Machine*; Fred Kaplan, *The Bomb: Presidents, Generals, and the Secret History of Nuclear War* (New York: Simon & Schuster, 2020).

38. Westad, *Cold War*, 289–290.

39. Ellsberg, *Doomsday Machine*, 136.

40. Boggs, *Origins of the Warfare State*, 133.

41. C. Wright Mills, *The Causes of World War III* (1958; New York: Ballantine Books, 1960).

42. Sherwin, *Gambling with Armageddon*, 4.

43. Sherwin, 4.

44. Mills, *Causes of World War III*, 90.

45. Sherwin, *Gambling with Armageddon*, 468.

46. Mills, *Causes of World War III*, 89.

47. Sherwin, *Gambling with Armageddon*, 9.

48. Sherwin, 469.

49. Kaplan, *The Bomb*, 86.

50. Kaplan, 88.

51. Evangelista, *Unarmed Forces*, 46.

52. Wittner, *Confronting the Bomb*, 82.

53. Schell, *Seventh Decade*, 105.

54. Jonathan R. Hunt, *The Nuclear Club: How America and the World Policed the Atom from Hiroshima to Vietnam* (Stanford, CA: Stanford University Press, 2022), 245.

55. Cirincione, *Bomb Scare*, 29.

56. Hunt, *Nuclear Club*, 12.

57. Hunt, 256.

58. Ronald C. Kramer and Amanda Marie Smith, "Death Flies Down: The Bombing of Civilians and the Paradox of International Law," in *Towards a Victimology of State Crime*, ed. Dawn Rothe and Dave Kauzlarich (London: Routledge, 2014), 100–130.

59. Kauzlarich and Kramer, *Crimes of the American Nuclear State*.

60. Ellsberg, *Doomsday Machine*, 311.

61. Kauzlarich and Kramer, *Crimes of the American Nuclear State*.

62. Joseph M. Siracusa, *Nuclear Weapons: A Very Short Introduction* (Oxford: Oxford University Press, 2008), 77.
63. McMahon, *Cold War*, 122.
64. McMahon, 122–123.
65. Siracusa, *Nuclear Weapons*, 68.
66. Michael R. Beschloss and Strobe Talbot, *At the Highest Levels: The Inside Story of the End of the Cold War* (Boston: Little, Brown, 1993), 112.
67. McMahon, *Cold War*, 124.
68. Reynolds, *America, Empire of Liberty*, 381.
69. McMahon, *Cold War*, 128.
70. Alva Myrdal, *The Game of Disarmament: How the United States and Russia Run the Arms Race* (New York: Pantheon Books, 1976).
71. McMahon, *Cold War*, 128.
72. Schell, *Seventh Decade*, 107–108.
73. Reynolds, *America, Empire of Liberty*, 413.
74. Kaplan, *The Bomb*, 130.
75. Andrew J. Bacevich, *America's War for the Greater Middle East: A Military History* (New York: Random House, 2016), 12.
76. Eric Schlosser, *Command and Control: Nuclear Weapons, the Damascus Accident, and the Illusion of Safety* (New York: Penguin, 2013), 362.
77. Kaplan, *The Bomb*, 121.
78. Andrew Hunt, *We Begin Bombing in Five Minutes: Late Cold War Culture in the Age of Reagan* (Amherst: University of Massachusetts Press, 2021), 9.
79. Schlosser, *Command and Control*, 362–363.
80. Hunt, *We Begin Bombing*, 8.
81. Hunt, 8.
82. McMahon, *Cold War*, 137.
83. Naomi Oreskes and Erik Conway, *Merchants of Doubt: How a Handful of Scientists Obscured the Truth on Issues from Tobacco to Global Warming* (New York: Bloomsbury, 2010), 17.
84. Oreskes and Conway.
85. David E. Hoffman, *The Dead Hand: The Untold Story of the Cold War Arms Race and Its Dangerous Legacy* (New York: Doubleday, 2009), 21.
86. Oreskes and Conway, *Merchants of Doubt*, 39.
87. Oreskes and Conway, 40.
88. Oreskes and Conway, 42.
89. Oreskes and Conway, 40.
90. Sjursen, *True History of the United States*, 550.
91. Kaplan, *The Bomb*, 128.
92. Kaplan, 129.
93. Kaplan, 130.
94. Kaplan, 132.
95. McMahon, *Cold War*, 138.
96. Reynolds, *America, Empire of Liberty*.
97. Sjursen, *True History of the United States*, 2021: 551.
98. Kaplan, *The Bomb*, 135.
99. McMahon, *Cold War*, 141.
100. Bacevich, *America's War*, 280.
101. Bacevich, 280, emphasis added.
102. Bacevich, 29.
103. Michael Klare, *Blood and Oil: The Dangers and Consequences of America's Growing Petroleum Dependency* (New York: Metropolitan Books, 2004).
104. Bacevich, *America's War*, 245.

105. Gerstle, *Rise and Fall of the Neoliberal Order.*
106. Gerstle, 141.
107. Reynolds, *America, Empire of Liberty.*
108. Gerstle, *Rise and Fall of the Neoliberal Order*, 116.
109. McMahon, *Cold War*, 145–146.
110. Wittner, *Confronting the Bomb*; Hunt, *We Begin Bombing.*
111. William M. Knoblauch, *Nuclear Freeze in a Cold War: The Reagan Administration, Cultural Activism, and the End of the Arms Race* (Amherst: University of Massachusetts Press, 2017).
112. Kevin M. Kruse and Julien E. Zelizer, *Fault Lines: A History of the United States since 1974* (New York: Norton, 2019), 123.
113. Kaplan, *The Bomb*, 147.
114. Oreskes and Conway, *Merchants of Doubt*, 40.
115. Kruse and Zelizer, *Fault Lines*, 123.
116. Hunt, *We Begin Bombing*, 108.
117. McMahon, *Cold War*, 146.
118. Kruse and Zelizer, *Fault Lines*, 124.
119. Kaplan, *The Bomb*, 148.
120. Glenda Elizabeth Gilmore and Thomas J. Sugrue, *These United States: A Nation in the Making, 1890 to the Present* (New York: Norton, 2015).
121. Westad, *Cold War*, 501.
122. Paul Boyer, *Fallout: A Historian Reflects on America's Half-Century Encounter with Nuclear Weapons* (Columbus: Ohio State University Press, 1998), 129.
123. Wittner, *Confronting the Bomb*, 141.
124. McMahon, *Cold War*, 154.
125. McMahon, 156.
126. Knoblauch, *Nuclear Freeze in a Cold War*, 11.
127. Jonathan Schell, *The Fate of the Earth* (New York: Knopf, 1982); Ground Zero, *Nuclear War: What's in It for You?* (New York: Pocket Books, 1982).
128. Wittner, *Confronting the Bomb*, 121.
129. Jonathan Schell, "The Spirit of June 12," *The Nation* 285 (July 2, 2007): 4.
130. Wittner, *Confronting the Bomb*, 152.
131. Wittner, 123.
132. Intondi, *Saving the World from Nuclear War*, 26.
133. Wittner, *Confronting the Bomb*, 123.
134. Schell, "Spirit of June 12," 4.
135. Intondi, *Saving the World from Nuclear War.*
136. Wittner, *Confronting the Bomb*, 154.
137. Schell, "Spirit of June 12," 4.
138. Wittner, *Confronting the Bomb*, 164.
139. Vincent J. Intondi, "The Fight Continues: Reflections on the June 12, 1982, Rally for Nuclear Disarmament," *Arms Control Now*, June 10, 2018, 2, https://www.armscontrol.org/blog/2018-06-10/fight-continues-reflections-june-12-1982-rally-nuclear-disarmament. See also Intondi, *Saving the World from Nuclear War*, 100–101.
140. Knoblauch, *Nuclear Freeze in a Cold War.*
141. Knoblauch, 34–35.
142. Lawrence Badash, *A Nuclear Winter's Tale: Science and Politics in the 1980s* (Cambridge, MA: MIT Press, 2009); Oreskes and Conway, *Merchants of Doubt*; Paul Rubinson, "The Global Effects of Nuclear Winter: Science and Antinuclear Protest in the United States and Soviet Union during the 1980s," *Cold War History* 14 (2014): 47–69; Knoblauch, *Nuclear Freeze in a Cold War.*
143. Knoblauch, *Nuclear Freeze in a Cold War*, 53.

144. Hunt, *We Begin Bombing*.
145. Knoblauch, *Nuclear Freeze in a Cold War*, 60.
146. Knoblauch, 63.
147. Hunt, *We Begin Bombing*, 107.
148. Hunt.
149. Kruse and Zelizer, *Fault Lines*, 128.
150. Kruse and Zelizer, 165.
151. Reynolds, *America, Empire of Liberty*, 422.
152. Kaplan, *The Bomb*, 150.
153. Kaplan, 150.
154. Knoblauch, *Nuclear Freeze in a Cold War*, 105.
155. Evangelista, *Unarmed Forces*, 390.
156. Hunt, *We Begin Bombing*, 120.
157. Kruse and Zelizer, *Fault Lines*, 165.
158. Evangelista, *Unarmed Forces*, 323.
159. McMahon, *Cold War*, 162.
160. Kaplan, *The Bomb*, 166.
161. Schell, *Seventh Decade*, 186.
162. Kaplan, *The Bomb*.
163. Wittner, *Confronting the Bomb*.
164. Mark Wolverton, *Nuclear Weapons* (Cambridge, MA: MIT Press, 2022), 170.
165. McMahon, *Cold War*, 162.
166. Schell, *Seventh Decade*, 107.
167. Kaplan, *The Bomb*, 170.
168. Kaplan, 171.
169. Evangelista, *Unarmed Forces*, 328.
170. McMahon, *Cold War*, 163.
171. Wolverton, *Nuclear Weapons*, 172.
172. McMahon, *Cold War*, 163.
173. Kruse and Zelizer, *Fault Lines*, 169.
174. McMahon, *Cold War*, 166.
175. Gerstle, *Rise and Fall of the Neoliberal Order*, 143.
176. Beschloss and Talbot, *At the Highest Levels*, 14.
177. Beschloss and Talbot, 28.
178. Evangelista, *Unarmed Forces*.
179. Beschloss and Talbot, 115.
180. Wolverton, *Nuclear Weapons*, 173.
181. Kaplan, *The Bomb*, 194.
182. Westad, *Cold War*, 616.
183. Westad, 616.

CHAPTER 6   AFTER THE COLD WAR

Epigraph 1: Michael Klare, *Rogue States and Nuclear Outlaws: America's Search for a New Foreign Policy* (New York: Hill & Wang, 1995), 27–28.

Epigraph 2: Matthew Evangelista, *Unarmed Forces: The Transnational Movement to End the Cold War* (Ithaca, NY: Cornell University Press, 1999), 39.

Epigraph 3: Jonathan Schell, *The Unfinished Twentieth Century* (London: Verso, 2001), 9.

1. Barack Obama, "Remarks by President Barack Obama in Prague as Delivered" (White House, April 5, 2009), https://obamawhitehouse.archives.gov/the-press-office/remarks-president-barack-obama-prague-delivered.

2. Joseph M. Siracusa, *Nuclear Weapons: A Very Short Introduction*, 3rd ed. (Oxford: Oxford University Press, 2020), 121.
3. Fred Kaplan, *The Bomb: Presidents, Generals, and the Secret History of Nuclear War* (New York: Simon & Schuster, 2020).
4. Kaplan, 223.
5. George P. Shultz, William J. Perry, Henry A. Kissinger, and Sam Nunn, "A World Free of Nuclear Weapons," *Wall Street Journal*, January 4, 2007, A15.
6. Kaplan, *The Bomb*, 225.
7. Kaplan, 225.
8. Obama, "Remarks."
9. Obama.
10. Obama.
11. Obama.
12. Tad Daley, *Apocalypse Never: Forging the Path to a Nuclear Weapon-Free World* (New Brunswick, NJ: Rutgers University Press, 2010), 15.
13. Obama, "Remarks."
14. Daley, *Apocalypse Never*; Jonathan Schell, "Reaching Zero," *The Nation* 290 (April 19, 2010): 11–18.
15. Christian Sorensen, *Understanding the War Industry* (Atlanta: Clarity Press, 2020).
16. Jonathan Schell, *The Gift of Time: The Case for Abolishing Nuclear Weapons Now* (New York: Metropolitan Books, 1998), 16.
17. Schell, *Gift of Time*, 11.
18. Klare, *Rogue States and Nuclear Outlaws*, 206.
19. Schell, *Gift of Time*, 11.
20. Schell, 12.
21. Schell, 16.
22. Jonathan Schell, *The Seventh Decade: The New Shape of Nuclear Danger* (New York: Metropolitan Books, 2007).
23. Schell, *Unfinished Twentieth Century*, 47.
24. Joseph Cirincione, *Bomb Scare: The History and Future of Nuclear Weapons* (New York: Columbia University Press, 2007), 42.
25. Hans M. Kristensen, Matt Korda, and Eliana Reynolds, "Status of World Nuclear Forces" (Federation of American Scientists, last updated March 28, 2023), 1, https://fas.org/issues/nuclear-weapons/status-world-nuclear-forces/.
26. Schell, *Seventh Decade*, 90.
27. Michael R. Beschloss and Strobe Talbot, *At the Highest Levels: The Inside Story of the End of the Cold War* (Boston: Little, Brown, 1993), 469.
28. Kaplan, *The Bomb*, 194.
29. Kaplan, 194.
30. Scott Ritter, *Dangerous Ground: America's Failed Arms Control Policy, from FDR to Obama* (New York: Nation Books, 2010), 304.
31. Ritter, *Dangerous Ground*; Siracusa, *Nuclear Weapons*.
32. Cirincione, *Bomb Scare*, 41.
33. Kaplan, *The Bomb*, 195.
34. Schell, *Unfinished Twentieth Century*, 70.
35. Klare, *Rogue States and Nuclear Outlaws*, 26.
36. Schell, *Seventh Decade*, 92.
37. Carl Boggs, *Origins of the Warfare State: World War II and the Transformation of American Politics* (New York: Routledge, 2017), 113.
38. Klare, *Rogue States and Nuclear Outlaws*, 6.
39. Klare, 10.
40. Schell, *Seventh Decade*, 93.
41. Klare, *Rogue States and Nuclear Outlaws*.

42. Klare, 121–122.
43. Schell, *Seventh Decade*, 94.
44. Klare, *Rogue States and Nuclear Outlaws*, 18.
45. Schell, *Seventh Decade*, 93.
46. Daley, *Apocalypse Never*; Shane J. Maddock, *Nuclear Apartheid: The Quest for American Atomic Supremacy from World War II to the Present* (Chapel Hill: University of North Carolina Press, 2010).
47. Andrew J. Bacevich, *America's War for the Greater Middle East: A Military History* (New York: Random House, 2016).
48. Larry Everest, *Oil, Power, and Empire: Iraq and the U.S. Global Agenda* (Monroe, ME: Common Courage Press, 2004), 32.
49. Michael Klare, *Blood and Oil: The Dangers and Consequences of America's Growing Petroleum Dependency* (New York: Metropolitan Books, 2004), xiv.
50. Andrew J. Bacevich, *The New American Militarism: How Americans Are Seduced by War* (New York: Oxford University Press, 2005).
51. Klare, *Blood and Oil*, 49.
52. Beschloss and Talbot, *At the Highest Levels*, 470.
53. Klare, *Rogue States and Nuclear Outlaws*.
54. Klare, *Blood and Oil*, 50.
55. Bacevich, *America's War for the Greater Middle East*, 13.
56. Klare, *Rogue States and Nuclear Outlaws*, 62.
57. Klare, 63.
58. Seymour Melman, *Pentagon Capitalism: The Political Economy of War* (New York: McGraw-Hill, 1970).
59. Sorensen, *Understanding the War Industry*.
60. Julia Gledhill and William Hartung, "Spending Unlimited: Contractors Cash in as Congress Adds Billions to the Pentagon Budget," *TomDispatch.com*, September 11, 2022, 3, https://tomdispatch.com/spending-unlimited/.
61. Klare, *Rogue States and Nuclear Outlaws*, 32.
62. Kenneth A. Gould, David N. Pellow, and Allan Schnaiberg, *The Treadmill of Production: Injustice and Unsustainability in the Global Economy* (Boulder, CO: Paradigm, 2008).
63. Gregory Hooks and Chad L. Smith, "The Treadmill of Destruction: National Sacrifice Areas and Native Americans," *American Sociological Review* 69 (2004): 558.
64. Robert J. Antonio and Brett Clark, "The Climate Change Divide in Social Theory," in *Climate Change and Society: Sociological Perspectives*, ed. Riley E. Dunlap and Robert J. Brulle (New York: Oxford University Press, 2015), 333–368.
65. Allan Schnaiberg, *The Environment: From Surplus to Scarcity* (New York: Oxford University Press, 1980); Gould, Pellow, and Schnaiberg, *Treadmill of Production*.
66. Paul B. Stretesky, Michael A. Long, and Michael J. Lynch, *The Treadmill of Crime: Political Economy and Green Criminology* (London: Routledge, 2014).
67. Gregory Hooks and Chad L. Smith, "Treadmills of Production and Destruction: Threats to the Environment Posed by Militarism," *Organizations & Environment* 18 (2005): 21.
68. Brett Clark and Andrew K. Jorgenson, "The Treadmill of Destruction and the Environmental Impacts of Militaries," *Sociology Compass* 6/7 (2012): 566.
69. Sorensen, *Understanding the War Industry*, 321–323.
70. David Reynolds, *America, Empire of Liberty: A New History of the United States* (New York: Basic Books, 2009), 442.
71. Glenda Elizabeth Gilmore and Thomas J. Sugrue, *These United States: A Nation in the Making, 1890 to the Present* (New York: Norton, 2015), 586.

72. Jill Lepore, *These Truths: A History of the United States* (New York: Norton, 2018), 699.

73. Gary Gerstle, *The Rise and Fall of the Neoliberal Order: America and the World in the Free Market Era* (New York: Oxford University Press, 2022), 156.

74. Kevin M. Kruse and Julian E. Zelizer, *Fault Lines: A History of the United States since 1974* (New York: Norton, 2019), 201.

75. Kaplan, *The Bomb*, 198.

76. Schell, *Seventh Decade*, 100.

77. Helen Caldicott, *The New Nuclear Danger: George W. Bush's Military-Industrial Complex* (New York: New Press, 2002), 3.

78. Schell, *Seventh Decade*, 88.

79. Andrew J. Bacevich, *American Empire: The Realities and Consequences of U.S. Diplomacy* (Cambridge, MA: Harvard University Press, 2002).

80. Gary Dorrien, *Imperial Designs: Neoconservatism and the New Pax Americana* (New York: Routledge, 2004), 225.

81. Gerstle, *Rise and Fall of the Neoliberal Order*, 145.

82. Medea Benjamin and Nicolas J. S. Davies, *War in Ukraine: Making Sense of a Senseless Conflict* (New York: OR Books, 2022), 16–17.

83. Benjamin and Davies, 103.

84. Ritter, *Dangerous Ground*, 322.

85. Benjamin and Davies, *War in Ukraine*, 103.

86. Benjamin and Davies, 103–105.

87. Klare, *Rogue States and Nuclear Outlaws*, 109.

88. Klare, 109.

89. Klare, 112.

90. Klare.

91. Schell, *Seventh Decade*, 87.

92. Schell.

93. Ritter, *Dangerous Ground*, 315.

94. Schell, *Seventh Decade*, 88.

95. Ritter, *Dangerous Ground*, 316.

96. Klare, *Rogue States and Nuclear Outlaws*, 124.

97. Schell, *Seventh Decade*, 88.

98. Klare, *Rogue States and Nuclear Outlaws*, 124.

99. Siracusa, *Nuclear Weapons*.

100. Ritter, *Dangerous Ground*, 317.

101. Ritter, 325.

102. Ritter, 327.

103. Ritter, 328.

104. Ritter, 331.

105. Ritter, 333.

106. Milan Rai, *Regime Unchanged: Why the War on Iraq Changed Nothing* (London: Pluto Press, 2003).

107. Rai, *Regime Unchanged*; Scott Ritter, *Frontier Justice: Weapons of Mass Destruction and the Bushwacking of America* (New York: Context Books, 2003); Ritter, *Dangerous Ground*; Geoff Simons, *Targeting Iraq: Sanctions and Bombing in U.S. Policy* (London: Saqi Books, 2002).

108. Ritter, *Dangerous Ground*, 332.

109. Schell, *Seventh Decade*, 97.

110. Schell, 97.

111. Kaplan, *The Bomb*, 210.

112. Kaplan, 210.

113. Ronald C. Kramer, Raymond J. Michalowski, and Dawn L. Rothe, "The Supreme International Crime: How the U.S. War in Iraq Threatens the Rule of Law," *Social Justice* 32 (2005): 52–81.
114. Ronald C. Kramer and Raymond J. Michalowski, "War, Aggression and State Crime: A Criminological Analysis of the Invasion and Occupation of Iraq," *British Journal of Criminology* 45 (July 2005): 446–469; Michael Schwartz, *War without End: The Iraq War in Context* (Chicago: Haymarket, 2008); Rebecca Gordon, *American Nuremberg: The US Officials Who Should Stand Trial for Post-9/11 War Crimes* (New York: Hot Books, 2016).
115. Ronald C. Kramer, *Carbon Criminals, Climate Crimes* (New Brunswick, NJ: Rutgers University Press, 2020).
116. Schell, *Seventh Decade*, 115.
117. Daley, *Apocalypse Never.*
118. Benjamin and Davies, *War in Ukraine.*
119. Dorrien, *Imperial Designs*, 9–10.
120. David Armstrong, "Dick Cheney's Song of America: Drafting a Plan for Global Dominance," *Harper's Magazine*, October 2001, 8.
121. Armstrong, "Dick Cheney's Song of America"; Stefan Halper and Jonathan Clarke, *America Alone: The Neoconservatives and the Global Order* (Cambridge: Cambridge University Press, 2004); James Mann, *The Rise of the Vulcans: The History of Bush's War Cabinet* (New York: Viking, 2004); Bacevich, *America's War for the Greater Middle East.*
122. Mann, *Rise of the Vulcans.*
123. Dorrien, *Imperial Designs*; Bacevich, *America's War for the Greater Middle East.*
124. Halper and Clarke, *America Alone*; Mann, *Rise of the Vulcans.*
125. Dorrien, *Imperial Designs.*
126. Dorrien.
127. Charles Krauthammer, "The Unipolar Moment," *Foreign Affairs* 70 (1991): 23–33.
128. Ira Chernus, *Monsters to Destroy: The Neoconservative War on Terror and Sin* (London: Routledge, 2006).
129. Kramer and Michalowski, "War, Aggression and State Crime."
130. Schell, *Seventh Decade*, 100.
131. Schell, *Seventh Decade*; Daley, *Apocalypse Never.*
132. Ritter, *Dangerous Ground*, 347–348.
133. Schell, *Seventh Decade*, 114.
134. Daley, *Apocalypse Never.*
135. Harald Muller, *The 2005 NPT Review Conference: Reasons and Consequences of Failure and Options for Repair* (Stockholm: Weapons of Mass Destruction Commission, 2005); Ritter, *Dangerous Ground.*
136. Schell, *Seventh Decade*, 108.
137. Cirincione, *Bomb Scare*, 114.
138. Daley, *Apocalypse Never*, 101.
139. Schell, *Seventh Decade*, 104.
140. Daley, *Apocalypse Never*, 100.
141. Schell, *Seventh Decade*; Ritter, *Dangerous Ground.*
142. Kaplan, *The Bomb*, 218.
143. Kaplan, 217.
144. Philippe Sands, *Lawless World* (New York: Penguin, 2005).
145. Daley, *Apocalypse Never*, 98.
146. Cirincione, *Bomb Scare*, 112.
147. Muller, *2005 NPT Review Conference*, 1.
148. Muller.
149. Ritter, *Dangerous Ground*, 342.

150. Ritter, 343.

151. Benjamin and Davies, *War in Ukraine*, 16–17.

152. Ritter, *Dangerous Ground*, 349.

153. Siracusa, *Nuclear Weapons*, 117.

154. Ritter, *Dangerous Ground*, 365.

155. Ronald C. Kramer and Elizabeth A. Bradshaw, "US State Crimes Related to Nuclear Weapons: Is There Hope for Change in the Obama Administration?," *International Journal of Comparative and Applied Criminal Justice* 35 (2011): 243–259.

156. Robert Scheer, "Earning His Nobel Prize," *CBS News*, April 7, 2010, https://www.cbsnews.com/news/earning-his-nobel-prize.

157. Kaplan, *The Bomb*, 227.

158. Kaplan, 227.

159. Jonathan Alter, *The Promise: President Obama, Year One* (New York: Simon & Schuster, 2010), 225.

160. Alter, 225.

161. Hans Blix, "A Season for Disarmament," *New York Times*, April 4, 2010, 1, https://www.nytimes.com/2010/04/05/opinion/05iht-edblix.html.

162. Schell, "Reaching Zero," 14.

163. Sorensen, *Understanding the War Industry*, 321.

164. Walter Pincus, "Nuclear Complex Upgrades Related to START Treaty to Cost $180 Billion," *Washington Post*, May 14, 2010, https://www.washingtonpost.com/wp-dyn/content/article/2010/05/13/AR2010051305031.html.

165. Kaplan, *The Bomb*, 236.

166. Kramer and Bradshaw, "US State Crimes."

167. Steven Pifer, "10 Years after Obama's Nuclear-Free Vision, the US and Russia Head in the Opposite Direction" (Brookings Institution, April 4, 2019), https://www.brookings.edu/articles/10-years-after-obamas-nuclear-free-vision-the-us-and-russia-head-in-the-opposite-direction/.

168. Kaplan, *The Bomb*, 247.

169. Benjamin and Davies, *War in Ukraine*, 17.

170. John Feffer, "Obama's Nuclear Paradox," *Foreign Policy in Focus*, June 1, 2016, 1, https://fpif.org/obamas-nuclear-paradox/.

171. Feffer, 1.

172. Feffer, 1.

173. Kaplan, *The Bomb*, 243.

174. Kaplan, 243.

175. Feffer, "Obama's Nuclear Paradox"; Kaplan, *The Bomb*.

CHAPTER 7   CURRENT APOCALYPTIC THREATS, THE AMERICAN EMPIRE, AND A PATHWAY TO THE ABOLITION OF NUCLEAR WEAPONS

Epigraph 1: Tad Daley, *Apocalypse Never: Forging the Path to a Nuclear Weapon-Free World* (New Brunswick, NJ: Rutgers University Press, 2010), 229.

Epigraph 2: Jonathan Schell, *The Unconquerable World: Power, Nonviolence, and the Will of the People* (New York: Metropolitan Books, 2003), 355.

1. Robert Jay Lifton and Richard Falk, *Indefensible Weapons: The Political and Psychological Case Against Nuclearism* (New York: Basic Books, 1982), 118.

2. Ronald C. Kramer and Sam Marullo, "Toward a Sociology of Nuclear Weapons," *Sociological Quarterly* 26, no. 3 (1985): 277–292.

3. David Kauzlarich, Ronald C. Kramer, and Brian Smith, "Toward the Study of Governmental Crime: Nuclear Weapons, Foreign Intervention, and International Law," *Humanity and Society* 16, no. 4 (1992): 543–563; David Kauzlarich

and Ronald C. Kramer, "State-Corporate Crime in the US Nuclear Weapons Production Complex," *Journal of Human Justice* 5 (1993): 4–28; David Kauzlarich and Ronald C. Kramer, "The Nuclear Terrorist State," *Peace Review* 7 (1995): 333–337; David Kauzlarich and Ronald C. Kramer, *Crimes of the American Nuclear State: At Home and Abroad* (Boston: Northeastern University Press, 1998).

4. Ronald C. Kramer and David Kauzlarich, "The Opinion of the International Court of Justice on the Use of Nuclear Weapons: Implications for Criminology," *Contemporary Justice Review* 2 (1999): 395–413.

5. Lifton and Falk, *Indefensible Weapons*, 125.

6. Jonathan Schell, *The Gift of Time: The Case for Abolishing Nuclear Weapons Now* (New York: Metropolitan Books, 1998).

7. Linda McQuaiq, "Western Leaders Don't Want Us to Worry about Nuclear War, but We Should," *Toronto Star*, June 29, 2023, https://www.thestar.com/opinion/contributors/2023/06/29/western-leaders-dont-want-us-to-worry-about-nuclear-war-but-we-should.html.

8. Michael Klare, "Surviving an Era of Pervasive Nuclear Instability: A Call for Grassroots Activism," *The Nation*, February 12, 2024, https://www.thenation.com/article/world/surviving-an-era-of-pervasive-nuclear-instability/.

9. Richard Falk, "A Radical World Order Challenge: Addressing Global Climate Change and the Threat of Nuclear Weapons," *Globalizations* 7 (2010): 137–153; Richard Falk, *Public Intellectual: The Life of a Citizen Pilgrim* (Atlanta: Clarity Press, 2021).

10. Richard Falk, "Geopolitical Crimes: A Preliminary Jurisprudential Proposal," *State Crime* 8, no. 1 (2019): 18.

11. Falk, "Radical World Order Challenge," 151.

12. Falk, *Public Intellectual*, 417.

13. Falk, "Radical World Order Challenge," 151.

14. Hans M. Kristensen, Matt Korda, and Eliana Reynolds, "Status of World Nuclear Forces" (Federation of American Scientists, last updated March 28, 2023), 1, https://fas.org/issues/nuclear-weapons/status-world-nuclear-forces/.

15. Kristensen, Korda, and Reynolds, 1.

16. Hans M. Kristensen and Matt Korda, "Nuclear Notebook: United States Nuclear Weapons, 2023," *Bulletin of the Atomic Scientists* 79 (2023): 28.

17. Kristensen and Korda, 28.

18. Kristensen and Korda, 28.

19. Kristensen and Korda, 28.

20. Hans M. Kristensen, Matt Korda, and Eliana Reynolds, "Nuclear Notebook: Russian Nuclear Weapons," *Bulletin of the Atomic Scientists* 79 (2023): 174.

21. Kristensen, Korda, and Reynolds, 174.

22. Kristensen, Korda, and Reynolds, 174.

23. Kristensen, Korda, and Reynolds, "Status of World Nuclear Forces," 1.

24. Jonathan Schell, *The Seventh Decade: The New Shape of Nuclear Danger* (New York: Metropolitan Books, 2007); Daley, *Apocalypse Never*.

25. Walter Pincus, "Nuclear Complex Upgrades Related to START Treaty to Cost $180 Billion," *Washington Post*, May 14, 2010, https://www.washingtonpost.com/wp-dyn/content/article/2010/05/13/AR2010051305031.html.

26. John Feffer, "Obama's Nuclear Paradox," *Foreign Policy in Focus*, June 1, 2016, https://fpif.org/obamas-nuclear-paradox/; Fred Kaplan, *The Bomb: Presidents, Generals, and the Secret History of Nuclear War* (New York: Simon & Schuster, 2020).

27. Jim Mattis, "Secretary of Defense Jim Mattis, House Armed Services Committee, Written Statement for the Record, February 6" (House Armed Services Committee, February 6, 2018), 10, emphasis added, https://docs.house.gov/meetings/AS/AS00/20180206/106833/HHRG-115-AS00-Wstate-MattisJ-20180206.pdf.

28. Michael Klare, "Making Nuclear Weapons Menacing Again: The Pentagon Plan to Overhaul the US Nuclear Arsenal Is as Costly as It Is Dangerous," *The Nation*, April 8, 2019, 17.

29. Klare, 17.

30. Center for Arms Control and Non-Proliferation, "2022 Nuclear Posture Review" (November 8, 2022), 1, https://armscontrolcenter.org/wp-content /uploads/2022/11/NPR-Fact-sheet.pdf.

31. Center for Arms Control and Non-Proliferation, "U.S. Nuclear Weapons Modernization: Costs & Constraints" (January 22, 2023), 1, https://arms controlcenter.org/fact-sheet-u-s-nuclear-weapons-modernization-costs -constraints/.

32. Vladimir Marakhonov, "How Chinese Military Aid to Russia Could Lead to a Strategic Reversal of Nuclear Forces," *Bulletin of the Atomic Scientists*, April 17, 2023, https://thebulletin.org/2023/04/how-chinese-military-aid-to-russia-could -lead-to-a-strategic-reversal-of-nuclear-forces/; David E. Sanger, William J. Broad, and Chris Buckley, "3 Nuclear Powers, Rather Than 2, Usher in a New Strategic Era," *New York Times*, April 19, 2023, https://www.nytimes.com/2023 /04/19/us/politics/china-nuclear-weapons-russia-arms-treaties.html.

33. Lisbeth Gronlund, "The New Nuclear Posture Review Is a Major Step Backward," *Bulletin of the Atomic Scientists*, November 4, 2022, 4, https:// thebulletin.org/2022/11/the-new-us-nuclear-posture-review-is-a-major-step -backward/.

34. Hans M. Kristensen, Matthew McKinzie, and Theodore Postal, "How US Nuclear Force Modernization Is Undermining Strategic Stability: The Burst-Height Compensating Super-Fuze," *Bulletin of the Atomic Scientists*, March 1, 2017, https://thebulletin.org/2017/03/how-us-nuclear-force-modernization-is -undermining-strategic-stability-the-burst-height-compensating-super-fuze/.

35. Daniel Ellsberg and Norman Solomon, "To Avoid Armageddon, Don't Modernize Missiles—Eliminate Them," *The Nation* 313 (November 1/8, 2021), 5–6. In July 2024, in an open letter to President Biden, more than 700 scientists called for an end to the US land-based nuclear weapons program that is set to be replaced. See Edward Carver, "Hundreds of Scientists Urge Biden to Cancel $100 Billion Nuclear Weapons Boondoggle," *Common Dreams*, July 8, 2024, 1, https://www .commondreams.org/news/scientists-end-land-based-nuclear-weapons.

36. John Mecklin, ed., "'A Time of Unprecedented Danger: It Is 90 Seconds to Midnight': 2023 Doomsday Clock Statement," *Bulletin of the Atomic Scientists*, January 24, 2023, 2.

37. Mecklin, 2.

38. John Mecklin, ed., "'A Moment of Historic Danger: It Is *Still* 90 Seconds to Midnight': 2024 Doomsday Clock Statement," *Bulletin of the Atomic Scientists*, January 23, 2024, 2.

39. Medea Benjamin and Nicolas J. S. Davies, *War in Ukraine: Making Sense of a Senseless Conflict* (New York: OR Books, 2022); Medea Benjamin and Nicolas J. S. Davies, "When Will US Join Global Call to End Ukraine War?," *Common Dreams*, May 30, 2023, https://www.commondreams.org/opinion/will-us-push-to-help -end-ukraine-war; Anatol Lieven, "A Peace Settlement in Ukraine: If the War Is to Ever End, It Will Have to Do So through Some Form of Pragmatic Compromise," *The Nation*, June 22, 2022, https://www.thenation.com/article/world/peace -settlement-ukraine/; Jessica Corbett, "Amid Fears over Russia-Belarus Nuke Deal, UN Official Calls for Talks to Ease Tensions," *Common Dreams*, March 31, 2023, https://www.commondreams.org/news/nakamitsu-united-nations-nuclear-russia; "The March of Folly," *The Nation* 316 (March 6–13, 2023): 4; Jeffrey D. Sachs, "The War in Ukraine Was Provoked—and Why That Matters to Achieve Peace,"

Common Dreams, May 23, 2023, https://www.commondreams.org/opinion/the
-war-in-ukraine-was-provoked-and-why-that-matters-if-we-want-peace.

40. Missy Ryan and Annabelle Timsit, "U.S. Wants Russian Military 'Weakened' from Ukraine Invasion, Austin Says," *Washington Post,* April 25, 2022, https://www.washingtonpost.com/world/2022/04/25/russia-weakened-lloyd-austin-ukraine-visit/; Andrew J. Bacevich, "On Missing Dr. Strangelove: Or How Americans Learned to Stop Worrying and Forget the Bomb," *TomDispatch.com,* March 19, 2023, https://tomdispatch.com/on-missing-dr-strangelove/.

41. "March of Folly," 1.

42. Benjamin and Davies, *War in Ukraine,* 181.

43. Michael Klare, *Rising Powers, Shrinking Planet: The New Geopolitics of Energy* (New York: Metropolitan Books, 2008), 6.

44. Alfred W. McCoy, *To Govern the Globe: World Orders and Catastrophic Change* (Chicago: Haymarket Books, 2021); Alfred W. McCoy, "The Rise of China (and the Fall of the U.S.?): Tectonic Eruptions in Eurasia Erode America's Global Power," *TomDispatch.Com,* April 27, 2023, https://tomdispatch.com/the-rise-of-china-and-the-fall-of-the-u-s/.

45. McCoy, *To Govern the Globe,* 286.

46. McCoy, 284.

47. Paul Krugman, "Why Is China in So Much Trouble?," *New York Times,* August 31, 2023, https://www.nytimes.com/2023/08/31/opinion/china-xi-jinping-policy-thrift.html; David Wallace-Wells, "What Can Replace China as a Global Economic Engine?," *New York Times,* August 23, 2023, https://www.nytimes.com/2023/08/23/opinion/columnists/what-can-replace-china-as-a-global-economic-engine.html.

48. Klare, *Rising Powers, Shrinking Planet*; McCoy, *To Govern the Globe.*

49. Jake Werner, "Spot the Difference: China and Russia Both Pose Major Challenges to US Foreign Policy," *The Nation* 315 (October 31 / November 7, 2022): 21.

50. Marakhonov, "How Chinese Military Aid," 1.

51. Michael Klare, "The New Cold War with China: How Will It Affect You?," *TomDispatch.Com,* June 11, 2020, https://tomdispatch.com/michael-klare-is-there-a-chinese-missile-crisis-in-our-future/.

52. McCoy, *To Govern the Globe,* 282.

53. McCoy, 272–273.

54. Helen Davidson, "Biden Raises Taiwan and Human Rights with Xi Jinping in First Phone Call," *Guardian,* February 10, 2021, 1, https://www.theguardian.com/world/2021/feb/11/biden-raises-taiwan-tensions-and-human-rights-with-xi-jinping-in-first-phone-call.

55. Michael Klare, "None Dare Call It Encirclement: Washington Tightens the Noose around China," *TomDispatch.Com,* January 13, 2022, 4, https://tomdispatch.com/none-dare-call-it-encirclement/.

56. Hans M. Christensen, Matt Korda, Eliana Johns, and Mackenzie Knight, "Chinese Nuclear Weapons, 2024," *Bulletin of the Atomic Scientists* 80 (2024): 49–72.

57. Washington Post Editorial Board, "Opinion: China Is Rising as a Nuclear Power. Its Ambitions Warrant Global Attention," *Washington Post,* November 8, 2021, 1, https://www.washingtonpost.com/opinions/2021/11/08/china-is-rising-nuclear-power-its-ambitions-warrant-global-attention/.

58. Washington Post Editorial Board, 1.

59. Sanger, Broad, and Buckley, "3 Nuclear Powers," 1. Also see Klare, "Surviving an Era of Pervasive Nuclear Instability," 2–3, for a discussion of "The Emerging Three-Way Nuclear Arms Race."

60. Michael Klare, "The Pentagon Inflates the Chinese Nuclear Threat in a Push for New Intercontinental Missiles," *The Nation*, May 19, 2021, 1, https://www.thenation.com/article/politics/pentagon-china-nuclear/.

61. Klare, 1.

62. Michael D. Swaine, "Threat Inflation and the Chinese Military," Quincy Paper no. 7 (Washington, DC: Quincy Institute for Responsible Statecraft, 2022), 2.

63. Joseph Gerson, "Alternatives to the Pentagon's China Nightmares," *Common Dreams*, November 6, 2021, 4, https://www.commondreams.org/views/2021/11/06/alternatives-pentagons-china-nightmares.

64. Michael Klare, "Is a Chinese Invasion of Taiwan Imminent? Or Is Washington in a Tizzy over Nothing?," *TomDispatch.Com*, March 14, 2023, 5, https://tomdispatch.com/is-a-chinese-invasion-of-taiwan-imminent/.

65. Klare, 9.

66. Michael Klare, "Countdown to World War III? It May Arrive Sooner Than You Think," *TomDispatch.Com*, December 2, 2021, 7, https://tomdispatch.com/countdown-to-world-war-iii/.

67. Klare, "Surviving an Era of Pervasive Nuclear Instability," 3.

68. Elaine Scarry, *Thermonuclear Monarchy: Choosing between Democracy and Doom* (New York: Norton, 2014), 5.

69. Langdon Winner, "Do Artifacts Have Politics?," *Daedalus* 109 (1980): 131.

70. Scarry, *Thermonuclear Monarchy*, 24.

71. Scarry, 27.

72. Garry Wills, *Bomb Power: The Modern Presidency and the National Security State* (New York: Penguin, 2010), 223.

73. Wills.

74. Wills, 222.

75. Scarry, *Thermonuclear Monarchy*, 38.

76. Scarry, 38.

77. Bandy X. Lee, *The Dangerous Case of Donald Trump: 37 Psychiatrists and Mental Health Experts Assess a President*, updated ed. (New York: Thomas Dunne Books, 2019); Bandy X. Lee, *The Dangerous Case of Donald Trump: 27 Psychiatrists and Mental Health Experts Assess a President* (New York: Thomas Dunne Books, 2017); John Gartner and Steven Buser, eds., *Rocket Man: Nuclear Madness and the Mind of Donald Trump* (Asheville, NC: Chiron, 2018).

78. Gartner and Buser, *Rocket Man*, 10.

79. Joe Cirincione, "The Greatest Danger to America Is Her Commander in Chief," in Gartner and Buser, *Rocket Man*, 107–114, 107.

80. Ruth Ben-Ghiat, "Trump's No Madman, He's Following the Strongman Playbook," in Gartner and Buser, *Rocket Man*, 71–74, 71.

81. Thomas Singer, "Extinction Anxiety and Donald Trump: Where the Spirit of the Depths Meets the Spirit of the Times," in Gartner and Buser, *Rocket Man*, 205–212, 205.

82. Quoted in Julian Borger, "My Jaw Dropped: Annie Jacobsen on Her Scenario for Nuclear War," *The Guardian* (March 31, 2024), 4, https://www.theguardian.com/books/2024/mar/31/annie-jacobsen-nuclear-war-scenario.

83. Eric Schlosser, *Command and Control: Nuclear Weapons, the Damascus Accident, and the Illusion of Safety* (New York: Penguin, 2013), 481. For more on what Daley (*Apocalypse Never*, 64) calls the potential for "accidental atomic apocalypse," see Dan Drollette, "Introduction: Near-Misses, Close Calls, and Early Warnings," *Bulletin of the Atomic Scientists*, May 9, 2023, https://thebulletin.org/premium/2023-05/introduction-near-misses-close-calls-and-early-warnings/; Daniel Ellsberg, *The Doomsday Machine: Confessions of a Nuclear War Planner*

(New York: Bloomsbury, 2017); and Charles Perrow, *Normal Accidents: Living with High-Risk Technologies* (New York: Basic Books, 1984).

84. Jurgen Scheffran, *The Climate-Nuclear Nexus: Exploring the Linkages between Climate Change and Nuclear Threats*, 2nd ed. (London: World Future Council, 2016). See also Timmon Wallis, *Warheads to Windmills: Preventing Climate Catastrophe and Nuclear War* (Northampton, MA: Indispensable Press, 2023).

85. Robert Jay Lifton, *The Climate Swerve: Reflections on Mind, Hope, and Survival* (New York: New Press, 2017), 30.

86. Robert Agnew, "Dire Forecast: A Theoretical Model of the Impact of Climate Change on Crime," *Theoretical Criminology* 16 (2011): 21–42; Alex Alvarez, *Unstable Ground: Climate Change, Conflict, and Genocide*, updated ed. (Lanham, MD: Rowman & Littlefield, 2021); John P. Crank and Linda S. Jacoby, *Crime, Violence, and Global Warming* (London: Routledge, 2015); Ronald C. Kramer, *Carbon Criminals, Climate Crimes* (New Brunswick, NJ: Rutgers University Press, 2020); Rob White, *Climate Change Criminology* (London: Bristol University Press, 2018).

87. Michael Klare, "Twin Threats: Climate Change Is Speeding Up—and So Is the Nuclear Arms Race," *The Nation* 308 (January 27, 2020): 17.

88. Michael Klare, *All Hell Breaking Loose: The Pentagon's Perspective on Climate Change* (New York: Metropolitan Books, 2019), 12.

89. Scheffran, *Climate-Nuclear Nexus*, 3.

90. Klare, "Twin Threats," 19.

91. Lili Xia, Alan Robock, Kim Scherrer, et al., "Global Food Insecurity and Famine from Reduced Crop, Marine Fishery and Livestock Production Due to Climate Disruption from Nuclear War Soot Injection," *Nature Food* 3 (2022): 586–596, 586.

92. Lifton, *Climate Swerve*, 23.

93. William M. Knoblauch, *Nuclear Freeze in a Cold War: The Reagan Administration, Cultural Activism, and the End of the Arms Race* (Amherst: University of Massachusetts Press, 2017), 34–35.

94. Matthias Dorries, "The Politics of Atmospheric Sciences: 'Nuclear Winter' and Global Climate Change," *OSIRIS* 26 (2011): 198–223, 199.

95. Jill Lepore, *These Truths: A History of the United States* (New York: Norton, 2018), 682.

96. Lepore, 683.

97. Kramer, *Carbon Criminals*.

98. Raymond Michalowski and Ronald C. Kramer, eds., *State-Corporate Crime: Wrongdoing at the Intersection of Business and Government* (New Brunswick, NJ: Rutgers University Press, 2006), 21.

99. Falk, "Geopolitical Crimes."

100. Kramer, *Carbon Criminals*.

101. Gregory Hooks and Chad L. Smith, "Treadmills of Production and Destruction: Threats to the Environment Posed by Militarism," *Organizations & Environment* 18 (2005): 19–37; Brett Clark and Andrew K. Jorgenson, "The Treadmill of Destruction and the Environmental Impacts of Militaries," *Sociology Compass* 6/7 (2012): 557–569.

102. Carl Boggs, *Origins of the Warfare State: World War II and the Transformation of American Politics* (New York: Routledge, 2017).

103. Lifton and Falk, *Indefensible Weapons*.

104. Joseph Gerson, *Empire and the Bomb: How the U.S. Uses Nuclear Weapons to Dominate the World* (London: Pluto Press, 2007).

105. Wallis, *Warheads to Windmills*, 214.

106. Falk, "Radical World Order Challenge," 139.

107. Noam Chomsky, *Internationalism or Extinction*, ed. Charles Derber, Suren Moodliar, and Paul Shannon (New York: Routledge, 2020).
108. Schell, *Gift of Time*, 11.
109. Antonio Guterres, "International Day for the Total Elimination of Nuclear Weapons: Secretary General's Message-United Nations 2022" (United Nations, September 22, 2022), 1, https://www.un.org/en/observances/nuclear-weapons -elimination-day/messages.
110. Jonathan Schell, "Reaching Zero," *The Nation* 290 (April 19, 2010): 11–18.
111. Toluse Olorunnipa and Michelle Ye Hee Lee, "At Hiroshima Summit, Japan to Push Against Nukes—But World Disagrees," *Washington Post*, May 17, 2023, 4, https://www.washingtonpost.com/politics/2023/05/17/biden-hiroshima-g7 -nuclear-threat/.
112. Schell, "Reaching Zero," 17.
113. Olorunnipa and Lee, "At Hiroshima Summit," 3.
114. John Mecklin, ed., "'A Moment of Historic Danger: It Is *Still* 90 Seconds to Midnight': 2024 Doomsday Clock Statement," *Bulletin of the Atomic Scientists*, January 23, 2024, 4.
115. Andrew J. Bacevich, *After the Apocalypse: America's Role in a World Transformed* (New York: Metropolitan Books, 2021), 11.
116. Bacevich, 10.
117. Chalmers Johnson, *Dismantling the Empire: America's Last Best Hope* (New York: Metropolitan Books, 2010).
118. Bacevich, *After the Apocalypse*, 11.
119. Noam Chomsky, *Imperial Ambitions: Conversations on the Post-9/11 World*, interviews with David Barsamian (New York: Metropolitan Books, 2005).
120. Anatol Lieven, "Seeking Peace: To Resolve the Conflict in Ukraine, We Need to Take an Honest Look at the End of the Cold War," *The Nation* 318, no. 2 (February 2024): 10.
121. Klare, "Surviving an Era of Pervasive Nuclear Instability," 5.
122. Falk, "Geopolitical Crimes," 5.
123. Paul Kennedy, *The Parliament of Man: The Past, Present, and Future of the United Nations* (New York: Random House, 2006), 76.
124. Philippe Sands, *Lawless World* (New York: Penguin, 2005).
125. Schell, *Unconquerable World*, 335.
126. Kennedy, *Parliament of Man*, 11.
127. Alexander Kmentt, "The Ban Treaty, Two Years After: A Ray of Hope for Nuclear Disarmament," *Bulletin of the Atomic Scientists*, January 23, 2023, 2, https://thebulletin.org/2023/01/the-ban-treaty-two-years-after-a-ray-of -hope-for-nuclear-disarmament/.
128. Kmentt, 4.
129. International Campaign to Abolish Nuclear Weapons, "Vienna Declaration and Action Plan" (June 23, 2022), 1, https://www.icanw.org/vienna_declaration _action_plan_overview.
130. Scott Ritter, *Dangerous Ground: America's Failed Arms Control Policy, from FDR to Obama* (New York: Nation Books, 2010), 377.
131. Boggs, *Origins of the Warfare State*, 101.
132. Schell, *Seventh Decade*, 166.
133. Schell, 176.
134. George P. Shultz, William J. Perry, Henry A. Kissinger, and Sam Nunn, "A World Free of Nuclear Weapons," *Wall Street Journal*, January 4, 2007, A15.
135. Lawrence S. Wittner, *Confronting the Bomb: A Short History of the World Nuclear Disarmament Movement* (Stanford, CA: Stanford University Press, 2009).

136. Kathleen Kingsbury, "Confronting a New Nuclear Age," *New York Times*, Sunday Opinion (March 10, 2024), 4.

137. Jim Carrier, "Where is the Protest? *The Progressive* (June/July 2024): 42–46.

138. Klare, "Twin Threats," 19.

139. Heather Gautney, *The New Power Elite* (New York: Oxford University Press, 2023), 228.

140. Arthur Laffin, ed., *Swords into Plowshares: A Chronology of Plowshares Disarmament Actions 1980–2003* (Marion, SD: Rose Hill Books, 2003).

141. Andreas Malm, *How to Blow Up a Pipeline: Learning to Fight in a World on Fire* (London: Verso, 2021).

142. Wendy Brown, *Nihilistic Times: Thinking with Max Weber* (Cambridge, MA: Belknap, 2023), 57–58, emphasis original.

143. Thomas Mann and Norman Ornstein, *It's Even Worse Than It (Looks) Was: How the American Constitutional System Collided with the New Politics of Extremism*, new ed. (New York: Basic Books, 2016); Noam Chomsky, *Illegitimate Authority: Facing the Challenges of Our Time*, ed. C. J. Polychroniou (Chicago: Haymarket Books, 2023).

144. John Nichols, *The Fight for the Soul of the Democratic Party: The Enduring Legacy of Henry Wallace's Antifascist and Antiracist Politics* (London: Verso, 2020).

145. Max Weber, "Politics as a Vocation," in *From Max Weber: Essays in Sociology*, ed. Hans Gerth and C. Wright Mills (New York: Oxford University Press, 1946), 77–128, 128.

146. Michael Burawoy, "For Public Sociology," in *Public Sociology: Fifteen Eminent Sociologists Debate Politics and the Profession in the Twenty-First Century*, ed. Dan Clawson, Robert Zussman, Joya Misra, Naomi Gerstel, Randall Stokes, Douglas Anderton, and Michael Burawoy (Berkeley: University of California Press, 2007), 23–64, 28.

147. William Julius Wilson, *More Than Just Race: Being Black and Poor in the Inner City* (New York: Norton, 2009), 139.

Index

About the Author

RONALD C. KRAMER is professor of sociology and the former director of the criminal justice program at Western Michigan University. He received his doctorate in sociology from the Ohio State University, specializing in criminology and law. His previous books include *Carbon Criminals, Climate Crimes*; *State-Corporate Crime: Wrongdoing at the Intersection of Business and Government* (with Raymond Michalowski); *State Crime in the Global Age* (edited with William J. Chambliss and Raymond Michalowski); and *Crimes of the American Nuclear State* (with David Kauzlarich). Dr. Kramer is the recipient of a Lifetime Achievement Award from the Division of Critical Criminology of the American Society of Criminology, and he has also been given the Larry T. Reynolds Award for Outstanding Teaching of Sociology and the Charles Horton Cooley Award for Distinguished Scholarship in Sociology from the Michigan Sociological Association. He lives in Kalamazoo, Michigan, with his wife Jane.

Clara S. Lewis, *Tough on Hate? The Cultural Politics of Hate Crimes*

Michael J. Lynch, *Big Prisons, Big Dreams: Crime and the Failure of America's Penal System*

Erik S. Maloney and Kevin A. Wright, *Imprisoned Minds: Lost Boys, Trapped Men, and Solutions from Within the Prison*

Liam Martin, *The Social Logic of Recidivism: Cultural Capital from Prisons to the Streets*

Allison McKim, *Addicted to Rehab: Race, Gender, and Drugs in the Era of Mass Incarceration*

Raymond J. Michalowski and Ronald C. Kramer, eds., *State-Corporate Crime: Wrongdoing at the Intersection of Business and Government*

Susan L. Miller, *Victims as Offenders: The Paradox of Women's Violence in Relationships*

Torin Monahan, *Surveillance in the Time of Insecurity*

Torin Monahan and Rodolfo D. Torres, eds., *Schools under Surveillance: Cultures of Control in Public Education*

Ana Muñiz, *Police, Power, and the Production of Racial Boundaries*

Marianne O. Nielsen and Linda M. Robyn, *Colonialism Is Crime*

Leslie Paik, *Discretionary Justice: Looking Inside a Juvenile Drug Court*

Yasser Arafat Payne, Brooklynn Hitchens, and Darryl L. Chambers, *Murder Town, USA: Homicide, Structural Violence, and Activism*

Anthony M. Platt, *The Child Savers: The Invention of Delinquency*, 40th anniversary edition with an introduction and critical commentaries compiled by Miroslava Chávez-García

Lois Presser, *Why We Harm*

Joshua M. Price, *Prison and Social Death*

Heidi Reynolds-Stenson, *Cultures of Resistance: Collective Action and Rationality in the Anti-Terror Age*

Diana Rickard, *Sex Offenders, Stigma, and Social Control*

Jeffrey Ian Ross, ed., *The Globalization of Supermax Prisons*

Dawn L. Rothe and Christopher W. Mullins, eds., *State Crime, Current Perspectives*

Jodi Schorb, *Reading Prisoners: Literature, Literacy, and the Transformation of American Punishment, 1700–1845*

Corinne Schwarz, *Policing Victimhood: Human Trafficking, Frontline Work, and the Carceral State*

Susan F. Sharp, *Hidden Victims: The Effects of the Death Penalty on Families of the Accused*

Susan F. Sharp, *Mean Lives, Mean Laws: Oklahoma's Women Prisoners*

Robert H. Tillman and Michael L. Indergaard, *Pump and Dump: The Rancid Rules of the New Economy*

Mariana Valverde, *Law and Order: Images, Meanings, Myths*

Michael Welch, *Crimes of Power and States of Impunity: The U.S. Response to Terror*

Michael Welch, *Scapegoats of September 11th: Hate Crimes and State Crimes in the War on Terror*

Saundra D. Westervelt and Kimberly J. Cook, *Life after Death Row: Exonerees' Search for Community and Identity*